MW01132712

A TRAITOR TO
HIS CLASS

A TRAITOR TO HIS CLASS

ROBERT A.G. MONKS AND THE BATTLE TO CHANGE CORPORATE AMERICA

HILARY ROSENBERG

JOHN WILEY & SONS, INC.

New York • Chichester • Weinheim • Brisbane • Singapore • Toronto

This publication is designed to provide accurate and authoritative information in regard to
the subject matter covered. It is sold with the understanding that the publisher is not
engaged in rendering professional services. If professional advice or other expert
assistance is required, the services of a competent professional person should be sought.

ISBN 0-471-17448-3

Printed in the United States of America.

10 9 8 7 6 5 4 3 2 1

For Mom and Dad
Sol and Ruth Rosenberg

Contents

Introduction

The chief executive officer of Stone & Webster, the old-line engineering firm, had just finished the annual exercise of touting the year's accomplishments to a packed shareholders' meeting in a Wilmington, Delaware, hotel ballroom. When he finally opened the floor to comments, a man in the back raised his hand and was called on. Dressed in a dark suit and conservative tie, hair neatly combed back, he appeared to be just another in the legions of investment managers doing his fiduciary duty by attending yet another annual meeting. The man stood up and took a microphone that had been handed him. And when those in the ballroom recognized him, they fell into a respectful silence.

"Listening to the president," he began in a steady voice. "I kept wondering, when is he going to commit this company to create value for shareholders? A day late and a dollar short? No. A year late and $60 million short. Please, Mr. CEO, make yourself accountable. When are you going to achieve these things?"

He approached the front of the room to direct questions to the three nominees to the board who were seated in the first few rows. As he came nearer, his six-foot-six frame loomed menacingly. The chairman of the board, eyebrows raised, stopped him by thrusting out his hand, and then, pointing to a microphone stand in the middle aisle, said, "I don't think we'll be sharing the podium with you. I am the chairman of this meeting, and I am going to control it. Why don't you stand back there before we get too close together?"

Somehow, this interloper talked the chairman into letting him stand at the front, but all the way to the left of the crowd, without a microphone. But he did not need one. His resonant voice carried to the back of the hall.

Still, as he usually does, the man in the dark suit got a bit too close for comfort that sunny day in May 1995. Although he did not share the podium, he, or more exactly his investment fund, the Lens fund, managed

to win 36 percent of all votes cast for a proxy resolution to hire an investment bank to study the idea of selling part or all of the underperforming
company—an impressive result for a shareholder-sponsored resolution.

That tall man in his mid 60s does not fit most people's stereotype of a
social activist. But then again, most people have not met Robert A.G.
Monks. Born into privilege—a New England family whose fortune
stretches back more than three generations—including greatly multiplying
his wealth through shrewd investing as a young man, he could have worked
little and lived in luxury. Instead, he chose to use his wealth and social position to wage a guerrilla war on big business. The goal: nothing less than
to make corporate America answerable both to its owners and, in accomplishing that, to society at large.

Both the goal and the tactics he employs to attain it are controversial.
Critics have branded Monks a publicity-seeking gadfly who has hurt corporations by hounding managements or encouraging big investors to rally
behind hostile takeovers. Many people have misread Monks' campaign as
merely an effort to make a quick buck for big investors by urging companies to take such drastic actions as laying off thousands of employees or
divesting businesses in one fell swoop. But, after years of work in business,
investments, and politics—including three runs for the U.S. Senate—
Monks has developed a leather skin that wears surprisingly well under constant disparagement of his work. Besides, he has found vast encouragement
in the change that he and his disciples have helped bring about at U.S. corporations and in the shareholder activist movement's progress abroad—not
to mention the kudos he has won from many admirers. Today, institutional
investors in the United States, including pension funds, own almost 50 percent of corporate America's equities, and due in great part to Monks' efforts, many of the largest public pension funds and investment managers
have learned how to flex their muscles and throw a mean punch as shareowners of corporations. There are now many instances of big shareholders
driving change at troubled or mediocre companies, and in more than a few
cases driving the CEOs out. What is more, corporate managements and
boards of directors are increasingly attentive to their shareholders' wants
and needs—which include having boards that are independent from management and are therefore trustworthy monitors of management.

Missionaries can be found in every field of endeavor from charitable
works to science to politics. In the business world, a person with a mission
might be a CEO who strives for his or her company's continued prosperity

or an investor building a track record and a fortune or a labor leader out to improve the lot of workers. Business world activist Monks has a broad agenda that he and his longtime partner Nell Minow have tried to communicate in the books and articles they have written: They would like their efforts to help cure some of the ills of society. What Monks is trying to do is to make the point—one case at a time—that companies need to be accountable to someone and that someone must be its shareholders. Since increasingly those shareholders are big institutional investors such as pension funds and mutual funds that represent millions of citizens with long-term goals, accountability to owners becomes, in his view, the same thing as accountability to society. Once institutional investors learn that they have to serve their constituency as the major owners of U.S. businesses, Monks reasons, they will have to demand that those businesses do more than make money; they also must, for example, maintain a clean environment and good working conditions for their employees around the world. "In the same way my owners are going to require the board to maximize profits, they are also going to hold them to other standards," Monks says. Those other standards may be nonprofit oriented, but they will be essential to the shareholders.

Certainly, Monks has not been the sole patriarch of shareholder activism and corporate governance in the United States. He himself gives great credit to the late Jesse Unruh, the former California Treasurer, corporate adviser Ira Millstein, former California pension fund chief Dale Hanson, and money manager Dean LeBaron, among others. But, he also does not hesitate to give himself a great portion of credit as a leader in the field. And some prominent figures in the investment community name him as the most influential figure of the movement. John Wilcox, chairman of the New York proxy solicitation firm Georgeson & Co., who has worked both for and against Monks in a number of shareholder campaigns challenging corporate managements, unabashedly calls him "a Jesus Christ of the activism movement—a kind of messiah." Richard Schlefer, investment officer at the nation's largest pension fund, the Teachers Insurance and Annuity Association—College Retirement Equities Fund, says that Monks is "Number 1" in corporate governance and that "without him, there wouldn't be the kind of corporate governance activity, particularly by institutions, that we have today." Richard Koppes, general counsel of the California Public Employee Retirement System in the 1980s, remarks: "I really view him as the grandfather of the movement. He was out there long before Dale and I." Al Sommer, a former commissioner of the Securities and

Exchange Commission (SEC), declares, "If I had to choose one person who's had singular impact, I'd have to say Bob Monks. He's been a crusader, a burr under the saddle of corporate management, a maverick." Finally, Anne Hanson, deputy director of the 110-member Council of Institutional Investors, says, "It is his name that pops up first when you think of the founders of the shareholder activist movement."

Monks is one of the few if not the only leader in this movement who both helped lay the groundwork for its development and has stayed with it to prod its momentum over the years. For the past 15 years, he has devoted nearly all his energies to the mission of improving corporate governance in this country. And before that he spent several years thinking deeply on the subject. He read the works of those who have pondered the modern corporation and its role in society, including Louis Brandeis, Frederick Hayek, James Willard Hurst, and Adolphe Berle and Gardiner Means, who first recognized that the dispersion of small shareholders in modern corporations separated ownership from control, which by default went to management. At the same time, he wrote long essays and letters to friends to clarify his thoughts and find the best way to approach the problem.

How Monks became so effective a reformer is really the story of a life. Unlike other protagonists in this story, generally institutional investors or corporate attorneys, Monks hails from a varied background as a businessman, venture capitalist, corporate lawyer, politician, and regulator. His character is similarly multi-faceted. He is an intellectual with a fascination for history and a highly logical mind. While he is a member of an old-line wealthy family with an appreciation for the power of money, he is also a minister's son with a need for spirituality and a desire to do some sort of public service. So, to him, the possession of wealth means he can satisfy these cravings: live well and make his mark in public service, as a regulator or entrepreneur working in the interest of bettering corporations. He likes having the security of money in the bank—he says his net worth is in the tens of millions—and he likes the luxuries—two beautiful homes in Maine, a Palm Beach retreat, land, and travel. But, for all his wealth, Monks is not a man of many indulgences. In fact, he prefers an old Jeep to a luxury car, comfortable clothes to spiffy suits, and he is more likely than not to leave a dinner table with a spot on his tie or shirt.

As a businessman, Monks is personable, but calculating, and gets impatient when things do not go his way. He has been known to hold a grudge against those who have stood in his path or not returned favors. As a negotiator, he can be crafty, annoyingly persistent, or even a bully using threats to get his way. He can use his size to his advantage—just by standing up. Once, he even picked up financier Sanford Weill and threatened to throw him out a window, though apparently in jest. But with friends, he is engaging and inquisitive, telling stories with a talent for pulling apt analogies out of the air, and finishing them with a deep, infectious laugh. His mood is often one of general enthusiasm, and he usually sees any glass as half full rather than half empty. "He'll walk in here with a big smile: 'Let's see what we can do to stir things up!'" says his friend and fellow Mainer William Cohen, who is now the Secretary of Defense. Business associates genuinely like Monks, though some find his tendency to show concern for them hard to believe. "He can make you think more of yourself and your abilities than you ever thought," says Jamie Heard, who once headed Institutional Shareholder Services, which Monks founded. "Sometimes I feel, 'He really believes in me, I should believe more in myself.' Other times I think he's buttering me up because he wants me to do something for him."

Earlier corporate gadflies—Louis and John Gilbert and Evelyn Davis are the best known—were outsiders viewed as eccentric. Monks, on the other hand, is an insider in terms of his background, education, wealth, Republican politics, and professional credentials. Says his friend and fellow activist Alan Kahn: "The analogy is Franklin Delano Roosevelt. He was an American patrician, born to wealth, who by all reason should have been conservative, Republican, a protector of property rights, whereas all the liberals were looked on as radical fringe, quasi nuts. He became the champion for the liberal cause. Bob Monks has become the champion for corporate establishment to make change." Others, too, refer to Roosevelt. In recalling her distinct impression of the controversy that surrounded Monks during his 1991 campaign for a seat on the board of Sears, Roebuck & Co., Olena Berg, who recently left her position as pensions regulator at the Department of Labor, says, "The reaction in Sears days reminded me of Roosevelt. The personal antipathy. Roosevelt's former classmates from prep school treated him almost like a traitor. To the chieftains of the corporate community, Bob is almost a traitor to his class." Certainly, Monks is no FDR and would not pretend to be. But there is no question that he is a renegade.

Often, he has seemed as much a traitor to his party as to his class. Frequently, for example, he has not voted the Republican ticket. And, dressing down corporate chiefs and boards is hardly on the Republican platform. "This is really a blue collar issue," says Cohen, "because you've got many individual investors in pension plans, and they have no idea what's going on with those programs. People have their life's savings in these. If you had a Democrat doing this, it might resonate more. To go after companies would be typically Democratic. But for a Republican it's harder to make a case."

Monks gained notoriety for the Sears effort and other battles he has waged on the public stage. At Sears, he advanced the movement considerably by demonstrating that it was virtually impossible for a shareholder nominee to come onto the board of a large corporation. Furthermore, he showed that the highly publicized efforts of one activist investor could inspire enough support to help restructure a major corporation. Monks is also known for his boldness as the Department of Labor's pensions administrator in 1984–1985, when he laid the foundation for much of today's scrutiny of corporations by big investors, by making it the government's policy that institutional shareholders had a fiduciary duty to behave as owners of corporations.

But what Monks has accomplished as an undercover agent of change has been equally vital to the progress of this movement over the years and, it can be argued, to that of corporate America. For example, he was the one who educated the officials of the California Public Employees Retirement System in the rudiments of shareholder activism and for a few years held their hands as they set out on the path to make Calpers the leading activist institution. For Calpers and others, he wrote many of the first shareholder resolutions demanding changes in corporate governance at major corporations. Moreover, from nothing, Monks built Institutional Shareholder Services, which today handles shareholder voting for hundreds of corporate and government pension funds and represents a deciding factor in many controversial proxy votes at large companies here and abroad. The forays of his Lens fund into such poorly managed corporations as Stone & Webster and Waste Management have set new precedents for shareholder activism.

From the beginning of his effort in governance, Monks habitually mapped out "governance agendas" that he then followed closely. Because he was so familiar with the development of ideas, politics, government, and business, and because he is a master strategist, he knew that certain steps were essential if he and other shareholder activists were to have an impact. What is remarkable is how he kept at it, though the odds were stacked against him. It is but one example of his characteristic tenacity, molded by a competitive spirit and a lust for achievement. His belief is that with enough effort and enough time, he could do just about anything. Of course, he could not; and he has failed time and again, suffering because his investment of emotion and time had been so great. But his self-confidence is a solid core of his personality, and it allows him to rebound. "I have tender feelings about the man, because I see that he gets hurt with a degree of regularity," says proxy solicitor Wilcox. "And yet he never gives up. He's incredibly persistent."

What have been his agendas? Monks realized early on that the government would have to set policy requiring attention to ownership duties. He personally began that process and helped make sure that others finished it. What is more, he knew that for any idea to blossom into reality, it needed an intellectual foundation; he needed to nurture a new academic discipline for corporate governance complete with new terminology. In the interest of this goal, he and his partners wrote articles and books, participated in forums and conferences, and developed associations with scholars. Later, Monks and Minow would attempt to raise corporate governance to the level of a profession by speaking at numerous universities worldwide and writing a textbook. Then there had to be activist owners—the pension funds and money managers. In Monks' view, they would emerge not only as a result of government decree but also when they saw value flow from activism. Monks patiently introduced the concept of activism to scores of institutional investors, one at a time, and then demonstrated to them the power they could have and the value they could achieve. From there, he moved abroad, for his methodical reasoning indicated that since multinationals could move anywhere and get their capital from anywhere, governance needed to be a global concept.

If others were working in one area of corporate governance, Monks, often working with Minow, would turn his attention to another where he saw a need. "I saw my role in this evolution as the person who would always be attempting to raise the next critical issue," he says. "I mean, why run for the board of Sears, Roebuck? You could sit and tell people til you were blue in the face that the election of boards of directors was the equivalent of the election of the Albanian government. And people would chuckle and they would go on to their next course. It didn't mean a goddamn thing. You finally had to get up and say, 'I'm a guy who's been a director of ten public corporations. I'm highly qualified. I legally will file the papers. I have a lot of support from institutional investors. And I can't get in the front door.' Only something like that makes it clear."

To be sure, Monks recognizes the limitations of his efforts—that his goals will never be reached in his lifetime and indeed may be unreachable. But he maintains his zeal for the mission, not unlike a scientist whose life-work may be to uncover something obscure and seemingly miniscule but that may enlarge the possibilities for future exploration. His hope is that as the structure of business and its ownership becomes international, competitive forces will fall much more in line with owners' standards for corporate behavior. At the same time, he recognizes the contributions that need always be made by other forces working for the interests of society, including the government and citizens' groups. "I don't claim exclusivity," he says. "I've got my hand on a piece of the puzzle. And all the pieces have one unifying link, which is, you were not put on earth to be a spectator."

A TRAITOR TO
HIS CLASS

1

The Minister's Son

His father felt second-rate in this elite culture. That had an overwhelming driving effect on my father. He was really driven to succeed.

Robert Monks Jr.

It is an afternoon in late October, and a stiff breeze blows in off the Atlantic, but Monks, standing outside in shirtsleeves, seems not to notice. At the age of 65, his powerful frame is still sturdy, his eyes still a cloudless blue, though his black hair has faded mostly to gray and is whitening at the curly edges. As usual, he is slightly stooped, perhaps from explaining his views of the world so earnestly to others (most of whom are much shorter). He walks toward his car, parked outside his shimmering, all-glass home in Maine, a 200-acre forest behind him and before him the vast ocean. Reflecting on the scene, he remarks to a guest, "I've got this beautiful place, a beautiful wife, more than anyone could ask for. What else should I do with my time but think about big important issues?"

To those who argue that the most effective reform comes from inside the system, the career of Robert A. G. Monks serves as illustration. Putting his mark on the world in some way, making changes that affect people's lives— these were the vague goals of Monks as a young student and lawyer. Yet, he would have to evolve into this role. The practice of law was not to be the means to any end for Monks, other than furnishing knowledge and contacts as well as legitimacy that would later prove most useful. It was only the first of many lines of work he would pursue—for the most part with great success—in thrashing about for personal satisfaction. "I am a creature of enthusiasms," he once told me. A restless soul. In time, he found something to do

1

that both matched his talents and moved his spirit, when he defined a "mission" of improving corporate governance and accountability by prodding shareholders to act as owners.

What helps explain the intensity of Monks' search and his ultimate inspiration is his upbringing as both a Boston Brahman and a minister's son. It was an unusual combination, replete with both contradictions and complements. Among other characteristics that emerged from that simmering pot was an overarching sense of history; a deep appreciation for family; and a reverence both for his Yankee heritage and for the work that his forebears put into the accumulation of wealth. Along with his love for the spiritual aspect of life was an equally strong craving for intellectual pursuits. Moreover, he always possessed almost an instinctive drive to make himself useful to the world. Indeed, his intellectual capacity gave him an unusual degree of confidence—often overconfidence—that he could make momentous changes.

Robert Augustus Gardner Monks was born in Boston, on December 4, 1933, the fourth of five children (the first died from a birth defect when only a few days old). He got his first name from his mother's older brother Robert Treat Knowles, an oil field wildcatter, and his father's uncle, Robert Monks, an impressionist painter. His two middle names come from his grandmother's cousin, Augustus Peabody Gardner, the only member of Congress—Monks likes to recount—to die in World War I. In a strange coincidence, Gardner had run against and defeated James Shaw, whose great granddaughter, Millicent Sprague, eventually married Bob Monks.

The Gardners were a great family of Boston that had moved to New England before the Revolution, in 1624. George Augustus Gardner, Monks' great-grandfather, came into a large inheritance from his ancestors, who had been involved in the East India trade. He himself went into real estate in Boston and became known as a tough bargainer, even when haggling with peddlers. But he was also a generous man. Many have described his great grandson in similarly contradictory terms. There is a story about a 84-year-old George Augustus going to visit legendary Boston Mayor James Michael Curley in 1913, to whom he said, "Mr. Curley, I think this winter is likely to be a difficult one so far as the economic picture is concerned, and I would like to give you $10,000 to be used by the city to give work to the unemployed on some project of civic improvement." He told the mayor that he would make the donation under the pseudonym "Mr. Smith," as he did not want to reveal himself as the benefactor. However, Mayor Curley did unveil the true donor in 1914 at a ceremony opening Gardner Way in South Boston, and Gardner was cheered by the 20,000 spectators for 15 minutes.[1] Immensely wealthy for his time, Gardner had three homes: in Boston, at Monument Beach on Cape Cod, and on the family-owned Roque Island off the northern coast of Maine. One of his brothers was married to Isabella Stewart Gardner, known in the Monks clan as Aunt Belle, an eccentric, headstrong woman who became one of this country's great patrons of the arts, establishing Boston's Isabella Stewart Gardner Museum.

George Augustus and his wife, Eliza Endicott Peabody, were actually blood relatives. Both of them were grandchildren of Joseph Peabody, another great New England family name. Peabody fought at sea in the Revolutionary War, and after the war headed a large fleet of merchant ships, becoming one of the foremost merchant traders of the time. He made much of his fortune by commandeering British merchant ships, towing them back to an American port, and selling their stock, a practice that was well within the law at the time. The Peabody name turns up all over Massachusetts, for example, in the Peabody Museum in Salem and the town of Peabody itself. Joseph also established roots in Maine, around 1800 acquiring a small group of islands off the coast, one of which, Roque Island, remains in the Monks/Gardner family and is used as a retreat by many of the 100 or so family descendants.[2] It continues to be one of Monks' favorite places on earth, where, he says, his "soul resides."

The oldest of George and Eliza's seven children, George Peabody Gardner, distinguished himself as one of the early directors of the General Electric Company—from 1895, its third year, to 1938. His son George Jr. served as a GE director for 20 years after that. Collectively, the Gardner family was at one time the largest holder of GE stock. Indeed, Bob Monks inherited a great deal of it and held it for many years.[3]

Bob's grandmother was George and Eliza Gardner's youngest child, Olga, who married George Howard Monks, a physician. The Monks family had arrived in America much more recently than the Gardners. Around 1820, Bob's great-grandfather, Irish immigrant John Patrick Monks, started a lumber business in Hampden, Maine. Later he moved the principal business to Boston, where it thrived. He even earned mention in an 1851 tome entitled, "The Rich Men of Massachusetts," a sort of Forbes 400 of its time, and is credited with having accumulated $200,000—a fortune much smaller than that of the Gardners and Peabodys, who had amassed their wealth over multiple generations.[4]

Olga Monks was known as an energetic and charitable woman in the Boston community, and her reputation endured long after her death in 1944. One day in the fall of 1958, when Bob had just started practicing law, he saw Mayor Curley at a restaurant having lunch. Bob approached the octogenarian and introduced himself. Curley recognized the Monks name at once. "You must be Olga Monks' grandson," he said. "You know, when we put parking meters in the Back Bay, there was no meter in front of her house. I believe there are some people who should enjoy the freedom of the city forever."

Her son, and Bob's father, George Gardner Monks—who went by the name Gardner because so many of his contemporary relations were George—was an extraordinarily bright man. Since childhood, he had an unusually strong affection for poetry, and in grade school chose to memorize and recite poems that were much longer than those assigned to the class as a whole. As an adult, he often quoted poetry and hymns in casual conversation, and even at the age of 80 he could still recite all 2,000 lines of Thomas Macauley's lyric poem *The Lays of Ancient Rome.* He was also fascinated with puzzles of all kinds, and as he grew older, became obsessed with crossword puzzles. He had the ability to complete an entire Sunday crossword from the Across clues alone.

Gardner Monks studied engineering at Harvard. But, his work as a volunteer in a church program for teenage boys convinced him to become a minister in the Episcopal order in which he was raised. "I was certainly one of those to whom much had been given. I accepted not grudgingly but gladly that of me much ought to be required. I could try to fulfill this responsibility through my work as an engineer," he once wrote. "But somehow mental and spiritual contributions seemed more basic and fundamental, issues of the spirit more urgent and crucial. The overwhelming impulse was to be of maximum service."[5] Perhaps because he was a mathematician as well as a spiritualist at heart, he later referred to religion as "the best bet he knew" for his own life. He married Katharine Knowles, a compassionate, voluble woman from a long line of Mainers. While she bore three boys and two girls, she was not a particularly hands-on mother, preferring to have household servants deal with the children. Instead, she put much of her energy into fulfilling the obligations of a minister's wife.

In his son's view, Gardner Monks was not a happy man. One reason he went into the clergy, believes his son, was to avoid the social obligations of his well-stationed family. "My father was not a people person," Bob says. "It was a very serious problem for a clergyman." Gardner openly admitted his preference for one-on-one contacts and long stretches of solitude over participation in groups. Yet, as a cleric he did well. In 1927, Gardner Monks took charge of a newly established Episcopal boys' high school in Lenox, Massachusetts, The Lenox School, where the students were responsible for running most of the basic functions. (It had a staff of three: a chef, a doctor, and an engineer for the boiler.) In 1948, after leaving the school to another cleric, the senior Monks moved to Washington as a canon in the Washington Cathedral, the home church for the presiding bishop of the Episcopal Church, and for a while also served as acting dean. While, in keeping with his reserved character, he appointed someone else to handle the ceremonial responsibilities of the cathedral, he periodically delivered sermons to crowds of thousands. Indeed, at one point he taught homiletics at the Episcopal Theological School, though his own sermons lacked the passion and drama of the most effective preachers. But his main charge as a canon was directing the work of finishing the cathedral, a project that, given his abiding interest in engineering, he loved. Later, he became more and more involved, particularly with his son Bob, in what became a great avocation: investing.

As a boy, Bob Monks looked to his father for attention and approval. And, in time he won both. For one thing, he developed a sense of humor that could break his father's severity, easing the son out of many a potentially tough scrape. Moreover, the young Monks showed an intellectual capacity that matched that of his bookish father. The two regularly engaged in arguments at the dinner table over such questions as, "What is the highest mountain in the state?" Once excused from the table, Bob would run to an atlas to find the answer. Monks also had a predilection for memorizing something to recite to his family. One year it was parts of the encyclopedia; other times it was baseball statistics. "He was fascinated by learning," observes his older brother George. "He was motivated by an internal drive to succeed, a bug that was inside him."

Like his father, Monks is contemplative and more comfortable one on one than in large groups of people. But, having inherited his mother's loquaciousness, he is much more at home among people than his father was. Perhaps most elemental to his success is that, like his father and his grandfathers, both of whom were doctors, Monks has a clear sense of duty. Not to God, in particular. In fact, the Monks children were turned off to religion by the weekly march to church and by inconsistencies they perceived in the behavior of the day's leaders of Christian institutions. But there is no doubt that Monks' sense of obligation came partly from daily exposure to religion and a religious school. The motto of the Lenox School was *non ministrari, sed ministrare,* "not to be ministered unto, but to minister."

It is also an aristocratic tradition to give something back to society, and both Bob and his father were undoubtedly shaped by their heritage. Over time, however, Bob grew cynical, indeed angry, about this image accorded the patrician class. What most disgusted him was that members of wealthy Boston families—including his own—were handed privileged positions in public service on account of their social standing, but then often they did not carry the weight of their jobs. He suffered a disillusionment as a young man. One of his uncles, for example, was president of The Children's Hospital, and was the third generation in his family to hold that title. But Monks found out that this uncle spent a good deal of his time arranging for a sculptor to do his bust, which he then ordered placed in the hospital's entrance hall. Later, as a lawyer, Monks ran across instances in which trustees acted for their own benefit rather than that of the trust beneficiaries. "It was just a culture that was so confident of itself and of its place, and I began to see that many of the assumed virtues were false," he says.

His friend Arthur Dubow tells a story about an awkward dinner he and Monks had at the fancy Somerset Club in Boston in the late 1970s. It was a summer evening, and they were sitting out on the club's patio. "As we were sitting there having dinner," Dubow says, "you could see that he began to get really uncomfortable. He looked around and said, 'All these people. Either I am related to them or I went to school with them. They are all ungiving people. I can't stand them. They're all mean-spirited.' The venom poured out of him. We almost had to leave before dinner was served. Here I am a Jewish member of a predominantly WASP club, and Bob is the one feeling uncomfortable."

While he has this queasy feeling about his own social class, Monks also has unmistakable pride in being included in a line of people that helped build New England. After all, in public life he has always used his two middle initials. And, he has lived the kind of life that has been passed down to him. Until the age of 10, he lived with his family at his father's school in Lenox, himself attending school in nearby Barrington. They resided in an old house that was so large it required a staff of six to maintain. A governess was on hand to help teach the young children, and they all read at an early age. After the United States went to war, domestic help was hard to come by in the region. So everyone but Monks' father moved to a smaller home in Cohasset, south of Boston, and Bob attended fifth and sixth grades at a nearby private school, Derby Academy. Often on weekends, taking a break from the rigorous academic routine, Bob and his older brother George would sneak up to the third floor of the house with Cokes® and piles of comic books, and would not be seen for the rest of the day. The family spent summers at Roque Island, where fishing was a great preoccupation and prizes were awarded (25 cents for the first catch, 25 cents for the biggest, and 50 cents for the most fish).

For seventh and eighth grades, Monks entered boarding school, the Fessenden School in West Newton, Massachusetts, outside Boston. After that, it was off to another Episcopal school, the prestigious St. Paul's in Concord, New Hampshire (Bob assumes that his father did not believe it was a good idea for a boy to attend his own father's school). These private schools were breeding grounds of future relationships in business and politics. At Derby, Frank Cahouet, the future CEO of Mellon Bank, was a classmate. Edward Kennedy was one of Monks' school- and dorm-mates in seventh grade at Fessenden. They were on opposing debating teams in 1945 when the topic was, "Should the U.S. cooperate more closely with Russia than Britain in the postwar world?" Both men also later attended Harvard. In 1962, when Kennedy, then 30 years old, was thinking of running for the Senate, he consulted with some old friends, including Monks, who was then practicing law. Monks advised him against entering the race, remarking, "Ted, do you remember our speech teacher at Harvard who got everybody's attention the first day by breaking a chair against the speaking podium? What'll happen is that your opponent will use you instead of the chair." Kennedy laughed at this and then went on to win every election he entered. They kept up a distant acquaintance. After the tragic incident at Chappaquiddick in which the car Kennedy was driving veered off a bridge and his female passenger drowned, Monks made a point of inviting him to his house after a college football game along with some mutual friends.

At St. Paul's, Monks befriended Minoru "Ben" Makihara, a student who later married into the Japanese family that ran Mitsubishi and who himself now heads that corporate giant. The year before Makihara arrived, St. Paul's rector got up in front of the assembled students and announced that the school was bringing over a Japanese student in part to counter a perceived attitude of intolerance among the students. Makihara, who was born in England, was happy to come to St. Paul's from his war-torn country and found the students welcoming and curious about Japan. Both he and Monks were seniors in 1949–1950, and they became fast friends. The two boys were amiably competitive, as in one essay contest on what U.S. foreign policy should be in Asia. "I felt this was a contest I would win," Makihara says. "But Bob won the thing. From those days, he was interested in Asia and what was going on." In that essay, Monks suggested a program whereby the U.S. government would work with American companies to develop trade in certain foreign locations, a sort of extension of the Marshall Plan.

When he graduated from St. Paul's, Monks was only 16, having skipped the fourth grade, and his father did not think he was ready for college. So, he sent his son to yet another school, L'École International in Geneva, where he learned to speak French. On the weekends, he would often catch a bus to the ski slopes of the French Alps. One day while skiing, he came across an image that would become indelible—a cross stuck in the snow inscribed with the words, "Maquisard, Mort pour la France." He didn't recognize the word *Maquisard,* but with a little research he found out it derived from the word *maqui,* which meant "underbrush," and that it was the name taken by the French resistance in this region.

The next year, when he was 17, Monks entered Harvard University as a sophomore, majoring in French history with the full intent of becoming a history scholar. Among his classmates were Makihara, who became a roommate, Ned Johnson, future chairman of Fidelity Management and Research, and Dean LeBaron, who as a money manager became a good friend and ally later in the corporate governance crusade. Monks was well aware that he was younger than his fellow students. In October of that year, he learned somehow that the second youngest person in the class was Arthur Dubow and through a mutual friend arranged to meet him. They met near the Charles River, behind the boathouse.

After shaking hands, Monks said to Dubow, "You're not the youngest person in our class any more."

"What? I didn't know I was the youngest person in the class," Dubow replied, surprised that someone would actually find a way to look this up.

They chatted and then said good-bye without plans to meet again. But, over the next three years, they became friends and, later, fellow investors.

Another friendship Monks initiated was with Thomas Jefferson Coolidge, who was descended from two presidents and was actually Monks' distant cousin. He introduced himself to Coolidge by informing him that they were related.

At Harvard, Monks joined the crew. While he had played baseball in high school, he was not good enough for college competition. His father had rowed at Oxford, and his sister's husband, Austin, had rowed for Yale and told him it would make all the difference in his life. So he decided to give it a try. In a sport made for tall, rugged men, Monks at 6′6″ and 210 pounds fit the bill. But it was still back- and limb-breaking work. The crew rowed along the Charles River six days a week, from 3 P.M. to almost 7 P.M., and had weekly races. Every day, Monks would mount the steps outside Newell boathouse feeling confident he had the stamina for the workout to come, but also anxious that if he performed well he would end up wishing he were dead. "Rowing is a head game," he recalls. "After you have acquired the physical capability, the whole question is, 'How much can I ask of myself?' If you ask a lot, you hurt a lot; if you don't ask a lot, you're wasting your time."

In the spring of his junior and senior years, 1953 and 1954, the crew spent a few weeks at a training camp in Connecticut to prepare for the four-mile race against Yale University. In his scanty spare time over both seasons, Monks managed to read the English translation of Marcel Proust's multipart novel, *À la recherche du temps perdu (Remembrance of Things Past)*. The magic of sensory experience opening doors to the past appealed to the young Monks' romantic tendencies. He has since reread the volumes twice.

The Harvard crew did well while he was on it. Monks went on to row for Cambridge University in a year spent there after college. "He was the biggest, strongest man in the crew," says one of his best friends and another rower, Torquil Norman. In a race down the Thames in London, viewed by millions, Monks helped the crew beat arch enemy Oxford by the largest margin ever recorded. Rowing reinforced Monks' already solid self-confidence because it showed him he was physically able to do something that initially seemed beyond his capacity. The sport also enhanced his already highly competitive nature. As Norman says, "He is not someone who likes to come in second—at all." What David Halberstam wrote about rowing in *The Amateurs* is revealing about Monks: "It was in its way a very macho world. The egos were immense—they had to be for so demanding a sport. Men of lesser will and ambition simply did not stay around. The oarsmen were almost to a man highly individualistic and exceptionally compulsive."[6]

Yet at the same time, they had to learn to work as a team. Monks, who was the sixth rower of eight in the boat, says he found that aspect of the sport especially gratifying. At times, however, he was accused by observers

of trying to be "the stroke," or the lead. He denies it. In fact, he was horri-
fied once when someone mistakenly introduced him as "Monks, the stroke of
the Varsity Crew." He says he enjoyed the anonymity of being in "the powerhouse" and simply doing the job. At the 40th reunion of Monks' Cambridge Crew, however, the president of the boat club told Milly Monks that,
given the force of her husband's rowing personality, they had no choice but
to build the crew around him. Try as he might to fit in, and somewhat under
the illusion that he did, Monks could not hide the force of his presence.

Disciplined and focused, Monks had little trouble handling his studies
while keeping his rowing commitments. The evidence was in his grades; he
graduated Phi Beta Kappa, magna cum laude, and Number 2 among history
majors. "I liked to work, and that's all I did," Monks says, as his friends
confirm. And then, in his senior year, he met Milly.

Millicent Carnegie Sprague came from another of New England's
wealthy families on her father's side and one of America's great families
on her mother's. Her mother was Lucy Carnegie, daughter of Andrew
Carnegie II. He was the son of Thomas Carnegie, whose brother and business partner was Andrew Carnegie, the founder of U.S. Steel and a great
philanthropist, who gave away the vast preponderance of his money. Lucy
grew up on Cumberland Island, a 25-mile stretch off the coast of southern
Georgia, where the Thomas Carnegie family had built mansions. Milly inherited a 200-acre strip of land, featuring her grandfather's beach house.
The U.S. government began negotiating with the Carnegie clan to acquire
the island during the Eisenhower administration, and when he was practicing law in the early 1960s Monks traveled there with his mother-in-law to
meet and negotiate with then Interior Secretary Stewart Udall. The government bought the land in the early 1970s and turned it into a national
park. Some family members chose to retain life interests in their homes;
Milly and Bob kept a 25-year lease on theirs.

Milly's father, Phineas Shaw Sprague, owned C. H. Sprague & Son, a
New England fuel distribution company that her great-grandfather Charles
Hill Sprague founded in 1870 with his son Phineas W. Sprague. Charles
Sprague was an MIT professor of geology who took samples of the black
outcroppings he had seen in the West Virginia hills and discovered rich
veins of marketable coal. The business grew very large and profitable, and
P. W. Sprague set up trusts for his heirs that included 2,500 acres of land he
had purchased in two nearby towns on the Maine Coast.

Milly's parents divorced when she was 13, in part because her mother
could not tolerate her husband's womanizing. A slender and attractive

brunette, Milly attended a private high school in Virginia. From there, she went to Sarah Lawrence College, but stayed only one year. At the time she met Monks, in the fall of 1953, she was studying to be an opera singer at the New England Conservatory of Music. Years later, she lost her voice, cutting short a promising operatic career. But she took up dancing with equal zeal and made a name for herself as a choreographer, both in Maine and Washington.

Bob and Milly first met at a dance, a coming-out party for one of her schoolmates. He stepped on her toes while dancing, so they talked and discovered that their families had known each other in Boston. They did not see each other again for some weeks, when they happened to meet on an airplane to Aspen, Colorado, during a school break. Both were traveling with groups of friends on separate ski trips. On the plane, Milly says, "He was impossible. I mean he talked the entire time. I couldn't read my book. When we got to Aspen he kept following me around. I skied faster, so I got away from him." On New Year's Eve, the two groups got together for the evening. For a while, Milly and Bob sat talking under a Christmas tree. "And he discussed my sex life," Milly recounts. "Well that did it. I simply wouldn't speak to him. He was just curious about what I'd be like. I'd seemed uptight." But on the trip home, things changed. "We got on the bus, we sat in the back of the bus, and on the way to the airport I fell in love with him. I was completely and totally in love with him. Something just clicked in my head."

But when they left the plane, she remained standoffish. So, the persistent suitor, seeing opportunity at the baggage carousel, decided to steal her skis. The next day, he showed up at her door with them, admitting that he had taken them so he could see her again. They were engaged in May and married in July 1954, shortly after graduation. "I liked the look of the man. I just liked to look at him," Milly says. "I liked his mind. I liked that quick intellect and that wonderful creative way of thinking. And the energy level. The energy level is enormous in Bobby."

At that time, Monks had his heart set on pursuing an academic life as an historian. He was also interested in politics and how the U.S. government was run, and in the U.S. and Japanese economies, according to his friend Ben Makihara. As yet, he showed no inclination to run for political office or go into business. "The instinct was in him to make a broader impact, but at that point he was simply very energetic," Makihara says.

And curious about the world. For his senior thesis, Monks chose to write about the Maquisard, the French resistance, whose cross he had encountered in the snow while attending school in Switzerland. The summer before his senior year at Harvard, he spent a few weeks in France to conduct his research. The region of Haute-Savoie had been occupied first by the Vichy government, then by the Italians, and ultimately by the Germans. Monks sought out people who had been involved in the resistance. "I saw guys who'd been tortured, and they took off their shirts [to show him the scars]. I went to places where they'd killed people. In retrospect it was folly that I went, because there was much too much residual violence. [During the war], communists from Paris had come in and blown up a German truck at which point the Germans took 10 [local] people and shot them. The communists' terrorism was much resented by the locals who had to pay the price of German reprisals. Those scores were still being settled." During his research, the history student discovered that the cross marked a spot where a Maquisard had been killed in a mountaintop battle.

Monks also chose to explore a different region of his own country, not by vacationing but by working there. Since high school, although surrounded by privilege, Monks felt compelled to work and earn his own money because, as he has said, "To me, earning money was always freedom." The summer after graduating from St. Paul's, the future investor worked as a runner delivering stock certificates for the Boston office of Paine, Webber, Jackson & Curtis, where he took home the minimum wage, amounting to $30 a week. In college, he worked in Michigan and Illinois as one of many laborers building a pipeline from St. Louis to Detroit. The young Monks was eager to get on with the experience of life, and here in the Midwest was something that was out of the realm of his patrician New England upbringing.

He got the job through his namesake uncle, Bob Knowles, the wildcatter who went broke in the Depression and later got a job as the person in charge of buying rights-of-way for Shell Oil pipelines. For two summers, 1952 and 1953, he worked seven days a week, up to 15 hours a day. He hitchhiked from Boston and then daily to the job sites, imagining himself to be the lanky Montgomery Clift at the beginning of *A Place in the Sun*, walking along the highway, lugging a battered suitcase, a jacket draped over his shoulder, just before Elizabeth Taylor swings by in her Buick Roadmaster convertible.

The first summer, he worked eight weeks on the maintenance crew for Phillips Petroleum, which meant digging lots of ditches. Then he spent four weeks serving as a welder's assistant in the construction of a pipeline for Shell, carrying metal rods from pipe joint to pipe joint as the welders fit them all together. There he learned the gospel of the welders: "Only God and us make steel," they would chant as they arrived on the job in their special bus.

The second summer, Monks worked eight weeks in the railyards in Jackson, Michigan, coating steel pipe with cement as insulation. Nights were a contrast; after working all day, he'd often read French writers like André Gide, Albert Camus, and André Malraux, and the American John Roderigo Dos Passos. Malraux, especially, inspired him, writing about the capacity of individuals to affect their surroundings.

One day, Monks' uncle Bob visited him in the small town of Jackson. As they drove together to the construction site, Monks said he was hungry, and his uncle offered to buy him a meal. "No, no," said the inspired youth. "I'm hungry for life, for experiences."

But this was dangerous work. It involved operating electric static leak detectors, moving cement, using pressurized bottled gas to fuel torches used to coat the cement on the pipe, and loading lime onto conveyor belts in 100-degree heat, all the while breathing in lime and cement dust. One morning just before noon, Monks heard a bone-chilling scream and turned to see one of his co-workers aflame like a human torch running through the cornfield, then rolling to put out the fire. One of the bottles of gas had exploded. Another day, a pipe length fell off a ramp and severed a co-worker's arm below the elbow.

Those doing most of the grunt work were college boys like Monks looking to earn some fast money. The deal with the company was double time after 60 hours a week and triple time after 80. The laborers easily fell in the triple-time range, sometimes working 105-hour weeks. Monks was in his sixth of eight weeks, having just worked 80 hours, when the foreman told the group that they'd run out of lime and there'd be no more work that week. The crew was furious. Monks and his friend Eric Sellin demanded the name of the lime supplier. The foreman shot back, "Are you calling me a liar?" But then he came out with the truth: there was no shortage of lime. It was, Monks says, a traditional management bait-and-switch. The two college students appealed to their boss's sense of fairness. When that did not work, they threatened to sue. And finally, Monks recounts, "We said, 'No lime, no work next week.'" The other laborers, mostly a group of students and young teachers from a local religious college who were planning to work longer that summer than Monks and Sellin were, were astounded at the nerve of these two Easterners. But they remained silent. After much yelling and screaming with the foreman, the young activists won the day, and the workers got their hours and their pay.

The income helped Monks pay his way through Harvard. Not that he really needed to pay for college himself. Even though he did not yet have access to his inheritance—a trust fund set up by his father for use after age 21 and a trust fund set up by his grandparents available only on the death of his parents—his father would gladly have paid his college expenses. But Monks was determined to earn the money himself; and his father, who came from a tradition of the Puritan ethic, was fully behind his son's desire.

By the time he graduated in 1954, Monks did not have any money to speak of. His father had put aside $3,000 a year for him in the trust, which was then invested in stocks and bonds, but he was only 20½ and by law could not draw on it for six months. So, his father advanced the funds for living expenses for the remaining period. That fall, Monks went on a Fiske Scholarship to Cambridge University for a year of study in history under a tutor.

The newlyweds did not live well in England. Some food was still rationed; Milly was able to get an extra milk allotment after she became pregnant. The only apartment they could get, at any price, was a three-room flat on two stories costing 7 pounds, six pence a week, translating into around $20. The place had coin-operated gas heaters, and, as Monks puts it, "A gas heater is good for toasting crumpets and English muffins, but it ain't good for anything else." Some nights were so cold that they were forced to pull the rug up over the bed. There was no telephone in the apartment, due to a general shortage. To make matters worse, the locals disliked Americans, apparently because of the U.S. air bases in the area. "I'd oftentimes be thumbing a ride on a road and they'd hear my voice and drive off," Monks maintains. Milly attended some classes with her husband and worked in the hospital helping the midwives. Between terms they went on a five-week excursion that included Egypt, Israel, Turkey, Greece, and skiing in Davos, Switzerland. After another month in Cambridge, they moved to London because the Cambridge crew was rowing nearby. Once a week, Monks would take the train to Cambridge to see his tutor.

At the end of the term, the tutor advised Monks not to pursue a career as a history professor because Monks seemed to have too much energy for the academic life. This was, of course, one person's opinion. But it came from someone Monks trusted. His tutor was an older man who had gone from serving as an officer in the British secret service to—when his cover was blown—teaching history. He spoke with an air of authority. "It really was a startling confrontation," Monks recalls, "because I worked hard and I really thought well of myself as an historian. I liked history. I liked the historians there very much. Then to be told that the work I did was excellent, but I couldn't do it was shocking to me." But at the same time, it rang true. Reconsidering his career options, Monks settled on law school because he knew the degree would be helpful in whatever else he decided to do. And, he says, "it seemed to be the thing that foreclosed the least. If you were a lawyer, you could be anything."

By the time he had made this decision, it was Labor Day and much too late to apply to Harvard Law School. So, he paid a visit to the dean, who told him that if he went to Boston College Law School that year and was first in his class, Harvard would take him the following year. Monks spent his last two years of law school at Harvard.

Now married and with a daughter, Monks did not need to worry about money. He had full access to the trust his father had set up for him, which by then had grown to $150,000. It was a lot of money at the time, and certainly he could be considered wealthy by Boston standards, though not on a broader scale. They bought a house in Cambridge and hired a maid. The family's second house in Cambridge needed extensive repair and refurbishing, and an uncle of Monks' who was an architect helped them map out and perform the work. The family lived there for 12 years to 1971—much of that time housing one of Monks' relatives as part of an effort that would last many years to help him overcome a drug addiction. All the while they summered in Maine on the property in Cape Elizabeth that they would later live on. When they left for Maine in 1971, Monks donated the Cambridge house to Harvard.

While at Harvard Law School, Monks met French Anderson, a medical student who would prove to be as creative and aggressive in his own field of gene therapy as Monks was in his field of shareholder activism. They served together on the Harvard-Cambridge Scholarship Committee, which awarded the Fiske and other scholarships. As Anderson relates: "We couldn't stand each other. We were too similar. We were both aggressive, focused, hard driving." Monks liked to tease Anderson in front of the committee by calling him "the Boy Scout" because Anderson didn't smoke, drink, or swear. By that definition, Monks himself was also a Boy Scout. But, Anderson was particularly annoyed because he actually had been a Boy Scout and was proud of it. In any case, the two young men soon found that they were allies on every single issue about each candidate and "the intensity of the negative feelings we had for each other turned into the reverse," Anderson says. "He's my lifelong best friend."

What the two men most had in common, which over the years reinforced the bond of their friendship, was a sense of purpose. "He can understand where I'm coming from," Says Anderson, who one day would perform the world's first successful gene therapy experiment. "We're the same in how totally obsessed we are with what we do." This was true of Monks in whatever pursuit he was engaged in at the time. Once, after a scholarship committee meeting, Anderson and another committee member dined at Monks' house in Cambridge. Monks and Anderson spent the entire meal grilling the other man about his job as a corporate senior vice president. They asked him about his vision. To them, their fellow committee member didn't appear to have any vision or passion for what he was doing.

"How can you work without a vision?" Monks and Anderson pressed him.

When he left, Milly, clearly annoyed, asked them, "Why did you give him such a hard time?"

"Because," Monks said, "he used to be one of us, and he's not any more."

2

Lawyer, Investor, Businessman

Whenever there was a problem, he always had an instant strategy, always a clear sense of what should be done.

T. Jefferson Coolidge

Monks is an organized, strategic thinker. He was a natural as a corporate lawyer. His goal was to be a partner in a law firm. Luck played a role in allowing him to pursue this objective right away. He reached draft age between wars, turning 21 in 1954, one year after the end of the Korean War. When he graduated from law school in 1958, he had a family and was therefore not interested in joining the military. He stepped directly into a career. Fresh out of Harvard Law, now with two children, a girl, Melinda, and a boy, Robert Jr., he joined Goodwin, Procter & Hoar, Boston's second biggest law firm.

At Goodwin, Procter, Monks met people who would later become partners in business and advisers in his political and shareholder activism pursuits. To some of them, he stood out as exceptional in an unexceptional crowd. Joshua Berman, the son of a New York City rabbi and today a prominent New York attorney, arrived at Goodwin, Procter in 1960 as a young summer clerk after his second year at Harvard Law School. He was the first Jewish employee in the history of the firm. At once, he struck up a friendship with Monks, another son of a clergyman albeit of a different faith who impressed him as "very very open" and not like anybody else. Monks, who'd already been at the firm for two years, was delighted to see a Jewish kid coming into the firm, believing it could only be good for the place. Anything that shook up the establishment was good in his view, even if he was part of the establishment. Monks and Berman often talked about the changes then taking place in Boston's corporate and financial world, with outsiders coming in to play important roles at hitherto Yankee-dominated institutions, and it was something that seemed right to the Gardner/Peabody heir. Berman, like others, found that Monks tended to think in unusually broad terms, placing events in a larger context and—as would become apparent later—often spouting ideas that were way ahead of his time.

A few years into his practice as a lawyer, Monks met Howard Goldenfarb, who was working at the firm as an office boy while attending college, with the intent of going on to law school. Goldenfarb took to Monks right away; in time Monks would become his mentor and later his business partner. Says Goldenfarb: "After about two days, it became clear to me that I didn't want to practice law, at least in that environment. Rigid, stiff, unpleasant, robotic people. But one person stood out, and not only because he was a big man. He was a different cut, marched to his own beat, had some compassion." One day, Monks asked Goldenfarb to deliver a package to Providence, and handed him the keys to his car. A few days later, when Goldenfarb got a check from the law firm for the mileage used on the trip, he brought it to Monks. "You keep it," Monks said. To Goldenfarb, who was making $55 a week, the $11 check was a windfall. Monks also gave Goldenfarb a break from his usual job of making deliveries and operating the copier by assigning him some research projects. In fact, Monks often encouraged those who worked for him to stretch themselves. He even paid to send his secretary to earn her master's degree in business school.

Monks' views on how someone should treat their employees became explicit in 1967 when he was advising his friend French Anderson, who was then building his lab at the National Institutes of Health. As he recalls, Monks told him, "When you hire key people, don't pay them what they're worth. Pay them *more* than they're worth. They'll bust themselves trying to earn the salary they're getting." Because Anderson worked for the government, it was impossible for him to do this. But he did delegate greater responsibilities to his people earlier than he would have otherwise, and it worked well.

Money quickly became a real issue for Monks. His first year he made $4,800 in salary—less than his secretary who was paid on a weekly basis and earned $100 a week. By 1961, his salary had grown to an uninspiring

$8,000. Meanwhile, he had spent a good chunk of his father's trust on his house and now had two children to raise. But, Monks pictured in his mind a lifestyle in which he would not only have enough money to live comfortably, but so much that he would be able to pursue whatever fancied him. This meant making a lot of money early on. To supplement his lawyer's income, he began moonlighting. He went into real estate with a couple of partners—one whose family was in the construction business and another who was an architect. Working evenings and weekends, the three men built government-assisted (Federal Housing Authority) housing for middle-income tenants—two high-rise projects in the Brookline section of Boston. In one of those projects, Monks' father joined as an investor.

While dabbling in real estate, Monks also had a hand in venture capital. In the spirit of President Kennedy's rallying cry of "Let's get America moving again!" Congress passed legislation encouraging the formation and growth of small businesses. One product of the Kennedy Administration was the Small Business Investment Company that provided government assistance for upstart companies. The government guaranteed a level of subordinated debt for a qualifying SBIC company; the minimum requirement was $150,000 in equity capital, which the government would match. Monks and a small group of friends obtained a SBIC license, named themselves Union Capital Corporation, and began their search for future Xerox Corporations. "We looked at glass that doesn't break, perpetual motion machines, centrifuges and all manner of the fruit of the capitalist creativity," Monks says. Union Capital invested in 10 companies, most of which were dismal failures. But a few successes more than made up for those. One, Damon Engineering, was a four-year-old venture that initially produced systems for use in radar tracking and missile control, and later branched into school and hobby products and then medical services. It was at this third stage that Monks and his partners invested in the company; Monks himself was so excited about the operation that he bought more stock personally with borrowed funds. He sold out his $2,000 position several years later for $200,000.

The lure of real estate tugged at Monks again when in 1964 Boston started an urban renewal program. Monks, his two real estate partners, and a third partner, Harvard classmate Jeff Coolidge, decided to jump into this highly competitive arena when the Boston Redevelopment Authority was auctioning off sites in the commercial district for new buildings. They put in a bid for Parcel 8, which was a prime site right next to the old statehouse on State Street. The winner of a design competition would win the bid, but then have to come up with financing. That seemed simple enough. Monks' group recruited an Italian architect and surprised everyone by winning the competition over other, more established outfits.

For the financing, Monks started by asking Dubow and others to invest, and even got Dubow's help with an introduction to the Rockefellers, David and Laurence, who at that time had a real estate development operation in New York. But it came to nothing. As Dubow tells it: "We had an 11 o'-clock appointment, and there was an incredible snowstorm. Bob's plane was delayed. I'm down there at the meeting with the guy who was the head of the company. David Rockefeller was next door and he was going to come in when Bob arrived. It gets to be 11, then 11:15 and 11:30, and we're looking outside and we don't think anyone's ever going to arrive. At quarter to twelve he arrived. David Rockefeller had just left. But we had the meeting. And they declined."

Monks did scrape together the financing. But in the end, the group did not get the Parcel 8 project. New England Merchants National Bank, which was then occupying the building on the Parcel 8 site, had pledged to be the prime tenant in a building constructed by one of Monks' rivals. When the Monks team won the contest, another, larger bank, the First National Bank of Boston, indicated its interest in locating in his group's building. But, the CEO of the Merchants phoned his counterpart at FNB to ask that he stay out of the matter, since Parcel 8 was after all the Merchants' traditional locale. The FNB chief complied, as he later told Monks. A newly formed Blue Ribbon Commission then officially recommended to the mayor that the project be awarded to Monks' rival.

Coincidentally, Merchants was also Goodwin, Procter's largest client. So when Monks lost Parcel 8, he uncharacteristically did not press the issue for fear that his job at the law firm would be in jeopardy. "It was devastating," Dubow says. "That was Bob's first big disappointment, realizing that you can't trust the establishment." He did no more real estate projects for a number of years.

Despite all the excitement of these evening and weekend ventures, Monks' main preoccupation was his law practice. Carrying himself with an air of authority despite his youth and inexperience, Monks was actively building his clientele. Among his many clients were his father-in-law's business, C. H. Sprague, as well as several small research and development enterprises of the type he was also investing in. Monks loved the intricacies of corporate law and proved himself to be a problem solver. He developed skills in financing, including selling securities and obtaining financial back-ing, to help his capital-hungry clients. In fact, he was so successful that sev-eral businesses that retained him as their legal counsel asked him to become a director on their boards. Two were: Codex Corp., which made a trans-mitting device that encoded messages, and instrument maker Esterline Cor-poration, which acquired 32 companies between 1967 and 1969.

Given his large measure of self-confidence, Monks was not easily fazed. Berman recalls the time he was working with Monks on a sizable deal in which a client was selling his company to a large German multinational. The two lawyers met with the client in their office the day before the clos-ing and then walked him to the elevator. Just as he was stepping into the el-evator, the client said, "Oh by the way Bob, I meant to tell you, I can't find my stock certificates. I must have misplaced them. This isn't going to be a problem is it?" Berman was alarmed, but Monks was composed. "No prob-lem," he said. "We'll take care of it. Just be here at 10 o'clock tomorrow." The elevator doors closed. Monks turned to his colleague and said, "Holy shit! The stupid sonofabitch lost his stock certificates! What the hell do we do?" By morning, they had figured a way out of the problem and got the deal done.

One of Monks' biggest clients was his father-in-law's family fuel distri-bution business, C. H. Sprague. After World War II, Sprague, then exclu-sively a coal company with mines in West Virginia, became one of the largest exporters of coal in America, and exporting coal was then big busi-ness since European mines had been devastated by war. The Marshall Plan paid for the initial few years of exports to Europe. Exports also went to Japan. Domestically, Sprague shipped much of its coal to utilities in New England. When the utilities and paper companies converted to oil starting around 1949, Sprague struck a deal with Royal Dutch Shell to distribute residual fuel known in the business as "black crap" from Shell's Asiatic Pe-troleum subsidiary in Venezuela. Sprague received the oil at its tidewater terminals and sold the bulk of it to paper companies and utilities in the Northeast. The company also owned a number of home heating oil distrib-utors in New England.

Monks' involvement started when his father-in-law, Phineas Shaw Sprague, asked him for legal advice concerning a family feud over the com-pany's fate. Sprague stock was in a trust for the benefit of the Sprague fam-ily, and 52 percent of the trust was in Shaw Sprague's name. The other trust beneficiaries, his two sisters, were increasingly resentful that the company was run preponderantly for their brother's benefit, given his majority position in the stock and the perks he got from that controlling position; for example, he used a yacht to travel around the world, supposedly to visit customers but often just for pleasure. They hoped to coerce the trustees into selling the trust property, C. H. Sprague & Son, by finding bidders. However, the trustees received only one offer, in 1961, from Consolidation Coal Company to buy the company at its book value, $32.6 million.

Monks' father-in-law protested that the offer was too cheap. The trustees of the company, meanwhile, were obligated to consider the Consolidated offer, but were squirming from the thought of being caught in a family quarrel. Monks figured out a way to make everybody happy by using what later became known as a leveraged buyout. His father-in-law could buy the company from the trust for the same price offered by Consolidation by putting up a small amount of equity, $2 million, and obtaining loans collateralized by the value of the company's assets. That would put the company's value at $4.50 a share. Sprague and Monks got about $30 million in loans by first obtaining $12 million of subordinated debt from a division of their oil supplier, Royal Dutch Shell. Shell had an interest in preventing someone else from getting this company, since C. H. Sprague had claim to a large oil import quota (oil imports being restricted at the time) and several terminals, and was Shell's largest customer for Venezuelan oil. Of the total loan, $3 million was convertible into stock at $20 a share after two years. The value of that option, which Shell itself calculated, was a clear indication that Shaw Sprague would be getting the company for a song at $4.50 a share. With their Shell loan in hand, the Monks/Sprague contingent was able to get the rest from Irving Trust, Shell's bank in New York.

Shaw Sprague still needed $2 million in equity. Monks' father agreed to put up $500,000. The other $1.5 million came from loans from Shaw's personal holding company and trusts for his children. When all the contracts were signed, in July 1963, Monks' family owned 62,500 of the 450,000 shares of company stock; his father-in-law owned 150,000; a trust for his first family had 67,500; a trust for his second family held 120,000; and employees had 50,000. "I was acting as my father-in-law's lawyer, and we bought it for nothing, in effect," Monks says. "We were able to borrow all of the money. My father-in-law now had the company and the trust. He thought this was a miracle." Monks, while still practicing law, was now also a director and the secretary of Sprague.

At the same time, though, there was more family intrigue. The very day after the sale closed, Shaw Sprague, then 60, informed Monks that he was planning to divorce his second wife and move on to a third. Monks had always admired Shaw Sprague's fun-loving attitude. But this plan did not sit well with the son-in-law. "I had spent a lot of time with the debris of his first wife" (Milly's mother), he says. "One more wife was something we didn't need. I felt it was very destructive." Monks took it on himself to refer the second wife to a lawyer and encouraged her to fight to keep her home and a large portion of Shaw Sprague's assets. She did not, however, retain much of anything. And by helping her, Monks angered his father-in-law, and the rift never healed. "I was wrong to get involved," Monks says today. "We fell out over that." But at the time, he wanted to take a stand when confronted with something he believed was wrong. It would not be the last time he would take a firm position, nor the last time he offended someone by doing so.

Shaw Sprague's long-term goal was to sell the company at a sizable profit, and that would become a new challenge for Monks as business manager. The process would involve developing favorable long-term contracts with all the company's suppliers, customers, and distributors such as the railroads that carried the coal. Many existing contracts with European and Japanese buyers, mostly utilities, were long-term fixed-price agreements. That circumstance could hurt the company if coal prices increased because Sprague's own mines represented only a portion of what it delivered to customers; it had to buy the rest from other mining companies. If coal prices rose, Sprague would be paying more but receiving the same price at sale. Monks soon began renegotiating contracts with all manner of accountants and lawyers, honing skills that he would find valuable later as a bank chairman and then as a shareholder activist bargaining with corporations.

Monks had never been committed to law as a long-term career, a fact amply demonstrated by his tendency to stray from it. To be sure, he was hoping his other activities would make him a fortune and free him for new, non-profit-oriented pursuits such as some sort of public service. But he was also excited by his ability to thrive in these new fields, and they offered tempting new avenues for him. At the same time, he thought that the one thing he had not yet tried that might give him a much better perspective on career opportunities was working for a first-class large corporation. "I always had a sense that I was trying to prepare myself for something," he says. "By then, I'd not had any structured training in business. I thought I could learn something."

He decided to call on James Stillman Rockefeller, who was then CEO of Citicorp and also happened to be married to Milly's aunt, Nancy

Carnegie. Monks had two questions for him: "What is the best company in America?" and "Do you know anyone there to whom I might talk about being employed?" Rockefeller didn't miss a beat in naming Jersey Standard, now Exxon, which the Rockefeller family had been instrumental in founding. At that time, Jersey Standard was in the process of diversifying away from oil and chemical operations into electronics, office products, and other areas. Rockefeller thought that Monks might be an ideal candidate for a senior level position overseeing these new businesses. He recommended his nephew to the company, and Monks had a series of meetings with the vice president of personnel, who liked Monks and encouraged him to propose a starting salary level. At the time, Monks was earning about $35,000 a year at the law firm, which was quite high for its time and certainly more than the Jersey Standard personnel officer was making. Monks met him for lunch with an unusual proposition: He would work for nothing for one year to prove himself capable of a high level job at Jersey, if the company assured him a chance at getting one. Monks recalls the baffled look on the face of the man eating lunch across from him. There was no place at the company for an outsider with this kind of ambition. "That look coalesced the whole range of doubts that I had about my capacity to fit into a huge bureaucracy," he recounts, "and the dinner continued with both the VP and I agreeably understanding that there was no way in God's earth that I was coming to work for Jersey."

At the end of 1964, Monks was made a partner at the law firm, at the age of 31 one of its youngest ever. He was astonished when the senior partner gave him the news, but then realized that he had been generating a sizable portion of the firm's billings. Within a few days of that promotion, however, he quit. Having achieved that milestone, he saw that he had got all he wanted out of the legal profession. Encouraged by his successes in venture capital, he decided to head in that direction. "My energies couldn't really be contained in taking care of other people's problems," he says. Getting involved in his own businesses was what captivated him now. Besides, given the extent of the law firm's clientele, he was sure that at some point he would become involved in a real estate or investment situation that would embarrass the firm. "We were all shocked," Berman says, "but we weren't really surprised."

Monks then formed a venture capital partnership with his college friend Jeff Coolidge—just back from Korea where he had been in the CIA and then in business—and a banker, Charlie Cunningham, another distant relative. The three partners called themselves Coolidge, Cunningham & Monks (CCM); they were all in their early 30s, all well connected, and in fact all related in one way or another to the Gardner family. They were going to be investors and do deals like a merchant banking organization. Goldenfarb, the law firm's office boy, went with them to continue his work/study program and stayed full time after graduating in 1967. Several months later, one of Monks' former law partners, Dwight Allison, joined the group. CCM invested in Damon Engineering and other small businesses. Before long, CCM folded into the Gardner family office, becoming Gardner Associates, which managed the family's investments.

One of their investments was in International Equipment Company (IEC), which made centrifuges, machines that generate centrifugal force. The company claimed to be on the verge of producing high-speed, "ultra" centrifuges that could create a force of one-half million times the force of gravity for use in biotechnology research and in making uranium. To check that claim, Monks—who with his partners had bought a 10 percent position—asked his close friend Anderson for his opinion. At the next big medical conference, Anderson, a scientist who had worked with centrifuges, spent an hour and a half talking with IEC sales and technical employees. They showed him one of the new centrifuges that they had on display and told him that its design was already being reviewed by outside experts. "I told them up front I was working with Bob Monks of Gardner Associates," he says. "They showed me everything. I concluded that they were not aware of the problems they'd face. I told Bob, and he immediately sold the company." Monks and the other venture capitalists in both IEC and Damon merged the two companies. IEC never did break into the ultra centrifuge market, Monks says. Ultimately, Damon was bought by Corning.

Over the years, Anderson has helped Monks in a number of investments. "He was always frustrated that he couldn't give me a cut of the profits because I was a government employee," Anderson says. However, Monks always returned these favors in kind, with legal or business advice. In the early 1970s, when Anderson was running a lab at the National Institutes of Health, he was distraught over one particularly aggressive physician who was trying to take over the best projects. When Monks saw Anderson at a January Harvard-Cambridge Scholarship Committee meeting, he took him aside and said, "You look like you're about to collapse." Anderson told him the story, and Monks immediately knew what his friend should do: "Call Kathy," Anderson recalls Monks saying. "Tell her you're not going back to

Washington; you're going to Maine with me." Anderson protested that he had work to do. But after the meeting, Monks led his friend out the door and over to his own car, put him in the passenger seat, got in, and drove the two hours to Cape Elizabeth. Anderson stayed for two days. "We walked together and talked about life, and about management," Anderson recalls. "Bob had one of those Finnish saunas—140 degrees, 100 percent humidity. You sit in the sauna and then run outside in the buff and roll in the snow. I'd never done that before or since. It was an interesting experience."

Monks then suggested that Anderson go to Puerto Rico and lie on the beach. This time Anderson didn't resist. "After five days down there, it dawned on me: I didn't work for that doctor. He worked for me. I'm not supposed to make him happy. He's supposed to make me happy. So I got on a plane and went back to Washington. I went into the office and said, 'Ron, from now on, you make me happy.' And he did!"

While developing other investments, Monks spent an increasing amount of time on C. H. Sprague. In 1965, Coolidge, Cunningham & Monks bought 50,000 shares from the Sprague second family trust at $20 a share, and, as scheduled, Shell exercised its option for 150,000 shares at the same price. C. H. Sprague may have had problems in coal, but its oil business was swimming in profits. Yet there was something about this happy situation that puzzled Monks. Although Royal Dutch Shell was one of three oil drillers in Venezuela, the other two wouldn't talk to Sprague about doing business together. "Why couldn't we get a better price? I'd been to Venezuela. I understood the logic of pricing. There were no costs allocated to the residual product, and therefore price could be set at any level and still show a profit. Why couldn't we make a deal with somebody else?" Monks says. "I was making a lot of money, but I couldn't get free of Shell. I made whatever money they wanted me to make. Everybody else was happy, but not me. It just didn't make sense to me." Unaware that the prices had been fixed—at the time, which was before OPEC (Organization of Petroleum Exporting Countries), there were secret pricing agreements among the world's oil companies—Monks became anxious that the company's situation was too fragile, relying as it did on one supplier.

As chance would have it, one of Monks' neighbors in Maine had a daughter who had married an Iranian. When Monks met the husband, Hussain, he learned about Hussain's great uncle (whom the young man had never actually met), who headed a national oil company in Iran. Some quick research confirmed for Monks that this story was true. The great uncle, Dr. Egbahl, was then head of the National Iranian Oil Company (NIOC), which was part of an effort by oil-producing countries to take back control of pricing from the oil companies. So, Monks and Allison decided to take the young couple to meet Dr. Egbahl in Tehran. The goal: to get a supply contract for oil from somebody other than Royal Dutch Shell.

Tehran, framed by the magnificent Elburz Mountains, was startling to Monks. Traveling through, he witnessed the grandeur of its wealthy sections and the diesel stench of the poor ones. On the streets, the frenzied traffic seemed to give way to complete chaos. Their host was another of Hussain's relatives, a lawyer. Monks and Allison stayed a couple of weeks, holing up in their host's offices, typing proposals, plotting strategy, breaking for lamb luncheons and meetings with officials of the NIOC. Those sessions led finally to a meeting with Dr. Egbahl. Since Dr. Egbahl knew very little English, he and Hussain would whisper in each other's ears. But the older man was quite knowledgeable and impressed with C. H. Sprague's control of deep water ports on the East Coast, its operation of ships in and out of those ports, and its large customers for residual fuel oil. To the NIOC, a regional company like Sprague represented an incursion onto major oil companies' turf. Monks and Allison then retreated to their temporary office to draft a letter agreement for Dr. Egbahl to sign. They left the country with a signed contract for the NIOC to supply them with their needs in oil at a good price, provided that they get the agreement of one Mr. Fallah, a power broker based in London. So, on their way back home, they stopped at Fallah's hotel suite in London. Regrettably for the two young oil tycoons, Fallah tore up the contract (a copy) before their eyes. Sorry, no deal. They knew they could try greasing the man's presumably well-oiled palm, but decided just to go home. Actually, they felt pretty proud of themselves for getting as far as they did, given that they were only a regional distributor. And they were fairly confident that sometime in the next few years they would be able to secure a better deal than their Shell contract, since from their experience it seemed evident that the oil companies were losing their grip on the market.

In 1967, Shaw Sprague, then 64, wanted to cash out of his stock in C. H. Sprague. After mulling alternatives, Monks and Allison decided that together they would borrow the money from banks to buy all of Shaw Sprague's 150,000 shares and so end up with the controlling interest. They approached him with an offer of either $20 a share—$3 million—plus half the profits realized over five years, or $30 a share. Sprague, who was still not on good terms with Monks, wanted the $30, $4.5 million for his

150,000 shares, but agreed to an arrangement by which they would pay the full amount in three installments from 1967 through 1969. Even so, the two young men were deeply in debt, borrowing $4.5 million over the two-year span, first from one bank in Boston and later from five small banks in Maine. "At one point in this period I had interest obligations of over $1,000 per day with nothing but my wits to find out how to pay it back," Monks says. His wits swiftly solved the problem, at least for the moment. He and Allison were paying themselves about $100,000 each in salary, which they used to make the interest payments. For living expenses, they had directors' and consulting fees. In addition, they began to sell stock in their venture capital investments; by chance, Damon and Codex were just going public.

Allison became Chairman of Sprague and Monks CEO. Given the extent of their debt and the volatility of the coal trade, they were, in a word, nervous. As Monks puts it, "The coal business makes money once every ten years and then it makes a lot of money. The other years you lose either a little or a lot. So it's a rotten business to be in if you've borrowed all the money to go into it, like Dwight and I had." It was a foregone conclusion that they would have to sell the business to pay their debts, and they hoped they could make a profit as well. So the goal was improve the bottom line.

At that time, C. H. Sprague was recording sales of about $250 million a year. Of that, coal represented some $215 million and oil accounted for the rest. But the oil division made money consistently, about $3 million after taxes, while coal swung from losses to $6 million in profits. In the mid 1960s, coal profitability was in a downdraft. One thing Monks and Allison did was find other products needed in the region that they could move through their New England docks, such as road salt, solar salt, and sulfur.

But that did not make up for the losses from the fixed-price contracts. A boat bound for a plant in Cherbourg, France, operated by Électricite de France would arrive at Newport News once a month to pick up 80,000 tons of coal. Each boatload represented a $1 million loss to Sprague. Fortunately, that contract only had a few months left on it when Monks and Allison took over. They were not so lucky with other customers. Their training as lawyers helped greatly with contract renegotiations, especially for a particularly tough-worded agreement with a German utility, Hamburg Gas, that was draining $400,000 to $500,000 a month from their coffers in a contract stretching out another dozen years. "Dwight invented a new law to get us out of the contract," Monks relates. "There's a thing called a *force majeur* provision in a contract that says you can't be made to perform if it's impossible, and Dwight got the word 'impossible' changed [in this contract] to 'commercially impractical.'" How they managed this had a lot to do with what Westinghouse Corporation was going through at the time. The company had announced that if it was forced to honor a fixed-price contract to deliver uranium, it could go broke. The matter was in the process of being resolved when Sprague was trying to deal with its German contract. Allison and Monks took the position that U.S. law could now be interpreted as saying that one did not have to deliver on a contract that could ruin the business, and they told Hamburg Gas that they would fight to defend this view. Luckily, the German company backed down and agreed to redo the contract. "We had to face down those Germans, who were very hard to face down," Monks says. "In that case, we never got sued. We just alleged that that was the law, and they put up with it, and ultimately we were vindicated because the court changed the law. But, whew! Heavy stuff. We could've gone down on that one. One contract."

On top of such financial complications that Monks could handle was an emotional one that he had more trouble coping with. One day, he learned that a Sprague miner had been killed by falling rocks. The mines employed about 4,000 men and on average every year four died in accidents, but this was the first time it had happened under Monks' watch. He had toured the mines and knew how perilous they were. The news saddened him, and despite the protestations of managers in the Boston office, he insisted on attending the man's funeral. He flew to Washington and drove to West Virginia to meet the mine manager, Jim McCurry. But before they left to drive the 40 miles to the funeral, McCurry told him straight out: "Bob, you don't know what you're doing. People who go into the mines are a different breed. They understand their situation, they understand their grief and how to deal with it. They have their own community. It would be wrong of you to impose yourself on their grief." Monks went home, feeling useless.

While they were working to improve the business, Monks and Allison were starting to look into how they might sell the coal operation. Since some of their big customers were Japanese steelmakers, Monks consulted his friend Makihara, who in the late 1960s was in charge of the Washington, DC, office of Mitsubishi Corporation, which among other things was then one of the biggest trading companies in the world (although it did not handle C. H. Sprague's sales to Japanese buyers). Makihara agreed to meet Monks and Allison at a Chinese restaurant in San Francisco with the head of Mitsubishi's coal trading. That man, Mr. Tomabechi, gave them the straight story on Japan's steelmakers and coal traders. In the short term, he said, they had an inexhaustible appetite for the type of coal Sprague produced—Pocahontas coal, which has good characteristics for making steel efficiently. Mitsubishi needed it. Japan needed it.

"If you have such an appetite for coal now, why don't you buy our coal mine?" Monks ventured.

"Aaaah!" said Tomabechi with a knowing smile. Over the long-term, given foreseeable advances in technology, he probably would not need to buy this high-quality grade of coal. And then, it would be cheaper to get poorer quality coal available in closer locales.

Monks and Allison returned to Boston convinced that they needed to sell the coal business as soon as possible. Their dilemma: Sprague's coal business had huge volume and prestige as an exporter, but, at the time, no profits. Yet to pay off their debts, Monks and Allison needed to make a profit on the sale of this business. They approached logical potential buyers, but no one was biting. Then, they got lucky. The new CEO of Westmoreland Coal Company, then the country's largest independent coal company, loved the coal business and believed in its future. To him, Sprague and Westmoreland seemed to be a good fit, since Westmoreland had very little export business and Sprague needed experienced management and capital resources. In late 1968, Monks and Allison traded their stock for Westmoreland stock and cash worth $21 million and ended up with a 20 percent interest in Westmoreland and seats on the board.

At that time, Monks and Allison were still running the petroleum division of Sprague, and Shell continued to be Sprague's sole supplier. That became a problem, even before the Westmoreland deal, when the two executives began plotting ways to attract bids to sell the oil part of their energy empire and make a profit. In the style of true marketing daredevils, they took full advantage of a competition among oil giants that was then developing in Maine. In 1967, Jack Evans, an independent oil promoter, came up with the idea of creating a deepwater port and refinery in Machias on the northern coast of Maine. He applied to the Secretary of Interior for an oil import quota that would be needed for an oil company to build and operate the refinery and the port. Monks saw that with the help of his Maine connections, he could insert C. H. Sprague into the Machias situation as a key player. The desired outcome: he would accumulate enough leverage so that someone would have to buy him out just to get rid of him. With the precision of an expert marksman, Monks moved in.

His plan was full of the moxie he became known for years later in the realm of shareholder activism. The shoreline in question was one Monks knew well. Roque Island was just a few miles away, and as a boy he had often fished for cod just where Evans was contemplating development. Guided by the theory that whoever controlled the land would control the refinery project, Monks formed a new Sprague subsidiary called Atlantic World Port and, in 1968, bought options on the strategic waterfront and island properties on which an oil terminal could be built. How he managed to do that was via sheer chutzpah. He dispatched a longtime Sprague employee by the name of Eddie Stilatis to Machias for a few months, assigning him to size up the coastal landowners and begin negotiating purchases. Stilatis visited with the landowners, went fishing with some, took some out for coffee. Many knew of the Monks family. One by one, they sold. Says Monks: "We were able over several months to assemble options to thousands of acres of land, including the ledges that would have been the unloading place for deepwater vessels." To secure the options, C. H. Sprague paid about $200,000. Monks then got the state on his side by pledging to hand over the options at cost if the state's application for a foreign trade zone was granted. As the incipient refinery company's counsel, he hired Washington attorney Charles Colson, who would shortly become special counsel to President Richard Nixon.

While Monks was negotiating to buy the land options, Armand Hammer, chief executive of Occidental Petroleum, registered his desire to be the operating oil company for the project and bought out Evans' interest. The year before, Occidental had struck oil in Libya but had no U.S. refinery or import quota, so the Machias Bay project appeared to be the answer to his dreams. The big oil companies reacted unfavorably to Occidental's move to get an import quota and took their case to Washington. Meanwhile, that October 1968, Monks attended a meeting of five New England independent oil and gas marketers with Hammer and Maine Governor Kenneth Curtis in Occidental's New York office. From the back of the room, Monks—without revealing his land-option purchases to date—demanded to know more about C. H. Sprague's future role in the refinery project, insisting that his company's ownership of terminals in Maine and elsewhere in New England gave him a controlling position. Annoyed, Hammer told his lawyer to "Get that man's name." But Monks shot back, "M-O-N-K-S!"

Later that year, when Hammer learned that Monks held all the land options, the Oxy oilman was furious. At one point, he arranged a meeting with Monks and Governor Curtis in Augusta. Traveling to Boston in his private plane, Hammer picked up Monks and then flew to Augusta, where in the presence of the governor he futilely tried to browbeat Monks into giving up the options. But Monks was a tough bargainer, demanding part ownership of the refinery and a role for Sprague in the development of satellite industries. No way, said Hammer. The following year, Monks' associate Howard Goldenfarb drove north for two or three days at a time over a span of two months to make sure the land options were renewed; the last renewals become official two weeks *after* they expired in a nail-biting episode for Goldenfarb and Monks.

In April 1969, newly energized by Nixon's election and the installation of a Republican administration, including a number of friends, Monks approached Hammer with a proposal to have C. H. Sprague take over the refinery project with a commitment to use Occidental's oil. Hammer rejected that idea out of hand. But the increasingly evident frustration of this international wheeler-dealer greatly encouraged regional oilman Bob Monks in the pursuit of his own goals: to corner Occidental or Royal Dutch Shell into a deal to buy his Sprague oil assets. Alarmed by Monks' intrusions, within a couple months Hammer offered to buy Sprague at an attractive price. Although the sale wouldn't include the land options, it would give Hammer a marketing outlet for his oil.

At once, Monks and Allison informed Shell that Hammer would soon become a direct competitor. Monks went to New York to visit Shell Asiatic Petroleum head Jack Ritchie. At Ritchie's office in Rockefeller Center, Monks told him more about Oxy's offer in an attempt to prompt a counteroffer. "In the words of my clergyman father," Monks said to Ritchie on leaving his office, "speak now or forever hold your peace." What ensued was described in a book written about Machiasport called *Fragile Structures,* by Peter Amory Bradford:[1]

> Ritchie wanted time for Shell to think about it, but Monks told him that he was on his way to Occidental's offices, implying that Hammer had made an acceptable offer. Ritchie replied, as Monks remembers it, to the effect that he wouldn't do business at gun point, and Monks departed for Occidental's offices. Arriving there, he found a call from Ritchie awaiting him and, when he returned it, a better offer.[1]

Shell agreed to acquire C. H. Sprague's oil assets in return for the redemption of its 150,000 shares of Sprague stock and a commitment to lease the company's tidewater facilities for $1.2 million a year for 15 years. The acquisition did not include control of or interest in Atlantic World Port. Shell, after all, was one of those big oil companies that opposed any opening for "outside," noncartel oil to get into the country. (While it had been 25 percent owner of Sprague, Shell had not received profits from the Atlantic venture.) Enraged by Monks' tactics, Hammer complained to the Justice Department that the sale to Shell was part of an attempt by the big oil companies to squelch any potential competition in New England. Later, the Justice Department did require Shell to divest Sprague, and Axel Johnson, the Swedish company, was the buyer.

In the meantime, Monks still had Atlantic World Port and its land options. He decided to see the process through in case he won himself a refinery site. "With a Republican President, the land position, no conflicts on account of other oil business, and a project 100 percent of whose economics depended on political, as opposed to economic, developments—Foreign Trade Zone status and oil import quotas—Atlantic World Port seemed like an attractive speculative venture," he says. "It had good entrepreneurial characteristics."[2] It was also a way for Monks, who was by then beginning to think in terms of his political chances in Maine, to raise his profile there.

In June 1969, the same month he sold out to Shell, Monks held a press conference with great fanfare in a caucus room in the U.S. House of Representatives to announce AtlanticWorld Port's just-filed oil-import quota application. The quota would allow Atlantic either to operate a refinery itself or build one and lease it to a refiner chosen by the New England states. Monks even prevailed on Governor Curtis, who was in favor of the port project because of the jobs it would bring to the state, to endorse his proposal.[3]

While they were embarking on this unlikely path to building a refinery, Monks and Allison were devising ways to cash in their Westmoreland stock. There was no avoiding the inevitable: they needed cash to pay off their debts. That year, 1969, their Boston lender abandoned them just when they needed to make their third payment to Shaw Sprague. Monks scrambled to find new money, phoning numerous small banks in Maine. "I remember sitting in my office on the phone with Wendell Phillips from a bank in Presque Isle," Monks says. "And I was thinking, if he says no, I don't know where else I'll go." But he said yes. And so did four others—all lending to Monks up to their limits.

The partners decided that the only way they could successfully obtain cash was first to do a hostile takeover—almost unheard of in those times— either by waging a proxy contest in which they would put up an opposing slate of director nominees, or, more likely, by launching a tender offer for shares. If they acquired control of the company's cash flow, they could then get bank financing backed by their ownership position to pay off their personal debts. Already, Monks was thinking like the shareholder activist he would one day become. They began by hiring as their lawyer Lewis Powell, from Westmoreland's home state of Virginia, but within two weeks he was named to the U.S. Supreme Court. As their lead counsel, they then engaged Arthur Fleischer, today senior partner at Fried Frank Harris Shriver & Jacobson in New York. For financing, they skirted U.S. banks, which they knew would not lend money for a hostile transaction, and approached Swiss financiers and French banks. It looked like they had a bankable deal.[4]

But in the middle of their plotting, Westmoreland stock began to inch up. The Japanese, it turned out, were buying coal. Just as Mitsubishi's Tomabechi had told Monks and Allison, in the short term, steelmakers needed certain types of coal from the United States. The surging stock price scotched Monks' and Allison's plans for a takeover. Instead, they hoped to do a secondary offering of their 20 percent stake, selling it into the general market in one lump. Out of the blue, a phone call came from Monks' cousin Nicholas Coolidge, a banker at Kidder, Peabody & Co. (and a distant cousin of Monks' former partner Jeff Coolidge), who was almost breathless in his enthusiasm for handling the sale of their Westmoreland stock and invited them to the firm's headquarters in New York. The issue was scheduled for December 1970.

Among the analysts who were researching the company was a young George Soros. Then a securities analyst and money manager at Arnold S. Bleischroder in New York, Soros traveled to Boston to meet with Allison. Early that fall, the stock inexplicably started climbing again. Monks soon learned that the source of the stock's strength was Soros, who had been steadily gathering shares. "Nobody had ever heard of Soros," Allison says. "He was an astute independent thinker and he came to the conclusion that there was an opportunity in a company that was a coal-only enterprise." The stock continued to rise to the point where the company decided to issue new shares alongside Monks' and Allison's stock sale. Negotiations with the underwriter began anew, this time at a higher starting price. Monks and Allison couldn't believe their good luck.

Monks took the initiative to ensure that whatever offering price was negotiated actually held up. He had learned in working as a corporate lawyer that the underwriter never makes a firm commitment on price. Often, he found, the issuer and underwriter would tentatively agree on a price based on the market price at the time, but then the market price would drop for no apparent reason and the underwriter would claim to be struggling to get the issue done at the lower price. After the offering, just as mysteriously, the stock would rise to or past the originally agreed-on price. Monks was among many who suspected the underwriters of profiting at the expense of the issuer and its shareholders, and he wanted to prevent this from happening to Westmoreland and himself. "I made arrangements with another brokerage house to be sure that there was continuing buying pressure so as to mitigate this predictable Wall Street underwriting scam," he says. He described the problem to a friend at Lehman Brothers, a former CIA agent, who promised to take care of it. Indeed, about a week before the underwriting, a huge order came in from a Swiss investor, and Monks assumed his friend was somehow behind it. He even sent him $100,000, as a fee for his services. However, Monks says that no one ever confirmed the Lehman connection.

Monks and Allison ended up getting $26.9 million in the sale. With that plus the value of the sale of the oil operations, the two partners ended up taking more than $36 million. After paying off his debt and paying taxes, Monks walked off with a fortune of $14 million in cash. The two men flew to New York to thank Soros personally. Soros, ensconced in his small midtown office, was greatly surprised and pleased by the visit. As Monks recalls, "He was patently a very different energy than that customary in the investment business—thoughtful, polite, and discerning." It would be many years until they would meet again.

In December 1996, Westmoreland Coal filed for bankruptcy under Chapter 11 of the federal bankruptcy code. The reason: it could not generate enough cash to pay employee benefits that had been required by legislation. All the C. H. Sprague mines were shut down. Says Monks: "And to think that we valued the properties based on hundreds of years of reserves!"

To Monks, money opened new opportunities, freeing him to choose a whole new direction in his life. Looking back, he believed he had mistakenly been seeking "medals" as if he were competing in some great race, wanting to be "something at the expense of being someone." And so he had gone to Harvard and Cambridge, and graduated with honors; then he became a partner in a law firm and a venture capital firm, built some build-ings, and ran a good-sized company. His assessment might be partly true. Yes, he had a natural desire to earn merit badges. But he also had an uncan-nily free spirit that took him from one challenge to the next, always pas-sionate, always wanting to learn more. Making money would now become but a pastime for him. Monks' next passion would be politics. It felt like a new beginning, filled with possibility, and it was. But as much as he dis-dained his goals of the past, he was still seeking medals.

3

Political Follies

I don't understand why he keeps hitting his head against a stone wall. This piece of the puzzle doesn't fit. Why would one keep trying to do something one is not good at? He's a loner. He is by nature a historian. He reflects on the past and tries to then reflect on the future. And he doesn't suffer fools gladly. He doesn't suffer them at all.

Monks' sister Ellen Higgins

In politics, the odds were stacked high against Monks from the start. The first problem was that some of the requirements of a politician went directly against his nature. Monks was not at ease in a large crowd or mingling at a cocktail party. He had always been more effective getting his ideas across one-on-one or in writing than in a speech. What is more, Monks was apt to think in broad terms, years ahead of his time, and so could appear out of touch with today's realities. His friend Mitsubishi executive Ben Makihara says of him: "Where we think about this year and next year, he's thinking about ten years ahead, which I think makes him not suitable to be a politician."

An even bigger problem was the state he chose to run in. Massachusetts with its Democratic leanings would have been enough of a challenge. But Maine, which is a poor state, had an electorate that was wary of outsiders, wary of people with money, and wary of intellectuals: three strikes against Monks. His intellectual nature made him inaccessible. His references to great thinkers and writers, in casual conversation, were way above the heads of the voters. Even his ability to computerize his campaign operation, which he did in 1972, when computers still seemed mysterious, made him suspect in the eyes of the voters. Then, although he had kept a summer residence in Maine his whole life and had become a permanent resident, Monks was a Bostonian to the natives. Looking back, Monks said in an interview, "The most pervasive problem of my political career in Maine was that—notwithstanding years of summer residency and ancestors—I was not born or educated in the state. My exposure was of a rich summer person who had never even seen the place with the leaves off (a condition that prevails for nine months every year). Notwithstanding my conscientious preparation, I really did not feel at home in the state, and I was not a good enough actor to conceal it."

Not only was he an outsider, he was a rich outsider. As his friend Howard Goldenfarb says he once remarked to him during a campaign: "No one is ever going to believe that anyone with four initials is anything but old money. And old money means, my ancestors worked for you, and probably weren't treated well."[1] During his first Senate race, he became known as the Cape Elizabeth Millionaire, an obviously derogatory sobriquet that confused him. Given his recent indebted state, he was thrilled to be called a millionaire and indeed thought others might be impressed that he, through good old honest sweat, had achieved the American dream. As he soon found out, even worse than being wealthy was spending some of that wealth in a political campaign.

Finally, and most importantly, there were the races he chose to run. As an outsider, Monks would have been wise to start small and build a reputation that would carry him to higher strata—he needed to pay his dues. His older sister Ellen, who tried repeatedly to sway him from the political path, would often tell him, "If people don't know you, how are they supposed to believe you?"[2] But he opted to shoot for the U.S. Senate all three times, twice turning down opportunities to run for governor. Not only did he aim high, but in his first two races his opponents had achieved legendary status, both in Maine and nationwide. Margaret Chase Smith, who started in the House in 1940 and served in the Senate for five terms starting in 1948, had no college education and a personal, down-home style that Mainers loved. In 1950, she won great renown for her "declaration of conscience" speech denouncing Wisconsin Senator Joseph McCarthy's anticommunist tactics. She also set the standard, at least in Maine, for frugality in political campaigns. Edmund Muskie was a liberal Democrat, defender of the environment, who by the time he came up against Monks had served as governor, Senator, presidential candidate, and vice presidential candidate.

At the time, none of these obstacles discouraged the highly confident multimillionaire. At a young age, Monks had already spun straw into gold and faced down the likes of Armand Hammer. Who was to say that he could not win in politics? Monks had seen two of his college classmates elected to national office—Edward Kennedy to the Senate and John Culver of Iowa to the House (and later the Senate)—and believed that he was as capable as they were. Besides, this was what he had decided he wanted to do. Through his studies, friendships, and travels, Monks had learned about governmental systems around the world and was practically in awe of the democratic system of self-government. "I'd always thought that politics was what people ought to do," he says today. "The great game. I thought it was the one thing America did better than other countries." He hoped to be part of that system.

Surely, it is easier to judge him a political failure in retrospect. If he had won—and he did win one primary—no one would have questioned the choices he made. After all, he did have some points in his favor. While he might not have been the Harry Truman of public speaking, Monks had been known to deliver an effective talk. And he came across as genuine and caring when talking to people individually. As Goldenfarb said of him: "If he could meet everyone one-on-one, he'd be President." Moreover, Monks truly loved the political process. Like the rower he was, he got a rush from the endurance test, stretching himself and his capacities ever further. As for his opponents, yes they were tough, but at least one of them was truly vulnerable. Margaret Chase Smith was running for a fifth term and her ideas were sounding clearly out of date. Before he ran, Monks did a straw poll with the question, "Do you think Senator Margaret Chase Smith should step down?" The majority of the replies were in the affirmative.

Whether or not Monks should have entered politics, it was fortunate for the shareholder activism movement that he did. The process of running for office involves thinking through issues, plotting strategy, meeting citizens, hearing their voices, and, most of all, selling yourself. In Monks' case that meant selling a product that nobody knew about or knew they wanted, which is the utmost challenge to a salesperson. It was one he would meet again in starting a business to handle pension plans' proxy voting and then in launching an activist investment fund. But most significant for the corporate governance movement was that Monks, as a candidate, gave considerable thought to what was important to the state, the country, and ultimately himself.

The idea of pursuing a career in politics had always been stirring in the back of Monks' mind, but for years he felt he could afford only limited involvement. Monks was 23 when he started working for the Republican Party in Massachusetts. At that time, he was part of the research team—headed by Elliot Richardson, later the Attorney General in the Nixon Administration—for the party's gubernatorial candidate, who lost. A Republican victory was rare in this most Democratic of states. In 1966, just before he and Allison bought C. H. Sprague, Monks became chairman of the state's GOP finance committee, in charge of fund-raising. Toward the end of his term, in the summer of 1968, Monks went to the Republican convention as a delegate for Nelson Rockefeller; of course, Nixon won the nomination.

By 1969, Monks was already thinking about the possibility of a future in electoral politics. Indeed, the idea of challenging Senator Smith in 1972 had crossed his mind more than once. Although he did not yet live in Maine full-time, he was beginning to make his name known through his Atlantic World Port endeavors. He delivered speeches in cities and towns along the Maine Coast in which he expressed his quite genuine environmental concerns and criticized the oil industry's past environmental misdeeds. With his grip on the land in Machias, he said, he would see to it that no one could build a refinery that would ravage the coastline, and asserted that certainly he himself would build the cleanest refinery. Astutely sensitive to the media's power, Monks gave reporters and editors a good portion of his attention, and the local press responded favorably toward him. He would follow a similar strategy in his shareholder activist campaigns, with similar results. Monks gives the media great credit in shaping the corporate governance movement. But it was Monks who coddled reporters so that they were inclined to hear his viewpoint, which was that of the beloved underdog.

In a further effort to win local support for Atlantic World Port—and enhance his own reputation—Monks sponsored a referendum in the towns abutting the proposed development and promised to be bound by the results. The idea came from Goldenfarb, who was Monks' first lieutenant in charge of handling many of the details of Machiasport. While at dinner with his fiancée one evening in January 1970, Goldenfarb brought up Monks' most recent directive: to develop good public relations on their refinery venture. The young woman suggested they sponsor a referendum in the Machias region on the proposed development and promise to abide by the public's wishes. Monks thought it was a great idea and ordered Goldenfarb to get to work on it. To those who suspected that this initiative was just a way to launch his by now rumored political career, Monks was coy. "I never make any plans more than six months in advance, and as far as I know, Mrs. Smith is planning to keep her seat until 1972," he told one questioner.[3]

The vote was scheduled for April 1970. Monks was evenhanded in his speaking and radio appearances, describing the real risks of oil spillage as well as the obvious advantages of job creation. Again, the media was charmed. Aware that Maine residents generally didn't know anything about modern oil refineries, Monks decided to put on a show. He asked Goldenfarb to take a group of about a dozen local citizens to visit a state-of-the-art refinery owned by Hess Oil in the U.S. Virgin Islands. Monks, however, had neglected to tell Hess that they were coming, so the group was barred from entering the refinery and had to view it from the outside.[4] Even so, the voters were impressed. The result was pro-refinery, 1,391 to 1,159. Monks was elated. When the tally was announced, Monks and Allison pulled Goldenfarb into a corner of the room and handed him an envelope. Inside was a note to the treasurer of C. H. Sprague (then consisting of the Westmoreland shares) authorizing Howard Goldenfarb to buy the car of his choice. He chose to buy a Corvette. For Monks, the vote was his very first political contest, and he suddenly felt a thrilling sense of power. It now seemed well within the realm of possibility for him to go to the Senate in 1972.

Twenty months later, at the end of 1971, Monks dissolved Atlantic World Port. The whole notion of building a refinery on the Maine coast had lost momentum as prices of foreign oil began rising and environmental concerns about oil spillage heightened. He turned his land options over to a nonprofit research group. Ultimately, control of most of the land reverted to the owners, the residents, while one island became a nature conservancy. There were those who doubted that Monks ever wanted to build a refinery, believing his efforts to be solely in the interest of his future political career. Monks denies this. "There were different scenarios," he says. "If someone had given me an oil import quota, I would have been happy to build a refinery. If my debts got paid off, I would go into politics."

He did not have to make a choice. By 1971, having just earned a $14 million fortune at the age of 31, Monks made his final decision to pursue a political path in Maine. Nervous about inflation and the stock market, he put his money in cash and flew to Kenya for a three-week safari with his family. When he returned, he began preparing for his new career by enrolling in the Kennedy School at Harvard to take courses in economics, the one field that intimidated him. "It bothered me to be bullied by people with a vocabulary I didn't understand," he says, meaning economists. To run for national office, he thought he'd need to be able to talk authoritatively about economic concepts. Anticipating a move to Maine sometime that year, Monks changed his legal residence to Cape Elizabeth, south of Portland, clearing the legal road to a run for Smith's seat. On assuming Maine citizenship, Monks went to the trouble of sending a bouquet of roses to Senator Smith on her 73rd birthday and making sure the press knew about it.[5] And he began taking his own polls of her prospects, which indicated a growing belief that she was getting too old to serve.

That summer of 1971, the Monks family left Cambridge to live full-time in Maine. Monks acquired a lease on eight acres (expanded to 200 in 1980) of the Sprague family's 2,000-acre property in Cape Elizabeth and made it his home. It had been called Ram Island Farm since Milly's grandfather bought it. Monks and his family later conducted business under the name Ram Trust Services, for Robert, his brother-in-law Austin, whose family also moved onto the property, and Milly. Because of Shaw Sprague's ill feelings toward his son-in-law, the arrival of the Monks family created some friction. Shortly after they moved into their home, Monks encountered a gate blocking his access to one of the two roads leading to the main artery. He soon found out it was the work of his father-in-law. Rather than create an uproar, Monks let the matter alone until Shaw Sprague's death in 1978. Then, he tore the gate down. But, several years later, Sprague's son—Milly's half brother—put up another gate. Attorney Monks and the Sprague Corporation run by Robert Monks Jr. then took Shaw Sprague Jr. to court, claiming that the Monks lease included the right to have access to that road. The court sided with Monks.

It was a difficult time for the Monks family in a more important way. Since early childhood, Monks' daughter Melinda had suffered from an emotional disorder diagnosed as schizophrenia. As Monks describes it, she was touched by every misfortune she saw, lacking the filter that most people have to protect them from the suffering around them. "We can walk by beggars in the streets," he says. "Melinda can't. It simply hurts her too much. The sense of what's wrong is too strong." When Monks was thinking of using pastureland near his new home in Maine for raising beef cattle, Melinda wouldn't hear of it. Instead, he started a tree nursery. In the spring of 1971, Melinda, then in her teens, fell ill once again. Sent home from where she had been attending school in Europe, she was admitted to McLean Hospital in Belmont, Massachusetts. Worried that Melinda might not be getting top-quality care at McLean, Monks called French Anderson in Washington and asked him to check the place out. The head of the hospital at the time had been one of Anderson's professors at Harvard medical school. Without hesitation, Anderson flew to the hospital and met with his former teacher. He then spent a couple of hours strolling with Melinda on the hospital grounds. From what he could tell, she was receiving the best care she could get anywhere, and that news was a great comfort to his friend.

A few years later, Monks and his wife, in continuing sorrow over their daughter's condition and finding few people to turn to for counsel, placed an ad in the Portland paper. It invited the parents of children with mental illness to a get-together at Milly's dance studio downtown. They expected perhaps 25 people. But 150 showed up, barely squeezing into the small studio. Even with the cramped conditions, though, the event was a huge success from the standpoint of the excited attendees. This and future meetings offered some solace to parents who had been feeling isolated and guilty. "There was huge therapy in the shared realization that a troubled child was not uniquely the fault of his or her parents," Monks says. Over the years, Monks would become involved in financing mental health residences and services in Maine.

Even before he announced his candidacy for the Senate, Monks and his campaign manager, Bill Webster, had devised a strategy to leverage Monks' name by having him sponsor a statewide referendum on some matter of general importance. They chose the issue of the "Big Box." Maine voters had always been able to check a box on top of the party symbol indicating that they were choosing the whole party ticket. Some thought that this straight ticket voting tended to help Democrats more than Republicans. Monks, and others who joined his campaign for this referendum, held that this device encouraged voters to ignore who was actually running, especially candidates for lower level offices. In the first half of 1971, Monks spent many weekends sitting behind tables at supermarkets all over the state, collecting signatures to get the item on the ballot. He did get the signatures he needed, and in the process learned a great deal about the state and the state about him. The referendum passed resoundingly in a special vote in June 1971.

The following month, Monks formally launched his campaign. Right away, he concocted another inventive scheme to raise interest in his candidacy: To entice other young Republican newcomers into the 1972 primaries, thereby drawing a younger Republican crowd to the polls that might be more likely to vote for him than for Smith. Monks says that he also wanted to demonstrate that he had interests in Maine and the Republican party beyond his own political goals. In any case, he had his eye on William Cohen, a baker's son who was then mayor of Bangor, the third largest city in Maine. Greatly impressed with the young mayor, Monks encouraged him to run for Congress and offered help with financing the campaign and with paying off any debts, win or lose. Cohen, who had not given any thought to running for federal office, declined. But Monks was persistent. He talked to other Republicans in Bangor, who agreed that it was a good idea to have two young Republicans in races for both the Senate and the House. They urged Cohen to grab the opportunity, and finally he did. "It worked to Bob's advantage as well, because the same people who'd be supporting me would be supporting him," Cohen says. "It was a nice synergy. And he was not well known in Bangor or in the north." Monks contributed to Cohen's campaign and introduced him to other potential donors. "It was easier for him to raise money for me than for himself," Cohen says. "As a millionaire in a state like Maine, it becomes hard to say, can you contribute to Bob Monks' campaign." Monks did, however, raise all the money for his campaign and did not resort to spending his own funds.

In his own campaigning, Monks chose not to make a big issue of Smith's advanced age. He believed that if he simply ran an energetic campaign touting his own abilities, people would get a sense of the contrast between his youthful vigor and her growing obsolescence. And so, he would walk 10 or 20 miles between towns, and keep constantly on the move from one speaking engagement to the next. In speeches and position papers, Monks stressed his experience in business, which could help retain industry and bring new jobs to Maine.

As Monks journeyed from town to town in the summer of 1971, staying in small run-down motels, he had the revelation that marked the birth of his corporate governance mission. He was staying in Bangor, which sits on the Penobscot River near the bay where Monks' European ancestors on his mother's side first settled. Just north of the city, several paper mills churned out products on the banks of the river. The plants were familiar to Monks, since they had been loyal customers of C. H. Sprague. What he did not know was that their general practice was to wait until the middle of the night to send their industrial effluent down the river. As Monks recounts: "I woke up in the middle of the night with my eyes streaming. I couldn't figure out what the matter was. I got up and went out and looked at the river, and there was a foam going down the river that was two or three feet high. White. Very white. I asked someone the next day, and they said, 'Oh hell. That's just stuff from the paper mill.'" He witnessed the same phenomenon in other paper mill towns across Maine. Driving into Livermore Falls on a windy day, he saw the white foam everywhere, on the ground and wafting into the air. Someone he met that day told him in all seriousness to be careful not to get the stuff on his car because it would sear off the finish.

To Monks, this ubiquitous foam, like the pollution from the oil industry he had spoken publicly about during Machias, represented something much larger: an evil force oozing through the cracks in the capitalist system. He thought about what had created it and allowed it to exist. As a former fuel supplier to the paper companies, he knew their top officers, directors, and plant managers personally. As a politician, he was meeting the people who worked in the plants and served on town and county governments. And so it occurred to him, he says, that "there wasn't anybody who wanted to have this effluent in the river. Nobody. That was what began to get my curiosity about the whole corporate system and whether we had invented some kind of Frankensteinian monster that was going to consume us all." How to control it? Who was responsible for controlling it? By then, Senator Muskie had earned a reputation as the environmentally concerned senator from Maine and had written legislation to stem pollution. Still, the foam flowed on. These were fleeting thoughts at the time. For all of Monks' professed concern about the environment, he didn't make pollution into a campaign issue. That, he says, was hardly on the Republican agenda, and his main concern was winning the primary.

Monks spent some $500,000 on his run against Smith, at the time a record for a Maine primary, outspending his opponent 50 to 1. For its advertising, the Monks campaign chose a strategy that was bold for its time. Instead of buying 30 or 60-second TV spots, he presented half-hour shows in prime time, from 8 to 8:30 P.M.—TV time in Maine being relatively cheap. The idea was to give people a real sense of this newcomer to politics. Still, Monks was the outsider and Smith so very familiar. She took the prize by a 2-to-1 margin, more than Monks had expected. However, Monks had been right about Smith's vulnerabilities. She lost the general election to U.S. Rep. William Hathaway. Some of her supporters blamed Monks for breaking her stride, because many of those who voted for Monks turned Democrat in the general election. In the race to fill Hathaway's seat, meanwhile, Cohen emerged victorious, and the baker's son went to Washington. In fact, he gives Monks great credit not only for getting him in the race and supporting him, but also for helping him win by doing away with the Big Box.

Monks was disappointed, but more in himself than in the voters. In retrospect, he saw that he had run on the strength of his personality and his resume, and on a promise of "new ideas," without any program or unifying theme. "It was just sheer arrogance," he admitted years later. "I liked to think of myself as a Senator." To succeed as a politician, he would have to have principles that resonated with the population. And so, that summer, he and his family went into seclusion for several weeks at Milly's beach house on Cumberland Island—the one she had inherited from her Carnegie grandfather—and began what he later called "the process of finding out what I really thought," or, really, articulating his core beliefs. The house was a single-story wooden structure with concrete footings in the sand. It had large windows on all sides and a porch overlooking tropical plants, dunes, and then a half-mile stretch of beach to the water. Originally just a one-room dwelling, Bob Monks and his family had added a bedroom, a shower, a deck, and a bunkroom for kids, as well as electricity. Over the years, it served as a southern retreat for the small family. They would charter a plane, load it with food and a TV set, land at a strip on the island, and take a Jeep to the house.

Sitting on the porch day after day that summer of 1972, Monks pounded away on a typewriter, filling page after page with his thoughts. Out came a philosophy shaped by his reading, his experiences in business and on the campaign trail, his summers in Maine, and his father's and family's commitment to service. He wrote about the problems of rural America, which seemed endemically caught in decline. One chapter was titled, "Jonesport, Maine does not have a constitutionally guaranteed right to life." Other sections focused on corporations in Maine and their opposition to new businesses on their turf. He amused himself by writing a satiric advertisement for companies to relocate: "Come to Maine. Get all the benefits of the Third World, and a Constitution and Army to defend you as well."

These thoughts led to the main subject he wrote about that summer: a trend in society to forsake responsibility. He complained about no-fault insurance, which was new at the time, divorce, statutory death limitations, and the brand-new health maintenance organization. All seemed to him to take the view that people would not be responsible for their own acts. "I came to feel that the integrity of any form of organization must be founded on the informed and responsible involvement of its members," he later summed up his writing. "The sense is that once you pay your taxes you have fully discharged all obligation to society. Everyone does what they are required to do by law; nobody considers themselves responsible to do more. Much falls between the cracks. There is no one who is considering the

whole. Solutions that did not take into account the need for individual responsibility had to be wrong." He hoped to turn the rough draft into a
book called *The No Fault Society,* which never materialized. In future years,
as he continued writing, he would include corporations under this theme,
as he began to understand their limited liability and hence their ability to
dump "externalities"—pollution, defective products, and poisonous products such as tobacco—on the rest of us without personal consequences for
management or directors. In addition, he saw that the limited liability of
shareholders and, in turn, their lack of active interest in the companies they
owned, had allowed managements to operate without accountability.

Between Senate campaigns, Monks' strategy was to enhance his image
in Maine while conducting business part-time outside the state, so as not to
reinforce the wealth factor in people's minds. His thinking was that he
couldn't help being a millionaire, but "people don't forgive you for making
a profit off of them," especially Mainers who are poor to begin with. Besides, to be honest, there wasn't much in Maine that caught his imagination. As evidenced by the national office he chose to seek, Monks could not
be hemmed in by state boundaries in business as well as politics.

The business he wanted to pursue came to him all at once the day after
he lost the 1972 primary. He was sitting in his living room with some friends
and business partners who had come to be with him on election day, and
they were discussing what he might do next. What could he do with his new
fortune, which was sitting around in cash? He hadn't used any of it for the
campaign, having raised all his funding. Then, all at once, it came to him,
every piece of the plan. With the country then so worried about inflation,
real assets were attractive and, given Monks' experience, oil and gas would
be the best choice. Where to invest was easy, in theory. The United States
seemed to be headed toward socialism. If Nixon was imposing wage and
price controls, who knew what a Democratic administration would do? In
many other places around the globe, governments were nationalizing industry and properties. So what he wanted was a capitalist country with an English legal system that respected property rights. After a bit of study, Monks
settled on the Canadian province of Alberta as the best available option. Unlike the rest of Canada, which was then socialist, Alberta, in the west, was
rock-hard capitalist.

There was, briefly, the possibility of working on the Nixon reelection
campaign—which, ultimately, of course, had disastrous results. Immediately after the primary, Charles Colson, who had been Monks' lawyer and

remained a friend, asked him to come to Washington to talk about what he might do. Monks flew down and met his old friend at his office in the White House. Colson urged him to go to a meeting of the campaign staff the next day, and he complied. But at that meeting, as the campaign chairman, former Attorney General John Mitchell, addressed strategy, Monks couldn't resist making a comment.

"I don't think that's a good idea, Mr. Mitchell," he began.

Mitchell didn't let him finish. *"I think. You do,"* he boomed.

Monks stood up. *"I think I'm in the wrong place,"* he said, and walked out.[6]

Colson was unrelenting. From a stack on his desk, he picked up the thick "plum book" of available administration jobs and threw it at Monks. "Take any job you want," he implored. His recommendation: "Take Under Secretary of Commerce. Rogers Morton, the Secretary, has cancer and you'll be Secretary in no time." The problem for Monks was, having just moved to Maine and launched an electoral political career there, he really didn't want to uproot himself and his plans with a move to Washington. The solution for him appeared to be a part-time position heading a Congressional commission to study the country's water resources from the perspectives of energy, pollution, and recreation. It looked like Monks was a shoo-in; all that was left was Senate confirmation. But at the last minute, New York Governor Nelson Rockefeller expressed his desire for the job, and Monks got bumped. Declining to serve as just a member of the commission, Monks opted instead to be a delegate to the second United Nations Environmental Protection Agency meeting that was to take place in Geneva in the summer of 1973. It was there that he realized that any real progress on environmental preservation would have to be a global effort, given the inexorable march of global competition. Any nation that imposed standards would force its domestic industry into an uncompetitive position. Industry itself would have to adopt standards voluntarily on a worldwide basis. How this process might start was the question he began thinking about more and more.

In the meantime, Monks had followed up on his notion of investing in Alberta. In August, he and Nicholas Coolidge, his friend from Kidder, Peabody who had helped him sell his Westmoreland stock, went to Alberta to visit a dozen or so small oil companies. Many had already been bought by foreign investors. One that welcomed his interest was Sulpetro of Canada, one of Canada's top 25 oil companies, one of whose directors was none other than Arthur Dubow, Monks' friend from Harvard. Dubow, it turned out, had got involved in Sulpetro not because of the natural gas but because of the sulfur, which comes out of the ground with gas. From April 1973 to the end of the year, Monks invested about $7.5 million into both the company's stock and a new drilling fund that allowed the company to expand into the United States. As owner of some 5 percent of Sulpetro, he then went on the board, became chairman of the finance committee, and was instrumental in plotting the company's strategy for the following three years.

In 1972, OPEC first made itself known in the world by raising the price of oil, which eventually led to the U.S. oil crisis in the mid-1970s. Anyone in the oil and gas business who had reserves just sat back and watched the value of their company grow. At the same time, Monks didn't feel the pain of a bear market that was devastating stock investors in 1973 and 1974. Even so, as Sulpetro continued to pump big-time cash, Monks became uneasy. Anything that was this successful was risky, especially when he was living so far away from the company and couldn't watch management's every move. So Monks, in the same style he would practice as a shareholder activist, pressured the board members to allow the investors to cash in, either by taking the company public or selling the proven reserves. The directors, all investors like Monks, resisted at first but then decided to sell proven reserves and keep the company as a development operation. "He likes liquidity," Dubow said in an interview with the author. "Part of it is I think he gets bored. Or just wants to do something new. He goes in, fights, understands the business, and says if you've made 20 times on your money the first three years, you doubt that in the next three years you'll make 20 times what you have now."

Dubow and Monks took turns traveling around the country with Coolidge, trying to sell the proven gas reserves. The buyer they found was Hudson Bay Oil and Gas Company, which paid $102 million in July 1975. Sulpetro used half the proceeds from the sale to buy out the investors who wanted to leave, primarily the U.S. shareholders. There was a little difficulty when Sulpetro's CEO tried to arrange a merger of his personal holding company into the surviving Sulpetro. One result of this transaction would have been some hefty tax payments for Monks, who as the most recent investor was subject to higher taxes than others. Monks, accompanied by his lawyer, confronted the CEO. He then laid out the situation to all the partners, asserting that he would be satisfied only if he were given a fee that made up for the extra taxes. Because of his work to sell the bulk of the company, he thought that the partners would acquiesce to his request. But they refused, and he decided against a court fight. Monks exited Sulpetro in 1976 with an after-tax profit of some $9 million. Eleven years later, Sulpetro collapsed under the weight of heavy debts from an acquisition and was forced to sell all its assets.

All this time, Monks was living in Maine and working on projects that would keep his name visible until the next Senate race in 1976. For example, he headed a state energy commission that had been formed to deal with the energy crisis. Appointed by Governor Curtis, who had supported him in Machias, he ordered a study of the state's energy needs and how they could be met, looking at all of Maine's indigenous energy sources. Once he had written an energy plan, he proposed that the commission, its job now done, be disbanded. The legislature disagreed, however, and kept it going for several more years. After leaving that office in 1975, Monks followed up on one of his commission's recommendations, to develop Maine's wood resources. Since the state chose not to invest taxpayer funds into such a risky project, he himself helped start Maine Wood Fuel with four partners. They were betting that waste wood and slash spewed from the state's many pulp and paper factories could be turned into pure energy. Maine Wood Fuel built several plants, which bought wood priced according to its BTU content. Monks left that effort when politics called, first buying out his partners and then selling to a Bangor investor, who carried on to great success. Also on a small scale, Monks founded two short-lived organizations that reflected his interests and concern for the state. Aid for Industrial Development and Expansion, or AIDE, aimed to bring clean industry to Maine and attracted two modular housing plants. Another organization, Senior Power, was designed to help senior citizens manage their problems.

In 1973, Monks became involved in real estate again at the instigation of Howard Goldenfarb, who had followed Monks to Maine and was helping him invest the family money. Largely as a result of Monks' influence, Goldenfarb wanted to get into business for himself and asked for his mentor's support and partnership. Monks gave him his blessing, and Goldenfarb set out in search of something to do. He found it by looking out the window of their office in Portland at Exchange Street and the surrounding area—the Old Port neighborhood running from City Hall to the water. It was an old, blighted section of the city with dilapidated buildings and some prostitution. Goldenfarb wanted to help revive the area, one building at a time; but he could only do so with Monks' help. Once Goldenfarb arranged to buy the first building, a relatively small one, Monks sealed the purchase by taking out a $300,000 bank loan. The deal was that 1 percent of the property belonged to Goldenfarb and 99 percent to Monks, and when they repaid the loan, the split would shift to 50/50. It was Goldenfarb's job to raise the money to repay the loan by rehabilitating the building and finding new tenants. He fixed up the building, offices above and stores on the ground floor, in a restoration that preserved the historic nature of the structure—a technique that would spread across the country and ultimately benefit from tax incentives.

That was later. But six months into the project the building had only one tenant occupying only 8 percent of the square footage. Goldenfarb was downcast, but Monks remained confident that the historic preservation concept was on target. "Don't worry," he told his friend. "It'll happen." And over time, the building did fill up. They went on to buy 21 buildings together over nine years—borrowing an average $1.5 million per building at lofty interest rates. Goldenfarb was the active, out-front person, who got all the press. Monks furnished loan guarantees and emotional support to his partner who was less experienced in the trials of entrepreneurship. As the project continued in the early 1980s, Monks even provided the trees for the development, including two new parks, from the nursery he ran on his family's Cape Elizabeth property. In the end, the refurbished Old Port district proved to be a vital part of Portland's renaissance.

At one time, Monks came very close to running for governor. Ever since his Senate race, Monks had been mentioned often as a potential gubernatorial candidate. Toward the end of 1973, he decided to announce his candidacy right away to preempt another candidate's expected bid. He reached Goldenfarb in Australia to tell him the news. (Monks had sent him there to get a feel for the country, on a whim of moving there to settle and have more children. Goldenfarb reported back that the place was socialist and not friendly to newcomers.) But then he changed his mind. The job of governor possessed neither the scope nor the work that inspired him. "It simply wasn't a job that involved questions the answers to which interested me," he later reflected.

Instead, he found himself getting interested in the 1976 Senate race. This time, the candidate to beat was a Democrat, Ed Muskie, another Maine legend. But there was no doubt in Monks' mind that Bill Cohen would have first dibs. As a freshman in Congress, Cohen had earned a reputation as an independent-minded politician when he voted with the majority on the House Judiciary Committee to impeach Richard Nixon. For a while, he seriously considered running for the Senate. "It would have been close. I might have won; I might have lost," Cohen, now Secretary of Defense, says today. "I was really popular at that time. I had high visibility as a result of the impeachment proceedings. The polls showed that I was ahead, but that was before a full campaign. Muskie could raise a ton of money from all over the country, because he was a national figure. While I felt that I had the potential to be a good senator, I thought Ed Muskie was still a great senator in terms of his stature and in terms of what he could do for the state. I decided that I really wasn't ready to make that move." He called Monks and told him he was not going to run.

To Cohen, Monks did not appear to have a burning desire to get into the race. But he did seem annoyed that nobody was going to challenge Muskie when just four years earlier, Margaret Chase Smith's defeat had proved that even legends can fall (though not to Bob Monks) and when Muskie had long been showing signs of being bored with the job of senator. Muskie had been Hubert Humphrey's running mate in the 1968 race against Nixon. Then, in 1971, he competed in the Democratic presidential primaries, and early on he was the front runner, but lost that standing when he wept on national television while defending his wife from talk that she told dirty jokes (George McGovern won the nomination). By 1975, Muskie's name was among those mentioned as possible candidates for vice president; if he was not chosen, he would run for re-election. The way Monks saw it, if no one else was going to mount this challenge, then he would do it. Of course, Monks also had a burning desire to run and to win this time. His competitive juices were flowing.

His opponent in the primary was one Plato Truman ("Two great names and one great American"), a staunch conservative who ran a lifeless campaign. When Monks' campaign manager fell ill, Milly took over until a new one could be found. "I did know how to manage a dance company, so I knew something about budgets and how to get good help," she recounts. Monks trounced his opponent, with 81 percent of the vote.

Naturally, Monks was hoping that Muskie would be chosen as Carter's running mate, leaving a less formidable candidate for himself to take on. Then, that summer, while watching a television report describing the sessions presidential nominee Jimmy Carter was having with prospective running mates, Monks saw the impossibility of a Carter-Muskie ticket. Muskie was simply too big. He towered over Carter. And indeed, Carter chose the more moderately sized Walter Mondale to be his campaign sidekick.

So it would be Bob versus Ed. Fully aware of the magnitude of this challenge, Monks threw himself into it, hooked on the excitement of political competition. He believed that Muskie could be beat. In addition, Monks could now run on a stronger record of helping Maine in job creation, urban redevelopment, and government service.

Given Muskie's reputation as Mr. Clean,® part of Monks' message was the ineffectiveness of the Senator's environmentalism, as evidenced in the air and water pollution throughout the state. Corporations simply found a way around restrictive laws of any kind, he held, including those Muskie had spearheaded. One theme present in many of Monks' speeches was that good pollution control was good business, and once government required business to clean up its practices, companies could be creative in figuring out how they would comply. As an example, he cited the government's new standards for the paper manufacturers, prohibiting further dumping of effluent into public waterways. The companies implemented processes to reuse the residue from waste boilers to make pulp, instead of floating it down the river at night. The result was a much more cost-effective practice with substantial savings, Monks pointed out. But he soon found that calling attention to polluted sites worked against him; the voters made their livelihood in the pulp and paper industry, pollution and all.

Monks had trouble finding a campaign manager to carry him through to the general election. The Republican Senatorial Committee suggested a few men, who came to Maine to visit with Monks, but the chemistry was not there. Instead, Monks hired Bob McKernan, the young nephew of the Maine Senate President, who had just graduated from college and had been working for the Monks campaign. But, in addition, Monks took counsel from two nationally known political advisers. Josiah Lee Auspitz, founder of the Ripon Society, which promotes moderate Republican principles, came north to work with the candidate the final eight weeks of the campaign. Roger Ailes, who had helped Nixon polish his style in 1968, came to Maine to coach Monks on his debating technique and speech delivery, trying to help him get over his discomfort addressing crowds. In addition, Ailes produced the campaign's commercials, which this time were 30- and 60-second spots plus one half-hour show at the end of the race.

Monks and Muskie debated several times. Just before one debate, literally as the count got down to one, Monks followed Ailes' advice and tweaked his opponent's ear. Muskie was famous for his short temper, and the Monks team was hoping for an explosion. Muskie ignored the ruse. The nagging subject of pollution came up repeatedly. At one debate, Monks challenged Muskie on the subject of the pollution of Moosehead Lake and the wastefulness of successive federal cleanup plans that he had pushed through Congress. Proud of his accomplishments on environmental matters, Muskie easily rose to anger. At their last scheduled debate on public television, Monks challenged him to yet a further debate at Greenville at the southernmost tip of the lake. It was not to be.

In 1978, Muskie told Monks that two weeks before the vote, his polls indicated that Monks was actually ahead (Monks himself was not taking daily polls). But, the last week of the race, Muskie turned on the spigot, and the endorsements and ads poured over the airwaves. Voters viewed him as someone who had been cheated out of the presidency in 1972 and the vice presidency in 1976, but also as Maine's figure on the national stage. He won the race by a resounding 60 to 40. Says Monks: "For me, it was the end of a long, tough process. For him, it was a chapter in a familiar book." Monks remained on friendly terms with his rival, who two years later resigned from the Senate to become Secretary of State in the final two years of the Carter administration. The last time he saw Muskie was at Senator Cohen's wedding in February 1996, where the two former opponents spoke amiably for half an hour. Muskie, who was 82, died later that week.

After his defeat, Monks decided against any further pursuit of an electoral career. But he retained a genuine appreciation for the experience. In 1979, he wrote in the Harvard College 25th Anniversary Report (in which he referred to himself under "Occupation" as "Citizen"):

> The greatest pleasure that I have gotten from my own actions has been in running for public office. In that my two efforts have been unsuccessful, I take particular pleasure in Speaker [Samuel] Rayburn's choice of words cautioning then Vice President Johnson's enthusiasm: "Well, Lyndon, you may be right and they may be every bit as intelligent as you say, but I'd feel a whole lot better about them if just one of them had run for sheriff once.". . . I recommend unhesitatingly to everyone to run for office. It is the great privilege and opportunity available to all Americans. I don't recommend losing, because it is too painful, but consider the alternative—"never to have loved at all." It is ultimate freedom to discover that you grow as a person even in losing something with which you have passionately identified yourself.

Actually, Monks did not leave politics after the Muskie race. In fact, shortly after his loss, in January 1977, he took over as chairman of the state

Republican party, on Cohen's recommendation. Cohen was in his third term in Congress and starting his run against Senator Bill Hathaway, the Democrat who had defeated Margaret Chase Smith back in 1972; a victory would put a Maine Republican back in the Senate. In June, 1977 Monks raised out-of-state money for Cohen by hosting a lunch at a club in Boston. As he wrote of the candidate in the invitations: "He is that rarest of treasures—a first class person who is Republican and who is electable."

But as state GOP chairman, Monks concentrated on the upcoming legislative races. At that time, the legislature was controlled by the Democrats, but in 1978 the Republicans had a fighting chance at stealing their glory. Monks plotted a strategy in which the party would assign one "old pro" to help each marginal legislative candidate. But before he had a chance to carry the scheme to completion, Monks' world fell apart.

In August 1978, his mother suffered a heart attack and had to have a pacemaker implanted. Within a few days, Milly was diagnosed with breast cancer and the very next day was admitted into the hospital for a mastectomy. Afterward, her doctor predicted that she would not survive. When Monks' father, just home from the hospital with his wife, heard this news, he was devastated, for he adored Milly. The next day, Gardner Monks put in his usual day's work, climbed three stories of a parking garage to redeem his car, drove home and, exhausted, went to bed. That night he woke suddenly and, short of breath, managed to tell his wife, "Don't let them prolong it," and then he died.

The week left Monks in a state of shock. Sure that Milly was going to die, he was terrified. He could not think. The master strategist did not have a clue as to what they should do. But Milly, in coming to terms with her illness, decided that she was going to put up a fight, and once she had made that determination, Monks fell in line right behind her. Says Milly: "I had made up my mind. I could either give this a go, say yes, or I could say no, and I said yes." What she wanted to do was to try traditional as well as alternative health care; so while she got chemotherapy treatments, she researched other options. The conclusion she and her husband reached was that stress makes people susceptible to cancer and that they needed to find ways to relieve it in as many aspects of life as possible. Monks would be her companion every step of the way. And so, they both instantly became vegetarians, on the theory that the processing of meat is more taxing on the system than the digestion of other foods. And together they took up yoga and meditation. At one point fairly early on when Milly was unable to receive further chemotherapy treatments because of a low white blood cell count, she spent a week doing intensive meditation. After that week, her white cell count had doubled, allowing treatments to resume.

Both she and her husband went on to advanced training in meditation, each taking two-week courses at a retreat—Milly at a center in Connecticut in the summer of 1981 and Bob the following winter in Sonoma County. They learned various sutras, including a levitation sutra that elicits the feeling of lightness. At her retreat, Milly met a young doctor named Deepak Chopra, who would become immensely popular as a writer and lecturer on how meditation and other techniques can help treat serious illnesses, and she and Monks became friends with Chopra and his wife Rita. At Monks' meditation retreat, his independent spirit clashed with the general atmosphere. When he asked questions about the methodology, he was told simply, "If Maharishi had wanted to talk about this differently, he would have done so. We only repeat the material we are given." Ten years later, he, Milly, and the Chopras joined thousands of others in a day-long birthday celebration for the Maharishi Mahesh Yogi in Maastrict, Holland. They were able to get an audience with the guru at 3 A.M. in the former nunnery where he had his European headquarters. He told Monks that his work with corporations was important, noting his belief that corporations should be like families with both relationships and accountability kept on a human scale. Then he asked Monks to try to get President Bush to finance 6,000 meditators to go to the movement's Iowa headquarters for the mass meditation that was necessary to achieve "national coherence." While Monks was delighted with the energy manifest at the birthday celebration, he was put off by the cult atmosphere. He was not, after all, a joiner. Still, he continued to find great benefits in meditation. As did his wife. Milly's cancer never recurred. Over the years, Monks introduced Chopra to friends like Cohen and Frank Baxter, CEO of the boutique brokerage firm Jefferies & Co., who are greatly appreciative for the experience. Says Cohen, "I brought Deepak Chopra to Maine to appear at a statewide conference before 800 people. He spoke in a low monotone and had everyone on the edge of their seats. And I had him come to Washington to meet a group of Senators all of whom had prostate cancer."

But back in the fall of 1978, the Maine state Republicans were left without their appointed leader at a crucial time. At once, other leading Republicans stepped in to see Monks' plan through. On election day, the results proved the brilliance of the strategy. The Republicans took the majority in the state legislature. Monks stepped down at the end of the year.

But, he remained hooked on politics. In late 1979 at Maine's pre-primary convention in the presidential race, he helped his friend and neighbor George Bush, whose home was on a peninsula in Kennebunkport, win a straw poll from Howard Baker, which, as Bush put it, moved him from being an asterix to being a favorite in the Republican primary contests. Here is how Monks describes the event:

> All of the state's principal Republicans except me were for Howard Baker—Cohen worked for him after all in the Senate, John McKernan (who would become governor) ran his campaign in Maine at this time. He arrived in Portland with the whole national press corps, as a Maine victory was going to be the kick-off for his presidential campaign.
>
> Bush was the penultimate speaker. His first words were: "I have always regretted that I wasn't born in Maine. But my mother was, and I have been here every year of my life except during World War II." They were eating out of his hand after that. I rushed [to] the platform and took his hand and slowly slowly worked our way through the crowd with him. Having just run for the Senate and been the State Chairman I knew everybody, and I introduced George to everybody. I asked them to vote for him, and they did. Midway through our progression through the crowd, the chair tried to establish order. But, we worked every last hand. Baker was the last speaker. He gave a 'We guys in the Senate' speech and turned everyone off. They voted, and George won. Maybe my happiest day in politics. George became a recognized candidate, held on well against Reagan, and was awarded the Vice Presidency.[7]

Monks took an active role in the campaign as the finance chairman for the New England Reagan-Bush campaign, raising some $750,000 at a Boston fund-raiser. In time, Monks' support of Bush would pay off, both for him and for the shareholder activist movement—though not as much as he hoped.

4

Epiphany

One weekend in 1980, Monks hosted French Anderson at his seaside home in Maine. The two old friends sat on a ledge overlooking the waves breaking against the shore and talked about where their lives were heading. Anderson said his ideas about the use of gene therapy seemed like an impossible dream. Monks spoke about his dream of making corporations accountable for their actions. As Anderson recalls: "We said that the chances were that neither one of us would be successful in our lifetimes, but that we could make a real impact. We were both wrong."

The years 1977 to 1980 brought Monks into a whole new realm of exploration and discovery as a new business opportunity opened to him. Since 1975, he had been serving as a director of The Boston Company and its subsidiary, The Boston Safe Deposit and Trust Company, at the request of his friend Dwight Allison, who was then chairman of the executive committee of this regional trust bank and money management firm. On election night, November 1976, Allison suggested that Monks join him working full-time in Boston as chairman of the finance committee so he could help turn around the stagnating institution. Monks agreed and bought some stock as well. This career move would be pivotal for Monks, for it would finally bring him to the recognition of shareholder activism as his life's work.

Before long, Allison became the bank's next CEO. Allison saw his mission as helping the company "figure out where it's going to fit in the spectrum of financial institutions," he recounts. When he became CEO, his predecessor ascended to become chairman for about a year; when the chairman retired in May 1979, Monks replaced him.

Reunited in 1977, the experienced team of Allison and Monks began looking over the company and pondering its future direction. In recent years, the bank's money management business had branched out from its traditional clientele of family trusts into pension funds. It had acquired a number of money management companies, which became separate subsidiaries and ran independently. But Allison came to feel strongly that these subsidiaries should be integrated so that The Boston Company would have marketing, research, and investment strategies common to all its money management outlets. In that way, it might be easier to reach out to national corporate pension plans as they grew under the newly enacted pension law, the Employee Retirement Income Security Act of 1974, ERISA, which applied the concept of fiduciary duty to the management of pension funds.

The managers running the subsidiaries—the operations' former owners—were not happy with this judgment. They had been assured independence and, moreover, this plan was going to cost them more in revenues committed to centralized research. Still, Allison and Monks were not prepared for the violent reactions they got from some of the men in these outposts. Monks was on the front line in dealing with those who were most uncooperative. In one case in Seattle, which became known in local papers as "The Battle in Seattle," the manager, "Duff" Kennedy, went against headquarters' wishes by making a major investment in real estate for a pension fund. Allison asked the firm to back out of the investment, thinking it imprudent under federal law. When the manager balked, Monks and a small team from Boston flew to Seattle to take physical possession of the firm. "We called in all the employees and said, 'We're the owners. Are you staying with us or going out the door with him?'" To Monks' dismay, all the employees went with Kennedy—as did the clients.

Over time, most of the subsidiaries were spun off to their original owners. Monks put his negotiating skills to work to hammer out the deals. He had the most difficulty with a Houston firm that The Boston Company had bought only two years earlier. According to Monks, the manager offered the bank a price that was much lower than what he had sold the firm for. In the end, Monks made a final demand and walked away. "I rolled over him," Monks says. The manager went with Monks' price.

Monks ended up owning a large position in The Boston Company stock. The bank had two classes of stock, A and B, the A stock possessing more voting rights. Monks and Allison bought the maximum A stock they were allowed (less than 1% apiece) and then B shares as well, with Monks ending up with quite a bit more than his partner. To a large degree, his stake grew independently of his own initiative. Monks' nephew John Higgins had been in Portland investing for Ram Trust Services, the Monks and Higgins family office, and had been buying B stock here and there in the market because it looked cheap. The family ended up owning 25 percent of the total outstanding shares.

As a director and then as chairman, Monks certainly didn't have to become intimately involved in the daily goings-on at the company. But, he was used to taking a prominent role in plotting strategy at companies where he was on the board and owned stock. And he had lots of ideas about what The Boston Company should be doing. "I had complete confidence in Bobby's goals and interest," Allison says. "Because he is such a free thinker and independent guy, it was a bit like being involved in what somebody described as a Nantucket sleigh ride where the harpoon gets stuck into the whale by Bobby, and then you hang on for dear life." When Monks became chairman, he did not run the board meetings; Allison did because he wanted Monks to do what he was best at: strategizing, innovating, and negotiating.

Given that license, Monks took the liberty of nosing into all the company's operations to find out what the company was doing and why. Occasionally, he found germinating ideas that needed a senior person's patronage. For example, Charles Clough, the bank's head of research supporting the money management operation—who years later became the chief strategist for Merrill Lynch—had a brainstorm for a mutual fund that was a basket of commodities and bonds. Monks picked up on this imaginative idea, and worked with Clough to design the fund and offer it to the public.

The project took three years to accomplish, from conception to launch in January 1980, and Monks stuck with it the whole way, challenged by an idea that was radical for its time. It sprang from concerns about inflation, which was continuing to build in the economy. The fund would provide a hedged investment so that if bonds were off, commodities would do well. The idea played to Monks' talent as an astute investor faced with a tall order: inflation—the same talent that drew him to the oil patch in 1972. However, the product crossed over two regulatory regimes. To bring the fund to market, The Boston Company needed to get approval from both the Securities and Exchange Commission (SEC) and the Commodity Futures Trading Commission, and later on it would have to file periodic reports with both agencies. Monks handled the initial administrative details with his usual persistence. But, even though the fund built up a respectable amount of assets, $28 million, there were horrendous administrative costs dealing with the regulators. Continuing it was not practical. A few years hence, the hybrid fund concept would take hold in the form of real estate investment trusts, which combine yield and inflation protection, but report only to the SEC. Later, some investment banks would launch bond/commodities funds similar to The Boston Company's. Clough and Monks view the experience as more of an adventure than a crushing disappointment. "If we'd stayed at The Boston Company, we probably would have developed other products based on the same idea," because inflation continued to plague the national psyche, Clough says.

During Monks' continuing investigation into the company's doings, he happened upon some proxies that had come in from the companies that the firm had invested in for clients. Proxy forms are ballots that shareholders vote, mostly at annual meetings in the spring; they address all sorts of topics, from the election of directors to the passage of executive stock option plans to controversial initiatives, then from such activists as Ralph Nader and the Gilbert brothers. As he was snooping around one area of the bank, Monks spotted a proxy from the Great Northern Paper Company, one of the paper mills that was churning out the foam he had encountered several years earlier while campaigning for office. He took the proxy form back to his office and, looking it over, experienced a kind of epiphany: "My bank was a stockholder in these companies that were floating the junk down the rivers in Maine."

At the time, Monks and Allison had an ongoing dialogue about the implications of ERISA, one of which was that there would be more corporate pension funds and that the assets under their watch would grow to outsize proportions. Much of those assets would be placed in the stocks of major U.S. and global corporations. This not only presented a business opportunity for The Boston Company; it also presented an important step in Monks' thinking about corporate ownership. There would be fewer and fewer owners, and they would be growing larger and larger, making it easier for corporations to be held accountable for their performance and their actions.

Mindful of that portion of ERISA that said that pension plans had to be operated exclusively for the benefit of employees, Monks realized that the voting of the shares that were owned by a pension plan was one of the characteristics of the plan that had to be dealt with exclusively for the benefit of the employees. Hence, not only were pension plans big enough to influence the companies they held stock in, but also Monks was convinced that they really were legally bound to do so. They had to use their proxy vote to benefit plan participants; so they also had to know what was going on at the companies and make voting decisions as owners of those companies. It struck him that pension plan participants were also citizens who wanted to live in a good world, for example, free of pollution, crime, and other hazards, and so investing for their benefit meant paying attention to such factors. But this logic was a far cry from reality. Monks soon learned that The Boston Company did not do anything with the proxy forms that came in the mail. Since nobody knew what to do with them, they got tossed out. Even so, Monks was very excited about this new frontier.

Another idea filled out the picture. Monks had been working actively with the bank's law firm on the changes he and Allison were implementing at The Boston Company. Their lawyer was Joshua Berman, Monks' and Allison's former partner at Goodwin, Procter, who had set up his own practice. One of Berman's partners was David Engel, a former professor of corporate law at Stanford Law School. While practicing law, he was also writing an article for the 1979 *Stanford Law Review*. It had to do with the basic role of a corporation in a society, in the context of prominent debates at the time on what makes a "good" corporation and whether companies should operate in places like South Africa where people suffer discrimination. Engel agreed with theorists who held that corporations should stick to the practice of seeking profit. If they instead insist on doing good works— for example, in making a product, deciding what is a safe level of toxic emissions—they really are usurping the power of government. Or as Monks puts it, "Who elected corporate officials to make social judgments?"

But Engel went beyond this notion to pose the question: in this context, what nonprofit-oriented objectives can corporations appropriately and should pursue while conducting their business of maximizing profit? He identified three: obedience of the law, disclosure of material facts about corporate functioning, and absence from the political process (so that it remains free of the interests of big business). Included in the disclosure area is what Engel called the Kew Gardens Principle. That refers to an incident in the 1960s when residents of that Queens neighborhood heard the screams of a woman, Kitty Genovese, who was being attacked on the street, but did nothing to help stop the murderer—clearly unacceptable behavior. In Engel's theoretical view, anything that comes up at a company that is clearly unacceptable, whether or not it has to do with profits and by whatever degree it may harm profits, must be disclosed at the earliest possible moment. If not, one possible consequence would be that later on litigation would bankrupt the enterprise. As Monks phrases it: "If at the outset about cigarettes, or at the outset about the use of silicone for cosmetic or medical purposes, people are given an understanding as to what are the consequences, that gives you a much better basis on which to have a corporation exist." He goes on that, if every company is required to have such a policy of disclosure—and the culture of the company in turn is one of encouraging such immediate disclosure—it takes away any competitive advantage of keeping information secret. From an economics point of view, that would then have a corrective effect on pricing.

Monks took Engel's thinking further based on his own experience and beliefs. For example, one unacceptable corporate behavior he'd personally encountered was the creation of "externalities" such as pollution. If those externalities were to be disclosed and recognized by accounting methods and thereby "internalized," it would greatly clarify the true costs of operation and relieve society of a burden. A logical result would be a reduction in such awful by-products of operation. Other, less quantifiable behaviors are more problematic. For example, if a company is using child labor in a Third World country, it may have no foreseeable cost. Monks recalled visiting Swedish coal mine operators while he was running C. H. Sprague and hearing them proudly assert that people didn't die in mines there. But then they told him that their mines were in Sierra Leone. "Well, does that make you feel a lot better to have a mine in Sierra Leone than in Sweden?" asked an incredulous Monks. "Well," they would reply, "It's better for the people. We don't have our people in the mines." But such a tactic is unacceptable to many people and could cost a company in the form of a boycott, government regulation, or just a poor public image. What was "unacceptable" in the South Africa situation was not clear-cut, Monks acknowledges. Was it better for human rights that a corporation respond to negative publicity by divesting its South African operations, or that it remain in the country to continue offering black people employment? In the end, Monks says, apartheid was abolished before the question could be resolved—although some credit was given to the publicity generated by the divestment movement.

If the government does not create acceptable standards and enforce them—which it cannot do in all situations, particularly in a global context—who would demand that corporations behave decently toward society? Certainly, human rights and citizens' organizations play some role, urging government to step in or smearing a company's image and in turn hurting the stock and the business. If the government does create such standards, who will demand that the corporations have the proper governance in place to assure adherence to the law?

It was becoming evident to Monks that in both cases, ultimate accountability had to fall to the shareholders, in particular the pension funds, which were bound to become the country's and then the world's biggest shareholders in a fairly short time. As Monks sums up his conclusions: "When you stop to think about what you want your shareholders to do, it is to hold management accountable for achieving financial objectives *plus* the Engel agenda." This was where a lot of the pieces began to come together for Monks: The idea of a global approach to pollution and the importance of shareholder involvement, comparable to what he'd been doing for years as a large shareholder at energy companies, technology enterprises, and The Boston Company. With his new worldview, Monks would become impatient with those who insisted that corporations should be accountable to so-called stakeholders—employees, suppliers, customers, communities—on the same level that they are accountable to shareholders. He had no doubt that a successful corporation must tend to these other groups. But, when it came to ultimate responsibility, he says, "There must be an effective way to require accountability. How do customers or suppliers enforce a corporations's accountability? It is difficult enough with owners, who have, after all, the fundamental ongoing interest of personal enrichment." With Engel's help, he worked on some papers that helped clarify his thinking, the beginnings of a book. Despite the immensity of the task, Monks was feeling a strong pull to become what he liked to call "an agent of change" in corporate governance.

In April 1979, Monks wrote to Derek Bok, then president of Harvard University. He knew Bok and his wife (who happened to have been Monks' first date), and thought that America's foremost university would be a good place to begin his crusade. Following are some excerpts from his letter:

> Is there literally no one responsible for the ethical conduct of corporations? . . . Literally, our system has licensed entities accountable to nobody beyond the perfunctory requirements of the state of incorporation. It is a part of our tradition that owners of property are required to maintain it so as not to become a nuisance to others; why, other than convenience, should the ownership of common stock be otherwise regarded. [sic]

Is it right for a shareholder to complain of his own inability to affect the corporation and at the same time be allowed to keep the benefits from that of which he disapproves? Shouldn't a shareholder have the affirmative burden to urge standards of corporate citizenship on his management?

Harvard has long been a vital force in American life; it is not inappropriate to look to Harvard for leadership in vital areas. Harvard has the resources—not just in its financial standing, but in the legal and scholarly talent available to it—to begin the process of establishing responsible corporate ownership. Corporate managements listen to Harvard. It is not enough simply to vote on resolutions proposed by others.

We may curse the times and the wretched fates that require this problem to be dealt with now. The fact is that it is wrong to abandon the world to the "morality" of "generally accepted accounting principles." It is wrong to ignore the awful problem of our times to co-exist decently with large institutions [corporations. Ed.]. This is the kind of situation in which Harvard should undertake the burden of leadership.

Bok's response was, essentially, that Harvard would not have the resources to do a proper job of investigating companies so as to initiate shareholder resolutions or divest holdings. And if it did begin to "police the social and ethical practices of corporations," that would open Harvard to similar scrutiny of its academic programs, endangering those very programs. Still, the dialogue continued. In July, Monks met Bok for lunch and handed him a draft of a paper he had been working on addressing the responsibility of investment managers to monitor corporations. After reading the paper, Bok wrote Monks that his one concern about endowing money managers with this obligation is that pension plan participants would disagree with their judgments. He thought that instead, the money managers might inform clients about controversial issues and solicit their opinions—"especially if such votes might support positions that would sacrifice earnings to achieve a greater social or ethical goal."

As he continued to ponder these issues and further develop his working paper on the subject, Monks wrote Bok one more time in early 1980. At the time, the issue of corporations divesting operations in South Africa was heating up:

I feel like the fabled blind man trying to describe an elephant, because there are such a myriad of important issues being considered in a fragmentary and uncoordinated way by many people. . . . The problem is in general terms the impact of business enterprise (corporations) on modern societies. More precisely, it is to answer the questions—who is responsible for the impact of corporations and how can accountability be developed within our existing governmental and economic structure so as to assure the compatibility of corporate existence with societal needs? . . . I have given a great deal of thought as to how to provoke the necessary dialogue out of which constructive solutions might emerge. . . . These are important questions, and we [The Boston Company. Ed.] are prepared to devote both personnel and financial resources to having them seriously analyzed.

Reflecting today on the exchange, Monks continues to believe that Bok's pragmatic view was shortsighted. "People cannot afford to be single-minded," Monks says. "If a guy as good as Derek is going to put the blinkers on, who's going to look out for the little people? Who should act as owner other than rich arrogant Harvard? I wanted to raise that issue. I've had a very long-range view of this. I knew I wasn't going to change Harvard immediately." Today, Harvard, and other schools, remain well on the fringe of the corporate governance movement.

Monks would not stay at The Boston Company much longer. During his and Allison's tenure, profits had steadily improved. In numerous discussions with Monks and others, Allison decided on the best strategic course for the firm. Part of it was a process of elimination. The firm was not positioned to go after individual investors on a national scale because it did not have an extensive sales network. It could not become a significant force in lending, both because it did not have the capital on which to build a large depositary base and because the banking business in Boston was so competitive. The best route was to go after the investment management business of large corporate pension plans, because that was obviously a growth market. Allison recommended that the company obtain the resources to pursue this path by selling out to a larger organization. Coincidentally, at the same time, Monks raised the value of the company by a stunning 100 percent— $30 million—in negotiating the sale of The Boston Company's fixed-price option on its headquarters building, which had ballooned in value in inflationary times.

In considering possible buyers, Allison, Monks, and other board members talked with people at a wide range of financial institutions, not just other banks. Allison had preliminary conversations with Donald Regan, chief executive of Merrill Lynch. But they led nowhere.

For a while, Monks and Allison weighed the possibility of buying the company themselves from the other shareholders—a so-called management buyout on the order of what they had done at C. H. Sprague, but from public shareholders. This option suddenly looked doable when they were offered financing. One of the banks that The Boston Company had contacted as a possible buyer, on the theory that financial services businesses were destined to become international, was the Banque de Paris et de Pays-Bas, or Paribas, which was then led by Gérard Eskenazi. He sent over two bank officers to interview Monks and Allison and take a close look at the bank and its books, and then the Boston bankers went to Paris for further meetings. In the end, the French bank was not interested in buying The Boston Company, but did offer to finance a management buyout. Early in 1981, Monks and Allison decided against that route. "It was a lose-lose situation," Monks says. "Either I pay too much for it, or I pay too little and everyone else gets screwed." Actually, though, the decision was made for them when another buyer appeared on the scene.

At the time, Monks was marketing the bond/commodities fund that he had developed with Chuck Clough. He was working with Hardwick Simmons, who was then an executive at Shearson Loeb Rhodes and later became president of Prudential Securities. In the midst of selling the fund, Shearson CEO Sanford Weill began thinking that his firm should be marketing its own products, not those of others. At the same time, says Allison, one of The Boston Company directors who knew Weill told him that The Boston Company was for sale. Weill was interested, and Simmons and Monks worked up the numbers. The parties talked and quickly shook hands on a deal in February 1981. They met again for further negotiations at Weill's house in Greenwich and about a week later signed a letter of intent. The deal would be an exchange of stock at a predetermined ratio to be completed early in the summer.

In the midst of closing the transaction, American Express and Shearson struck a deal to merge. Shearson's stock shot up. That meant that the owners of The Boston Company would now take double the amount originally expected based on the same share exchange ratio. Great—if the bank's deal actually took place. The Boston Company team became increasingly nervous that it would not. After all, they were operating only under a letter of intent, although both sides had been reviewing drafts of the final documents. When the bank management heard about the new merger, its lawyer, Josh Berman, called Shearson repeatedly, but no one returned the calls. Says his partner Engel: "They without question wanted to walk away from the deal. It seemed very clear to us." The Boston Company assumed that American Express and Shearson, whose proposed combination had been highly publicized and would create a financial powerhouse, were concerned that regulators would step in once they learned that they were also to acquire a "bank," even though this bank was not making commercial loans. Monks' determination to see the merger through energized the whole team. He was absolutely confident that if they looked at the situation from all angles, they would be able to handle it.

Finally, Shearson's Weill and Peter Cohen and American Express's James Robinson agreed to a lunch with Monks and Allison, hosting them in AmEx's offices at the top of the World Trade Center. The guests took the position that they were entitled to the fruits of their arrangement. They insisted that they would not take kindly to being put on hold until the larger transaction was consummated. Monks, who acted as the lead negotiator for his side, asserted that, "You came to the dance with one person, you can't decide you're going to go home with somebody else." He promised to make life hard for them if they did not adhere to the deal.

At one point, Monks glared at Weill and said, "Sandy I've visited your house out in Greenwich. It's a very nice house. But you're not offering to give me your house."

"What do you mean?" Weill asked.

"It was you that wanted us to sign up," Monks said. "It was you that insisted on these terms. Now you're asking me to change the terms, to give it all up."

After a few minutes of back and forth, Monks took a threatening tone. In a steady voice, he asserted: "Sandy, if you don't stop screwing around I'm going to pick you up and throw you out the window." And he actually went over to him and lifted him up. Weill was a bit startled.[1]

At the end of the lunch, Robinson pledged in a written, legally binding guarantee that if The Boston Company would allow his deal to close first, then the new Shearson American Express would carry out the merger with the bank. The Boston Company sold for $47.2 million, some $12 million of which went directly into Monks' pocket as profit. (Weill did not return calls by the author requesting comments on this episode.)[2]

As Berman tells it, Monks provided the sheer force of will that pushed the transaction through: "Bob got that deal done. He was relentless. As the situation got tougher Bob's great strength came to the fore. Not just by being tough, but by keeping everything in perspective and being a very big person. You cannot intimidate him. You cannot embarrass him. He doesn't care if nobody agrees with him. This is what he thinks is right. This is what he's going to do."

Later in 1981, the international connection Monks had made with Paribas led to an unexpected opportunity for him. Charles Bouzanquet, Paribas' customer liaison who had met with Monks regarding a possible Boston Company privatization, came to Boston once again and dined with Monks at the Parker House. He had a proposition. With François Mitterand's election that year, the Socialist government intended to nationalize Paribas. But the bank's executives including Eskenazi acted swiftly to have the Swiss subsidiary issue stock to give a new group control and the nationalized bank a minority position. That new group was Pargesa, a consortium of Paribas' largest customers including Albert Frère and Leon Lambert of Belgium, and Paul desMarais of Canada. Bouzanquet suggested Monks become involved as a U.S.-based director. Monks invested $10 million in non-voting stock (all that was then available) and went on the board of the U.S. subsidiary, Lambert Bruxelles Corporation. That subsidiary, and in turn Pargesa, had taken over the 35 percent stake in the maverick brokerage house Drexel Burnham Lambert that was held by Leon Lambert's Banque Lambert.

Turning to his next endeavor, Monks took on another tough corporate situation. The election of Ronald Reagan and George Bush opened up opportunities for him just when he was free to take them. In the spring, Monks was nominated—by his friend Senator Cohen—to be a director of the U.S. Synthetic Fuels Corporation, a Carter administration initiative to subsidize the development of energy alternatives to foreign oil. In June 1980, seven years after the start of the oil crisis, Congress authorized the new corporation to spend a huge sum of money, up to $88 billion—$20 billion in a first phase and, subject to later approval, another $68 billion in a second phase. During the election campaign, Synfuels was one of the projects that Reagan pointed to as a symbol of government's intrusion into the private sector. But when he took office, he could not eliminate the agency, because Congress supported it. Since Synfuels was an executive branch agency, however, the President could appoint his own board of directors. Monks had headed the Industry Advisory Panel to the Synfuels Corporation Transition Team that December and therefore stood as a prime candidate to chair Synfuels. But because he was still involved in The Boston Company, he had not been considered for the top job or, for that matter, for any other, high-ranking job in the Reagan-Bush administration. Instead, the chairmanship went to Ed Noble, an oilman from Oklahoma. Noble had headed a Reagan transition task force calling for Synfuels' abolition, but said he hoped now to make it succeed. Monks, who as head of the advisory group saw a potentially strong role for Synfuels and indicated no desire to phase it out, was nominated as a director and confirmed by the Senate. He took the position without pay.

That summer of 1981, before actually starting at Synfuels, Monks for the second time in his life took time out to organize his thoughts. Again, as he did after losing his first Senate race, Monks chose a spot overlooking the Atlantic, this time from his home in Maine. On his computer this time, he wrote and wrote. Part of what he did was to look up every single footnote in David Engel's 100-page *Stanford Law Review* article. Every day, he gave a list of references to a friend of the family who was then studying at the University of Maine Law School, and in the evenings that person would bring back Xeroxed copies of articles and cases from the school library. In his research, Monks delved into the writings of Louis Brandeis and historian James Willard Hurst about the place of the corporation in a democracy. Brandeis was always wary of corporate power and warned it must be watched and challenged. Hurst, who traced over 100 years of efforts to contain corporate power (by limiting its life, size, and purposes, regulating it, and requiring minimum standards for safety, pollution, and discrimination, among other things), insisted that corporations are creatures of limited power and that a free society depends on that power being strictly limited. Engel expanded on this thinking by pointing out that there is no implicit authority for corporate leaders to go beyond the profit maximizing charter granted by the state, but then detailed the three acceptable ways he had found that they could. Monks put all of this together in his paper as a consolidation of the thinking in the field, and then tried to articulate where it should all lead. In personal terms, he was making it his mission to find the answer.

Those who would best bring this vision to fruition, he wrote, would be the owners. By this time, Monks had come to the understanding that the growing set of international pension funds of all kinds, already the largest shareholders in the United Kingdom and the United States, "comprised a continuing base of ownership for all of the large companies in the world." It seemed to him that these funds, given the nature of their beneficiaries, would inevitably be long-term owners of public corporations in the mold of the individual owners of privately owned companies. And because of their increasing size, they would over time end up owning essentially all public corporations. The key problem was how to energize owners to do the job of making sure that their corporations were behaving as responsible citizens in a democratic society. There was much that needed to be done. Monks tossed around the notion of the need to develop an intellectual basis for corporate governance by cultivating an academic interest. And, recognizing an inherent conflict of interest for private pension fund fiduciaries beholden both to their employers and to the beneficiaries, he considered ways of involving beneficiaries themselves as owners and also dreamed up the idea of special purpose, neutral voting institutions. The result of all this cogitation was a 100-page "governance agenda." Over the next 15 years, Monks regularly wrote actual agendas for action—usually at the end of a year—that went into much greater detail about the immediate and far-ranging challenges and how they should be tackled.

Shearson's acquisition of The Boston Company closed on Friday, September 30, and the next day Monks moved to Washington to start at Synfuels. While that job was certainly interesting to Monks, he thought that his friend George Bush might find something more for him now that he was in Washington full time—even though the Secretarial posts had been filled. Bush found room for him on the Vice President's Task Force on Regulatory Relief, headed by Bush's general counsel C. Boyden Gray. And so Monks wandered through the halls of the Executive Office Building and settled into an office occupied by someone who was on assignment in Asia.

The task force's mandate was to find ways in which government could get out of the way of the operation of the free market. Which regulations could be eased or eliminated? The panel tried to answer those questions by meeting with company executives to go over regulations. They were working alongside the Office of Management and Budget (OMB), which was trying to control the flow of new regulations. Monks attacked the issue at hand with his usual enthusiasm, asking characteristically provocative questions. But, although the task force was only part-time work, two or so days a week, it quickly became tiresome to Monks. "I found out early on that the large corporations liked regulations," he recounts. "In other words, what regulation means is it protects them against competition. It makes entry very difficult." Company executives didn't appear to want to change anything. "Any effort to simplify or make the rules more user-friendly, forget it," Monks says. Coincidentally at OMB, which had to review all proposed regulations to coordinate among agencies, Monks' future partner Nell Minow was finding much the same thing. The main result of the deregulatory task force's work, Monks maintains, was a small reduction in the number of pages of new regulations published in the *Federal Register*. It should be noted that because of his ownership of American Express stock stemming from the sale of The Boston Company, Monks was not involved in deliberations on the deregulation of the S&L industry.

From 1981 through 1983, Monks was spending most of his time at Synfuels. At the start, he described Synfuels as "a grand experiment," the biggest of its kind, where the government awarded a huge amount of money to start up a new industry. So, he entered into it with great gusto. "Notwithstanding his profession of adherence to the Reagan administration ideology that government doesn't belong in the energy industry, I don't think Bob ever believed that," says Frances Lilly, who was the executive assistant to the chairman. "Bob believed that, if designed and structured properly, government could in fact make a helluva difference in developing something like a synthetic fuels industry. Eventually it could go into the hands of the private sector; but in terms of getting there, the government could be a tremendous help."

Monks and Noble were two very different Republicans. Monks was a liberal thinker. The chairman was a rock-ribbed conservative, who literally spoke in a whisper for fear of being overheard by the press. Howard Wilkins, Jr., a Synfuels director and major Pizza Hut franchisee, tells this story about him. In the summer of 1982, the board went to South Africa to look at its developing synfuels industry. "The chairman was going through customs and they opened his briefcase," says Wilkins, "And in it there was a 38-caliber long barrel. He said he forgot he had it with him. Sort of a different kind of guy."

One of the board's first priorities was staffing. They needed to decide which of the Democrat-appointed staffers would stay and who would be brought in to replace those who left. Monks became increasingly irritated at the chairman and the top management for not bringing in any people he was recommending and for appointing Noble's former business partner, Victor Schroeder, as president in late 1981. Then, there was the matter of distributing the funds. By the time Reagan was elected, Synfuels was only six months old but had already spent $4 billion of its $20 billion. The new directors slowed down the project approvals temporarily so they could figure out their own policies of how the agency would operate. This approach was in line with what Monks had said at the confirmation hearing, that he agreed with the Reagan administration that the agency had to be carefully looked at. And he meant it quite literally. He not only read the statute authorizing Synfuels from start to finish, but he also brought the book with the statute in it to every board meeting and kept it on the table. Says Wilkins: "Bob was the most prepared, the most concerned. He took a leadership role in protecting the taxpayers' money. We had a genius on our hands who understood far more the potential of what we were going to be doing, and was sensitive to the consequences of what we would be doing in handing out such big grants." Lilly agrees: "After about three or four months I started to get the distinct idea that the way Bob analyzed things was in much greater depth, with much greater perceptivity and a different ideological spin than the rest of the group, and that there was going to be a possible confrontation building in terms of the two different camps." On that trip to South Africa, Monks and Wilkins told Noble flat out that he wasn't committing enough time to the job and should either become genuinely full-time or quit and let Schroeder do it. Noble appeared to lean toward quitting, until the next morning when he changed his mind.

Before long, Monks and others were disturbed by the management's cronyism not only in hiring but also in making awards to businesses run by friends. In one questionable episode, Schroeder offered a director help for his business and also got that director's support for Schroeder's plan to reorganize the corporation.[3] Schroeder denied that the two actions were connected. On top of these issues, even Monks, cautious as he was, thought the management was being far too indecisive and bureaucratic in granting contracts. He wanted things sped up.

Monks was writing regular memos on these and other concerns to Senator Cohen, who was chairman of the Senate Governmental Affairs Subcommittee on Oversight of Government Management. As Cohen relates: "Bob said, 'These people are trying to kill this corporation. They're not interested in seeing whether or not they could produce synthetic fuel. They're ripping it off, flying first class, best accommodations, lavish lifestyle, all at taxpayers' expense.' He would inform me of it, and we would complain about it. There was a series of letters going back and forth, to the head of Synfuels, asking for accountings of internal activities."

After a while, Schroeder and the chairman's group of cohorts on the board were doing their best to shut out Monks, Wilkins, and Jack Carter Jr., the three more independently minded directors. "It was sheer silliness," Wilkins says. "The day before a board meeting, each of us would get a briefing book and three huge boxes, 2 ft. cubic. No way could we get ourselves up to speed overnight. It infuriated the three of us. The other four didn't seem to care. It put us at the mercy of the staff. We on the board progressed from quiet arguments to outright warfare. We could never get a mission statement from the chairman. So after a while, we refused to vote or even speak. Even in the roll call, they'd say our names and Mr. Monks would say "abstain" instead of "present." We decided we were putting ourselves in jeopardy by acquiescing. We did not have good information on big big projects."

Monks went to Senator Cohen and asked for hearings. Cohen agreed that questions needed to be answered and that the lack of accountability was fertile ground for corruption. Hearings were held in July 1983. (One of Cohen's top aides at the time was Susan Collins, who would one day oppose Monks in his third Senate race.) In August, the three dissident directors, led by Monks, succeeded in their months-long effort to force Schroeder to resign. Yet, Monks was charitable in his public criticism. He was quoted in *Business Week* as saying, "Vic Schroeder is a good and decent man, but he is neither the manager that a $15 billion program needs, nor does he have the credibility to get the private sector to commit the billions of dollars needed to build these plants."

In the meantime, the whole notion behind Synfuels began to seem obsolete as oil prices in the early 1980s started their decline. Potential sponsors of projects shelved their plans. Monks, Wilkins, and Carter appealed to Bush to shut it down. "I had talked to Bush about the Synfuels problems until it was unmistakable that I was wasting our time," Monks says. Congressional opposition, meanwhile, had grown on both sides of the aisle. Congress did not vote to close Synfuels until the end of 1985, but even by then, the corporation had spent only a small portion of its allotted funds.

Given his frustrating experiences with both Synfuels and the deregulation commission, Monks became disillusioned with his old political friend George Bush. Monks' work at the Department of Labor in 1984–85 would do little to change that. Years later, as the 1988 presidential campaign got underway, Monks wrote to David S. Broder, the *Washington Post* reporter, who had just interviewed Bush on NBC's *Meet the Press*. The December

1987 letter is as much a reflection of Monks' own political idealism as it is of his personal distaste for Bush:[4]

Dear Mr. Broder:

I write to congratulate and thank you for your timely and revealing questions to George Bush last Sunday. In that George clearly is the "front runner," all Americans really want to know the answer to what I understood your question to be—*What kind of person are you?*

I felt that in asking three questions of fact you were probing for the most important of answers. On one level what you were asking was, after seven years of shelter in high executive position, to what extent are you in touch with the reality of the needs of American people; on another, you seemed to be asking, as a person sometimes accused of elitism, are you really cognizant of the problems of less fortunate Americans?

George Bush answered your questions unequivocally and the answer was no.

The answer that I would most welcome from a candidate for President of the United States would have been—

'I feel acutely the unfairness and the wrong in having *any* American in a position where they do not have access either to job, to unemployment insurance or the medical insurance. I would as President undertake, whether through better economic programs or through more comprehensive public and private aid programs, to assure that no American be in such a position.'

This answer would tell me that *President Bush* had feeling, that he knows what it is like to be "outside" and that he would for these reasons be someone who could be entrusted as our Chief Executive.

Instead, we got Yale, Phi Beta Kappa, too many years removed, from the people in high office, (sic), almost legalisms, impatience with your questions, as if it was demeaning to think that a public official could know such minutiae, almost contempt in giving guess answers and *no* feeling for people to whom the bounty of our society has been denied.

Broder replied, in part:

You understood exactly why I asked those questions of the Vice President and what I was hoping to learn. My judgment on his answers would be somewhat less critical than yours, but I think they point to the underlying question about a Bush presidency—not what its values would be but what its fix on the nation's needs would be, and who would supply the information that Mr. Bush clearly needs.

Monks ended up voting for the governor of his home state of Massachusetts: Michael Dukakis. Of course, Monks and Bush had some basic traits in common. Both were born into prosperous families and also earned great wealth in their careers. Both had been in the energy industry, and both were political animals. Indeed, in a 1997 interview with the author, Monks expressed some sympathy for Bush as a candidate:

> As I witness George Bush to this day struggling with the public perception of being born with a "silver spoon" in his mouth, I empathize hugely. It took me two elections to stop trying to persuade people that I really was a competent hard working guy who had succeeded in a competitive environment. As . . . the late McGeorge Bundy used to put it, "It won't wash, Bob." I once told this to George directly and told him— from the pain of my own experience—that it just made him appear foolish. He was not born in a log cabin: this made him neither worse nor better than other people; it was a fact. He should focus on what he had done with what he had. George and I are a good example of how two people with many characteristics in common assessed life in utterly different ways. George very simply wanted to be President, and I, with comparable megalomania, wanted to make the world a better place. That George actually got to be President must be accounted an extraordinary accomplishment. When you think of the work and the discipline that went into that achievement, you have to be very humble. I was a witness to a lot of it. For example, in asking George about an agenda during his vice presidency, it was plain that the entire agenda was get Reagan's support for 1988. Period. He would do absolutely nothing to help in difficult situations. I ultimately couldn't stand it.

5

Wielding the Stick

If you think about Bobby it was a natural kind of evolution. He's interested in the voting process, whether it's for electoral office or otherwise; he has a strong moral ethos that comes from his upbringing as the son of a clergyman; he was a lawyer and understood ERISA; he had an instinct for power. He knew that the money that was invested in these pension plans and their ownership of stock gave them a power to do things that hadn't really been appreciated. Whereas in the past, some trustee bank might have been receiving the proxies for these pension plans and doing god knows what with them, Bobby was quick enough to see that that's a real asset of the pension plan. It represents real power. These pension plans have the ability to exercise that power.

Dwight Allison

Watching the events at Synfuels unfold from afar was Noble's former executive assistant Frank Lilly. In late 1981, Lilly was offered the job of Deputy Solicitor of Labor, working for the Department of Labor's chief lawyer. Monks encouraged him to go. As Lilly recounts: "Bob said, "They've got one of the greatest acts down there ever invented that they're responsible for, and I think it's going to be one of the most important ones in the U.S." I said, "What's that?" And he said, "ERISA." And I said "What?" He said, "It's the pension law." I hadn't heard of it. It wasn't like OSHA. It wasn't on the tip of everyone's tongue at that time. But Bob was saying that this is the greatest thing going and it's going to have a great impact on the U.S., from a financial perspective. His analysis had a lot to do with my going down to the DOL. To this day I'm grateful to him." But he would do a great favor for Monks as well.

In the summer of 1983, Lilly stopped in to see his boss, Secretary of Labor Raymond Donovan. Lilly was now the Acting Solicitor of Labor. His concern today was that the department would not move aggressively enough to find a timely replacement for pensions administrator Jeffrey Clayton, who had announced his intention to leave in September. "This is an important position, in my view," Lilly told Donovan.

The Secretary agreed. In the years he'd been at this job, he had taken pride in the notion that his department shielded millions of citizens in every stage of their lives, from childhood, with child labor laws, to retirement, with ERISA. The latter was the direct responsibility of the pensions administrator. "Why don't you draw up your list of recommendations," Donovan instructed. Lilly called a few people to gauge their interest. Of course, he already knew about Monks' fascination with pension funds and phoned him at his Synfuels office. "Look, Bob," he said. "There's an opening here for the job of running the ERISA program. You know you probably can have the job if you want it."

Monks was intrigued by this news. He had been working at Synfuels full time (the deregulatory commission having petered out), and he had the vague notion of using his contacts in government at some point to stir up interest in the growth of institutional—namely pension fund—investors. Given his then solid relationship with the vice president and his other connections in the Republican party, he had some confidence that he would be able to create a commission to study big institutional investors and their growing impact on the companies in which they held stock and in turn on the economy. Monks had never considered taking the regulator's job. But when it became available, he recognized its potential. Being in the job himself would allow him to begin influencing the way pension funds used their latent powers.

Still, politically it seemed a bad move. Labor issues were low on the priority list in a Republican administration. Plus, he was the first to admit that, as he put it, "when the subject of pension funds or ERISA is raised, most eyes glaze over,"[1] and therefore it might be difficult to get things done. Moreover, the post would be a step down from the directorship at Synfuels, which was a high-ranking job, requiring a presidential appointment and Senate approval. The pensions administrator didn't even rank as an Assistant Secretary of Labor. Indeed, it was viewed as a good stepping-stone for a young political aspirant, not someone of Monks' experience and political stature. What's more, the Synfuels position was a so-called Level 3 job, meaning that Monks was not subject to the Hatch Act, which limits the political activities of lower level government employees. Anything lower would rank him as a civil servant and bar him from the political fund-raising, campaigning, and hobnobbing that had become such an integral part of his life. At that time, Monks was making some $30,000 a year in campaign contributions, mostly for Maine candidates.

In a brief interview that fall, Monks' views struck the right chord with the Secretary of Labor, stressing the importance of the pensions area and that the agency needed to be more effective.

"Mr. Secretary, if you decide to hire me, I'm a very hard working horse," he told Donovan.

And Donovan replied: "I want you to recognize, if you do get the job, that you're my horse, and I own the stables, and in addition I own the glue factory."

Monks was ready with a retort: "I hope with the job I'll do, you won't have to bring the glue factory into operation."

Monks was qualified—overqualified. But he told Donovan at that interview that he would only take the job if he could stay on as a director at Synfuels.

All the people the Secretary spoke with about Monks, including Senator Cohen and Vice President Bush, were enthusiastic about his taking the pensions job. Before long, Donovan called Monks with an offer to take the position. The catch was, the laws governing the Synfuels corporation forbid directors from holding other paid government jobs—even though Monks was donating his services at Synfuels. A couple of months later, however, as it became increasingly obvious that Synfuels was going to be phased out, Donovan allowed Monks to take the pensions job and stay on at Synfuels to help wind it down. Monks said he would get around the corporation's restriction by not accepting his $67,000 pay from the DOL. He did not need or want the money anyway and thought he could simply refuse it as he had done at Synfuels. "I consider it a privilege to work for the government," he told the *Washington Post*.

Monks also wanted Donovan to upgrade the rank of the position. But he did not receive assistant secretary, Level 3 status that would have allowed him to maintain his work in politics after the Synfuels directorship expired. Even so, Monks could not resist being the person in charge of policing America's growing pension funds, about which he had been thinking so deeply for several years. So in December 1983, he accepted Donovan's offer.

As it turned out, he had to forsake Synfuels and politics right away, because he soon discovered that by law he had no choice but to take payment for working at the Department of Labor. Hence, he had to resign his Level-3 Synfuels post. But by then he was so involved in starting his new job that he was not really upset about not being able to participate in President Reagan's reelection effort. And while he took his paycheck, as required, he turned it immediately over to a charity, the Spurwink School for emotionally disturbed children located on the outskirts of Portland, Maine. (In the late 1970s, Monks had bought Spurwink, contributing new capital and installing a new director, and years later he combined it with his daughter Melinda's own school, Creative Health Foundation.)

On taking the pensions job, Monks vowed—to himself and his family—that he would stay in the position for just one year. Milly did not think much of this plan. Monks later recounted her reaction: "Look," she told him, "if you really want to do this, you can't have any power. You tell people you're going to go in for a year, they'll know you're a lame duck. It's just silly. If you're going to go there, just stay there."

But Monks was confident this was the way to go, and in his typically global mode of thinking, he told his wife so. "Trust me," he remembers saying to her, in a recollection that may be colored by subsequent events. "I know my own temperament in the government. I have a single agenda for this. I'm not going into this because I want to be a career public servant. I'm going into this because it's in aid of my long-term project in trying to create change in the way that corporations function. I can't afford more than a year's time here. Also, because what I'm doing is going to be considered somewhat different, and it will elicit a fair amount of negative response, I probably have got only a year's credit there before people decide it's worthwhile bringing up the heavy artillery and doing me in. So long as it's clear that I'm going there to do one thing and one thing only, I'll have some chance of getting it done in a year."

After spending Christmas at a holistic retreat at Murietta Hot Springs in the Southern California desert, Monks leapt into his job. His first item of business was a variety of potential conflicts of interest that had to be resolved. This was not so unusual for a business person and investor coming into a regulatory role, since he might now be in a position to regulate/prosecute/investigate one of the companies he was personally associated with. But the intricacies of Monks' portfolio were such that it would take time to resolve all potential conflicts—if that were even possible.

First, the department had to identify the possible conflicts. With the help of his legal advisers, Monks completed Form 278, the financial disclosure report detailing the subject's finances and investments. He then walked it over to Lilly, who as part of his job as Acting Solicitor of Labor was the Designated Agency Ethics Officer (DAEO). Lilly himself had filled out a 278; his was seven pages long. Monks' was 38 pages. It included investments held by Monks and his wife, a trust for the Monks' children, and six trusts that had been created either for Monks or his wife. Monks and four of the six trusts had interests in various investment pools. Among the investments were a number of partnerships. For instance, Bar & Co. consisted of an investment of $5.2 million in the Lambert Bruxelles Corp., made in August 1983, amounting to more than 2 percent of Class A common stock and more than 2 percent of Series A convertible subordinated notes. At the time, LBC owned about 36 percent of the stock and convertible debentures of Drexel Burnham Lambert.

Monks wanted to know what Lilly would do with the report.

"I give it to Seth Zinman," said Lilly, referring to the Alternate DAEO—otherwise known around the department as Dr. Z or Dr. No.

"Can we have a meeting with this guy?"

"Yeah," Lilly shrugged.

"I don't want to give this to you until I have the guy here," Monks said.

"What are you going to do? Try to intimidate him?" Lilly asked.

"No. I just want to have a conversation with him, if that's okay."

"What's it going to be about?" Lilly asked.

"I just want to explain to him how confidential, personal, and sensitive this is."

So Lilly got Zinman and Monks in a room together. After a cordial greeting, Monks looked Zinman in the eye and said in a steady voice: "I'm going to give you this, and I'm going to promise you two things. One is, if I ever read anything in the paper about it, your government job will be in jeopardy. I'm just promising you that, because there's very sensitive, confidential personal and financial information in there. And I take it very seriously. I will do everything I can to see that you don't keep your government job, since we're supposed to have a confidential relationship here. I'm not threatening you. I'm just telling you this. The second thing is, in the year that I'm at the department, you are not going to finish going through this [to determine whether there were conflicts with the businesses he was invested in]."[2]

Monks did have to do some maneuvering to remove the potential conflicts of interest. For one thing, he took a leave of absence from his consulting arrangement with American Express stemming from the sale of The Boston Company. (He was to be paid $100,000 a year for five years ending in 1986, whether or not he actually provided consulting services, which to date he had not.) He also resigned from his positions as a director of Ram and Co. (which managed real estate and provided investment advice to the investment pools), Ram Trust Services, and Lambert Bruxelles Corp. (where he was also on the executive and compensation committees), and resigned from his position as general partner of the investment pools, instead becoming a passive investor.

But even then, one problem remained. And while he was allowed to proceed with the duties of his government job, Monks spent his entire year at DOL sparring with the ethics officials over this one point. The root of the problem was a trust set up by Phineas Sprague (1920) for whomever of his descendents would be alive when it expires in 2019, including one of his granddaughters, Millicent Monks or her descendents. That trust was divided into two parts, only one of which involved Milly; she had an 11 percent interest in it, valued in 1983 at more than $750,000. While Monks had knowledge of the trust's holdings (a vast portfolio of stocks and bond investments, the largest being about $100,000 in Chemical New York Corp.) since he got an annual report and read it, he had no control over them. Even so, his knowledge of the portfolio companies was considered to be a potential conflict of interest since he might have to deal with those companies at the DOL. Monks hired an attorney to help him work out the problem. But since Monks was only in office for a year, he left before the matter could be resolved. Fortunately, no conflicts arose that would have forced the issue.

On several occasions, though, Monks found himself involved in a meeting in which the subject under discussion related to or looked like it might relate to one of the many Sprague trust portfolio companies. In those cases, Monks would excuse himself, explaining that he might have a conflict. However, there was often another reason for his departure, as one former staffer tells it: "Invariably if the meeting was boring, Bob would say, 'You know what, based on this discussion, I think I may have a conflict. I'd better go check with Seth before I participate in this meeting.' And he'd go. I'd go back and say to him, 'Bob, there's no difference between this meeting where you didn't have a conflict and this one where you might have had one.' And he'd say, 'You think I'd sit in that boring meeting?' But he always had a legitimate claim to say he'd better go check, because no matter what company came in, Bob had some form of ownership or account."[3] And Monks does confirm that, given the limited time he had given himself at the Labor Department, "I did not want to get caught up in anything at DOL that detracted from my own agenda."

In his boyish way, Monks was terribly excited about his new job. But outsiders were baffled. When the press queried him on why he at the age of 50 with his extensive background in politics and business would take the lowly pensions administrator assignment, he was candid: He wanted to be "a public servant," involved in "hands-on management" in government. The pension program was more important than it seemed, he added, since it oversees "a substantial part of all of the long-term capital of the country" (some $840 million in plan assets as of 1983 expected to rise to $1 trillion by 1985) and protects nearly 70 million people in more than 700,000 plans.[4] He spoke of himself as "an agent of change," as he had been doing since the mid-1960s when first as an attorney and later as a manager and investor he was helping businesses solve problems. A bit later in the year, he even compared himself in his DOL guise with Moses in a brief *New York Times* article. In an oblique response to the question of whether he would stick around long enough to oversee some of the ambitious changes he sought, he remarked, "The price for being Moses is that I will never be Joshua." It would take a few years, but he would show the world what a hands-on manager of so vast a field of assets was capable of changing, especially in the area of corporate accountability and ownership duties.

The only reason Monks took this job was to advance his governance agenda, but he would not be able to spend all his time setting revolutionary policies about ownership responsibility. The pensions chief had to attend to a wide range of bureaucratic duties and lots of unfinished business inherited from predecessors. However, he had some major points in his favor. For one thing, Monks already had experience working in the federal government, and he was well aware of the time constraints. "In a government agency, you have control over about 20 percent of your time," he explains. "The other 80 is tied up with bureaucratic procedure and stuff that you just cannot fail to do. But I had 20 percent of my time, and that turned out to be enough." But Monks took the 80 percent very seriously, and what he did with it gave him a certain legitimacy that year and beyond that allowed him to raise his own agenda and complete much of it.

Also, he knew he'd be able to work long hours, since his wife was fully employed with her dancing, and he didn't have young children. Most important was a restructuring of the pensions division that took place just as he was coming in. The operation had been part of a larger group, the Labor-Management Services Administration, but was now split off as an independent unit, the Office of Pension and Welfare Benefit Plans (today the Pension and Welfare Benefits Administration), reporting directly to the Secretary of Labor. In addition—and this was equally important—Monks now had the enforcement authority over ERISA that his predecessor lacked.

He did not have a moment to waste in getting to work on his main concern: establishing the position that pension funds had fiduciary duties to act as owners of corporations. To Monks, it was a "simple legal proposition," that an ERISA fiduciary was obligated to concern himself or herself with the ownership element of portfolio securities, which started with simply exercising the proxy vote. Monks wanted to introduce this idea to the world at large. But first he had to lay the groundwork.

For all his career switching, Monks is 100 percent focused on whatever he is involved with at any one time. And as a strategic thinker, he is nothing if not methodical in his approach. He knew that the first step in this project had to be winning over the staff. As a businessman, he could not accomplish much by himself, and certainly as a newcomer to the DOL he would need support in carrying out a brand-new project. His two chief deputies would be Morton Klevan and Alan Lebowitz. Klevan, bespectacled, a few years Monks' junior, was the director for policy development and evaluation in the pension agency. Monks had already heard much about Klevan from others, and found him to be well worth listening to. A Brooklyn native with a dry humor and an ability to capture the essence of a situation plainly, Klevan was someone who knew the ins and outs of ERISA and the pension agency. He himself wrote many of the regulations, and Monks recognized his value at once. "I learned how to deal with Mort," he says. "And that was, every morning I saw him first, and every night when I left I saw him last. And it was simple. As long as Mort understood that I cared like hell about him—it's a matter of love, really—I got tremendous value added." The younger Lebowitz who was from Monks' native Massachusetts and was another store of knowledge, had been acting head of the agency since Clayton's departure in September and was the department's senior bureaucratic official.

One day before he actually started working, Monks came to the Labor Department in the Francis Perkins building to meet his new top staffers.

From the start, they knew they were dealing with an unusual person. "Whoever brought him in, Bob just quickly dismissed him because he just wanted to sit down with me," Lebowitz recalls. "And it was clear what Bob wanted to do. He wanted to get a sense of me. You could almost see his mind working to figure out who he'd be dealing with. Who are these people? It was just an informal discussion about what was going on here, who I was, and why I was there. It was all designed to help him figure out how he was going to deal with me. He wanted to take my measure. Find out what made us tick. It doesn't take Bob long to figure out what people are made of." Even so, he continued this sort of probe in future encounters so he could discover how they could best work together. For their part, Klevan and Lebowitz truly believed that Monks did not just want to pump work out of them, like a typical boss. "He made an effort to try to relate to the two of us," Klevan says. "And it wasn't just us." Among others Monks introduced himself to was his future secretary, Barbara Sleasman. "He came bounding in and pulled up a chair by my desk and said, 'So, tell me about yourself!'" she recalls. (A few weeks later, she was somewhat surprised, given what she already knew of his intellectual powers, to find him hanging up paintings in his office using a shoe to drive the nails into the wall.)

In the interest of creating a productive relationship, Monks, in his first meetings with Klevan and Lebowitz, proceeded to tell them something about himself, his background, and his goals. They already knew about his heritage and wealth from the press coverage of his appointment. At that initial meeting, he referred to himself as "a clergyman's son"—as he began doing habitually to make people "less uncomfortable with me," he explains, and in a shorthand way clear up the confusion generated by this blue blood's decision to take the lowly pensions job. As the conversation proceeded, the two staffers began to get the idea, which became increasingly clear as they worked together, that here was someone who, as Lebowitz puts it, "views public service as traditionally people of aristocratic backgrounds think of public service. He views his responsibility to the society at large. He's the Episcopal minister's son, a moralist."

Straight out, he explained to them why he was interested in this job. He said he'd been thinking about pension funds and corporate ownership for a long time and was in the process of writing a book on the topic of the potential power of institutional investors and the growing influence of ERISA on capital formation. Where better to finish the book, he told them, than right there at the virtual cerebrum of ERISA, where all the data he wanted could be found? Equally important, he said, he wanted to make his mark at the agency by helping the agency make its mark on the department and the administration. In his grand vision for the program, it would receive more resources and perhaps even combine with the Pension Benefit Guaranty Corporation, corporate pensions' insurance program, and the pension authority at the Internal Revenue Service to form a new, independent agency devoted to administering ERISA, similar in scope and power to the SEC. In short, he wanted to help usher in a new era for pension funds in the economy.

He told Klevan and Lebowitz, humbly and honestly, that while he was good at coming up with ideas, he was not very good at implementation and that that was where they came in. And it would take a lot of work, since, he revealed, he would be spending only one year at the department. "That absolutely shocked us," Klevan told the author in an interview, "because decent bureaucrats think anybody who says he's only going to stay a year will never get anything done. And yet in that year, he got more done than anybody else did in a year or two or three years. It was remarkable, first that he'd say that and second that he'd get so much done."

As a start, Monks asked his deputies for briefing books on all the division's major projects to review over the weekend. What he wanted were the actual documents, not just summaries of the goings-on. Surprised, but compliant, Klevan and Lebowitz handed him seven hefty volumes. Klevan had never seen and never would see anyone who asked for such an extensive briefing. And to his amazement, shortly thereafter, Monks appeared to have read and understood the documents. Granted, Monks had practiced law, knew something about ERISA, and had more than a passing interest in pension funds. Still, it was impressive how fast his mind worked. As Klevan and others would discover, it also took an indirect path. "Bob has an intuitive intelligence," Klevan later remarked. "A lot of people who are very creative can get to Z, but not by going through the alphabet in order. He'll start with A, then C, jump to R, go back to N, to Z."

Now cognizant of the department's recent work and its capabilities, Monks drew up a fairly short, yet ambitious, list of projects he wanted to accomplish that year. Included in that list, was his goal to introduce new thinking about corporate ownership. But there was a host of other items as well: computerization of the pension fund reporting process, sweeping away restrictions for pension plans to invest in venture capital and other types of investment pools, beefing up enforcement activity, introducing a means for asset managers to receive incentive compensation, and clarifying the ownership of surplus pension assets. Monks also wanted to put his stamp on the agency in a broad way, and as luck would have it his year would be ERISA's 10-year anniversary. So he had his heart set on performing a review of the Labor Department's handling of ERISA since the law's passage. By March, in office only a bit over two months, Monks was developing a reputation as a man of action. He appeared on the cover of that month's *Institutional Investor* magazine with the headline: "How Bob Monks Plans to Shake up Pensionland."[5]

So far, Klevan and Lebowitz very much liked their unorthodox new boss. But at times it seemed he was trying just a bit too hard to figure them out. Not knowing how much he could rely on his top men, he appeared to be setting them against each other so that they each would compete for his loyalty, and he would then know what was really going on with the staff. "I think it was a real surprise to him that we wouldn't play that game," Klevan says, "and that we'd tell him what was going on and that we'd do what he wanted to do. We'd argue with him, but once he said do it, we'd do it. And once he realized that he had a staff that was loyal and competent, I think he had a ball with the job."

While he wouldn't have very much time at the DOL, Monks was determined to do the best job he humanly could—and to use his authoritative position to learn as much as he could about pension funds' role in the markets. He not only threw himself into the details, but also he planned trips abroad to discover how other countries ran their pension systems—something no previous pensions administrator had done. He reasoned that a fresh perspective could only be valuable to the ERISA program and to his own personal agenda as well. "I wanted to use the year I had as a government official with the maximum leverage to find out what really was going on in the world," he later recounted. "I wanted to see specifically how other countries dealt with the questions of the effect of the pension assets on the economy." Paying his own way, he chose to visit countries with a wide range of experience in pensions, from France, which had no private pension system, to Sweden, which had the largest pension system in the world and the most advanced ideas, particularly in the area of fund activism, to Japan, which was then restricting its pension funds largely to domestic bonds, to the United Kingdom, where some institutional investors, including pension funds, already had large positions in corporations and were beginning to throw their weight around in the boardroom.

During his visit to the United Kingdom, Monks stopped in to meet Lord Henry Benson, who had been an assistant to the head of The Bank of England. In 1982, he—along with Adrian Cadbury, head of soft drink maker

Cadbury-Schweppes and then a non-executive director of the Bank of England, and Jonathan Charkham, who would become an adviser to the governor of the Bank—created an organization called Pro-Ned (Promotion of Non-Executive Directors), which acted as a clearinghouse for qualified candidates for selection as independent corporate directors. Monks was greatly impressed with and inspired by this development.

Monks was in England only a brief time when he discovered that his years at Cambridge, and specifically on the Cambridge crew, served as almost an honorary British citizenship in the way he was treated by prominent figures in the country. As he describes it: "If you rowed on the Cambridge crew, as I did, and won, everybody knows who you are forever. It's not the right way to be known, but it's a way to be known." He began to find that by the time he arrived for an appointment, his host knew that he had been a Cambridge Blue on the 1955 winning team. And any time he delivered a speech in England, that year and in future years, that fact would not fail to be mentioned. This passport to British society proved useful to Monks over the years as he continued to forge ties with the corporate governance movement there.

Back at home, Klevan and Lebowitz were quick to catch onto Monks' idea about fiduciary duty and ownership. "I had to be sure that they were copacetic with the idea," Monks says, "because if they were not, I could promulgate it, but after I was gone it would die." Not only did the two labor professionals agree with Monks' view, but Klevan in particular helped place it in the appropriate framework as an ERISA regulation. ERISA's so-called prudent man rule obligated pension fund trustees to be "prudent" in their management of plan assets. Klevan's idea was that since pension funds had to be "prudent" in their treatment of plan assets, they had to prudently manage the proxy vote—part of the owned security—as part of the management of the plan asset. That meant considering each vote carefully, as an owner of the corporation in question.

It was clear to Monks that the resources of the agency were so limited and the regulation-production process so tangled with requirements, from filings to public hearings and comment periods, that he would not succeed during his one year in office in turning his fiduciary duty concept into the law of the land. So, he had to find some other, less formal way of "making the law." Not that this was so exceptional. This was indeed the way that things had to be done in government. Years later, perhaps, an informal rule would get written down in black and white—and that did happen. But actually, the two bureaucrats informed Monks that a letter or even a speech had pretty much the same effect.

On top of that, Monks indicated that the enforcement office should begin working on the subject, thereby informing the world that he and the government were serious about this issue. The dirty little secret was that the enforcement arm of the pension agency was not likely to come up with something to prosecute in this area, at least for a while. That is because while it might be shown that not voting on an issue that affected the value of the stock held by a plan was a fiduciary breach, it would be virtually impossible to make a case that a fund that voted a certain way or did not vote at all made a difference in the result that caused a quantifiable loss. Indeed, formal proxy voting investigations did not begin for a few years. But, Lebowitz says, it was enough that enforcement was out there asking questions. "People don't like the government going in and looking at their books because you never know what it can find," he says. "Monks was the first pensions administrator to see that using enforcement to get a regulatory result would be a productive use of the agency's assets."

Monks used this notion of regulation-by-putting-the-fear-of-God-into-people in another, much bigger way during his year at DOL. In the summer of 1984, he directed his enforcement division to launch an investigation of the value that pension funds were getting from their use of soft dollars—a portion of their fees to brokers that pays for research and other purposes. He was convinced that they were not getting much. While he was at The Boston Company in the late 1970s and very early 1980s, Monks was startled by the lavishness of the conferences, trips, and perks provided by brokers to investment management firms such as his own. As Monks remarks today: "Soft dollars became a way in which brokerage houses could compete effectively without necessarily any net cost to themselves. If one concludes with a rather puritanical logic that the money had to come from somewhere, it came from the customers." That is, the pension funds were somehow paying larger commissions than necessary for their stock and bond trades to finance the extras that went to the funds' investment managers. (Monks was not endeared to brokerage firms. In a press interview in 1984, he referred to the people at Morgan Stanley as "thugs in pin stripes" because they were earning a substantial fee for being what he believed was a redundant fiduciary of the Teamsters Central States Pension Fund.)

The soft dollars assignment was a big challenge to a department that had in the past done virtually no enforcement in the financial arena; most of its time was spent playing cops to pension fund robbers—unions or others who were misusing money from the funds. But Monks added to the task by insisting that every field enforcement office spend 25 percent of its time on the project. "Alan and I both thought the agency was incapable of doing it," Klevan says. "We told him that the odds were there weren't three people in the field who knew what soft dollars were, much less were capable of making determinations about things like what is best execution (of a security trade)." The other problem was that the regional enforcement directors were accustomed to working on cases that achieved a numerical result such as an amount of money collected or a number of lawsuits filed as a result of their investigatory work. But from the start, they knew that it would be difficult if not impossible to catch anybody abusing soft dollars to such a degree that the department would file a suit. Hence, they grumbled about the unorthodox assignment.

"We recommended very strongly that we take one office and train a select group of people to do a small pilot project," Lebowitz says. "But Bob said, 'Nothing doing. Across the board. Twenty five percent.' We thought he was crazy. But basically he was right. I don't know if he knew it rationally, but he knew intuitively, that if people in all the major brokerage firms had people from the Department of Labor sitting there for weeks asking them questions, threatening to bring cases—that were unbringable in many respects—that people would pay attention and would clean up their acts. And whether it was coincidence or not, in that same period of time, the brokerage rates went down fairly dramatically."

But it was not just that Monks had made the pension division staff realize they were capable of much more than they had thought. More importantly, say his former deputies, he got his staff to start thinking like financial regulators. "Soft dollars in his mind was a good way to start that," Lebowitz says. "It was an issue that we may not have been familiar with, but we could understand it. And we could make an impact, not so much in terms of litigation, but at least in terms of getting people in the financial world to know who we were and to realize over time that we were going to have to be dealt with and that they were going to have to take into account issues relating to ERISA that they had never really thought much about."

Chuck Lerner who Monks hired as enforcement chief from the SEC and who picked up the soft dollars project when he started in September, also was impressed, as he reflects: "I think he's a visionary of a rare kind. He got the agency and separated it away from the union focus. He got everyone looking at the financial institutions. And he got everyone beating the same drum," that is working together on the same project. In 1986, the work that Monks had started resulted in the pension administration office's first soft dollar case. The department reached a private settlement with Bank of America, where one subsidiary had been using soft dollars to pay for errors it made. Says Lerner: "Enforcement staff had no idea what a brokerage firm was like. They were used to going into pension plans. People really didn't know what they were doing. They wrote a report. They slogged on. It really raised the issue, and the world took notice."

However, the department would not have been able to do this work without Lerner himself. Monks had inherited an operation with a weak enforcement arm. He took the initiative to rejuvenate this area by convening an enforcement task force and bringing Lerner in from the SEC, where the latter had worked on companion cases to Labor Department pension lawsuits. With Lerner in place, Monks redesigned the enforcement division by reducing the number of field offices and directing field officers to report to a national enforcement division. Then, realizing that one reason the enforcement staff had been ineffective was that its relatively small army of some 200 field investigators was addressing multiple issues, he got the staff to focus a large portion of its energies on this one issue of soft dollars. By 1986, the department had developed an official "significant issues" strategy based on this idea. "Our strategy was to pick areas, focus on them, get some publicity, alert people to them, and go onto the next one," Lerner says.

One of those areas was proxy voting. When he set the department in this direction, Monks was fully aware that a regulation forcing pension plan trustees to behave like owners of the corporations in their stock portfolios would be years in the making. Monks would be the one to plant the idea. Later, most of his successors would pick up on the theme and develop it further, while Monks would cultivate it in the private sector. Ultimately, this notion in combination with other factors would cost a number of CEOs and other corporate officers their jobs—and arguably that of many of the lower level employees who became caught in the downsizing gears of the 1990s. This idea would also help make U.S. corporations more competitive than they would have been without vigilant owners.

After only two months on the job, Monks was ready to present his revolutionary notion to the public. In discussions with the press, he let it be known that he planned "to raise for congressional and national consideration the issue of how pension beneficiaries might be able to vote on corporate matters related to their ownership," reported the *Los Angeles Times*.[6] To *Institutional Investor*, he noted, "The only people who can change the contract under which corporations can function are the owners. And the owners are increasingly pension funds. . . . Is it part of a fiduciary responsibility to exercise the right to vote?" The article expanded further on his thinking, striking at the essence of his motivations: "If pension funds used their ownership clout, he suggests, they could force corporations to look at social values as well as the bottom line."[7]

Then, on Thursday, April 5, 1984, he walked in the rain from his home in the Watergate complex up Rock Creek Parkway to the Four Seasons hotel in Georgetown, where he was scheduled to be the featured dinner speaker at a conference of pension plan officers hosted by *Institutional Investor*. The speech, called "The Institutional Shareholder as a Corporate Citizen," would be Monks' regulatory debut; and to the assembled crowd it was a complete surprise. "I proceeded to explain to the people there that they were now going to have the great honor to be responsible for how they voted for portfolio securities, which they had never done before," Monks later recalled. Following are excerpts from his talk, which subsequent pension administrators as well as leaders in the corporate governance field would come to call "seminal":

> When institutional investors don't vote, or vote without paying close attention to the implications of their vote for the ultimate value of their holdings, they are hurting not only themselves but beneficiaries of the funds they hold in trust. Therefore, it seems to me to be a self-evident proposition, that institutional investors have to be activist corporate citizens. . . . Given the huge blocks of stocks owned by institutions in all of our major companies, it is not always practical to quietly support management or sit on the sidelines and then sell if you don't approve of management's handling of the company. Also, it may not be legal. . . .
>
> I would suggest that it behooves institutional investors, in the exercise of their corporate citizenship, to take the lead in proposing, and passing, provisions which ensure, before takeover battles occur, that all [takeover defenses] are submitted either to the shareholders or to an outside committee for their approval. If that were done, I am sure that many of [them] would never see the light of day. . . . I believe that the time has come for institutional investors, as good corporate citizens, to initiate such proposals, rather than merely to wait and support them when they come up. . . . How can you be doing a proper job on behalf of your clients if you do not take the initiative to prevent actions from being

taken that may either prevent a company's stock from being properly valued or which may involve waste of the company's assets? I think this question is particularly acute today, because institutional investors, in bulk, own corporate America. Even if you wanted to run away from a poorly managed company, you couldn't all do it at once—it would too greatly affect the price of the stock. So, like it or not, it seems to me that, as a practical business matter, institutional investors are going to have to become more and more active shareholder-owners, and less and less passive investors, . . . good corporate citizens, not only analyzing and voting on the issues but, where necessary, taking the initiative to put items of vital interest to them on the corporate ballot.

In his talk, Monks was specific about the antitakeover devices that he felt institutional investors should be analyzing and in many cases opposing. Among them: Staggered elections of boards of directors, "supermajority" vote provisions (requiring much more than a simple majority for approval of an acquisition), fair price amendments requiring an acquirer to pay the same price for all shares that it paid to gain control, the creation of new classes of stock with enhanced voting rights, the granting of "golden parachutes" that give top management hefty severance payments in the wake of a takeover, greenmail (the purchase of a raider's stock at a price that is higher than the market price), and the sale of a company's "crown jewels," those operations that make it an attractive takeover candidate. Some money managers had already voted for and sometimes approved—though not themselves proposed—resolutions against proposed defenses in the most recent, 1983 proxy season (the spring annual meeting season was also known as the proxy season because proxies on company and shareholder proposals and director elections are cast at annual meetings), and some had filed suit against corporations for greenmail or for not considering takeover offers. But never before had a regulator stated that such actions as well as the initiation of those actions are duties under the law. Indeed, he came close to threatening his audience: "It is only a question of time before the department discovers a plan or a third party voting on a corporate takeover issue not solely in the interest of plan participants and beneficiaries," he declared.

Those present were not pleased with what they had just heard. The question and answer period was cordial enough. "Are you suggesting that there is only one right answer concerning ownership and responsibility to corporate America?" asked one man. Monks' reply: "Neither the Department of Labor nor any other governmental body should provide answers to how people should vote. But owners should require that they be allowed to vote on matters concerning corporate business." But Monks had discerned disapproval, even incredulity on many faces. And after the session broke up, he and Klevan had the distinct impression that people were avoiding him. The members of this audience did not hear that this is a way they could create new value, even though that really was a key part of Monks' point. Rather, what they heard was here was another government hack telling them that they would have to incur another responsibility and with it another expense to cut into their profit margins. And, of course, here was the government also telling them that they might have to vote against the management of potential clients.

What was he really thinking about the reaction to his statements? "They all make so damn much money out of this, that they can't really quarrel about having a little additional duty," Monks recalls his judgement. "But what they're really worried about is having to take a position that might inhibit their ability to get new business or make their existing relationships more contentious." Over the years, Monks would experience growing frustration as his ideal world of an ownership obligation would be plagued by this conflict-of-interest demon that he as just one man was powerless to vanquish.

Not for lack of trying. That April, the department began investigating a developing situation at Los Angeles department store chain operator Carter Hawley Hale, which was trying to fight off a takeover bid from The Limited Inc. of Columbus, Ohio. The department suspected that Bank of America, the trustee of the company's employee stock ownership plan and a major lender to the company, was more concerned about its client, Carter Hawley management, than about plan participants. ERISA, meanwhile, required that trustees act solely in the interest of plan beneficiaries.

To the pensions administrator, Bank of America had clear conflicts of interest. Not only was the bank a primary lender to Carter Hawley, but it played a pivotal role in helping the company fend off its suitor with a major new loan. Moreover, Carter Hawley CEO Philip Hawley was on Bank of America's board of directors and was chairman of its executive compensation committee.[8] (The bank has said that it had eliminated any procedural chance for conflict.) Meanwhile, the employee stock ownership plan held more than 18 percent of the company's stock, certainly a potentially decisive amount in a takeover battle. As trustee, Bank of America would take on the duty of tendering stock on behalf of plan participants. But, according to its policy, in such a situation of apparent conflicts of interest, it passed the voting responsibility on to plan participants. Generally, that policy guaranteed participants' confidentiality in how they voted. But this time, the bank told employees that it would not be able to prevent management from finding out how they cast their shares. This meant that employees would be likely either to side with management or do nothing at all (in which case the bank said their shares would go to management), even though The Limited's tender offer was some 50 percent over the market price of Carter Hawley's shares.

In April and May, the pension agency under Monks' direction prepared a lawsuit against the bank, charging violations of ERISA and seeking to replace the bank as plan trustee. In the midst of preparing the case, Monks wrote a letter to Bank of America attorneys, notifying them that the department was still investigating the case. The letter also detailed the way in which—in the department's opinion, with reference to its traditional view of any kind of proxy contest or tender offer—a procedure for obtaining voting instructions from plan participants might lawfully be put into effect. This could only be done, he wrote, "when the trustee had determined that the participants had in fact rendered an independent decision in directing the trustee, without pressure from their employer as to how to vote their shares. . . . If, among other things, the participants-employees are subjected to pressure from the employer to vote their shares in a particular manner, it would be the duty of the trustee to ignore any direction given which is the result of such pressure, as it could not be considered 'proper direction.'" Moreover, the letter went on, "A trustee cannot rely on a plan provision requiring that participants who do not specifically provide instructions be deemed to have issued a specific instruction regarding the tender of the shares allocated to their accounts," that is, that the shares would automatically go to management. Monks concluded with, "We hope this information will be useful to you in advising your client respecting carrying out its fiduciary responsibilities to the plan."[9]

(This established principle would come in handy for Monks a few years hence when he would run for the board of Sears, Roebuck & Co. Here was another case in which the employee pension plan held a large portion of stock and the plan trustees planned to take direction from the participants—this time in voting for directors. However, Monks would show that the plan participants could not "render an independent decision in directing the trustee" how to vote because they had not been fully informed on all candidates, and the pensions administrator agreed. Therefore, in the Sears case, the trustees had to take on the voting responsibility themselves and do the research required for them to meet this fiduciary duty. "That's why being there [at the Labor Department] was so important. Because you could put your spin on it," Monks says.[10])

But that letter was where it ended. The Department of Justice, whose approval was necessary for the DOL to bring lawsuits, decided against approving this one. Monks got a phone call from Lilly, who indicated that there were "political considerations," Monks told *Barron's*[11] (Lilly says he doesn't recall this). The U.S. Attorney General at the time was William French Smith, who, by remarkable coincidence, was a lifetime friend of Philip Hawley's, and of course both President Reagan and Hawley were Californians. But, Monks suspects that other forces within the Administration were also at work, given some Reaganites' professed determination to hold to the precept that the best government is the least government. For its part, Carter Hawley Hale told *Barron's* that the suit was not dropped for political reasons. In any case, with Carter Hawley's strong defense and the DOL threat removed, The Limited gave up before there was a vote.

To this day, Monks remains bitter over the Carter Hawley incident. Bringing the case, he says, would have accomplished a great deal in the interest of shareholder rights and corporate accountability. The agency has brought other cases, which have had limited impact on the overall problem. Over the years, as a regulator, an expert testifying at Congressional hearings, and a shareholder activist, Monks did his best to attack the conflict-of-interest problem and persuade lawmakers of the need for better enforcement to avoid it. But, the resistance to resolving the conflict has appeared too great for him to overcome.

One way Monks was trying to combat the conflict-of-interest dilemma during his year at Labor was by getting pension fund executives at major corporations thinking about their funds' responsibility as, effectively, permanent owners of portfolio companies. In the press, he forwarded the notion that pension funds should become long-term shareholders, and even mused about writing a statute defining prudence, under ERISA, as holding shares in a company for at least four years.[12] He also repeatedly made the point that institutional investors' stake in U.S. corporations was growing inexorably and would at some time in the not too distant future exceed 50 percent of total equity. With that kind of position in the economy, he noted—in a clear indication that he never stopped thinking about his own long-term goals of making corporations accountable to the society at large—long-term stockholders would begin thinking about broader issues. "People are not going to be able to ignore the notion that they need something a little bit wider—they need people a little bit broader than pure economic decision makers—in order to guide the American economy," he said in one publication. "To say that the majority owner of American companies—which the ERISA plans [plus other institutions] will be—is, in a sense, deaf, dumb and blind to anything other than narrow economic considerations is to consign the economy to be rudderless."[13] To a reporter from his home state of Maine, Monks remarked, "Everybody turns to the law to solve corporation problems. But there is also more and more looking to the owners of the corporations to help with such problems. The pension funds are very large shareholders in many companies. They have the power to influence corporations' decisions if they wish to. Ethics is involved in this. The pension fund trustees have to work for those coming under the pensions."[14]

More concretely, that spring Monks invited about 25 managers of the largest U.S. corporate pension funds to a luncheon at the Sky Club, an old-style businessmen's (and businesswomen's) club perched on the top floor of Manhattan's Pan Am Building. One of those was Gordon Binns, who ran General Motors' pension fund. As Binns recalls: "He said to us, 'You guys who are responsible for the assets of the pension fund don't have any voice in Washington. Meanwhile, it's the groups on the benefit administration and plan design side that do. You ought to do something about that."

Binns and the other listeners were intrigued by what they had heard, and a half dozen of the largest players asked Binns to arrange a follow-up meeting with Monks to talk further. Binns set up a dinner at the Harvard Club in Manhattan with the managers of the funds at General Motors, Bethlehem Steel, AT&T, U.S. Steel, IBM, General Electric, and Du Pont. Of course, Monks was happy to come. He hoped that by telling these people they were powerful, even if it was not completely true, they would start to use that power ("If you tell people they're powerful, they're apt to believe you," he says.). And he hoped that these were people who could think independently of management since, he reasoned, their companies were then viewed as being too large to be taken over and their top managements were therefore not concerned about that eventuality. Interestingly, Monks did not preach to them in this setting about fiduciary duty and the vote. It would be more effective, he thought, to appeal to their egos than to declare them subject to some vague notion of regulation that at the time they would have probably viewed as just another obstacle their lawyers could overcome.

Monks recalls the essence of his talk that day at the Harvard Club this way:

> It's wonderful to see you. One of the ironies is that each one of you is responsible for assets that in many cases are worth more than your company's market value. [This phenomenon had just begun to appear.] And yet, if you had a meeting of the top 50 executives of your company, you wouldn't be invited. [Pension officer was generally still a lowly, assistant treasurer or lesser type of position.] The fact is, you control a lot of assets, and if you don't understand that you have that power, you will be ceding it to other people. And if you don't use that power, you are encouraging abuse.

As an example, he invoked the name of T. Boone Pickens—the name that became synonymous in the 1980s with corporate raider:

> Why can Boone Pickens come in and take over companies? The reason he can is that the institutional investors act like they're dead! And the only thing they can do is either hold or sell, and as a practical matter they've got to sell when they have a high price. But, you're owners. The same as Boone Pickens is. You own more than Boone Pickens. But if you don't start thinking of yourselves as owners, you're conferring all this power on Boone. Boone doesn't need 50 percent to take over a company. He only needs 1 percent and a bank loan, and he can make the rest of you guys who can't do anything sell to him and, bingo, there goes the company. And there goes the company because you have behaved not like owners, but like dead pieces of wood who had no alternative here except to sell. So, you'd better get together as a group and understand that collectively you are the controlling shareholders of corporate America. And if you don't want to have hostile takeovers, it's very simple. The bunch of you have got to get together and understand what you're doing.

Following that encounter with the Labor Department's pension authority, the pension officers put together an ad hoc committee to consider a course of action—if any. The question was, how were they going to form a collective voice? At first they thought that they could find an existing organization to associate with. But the employee benefits lobbying groups were focused on benefits and not inclined to take an interest in the investment of plan assets. Over time, they decided to create a new committee under the auspices of the Financial Executives Institute (FEI) that would comprise only those people who were investing plan assets. The FEI's Committee on Investment of Employee Benefit Assets (CIEBA) convened its first session in November 1985, chaired by Gordon Binns, at the then AT&T Building in midtown Manhattan. About 25 companies were represented. Today, CIEBA has 154 members.

Also in his year at the DOL, Monks played a small but influential role in the formation of what would become a powerful Washington-based group of government and union pension funds called the Council of Institutional Investors. In August, Monks got a phone call from Jesse Unruh. Unruh was a mighty politician from California, nicknamed "Big Daddy," both for his size and his political abilities in delivering the state's Democratic delegation to John Kennedy in the 1960 primary. He then went on to nearly defeat Ronald Reagan in the latter's reelection campaign for governor, and later became state Treasurer. At the time he called Monks, he had been doing a lot of thinking about the importance of shareholder activism. In particular, he was upset that in March (1984) Texaco had got rid of a potentially hostile suitor, the Bass Brothers of Texas, by paying them off in greenmail. Texaco paid the Basses $1.3 billion, a 12 percent premium over the market price. Unruh, who had been following Monks' words and actions on the subject of shareholders' ownership responsibilities including reports in the press of Monks' concern about the growing practice of greenmail, very much wanted to meet him to talk about a project he was working on. They decided to meet half way—in Chicago.

On the Thursday before Labor Day, Monks flew there with his confidential assistant, Chicago native Donald Thibeau, whom he had brought to the department from Synfuels. In the sweltering, 100-degree heat, they took a cab to the Drake Hotel in midtown, where they found the mustachioed politician, looking much leaner these days, accompanied by his lawyer, none other than Ian Lanoff, a former pensions administrator who was now an attorney specializing in the pensions field. For almost three hours, first over dinner and later in the hotel bar, the four men discussed Unruh's idea of founding an association of big pension funds that would try to do something about takeover defenses that he perceived as abusive toward shareholder value.

Monks was enthusiastic. The assembly of large institutional shareholders seemed to him to be the first essential step in effective corporate governance, and he told Unruh so. "I said that I thought it was a good idea, and I would give any Republican institutional support to the idea of forming an organization of institutional investors, but that I thought it should be bipartisan," Monks recalls. "I said that he could count on me to back him and not to say that this was some Democrat trying to back-door socialize [take over businesses]. I said I would speak up, and say that what he was doing was compatible with Republican party principles." Monks mentioned Unruh's plans in his speeches to various groups during the rest of his term and beyond. For example, in an October speech to a group of institutional investors gathered in Washington,[15] he said: "The natives are restless. A gifted politician, state Treasurer of California Jesse Unruh, has just finished a nationwide series of meetings picking up encouragement, endorsements, and membership from public and private plans. Their aim: the soft underbelly of corporate America—the shareholders' vote at annual meetings. Their target: those devices now infamous that benefit management at the expense of the shareholders. 'Golden parachutes,' 'greenmail,' and a host of takeover tactics are signs of the times."

Actually, the Council took shape sooner than CIEBA, starting up early in 1985. Indeed, some people thought CIEBA was formed as a corporate reaction to the Council although its founders did not even know the Council was being formed. Briefly in 1986, CIEBA discussed joining the Council, but rejected that notion in favor of remaining independent.

Throughout the year, in speech after speech, Monks continued to use the bully pulpit to alert institutional investors to their ownership duties. He urged investors to pay the small cost of initiating a proxy fight or bringing suit against directors who abuse their positions. "In many circumstances, the returns to the funds which an institutional investor manages would be significant enough to weigh in favor of taking such action, although other shareholders might get a free ride," he told a crowd at a Financial Analysts Foundation conference in late October. He also expanded the list of areas that he believed investors were obligated to monitor to include salary levels and managerial benefits.

In his later speeches, Monks seemed to be beginning what would be his future career of influencing investors' votes during proxy season. Although he made it clear that each situation must be weighed individually and that investors must carefully evaluate both sides of the contest in terms of the long-term benefit to the company and to beneficiaries, he also indicated a bias against certain management tactics. He told the FAF meeting, "I would like to see institutional investors fighting for repeal of shark repellent provisions [defensive maneuvers] or at least to have existing shark repellents put on the ballot at annual stockholders' meetings." In a speech delivered the day after he left the Labor Department in late January 1985, Monks noted two areas that he felt required particular attention. One was the issuance of different classes of stock with different voting rights, concentrating power in a few friendly hands. The other was what he termed an "exploding right," the issuance of "rights to purchase common stock of the company or a greater number of shares of any surviving company at the same fixed price in the event of a hostile takeover . . . [which is] a blatant attempt to make a company takeover proof, and cannot be justified." This technique would become popularly known as a poison pill. Monks warned investors that these defensive maneuvers would likely reduce a company's stock value.

As a group, he explained, pension funds and other large institutions have grown to such a degree that they can no longer sell out of a company they don't like since the only buyer willing to take such a big block would be another institutional investor. Like it or not, pension funds were permanent investors in corporate America and becoming more so by the day. Increasingly, they were the deciding factor in ongoing battles for corporate control. In winding up his FAF speech, Monks tried to convey the revolutionary nature of this development: "After some 50 years of corporations dominated by management, with a largely anonymous, fragmented shareholder body, the rise of the institutional investor as an active corporate participant will allow the corporation in the real world to return, at least in its corporate governance aspects, to its original theoretical model: that of an entity governed by officers and a board of directors who are responsible to a vigorous and ever vigilant body of shareholders."

Inevitably, Monks' position was misinterpreted by some as a legal obligation for pension fund managers to go with the highest price in a takeover situation, frequently offered by a raider. In November 1984, management guru Peter Drucker published an essay in the *Wall Street Journal* in which he remarked that pension funds were compelled by law to sell out to the highest bidder. Monks actually knew Drucker from one of the regulator's previous careers. After Monks sold his energy company and then the stock he had received in the sale in 1970, his partner Dwight Allison suggested that they ask Drucker to talk with them about the various directions they might take next. They only knew Drucker through his book, "The Age of Discontinuity," published in the late 1960s, which had impressed them immensely because of the author's ability to view current events in a wider perspective. So, they invited him, for $1,000 a day, to sit down with them and a few associates and just talk. He agreed, and they met at the University Club on 5th Avenue in midtown Manhattan. "We asked him everything we could think of," Monks recalls. And, like the political science professor Drucker had been, he talked and talked and talked, and his hosts, a bit frustrated at first that he wasn't willing to be interrupted to hear their comments, sat back and just listened. The one thing Monks remembers about the two days: He and Drucker were standing together in the mens room, and Monks mentioned some idea he had. Drucker remarked, in his Viennese accent, "Bob, you have a very original mind. You must not be discouraged, because not many people have an appetite for original minds."

Monks later said he was "saddened" to see such a great man write so carelessly and irresponsibly in the *Journal* about pension trustees' obligations under the law—that they had to sell out to the highest bidder. "While there was an atmosphere of hostility against raiders, the notion that the trustees were legally obligated to sell was not only wrong but it was pernicious," Monks told me. "It let them off the hook. I was then early in my efforts to require that the trustees be sentient and responsible, so it was really sad for my old tutor to give them an excuse to act like automatons." Monks swiftly cleared up the matter—or at least tried to—with a letter to the editor stating that Drucker's statement simply was not true; according to ERISA, prudence ruled the decision, not price. And prudence as he saw it and explained in subsequent congressional testimony, requires "a solid, careful evaluation of long-term prospects of the company under existing management as against the short-term prospects presented by the takeover offer and by the ability to invest the proceeds of the takeover offer in another enterprise."

Meantime, all this talk of ownership responsibilities begged the question: How could pension fund officials and portfolio managers trained in asset allocation and securities investment be expected to behave as corporate owners? Monks addressed this matter briefly in later speeches. For example, in December 1984 he suggested to the Investment Technology Association: "Clearly this will involve the requirement for new skills and competencies. Current fiduciaries have neither the inclination nor the training to act as proprietors. Either they will have to acquire them, or a new institution will be developed. Obviously, the traditional lines between owner and management will have to be redefined to accommodate a more active owner." Developing such a new institution would shortly become Monks' next career goal.

While he was setting new policy about proxy voting, Monks had his staff working hard on writing a regulation relating to another field that he cared about dearly, since he had practiced in it: venture capital. In this endeavor, unlike his proxy voting work, Monks would be able to reach the formal, final, in-print stage of making regulation. The issue was this: pension funds had a problem investing in pooled vehicles such as venture capital, real estate, and oil and gas partnerships, because ERISA's prohibited transaction rules would bar certain common forms of compensation and many common transactions if the partnership assets were considered to be plan assets. While in theory ERISA allowed for high risk or speculative investments under its "prudent man rule" governing the fiduciary obligations of plan trustees, these kinds of partnerships appeared to be unavailable to pension funds. That is because under the law the managers of these pools would appear to be fiduciaries of whatever pension funds were invested in them and therefore subject to ERISA's prohibited transaction restrictions on use of the assets.

Monks was also convinced that the prudent man rule as it stood was forcing pension funds to be too conservative by leading them to invest too heavily in just traditional stocks and bonds and to hire consultants to verify prudence in choosing managers and allocating assets.

He cited evidence that the funds as a whole, by making conservative investments, did not appear to be making a real rate of return over the long term (after investment management, transaction, and consulting fees). Some pension experts complained that the pensions administrator had chosen a time period—1961 to 1981—that delivered mediocre returns (1982 marked the beginning of the long bull market) and looked only at the Dow Jones Industrial Average, without considering new contributions to funds, income earned, or asset mix. Others argued that the funds had been investing for returns, but also were keeping risk in mind.

To clarify the more recent situation to his boss, Klevan showed Monks evidence that pension funds were actually increasingly taking bigger risks for bigger returns by making more investments in venture capital, real estate, and foreign securities. To do so, many had been granted or were seeking exemptions from ERISA's fiduciary rules. Klevan says Monks "recognized it and didn't recognize it at the same time. He could hold the two beliefs at once." But Monks was adamant in his belief that pension funds were not performing as well as they could.

However, there were no facts. No one really knew how the pension plans were performing. So, Monks asked his deputies to commission a rate-of-return study to prove his suspicion that pension funds were underperforming the market and other institutional investors. The study was not completed by the time the agency held hearings on investment performance and corporate governance in January 1985, where Monks described the problem:

> Nobody ever seems to perform worse than the averages. . . . It reminds me of one of the times that I ran for office, that I never met anybody who voted for my opponent. But when they counted the votes on election day, she'd won. And the same thing is true with our talks with plan sponsors and with money managers. Everybody you ever talk to has performance that is better than average and everybody beats the averages. The numbers are reported in terms that are not absolute. You never find out how anybody performed as against a real standard. You always find out how people perform with reference to other people. . . . Almost no evidence is available as to how the plan as a whole performs.[16]

The performance study appeared in 1985. It was not conclusive—in part because different types of institutions invested in different types of assets. But it did indicate that Monks was essentially right.

From what information he had during his tenure, Monks saw a few different problems. For funds that were "fully funded"—that is, had the assets needed to meet their obligations—there was little justification for taking additional risks in their investments; still, though, these funds were not recording positive net returns. Meanwhile, those pension plans that were "underfunded" or did not have sufficient assets to meet their obligations (and most corporate funds were in this position) were not taking the necessary risks in their investing to generate the higher returns needed to build an adequate store of assets. Both types of funds in his view were victims of a system in which money managers are paid irrespective of whether they add value to the plan's portfolio; there were no incentive fees encouraging better performance. Also, he believed that whatever managers were doing in "alternative" (non-stock and bond) investments for underfunded plans, they could do more. But, he argued, it often took over a year for a plan to obtain a DOL exemption from the fiduciary rules. Moreover, many plans invested in pools without applying for exemptions, thereby taking a risk that the government would go after them or that an investment would sour, inviting lawsuits from beneficiaries and regulators. And who knew how many funds were just too nervous or conservative to take such a chance?

In any event, Monks believed that in his regulatory position he could create ways in which pension funds could begin to turn in better performance. First, he advanced the idea of incentive fees for managers. Also, for fully funded pension plans or as a core portfolio investment for other plans, he proposed the introduction of inflation-indexed bonds, instruments geared to provide a real annual return (over inflation) of 2 to 3 percent. Others at the time had been weighing the advantages of inflation-adjusted bonds in reducing the federal deficit, then at around $200 billion; Monks was the first to be interested mainly in their potential as an investment for pension funds. If pension plans were required to achieve a real rate of return over time, Monks reasoned, they would be highly likely to place a portion of their assets in the new bonds. On the other hand, critics pointed out, the securities might prove so popular that to buy them, pension funds would sell some of their stocks and bonds, in turn depressing market prices, which in turn would impact pension fund portfolios—although probably only temporarily. Monks countered that the likely sales would be of government bond holdings. Britain, among other countries, already had issued such securities with good results. In the spring of 1985, Monks testified in support of his views at a hearing on inflation-indexed bonds before the Joint Economic Committee. Nothing ensued. Years later, in 1997, the Clinton Administration finally did issue inflation-indexed bonds; their initial success was only modest, however, given the low inflation and bounding stock market at the time.

In addition to the bond idea, Monks believed that he could help by providing more liberal regulation on riskier, alternative investments including pooled funds for venture capital, oil and gas, and real estate. Monks' predecessors had started a project to define what exactly constitutes a plan's assets when a plan invests its money in securities. If the underlying assets of the issuer of the securities constitute plan assets, then the manager of the issuer would be a plan fiduciary and subject to certain restrictions as to handling the assets; if the assets are the unit of investment (stock, bond, participation in a pool), on the other hand, the manager of the issuer would not be a fund fiduciary. The decision was made that plan assets are the underlying assets of the investment; exceptions could be made for investments in widely held public securities and in operating companies including venture capital and real estate pooled partnerships.

The proposed regulation, which replaced a prior proposal, was drafted in 1982 and had made it all the way to the Office of Management and Budget (OMB) the clearinghouse for all regulations. And there it had stalled. It was Monks' job to arrive at a definition of what was and was not a venture capital operating company—as opposed to a venture capital investment management firm with all sorts of potential conflicts of interest in the use of its assets—that would please the people at the OMB and the venture capital industry and would be consistent with the general principle that the underlying assets of an investment pool were plan assets and the underlying assets of an operating company were not. Klevan assured him that this was something he could accomplish in his one year in office. For his part, Monks, an erstwhile investor in venture capital and energy, considered this task to be a top priority. In his characteristically grand language, he told one publication that he was now sitting in a place that allowed him to "set the rules for how an enormous conglomeration of capital" could be invested.[17]

In an indication of how much importance he placed on this measure, Monks personally walked to the OMB to present his case. It was then that he first met Nell Minow, then 32 years old, who was to become his partner in shareholder activism. Minow, who is the daughter of former Federal Communications Commission chairman Newton Minow (television is a "vast wasteland"), is idealistic, though also realistic about how the world works. Extremely bright and articulate, she has a childlike enthusiasm for whatever she is involved in. She earned a law degree at the University of Chicago and then went to work in government, at the Environmental Protection Agency during the Carter Administration. It was there that she became fascinated by the regulatory process and how painstakingly produced rules so often have perverse consequences. Later she shifted to OMB to pursue that interest. Within a couple of years, Minow became the assistant to Douglas Ginsburg, the director of new regulations at OMB. She was actually working on the same deregulatory effort as that of Vice President Bush's Task Force on Regulatory Relief, but had not met Monks while he was on it.

When she heard that Monks was coming over, she recalled something someone had told her about him. As she recounts: "One of my colleagues at OMB was telling me about this very interesting guy, who was complaining about something and said to her, 'They're not just rearranging the deck chairs on the *Titanic,* they're reweaving them.' I thought that was a very funny thing to say, and it made me remember his name." When Monks made the appointment with her, Minow was doubly impressed, since normally a department head would not show up at her door but instead just send a proposed regulation over for review or a low-level staffer to explain the matter at hand. "In my experience there," Minow says, "the only political appointee who decided to bring the regulation over and make sure that it went all right was Bob."

According to Minow, the problem was coming up with a definition of venture capitalist that everyone from the DOL to OMB to the investment advisory industry could feel comfortable with. Monks, Minow, Ginsburg, a couple OMB staffers, and three venture capitalists sat down to decide the matter. As Minow recalls the proceedings: "If we'd said we were coming up with a definition of fishermen, we'd be able to do it. But venture capitalists, by definition, or the people who go into that field, are people who hate to be confined in any way. No matter what you say to them, it's just their nature; you could not get them to agree to a definition. We'd say, 'How about if we say this?' And one of them would say, 'No, I had a deal once that wouldn't fit that.' We'd say, 'You give us a definition, you tell us, we'll use it. We're trying to help you here. We're trying to get you [a regulation that won't confine you]. Let us help you by just giving us some words to fill in.' And they would not do it. They could not bring themselves to define themselves in any way."

Monks was particularly frustrated because the venture capitalists in the room were people he knew as heads of venture capital associations he had dealt with. "All they wanted was more. Push push push," he recounts. At the time, Klevan referred to them with a Yiddish word that Monks did not forget: *chazzah,* or "pig." In the end, Labor wrote up and OMB cleared a definition that it imposed on the industry, giving the venture capitalists much but not all of what they wanted in terms of what they had to do to qualify for an exemption. Even today, Klevan marvels that it took them only 11 months to accomplish this regulation, even while doing so many other things.

Monks visited Minow one more time during his year at the Labor Department while drafting a much less important regulation. This time, Minow was taken by another aspect of his style. "I had marked up his draft, and I was expecting a big argument because most of the time people from the agencies felt that they were the experts and who was OMB to tell them what to do. And if he'd had a reason for doing it his way, I would have said fine. So I was reading off this small list of changes I was going to ask him about, and he just said, 'OK, fine, all right. Next.' I thought, 'This guy has less ego invested in the document and more commitment to getting the substance of it through than anybody I'd ever seen before. What an interesting person.'"

One reason Monks accomplished so much in his short span of service was that Secretary of Labor Donovan, then plagued by charges of corruption at his New Jersey construction business, did not get in his way. (Donovan was acquitted of fraud charges in 1987.) The pensions administrator did, however, have a few run-ins with politicians in charge of pensions oversight. At one point, for example, he commissioned a simplification of Form 5500, which pension plan sponsors have to fill out annually for the Labor Department. Next thing he knew, he was summoned to the office of Representative William Clay, chairman of the House Committee of Labor-Management Relations. In his office, the Congressman from Missouri lectured Monks like a school marm with a ruler. He started by pointing out that every single line in the form was required by the ERISA statute. And then he made it clear that he, as a legislator, made the laws and that Monks' responsibility was to carry them out, and not to amend them. Incidentally, 13 years later, pensions administrator Olena Berg commissioned a simplification of Form 5500. In any event, the political element did little to chill Monks' vast energies.

One time, an old school connection helped him out in this regard. Democratic Senator Howard Metzenbaum, while in the minority on a Senate Labor Committee subcommittee, had persuaded the leadership to let him conduct a hearing concerning a corporate takeover that he suspected was accomplished through a looting of the pension fund. Since Metzenbaum was notorious for unceremoniously grilling Reagan political appointees, Monks was apprehensive when he was summoned to testify. While he was conferring with Metzenbaum before the hearing began, Monks felt a large arm encircle his shoulders. It was Ted Kennedy. "Howard," Kennedy said, "I want you to know that Bob Monks is one of my oldest friends, and you should know that he is OK." Monks had no idea that Kennedy knew about this hearing; he was not on the subcommittee. But he was glad to see his seventh-grade school chum. Metzenbaum not only treated Monks kindly at the hearing, but he became so friendly with him that he even attended his going-away party at the DOL.

While working on the regulation and enforcement fronts, Monks was also forcing the pensions administration to take a good look at itself in his National Pension Forum hearings that marked the 10th anniversary of ERISA. Indeed, as the hearings began, Secretary Donovan recounted "some

considerable discussion on my staff as to the wisdom of embarking on a public self-critical examination of ERISA during an election year or, for that
matter, any year." But he went ahead with it, and many who testified praised
both him and Monks for doing so.

In arranging the hearings, Monks and his assistant Don Thibeau got together all of the original players to ask them whether they would write
ERISA the same way today in light of what had transpired. They included
Senator Jacob Javits of New York, the chief sponsor of the legislation, who
was seriously ill, confined to a wheelchair, and able to speak only with the
aid of an oxygen device. In responding to queries on one particular aspect
of the law, Javits asked to be excused until the afternoon to consult on the
matter. Later he returned and confidently affirmed the wisdom of the provision as written. Monks often repeats the story of asking Javits whether he
had any idea when he sponsored ERISA that pension assets would grow to
such a great extent. The senator replied: "I have never been accused of
modesty, but I will tell you in all sincerity that it never occurred to me."

The hearings also featured a number of witnesses from both inside the
agency and inside the pensions, benefits, and money management industries.
Many called for a national retirement policy. And a few urged the department to assess the impact of pension funds on the economy as a whole, most
prominently Congressman John Erlenborn and Randy Barber, director of
the Center for Economic Organizing in Washington. Here Barber struck at
the heart of Monks' personal goals: "The current administrator has correctly
urged pension fund managers and trustees to become more directly involved
in the governance of corporations whose equities they own in such increasing proportions. However, it should be evident that such reforms will be effective in making corporations more responsive to participants' needs only
when the fund managers and trustees themselves are made much more directly accountable to the desires and interests of those participants."[18] The
forum's recommendations included computerizing pension fund information processing; enhancing the enforcement program by adding funds and
investigators; creating a single agency to administer ERISA, and creating a
self-regulatory organization to monitor the Department of Labor's activity.
"It was a very worthwhile and productive series of events that told the investment community that the Labor Department is there with its eyes
open," Lilly says.

When Monks announced his resignation in December, as he had always
planned to do, the press was astounded. Why would someone abandon his

own projects in midstream? He got decidedly mixed reviews. *Pensions & Investments Age* praised him for raising provocative questions and remarked, "He inspired a fundamental re-examination of the nature of the private pension system, particularly how pension assets are invested and the role of the institutional investor as corporate citizen," and his ideas "stirred up the private pension system like none of his predecessors." But the article then criticized him for leaving major issues to be resolved by his successors.[19]

Others were even more critical. "Mr. Monks will leave behind a record of outspokenness, but also one that failed to live up to expectations that he had raised," proclaimed the *Wall Street Journal*. The article went on to note that Monks' desire to expand the program and make it more professional went against the Reagan administration's deregulatory bent—an irony considering his first position in the administration. Moreover, it pointed out that his only major enforcement action was scuttled by the Justice Department.[20] Former pensions administrator Ian Lanoff posed the nagging question: "Will the ideas he raised just sort of disappear, or will whoever replaces him pursue them further?" For his part, Monks remarked, "I think I've left you a number of acorns that I'm very confident will be the agenda for the next five years, and better cultivated by others."[21]

Whether they were *better* cultivated by others can not be answered. That they *were* cultivated by others is a fact. In organizing task forces, pilot projects, and hearings, Monks was trying his best to assure follow-up on some of his priorities. To address performance and governance issues, Monks had the pension agency hold hearings in January 1985, the month of his departure. Some 50 private sector experts in pensions and money management appeared in two days of testimony in San Francisco at a Holiday Inn and two days at the New York Plaza Hotel. Rapt by the presentations, Monks did not leave the podium for any reason during those four days. Then, largely due to his connection with Senator Cohen, the senator's government management oversight committee held hearings that summer on the growth of private pension plans, the administration of them by the DOL, and inherent conflicts of interest among private pension funds—illustrated by a study done for Monks by Jamie Heard of the Investor Responsibility Research Center that showed that many ERISA plan managers were either not voting at all or with company management 100 percent of the time. Says Cohen in an interview with the author, "When Bob looked at the responsibility of those in charge of administering these pension funds solely for the benefit of the beneficiaries, he saw all of the interlocking interests and said, here's a clear conflict of interest and no one's paying any attention to it. I was unaware of it. Most people, unless you're a student of ERISA, would have absolutely no idea how the entire system worked."

One example of the endurance of Monks' agenda was the issue of improving data collection at the pension agency. Monks, who as Chairman of The Boston Company had spearheaded the computerization of pension plan filings there, was the first pensions administrator to talk about automating the filing of annual reports by pension funds, hence saving money and time and aiding enforcement efforts. Under Monks, the agency did a pilot project and started mapping out the basics of an electronic network. He also put the matter on the agenda of both sets of Labor Department hearings and testified on its importance at the Cohen hearings. There, he laid out the problem:

> Currently, the 900,000 forms submitted each year are completed by hand. Once they reach the government, a lengthy and expensive process starts in which all the [Form] 5500 data are manually key entered on computer tape. . . . They are full of errors, incomplete, and up to several years old. . . . It means there is no way to even start to assess whether the program is cost-effective because no one can measure the benefits. . . . It means that enforcement staff must base their investigations on newspaper articles and phone calls—because by the time they have access to 5500 data, the statute of limitations has usually run. . . . To a great extent compliance with any law turns on some degree of public belief that if a federal return is required, someone in the government will open that return, read it, and act on it if warranted. No such belief whatsoever exists in the ERISA community. . . . Every year, the executive branch spends between $10 and $20 million and 100 full-time staff years to process ERISA data. Every year, it is conservatively estimated that the private sector spends $120 million just filling out 5500 forms. Yet the end result of the entire process is useless information, and disfunctionality in the programs that depend on it.

"He was, as with other things, ten years ahead of his time," Lebowitz says. "It was something that nobody in the government had ever attempted on that scale: To create an electronic filing network for a million filers. It really was not feasible to go ahead and build it. It wasn't even clear it could be done technologically. But again, as with the corporate governance issues, he planted the seed, and he hoped. And it turns out he was right, that the people he left behind would continue to tend this garden and that these things would grow over time. And it has."

The Cohen hearings led to a series of congressional recommendations on updating technology. The Reagan administration responded by providing funds to the pension agency and to the IRS to modernize the computer system for processing pension fund annual reports, which helped cross-reference data on payments into pension funds with IRS data on deductions and generally speed up the filing process. But it did not go far enough; the pension agency still had to input data manually into its systems. Only in 1996 did the government move to implement what Monks dreamed of 12 years earlier. The Clinton administration requested and Congress approved funds for fully automating the filing process. "This really was Bob's idea," Lebowitz says. "The technology wasn't there at the time, but he knew it would be. He knew that we had to begin thinking about it. Our computer people would say, 'What? We can't do that.' And he'd say, 'Sure you can. Go out and start talking to people and bring in a couple of contractors to sketch out what it might look like.'"

Monks' notions of corporate governance also had lasting effect in the department, and throughout the pensions and investment management communities. Not only did Monks set effective policy through his speeches, but he made governance a major topic for discussion in the various hearings. The January 1985 investment issues hearings and the Cohen hearings brought up the question of who should exercise the fiduciary duty of voting, given the inherent conflicts of interest and administrative difficulties for the money managers. Many witnesses agreed that in light of these problems the plan sponsors—the corporations themselves—should assume that duty. But how? At the hearings, as Monks formally summarized, there was "the birth of the notion of a yet undefined institution to exercise franchise power for trust holdings. If the trustee cannot do it, and if it must be done in order to preserve the value of trust assets, then some formal process must be devised to effect the desired goal." This idea also marked the birth of a new business and career for Monks, his next calling, as he moved to create a company that would try to fill this role.

The department followed up many of the corporate governance issues raised during Monks' tenure over the next few years with three proxy voting investigations and letter rulings. It finally codified its views in an interpretive bulletin published in 1994 encompassing all of the concepts the agency had expressed on proxy voting responsibilities over the preceding decade beginning with Monks' speech on the institutional investor as corporate citizen. "Coming into this job in 1993, a lot of the corporate governance movement had caught up to where Bob was a decade before," says Olena Berg, the department's pensions administrator from 1993 through June 1998 who issued that bulletin. "Bob is responsible for shaping the view at the department that the proxy vote is a plan asset that has to be managed for the best long-term interest of beneficiaries." The regulation also listed those issues that pension funds should be actively monitoring and, where necessary and cost-effective, on which they should take action, including the independence and expertise of candidates for the board, executive pay, mergers and acquisitions policy, the extent of debt financing, the nature of long-term business plans, investment in training, workplace practices, and financial and nonfinancial measures of corporate performance.

"With each one of these departmental actions, we've seen more and more compliance in the sense of people voting shares, having voting policies and guidelines, and keeping records," Lebowitz says. "Monks started that." However, in Monks' view, the issue of conflict of interest remains unaddressed by the government, and he believes that in the near term it will not be. He continues to this day to search for a way to approach the problem in the private sector. As Berg said in 1997, "We continue to talk about proxy voting here because activism is not the corporate pension plans. The corporate plans are lax. But it's difficult to enforce. My interpretive bulletin, which has the force of regulation, was meant to remind the ERISA plans of their obligations."[22]

"In many ways, we're still working off his agenda," Lebowitz said in 1997. "We probably would be working on many of these issues anyway; it's the evolution of ERISA. But he was there at the creation, and he crystallized our thinking on these earlier than we would have—in terms of our concern about proxy voting and corporate governance, long-term investing, and more mundane aspects of running the agency." Klevan and Lebowitz agree that Monks' single year in office was the most productive they had ever seen. As a result, he raised the profile of the agency to such a degree that the position of pensions administrator was elevated to the level of Assistant Secretary and the agency itself was also upgraded, from an "office" to an official "agency."

Looking back, Monks himself sees his year at Labor as absolutely critical to his future success as an advocate for shareholder activism and better corporate governance. Not only did he create the regulatory framework that served as the stick driving pension funds to pursue activism (cultivating the carrot would be a future project), he also earned the legitimacy of having been a federal government official. This background allowed him to speak and act with authority and credibility later on. And, of course, he also made the important contacts that come with such a position. "I basically made myself a Rolodex for the next 15 years," he says. The way it worked out for him and his battle plan for governance reform could not have been better.

6

The Double Helix

*Occasionally I dream about Bob. And my favorite dream about him,
which I just love because it's a very revealing dream, is that he took
me to a movie theater and all they played were coming attractions.
That really is the essence of what my experience with him has been.
No matter what we do there's always something else down the road
it's taking us closer to, and it's going to be great. It's a thrill to be
around somebody like that because most people don't think past lunch.
I can't stand to be around people who are threatened by challenging
ideas. He's never threatened by a challenging idea.*

Nell Minow

It was 1985, and the takeover boom was now nearly three years old and
growing. By the end of 1984, corporate raiders had begun using junk
bonds to finance their attacks on ever larger corporations. They were
now out in force, scouting out undervalued stocks of which there were
many, and then charging in and offering to take over the companies at a
higher value. If they did not capture the company, they frequently put it "in
play" so that more often than not someone else would. And then every
shareholder would make a bundle.

Among the major parties who were happily raking in these dollars were
pension funds. In fact, by this time, pension funds were big owners of corporate America. The 800,000 ERISA-governed corporate funds alone represented $1.25 trillion in value, holding about one fifth of the equity in
publicly traded U.S. corporations and one half the debt. Government employee funds also had ballooned in size, to some $440 billion. Government
projections indicated that these and other institutional funds would own

half the equity of U.S. corporations by the year 2000. And so, pension funds, as Monks and others had foreseen, were in a powerful position. How they were using this power—by galloping after the highest price offered them by a hostile raider—was unnerving to corporations. Suddenly, the managers of pension money—either the pension funds themselves or their hired money managers—were deciding the fates of some major companies.

In response, many companies were protecting themselves by erecting antitakeover defenses. In 1984 and 1985, more than 770 corporations adopted antitakeover provisions of many kinds, often with shareholder approval. So, not only were big institutional investors making decisions about raiders' tender offers and eager to take them, but at proxy season time in the spring they also were faced with voting in management's antitakeover provisions. So far, corporate America was having no problem putting up defenses; in fact, that effort was becoming easier and easier.

Money managers and trustee banks had a clear conflict of interest in voting on takeover defenses, given their desire to obtain business from corporations. In the DOL's January 1985 hearings, Monks elicited testimony from money managers confirming pressure from clients to approve defenses. In the summer of 1985, in the Cohen committee hearings, Monks commented on conflicts of interests that a money manager faces in voting on antitakeover measures. "Voting against the antitakeover proposals of a current or prospective client is seldom perceived as the best way to establish a warm relationship," he told the panel. However, the firm also "holds trustee responsibility for other [companies'] pension portfolios, whose best interest may well lie in Company A being available for acquisition." There was a further, related problem. Many plan sponsors and managers simply did not care how they voted their shares, so they just voted in favor of management as a rule. While he was at the Labor Department, Monks had made it clear that these investors had a fiduciary duty to start caring; and many institutions were well aware of this. But more work needed to be done to awaken a sense of ownership duty in the country's biggest investors.

Monks said it in a speech to corporate plan sponsors that summer, characteristically conjuring up an image to make the point: "One way to think about its [ERISA's] meaning is to consider the way a large mountain on a tropical island creates its own weather system. Due to its predominance, ERISA has created an economic climate unto itself, largely due to consequences that were not foreseen by its congressional sponsors. Not to get carried away, but clouds have begun to gather on the ERISA horizon; the question is, who's in charge of raincoats?" Those clouds were the very real conflicts of interest that were emerging in the hostile takeover environment. As reported in one article in mid-1985, Monks suggested that his former government agency "order corporations and money managers to disclose their policies on voting charter amendments," which in the next couple of years it would actually do.[1] But, though he kept in touch with his friends at the Labor Department, he no longer had control over the regulatory machine and was not particularly friendly with his successor.

But there was something he could do. It was time, he thought, for corporate, ERISA-covered pension fund sponsors and their managers to assign the vote to a third, neutral, party—the "institution" that had been talked about in the Labor Department hearings. Monks made that need clear in speeches to plan sponsors and fund managers. One fund manager anticipated Monks' next career step. "Monks, goddamn you. Guys like you, you go into the government and you start a forest fire and then you come out and try to sell us all fire extinguishers." Monks was astonished. Here was someone who saw right through him. He was indeed interested in selling the idea of a company that carried out voting tasks for funds—although he had no interest in the money he could earn from such a venture.

As would be Monks' good fortune throughout his efforts in governance, the press came along at just the right time to amplify his message. While he was still at Labor, Reuven Frank, the former president of NBC, had called on Monks with a request to interview him for a one-hour special he was producing for the network. Back in 1972, Frank was the creative force behind the production of the network's 1972 documentary, "Pensions: The Broken Promise," which was credited with helping to inspire passage of ERISA two years later. Now he was back for another look. "The Biggest Lump of Money in the World" aired on NBC on July 27, 1985. The show illustrated the growing part that ERISA and government funds play in the economy—including their voting powers—and it featured Monks prominently. The show even chose one of his comments as the title. Just before the show aired, the NBC correspondent who presented the show, Steve Delaney, remarked to a newspaper reporter that Monks "was the only one who looked beyond the system to see how it works and its impact on society" and called him a "visionary." He noted, however, "There are some in the investment community who see him as a loose cannon [and others] as worth listening to."[2] In any case, just when Monks was about to go out and spread the voting gospel, the major press was recognizing this issue as a legitimate one.

Monks' proposed company would be called Institutional Investor Services, or IIS. It would offer assistance to pension plans and their asset managers in doing their fiduciary duty of voting during proxy season. The company would analyze corporate governance proxy issues such as anti-takeover defenses, directors' and executives' compensation, and greenmail, based on a set of to-be-determined principles, and make recommendations on how to vote. Those services would all be done in the interest of Monks' larger mission: to get owners of corporations to feel and act like owners.

He decided to be what he liked to call an "entrepreneur of the idea of corporate governance." The central notion was to pursue the development of corporate governance through the structure of a profit-making business. Initially, he thought he could just set up a think tank. But, Monks shied away from this approach, believing that he could sell his idea to others most effectively by speaking from the standpoint of a businessman. "I saw the problem of rich men's hobbies. All that they prove is that a guy has enough money to pay the bills. They don't prove that they are valid ideas," Monks says. "As a business, my ideas had to be made relevant to people who were accustomed to paying only for something that was in fact valuable to them. I had to demonstrate that year in and year out good governance was good business." Later, Monks used the image of the "double helix" to describe his own approach to the subject. The double helix is the structure of DNA consisting of two strands of genes twisted together. One strand of Monks' double helix represented "money," his profit motive, and the other represented the "mission" of getting owners of corporations to protect their rights and their property and, in turn, society. "The parallel spiral forces of the double helix do not touch but are indispensable to each other," he wrote.[3]

The main problem was how to persuade investors that in fact his new services were valuable to them. After all, they were making plenty of money just doing what they had always done. The way Monks started out on what was going to be a very long and arduous journey was by continuing his public campaign to encourage the fiduciary duty of voting (giving speeches, writing articles, etc.), and at the same time sitting down with lots of institutional investors, one at a time. In May 1985, Monks met with three of the country's largest and most prestigious money managers: Robert G. Kirby, chairman of the Capital Guardian Trust Company in Los Angeles, David

Williams of Alliance Capital in New York, and Nick Potter of J.P. Morgan Investment Management, also in New York.

All agreed in theory on the need for a voting services company. They also concurred with Monks' view that there was a certain urgency in setting up the firm to forestall possible new, constraining legislation or regulation and the loss of certain basic shareholder rights. Congressional hearings were then being held on the takeover phenomenon and its dangers, and the New York Stock Exchange had proposed doing away with its 60-year-old requirement that its listed companies grant equal voting rights to all shares of common stock—the so-called one share/one vote rule.

Once he had spoken to these few big investors who showed interest in his idea, Monks twisted reality somewhat to help him market this brand-new concept. He introduced himself to new contacts by writing to them not that he himself had invented this idea for a voting service, but that a few "big institutional investors had asked him to look into this." Armed with these unofficial endorsements, Monks swiftly began looking for funding sources, since he felt he needed some private sector backing to be credible. He himself planned to take a minority equity stake worth some $450,000, while other founders would hopefully contribute $550,000 in equity and $5 million in debt. From June to September, he met with 26 institutional investors, including pension plan officials like Gordon Binns of General Motors as well as heads of money management firms, to gauge their interest in the concept of a voting organization and in the possibility of participating as an investor, member of management, or client, as well as to do research on exactly how proxies were being voted at big funds. Many seemed sympathetic to his cause—at least when he was in the room. As GM's Binns relates, "For some reason, Bob, who I considered a friend to the pension community, was not viewed that way. He'd give speeches [about how pension funds can't always vote with corporate managements and that corporations were abusing their shareholders], and after he left there was discussion about him and a lot of hostility and suspicion. He wanted to organize a group to make the decisions on how to vote. People would say, 'He just wants to get in the limelight and charge us a fee.' I said to them, 'You don't understand. He doesn't need any money. He's got plenty of money.'" For a while, Monks encouraged Binns, as head of the corporate pension plan officers' group CIEBA, to take the lead in the shareholder activism movement by using CIEBA to confront companies that were doing poorly. Binns declined the role. "I agreed with much of what Monks was saying," Binns says. "But he wanted me to devote my full attention to this. I said no, I don't think I can do this. I didn't like to be taking a position that would likely result in a lot of negative reactions. I sensed that even if I tried to lead, most of my counterparts at other pension funds would not follow. Many disagreed with Monks. Others might have agreed but feared taking a stand that was antagonistic to their own companies' top managements. People thought, 'We're going to get caught in the middle.' "

Meanwhile, Monks began drawing up a blueprint of the proposed organization so as to be up and running for the 1985–1986 proxy season. Initially, the idea was for some group, such as pension plan sponsors as a whole, to nominate candidates to be IIS's trustees, who would decide how proxy issues should be voted and do the actual voting; the new company's board would then select five from that group. That blueprint had to be redrawn as reality set in. Monks just was not getting the support of the plan sponsors and managers. By the end of September, he had only one commitment—from Dean LeBaron, president of Batterymarch Financial Management in Boston, and an old friend. LeBaron had long been a maverick in the money management field, an outspoken advocate of the need for more effective proxy voting by institutional investors. His view was that the vote should actually be separated out of a stock and trade on its own. Monks knew him from Harvard, where they lived across the hall from each other. Naturally, Monks felt comfortable approaching his former schoolmate about his idea for a new business.

They met briefly at Batterymarch's office in Boston in September of 1985, and LeBaron instantly caught onto the idea and signed up as the first client at a fee of $50,000 a year. Although he declined to come in as an investor, LeBaron did offer Monks a $250,000, three-year prime rate loan, which was accepted. Monks personally guaranteed the loan. "I hoped he'd give me a lot more than he did," Monks says, noting that he first tried for a fee of $150,000, "but at least he was my first customer. I had a customer." But, no one was willing to be Monks' partner in this venture. "It was too much of a PR risk for the potential partners," he later told me. As a result, he himself would finance the new company, and he himself, aided by a small staff, would provide the voting recommendations. IIS was born.

In the fall of 1985, IIS consisted of three people—Monks, Janet Brown, and Barbara Sleasman, both of whom had worked for him at the Labor Department. The three of them worked out of a cramped, two-room office on

M Street in Washington. Joshua Berman joined the organization as a director, and Monks recruited Arthur Dubow, Monks' college buddy and investment partner, to chair the board of directors. Dubow was not only well connected in the investment world, but also, as Monks wrote Berman, in a keen observation of his own character, "He is not at all daunted by telling me that I am wrong. I think this is a particularly important element for our organization because I obviously am deeply committed to the new ownership concept and am apt to be somewhat insensitive to negative input. I personally feel that the idea is of such great merit that the organization needs a structure that will permit the highest probability of its surviving skepticism and hostility in the early days. This will require restraint of some of my normal tendencies." Dubow's first act as a director was to urge Monks to change the name of the new company to Institutional Shareholder Services (so as not to offend Dubow's friend Gilbert Kaplan, the editor of *Institutional Investor* magazine, which had run a glowing cover story on Monks while he was at DOL).

Starting in the fall of 1985, Monks worked diligently to set down on paper ISS's philosophy and business practice. In October, he wrote Berman:

[ISS] will define the responsibilities and prerogatives appertaining to ownership of business corporations in America. . . . Large American corporations have in this century existed without reference to the expression of ownership opinion and have been dominated by a self perpetuating dominant management bureaucracy. It is, therefore, time for the re-expression of ownership concepts. . . .

We would hope that our expression of a role for ownership can be expressed positively involving increasing values not only for shareholders but also for society. The essential perception is that informed and active shareholders hold a proxy for the public interest lessening the need for the far more troublesome and expensive involvement by government that has characterized the last 50 years. Obviously this will require great skill, substantial luck and very competent personnel.

We do not feel that the full mission should be widely publicized at the beginning of our existence, rather we feel that we should focus on doing a first class job on proxies; that we should develop a reputation as a reliable, thoughtful voter; and we should permit the larger concerns of the mission to emerge as our public becomes more comfortable with us. Our immediate mission is to be able to respond to the proxy issues presented during 1986.[4]

He did not, however, hesitate to communicate the broader mission to the Council of Institutional Investors when he spoke at its first conference that month in Atlanta. After all, he was preaching to the converted: 20-odd public pension plans who had organized the previous January in the name of shareholder rights in response to the Bass brothers' greenmailing of Texaco the previous year. To this group—which Monks the regulator had discussed in Chicago with its founder, Jesse Unruh—Monks described pension plans as "the new shareholder." Inevitably, because of ERISA's requirements and the growing size of the funds, these shareholders would have to become increasingly long-term in nature and, hence, increasingly involved as owners of corporations, he argued. Then he declared, "I have long felt not only that trustee involvement is legally required, but that it can provide great benefits to corporations and society. . . . The beneficiaries of employee benefit plans are working people and retirees who have an interest in this country's stability, its adherence to laws, its care of the environment, and the strength of its economy. They have a long-term interest in the conduct and profitability of the corporations whose shares will support their future retirement."

Monks was already thinking in terms of using ISS to help activists go after corporations—foreshadowing the proxy battles to come in the late 1980s and the 1990s. As he noted to Berman: "A significant part of our mission, which probably should be deferred until 1987, is the initiation of proposals for consideration by shareholders and the recommendation of other acts, such as litigation by owners."

But, before he could proceed down that path, he had to convince shareholders to sign up as clients to receive recommendations on how to vote their proxies in the spring 1986 annual meetings and demonstrate ISS's usefulness. The range of services ISS would offer looked attractive on paper: (1) the development of a code of ethics that would serve as guidelines for financial institutions in voting their proxies; (2) the tracking of companies, analyzing their proxy issues, and making voting recommendations for clients that reflect ERISA's rule that pension funds be invested for the exclusive benefit of plan participants—the basic proxy voting advisory service; and (3) the organization of roundtable meetings during proxy season to hash over current governance issues with federal regulators and members of Congress. The fee for the basic research and recommendation service: $50,000 a year.

To recruit clients, it was essential that Monks and ISS create an ongoing dialogue with the largest pension funds, as a group and individually, about the importance of their involvement in proxy voting. How was he going to get this message across? Monks' experience in business and government told him that, at least in the beginning, most people would only be persuaded of their obligation to vote and in turn their need for ISS if they were forced to do so: if legislation were passed or, at least, a congressional investigative committee formed to make that duty clear. There was at the time the possibility that the Cohen hearings the previous year on conflicts of interest would lead to such an investigative panel. But how long could Monks wait for that? (There never was an investigation.) Even without that, though, he believed that if he could effectively argue that the government would eventually take action, at least some people would sign up to do business with him. "The plan sponsor should understand that the question of voting rights is so important that it will ultimately be the subject of government action if effective private action is not taken first," Monks wrote.[5]

A key part of the dialogue would be ISS's research and commentary on current governance issues. For example, Monks wrote in his business plan for ISS with extraordinary foresight about issues that would occupy corporate America and investors in the 1980s and 1990s: "We should attempt to establish directoral responsibility for corporate actions that do not reflect adequate concern for owners' interest. In the area of compensation, opinions differ as to what constitutes 'excess.' In the area of takeover defense, a great deal of latitude has been extended to the business judgement of management. Our efforts should be to identify those particular actions that indicate the most blatant concern for management and the least for owners. Among these might be greenmail and poison pills." (Poison pills essentially gave shareholders the right to buy additional securities at attractive prices in the event of a hostile takeover attempt, hence increasing the raider's overall purchase price.) The ISS business plan went on to say that if ISS finds poison pills are not in the shareholders' interest, then the proxy advisory company should identify the companies that have adopted the pills, keep track of 1986 proxies for new poison pill authorization, and consider recommending against the reelection of directors at those companies and/or "demand the repeal of either proposed or existing poison pill authority." This last idea—in a slightly changed form—would ultimately prove to be the best in assisting ISS's struggle for recognition and growth.

To spread these notions of ownership responsibility and how ISS could help investors carry them out, Monks continued calling on big investors. Monks' assistant Sleasman took on the task of contacting numerous people at a variety of organizations to request a meeting with her boss. "That was the hardest part of my job, trying to get people to see Bob," she says. It was these conversations as well as the speeches Monks made at every opportunity that helped define the themes that shareholder activists, mainly public pension plans, would take up in the second half of the 1980s. He found the government pension plan sponsors, which are often political in nature, particularly open to these new ideas.

As Monks saw it—and as he had anticipated in his 1981 100-page "governance agenda"—a large part of the nascent company's early efforts had to be geared toward developing credibility for ISS and for its ideas of shareholder ownership responsibilities within "the legal, scholarly and philosophical/sociological communities." At the start, the plan was to find a foundation interested in corporate governance and secure a research grant for it to study the current chaotic state of proxy voting, which would "illuminate the unacceptable nature of the status quo."[6] Another idea was to arrange for the Kennedy School at Harvard to host a conference on ownership issues. Early on, in July 1985, Monks began meeting with Charles Morin, Charles Colson's law partner and the benefactor of Boston University's Morin Center for Banking Law Studies, to discuss the notion of setting up a study of pension fund voting practices. That and subsequent discussions eventually led to a dinner meeting with Prof. Betty Krikorian in May 1986 at the F Street Club in Washington. She went on to write a book called *Fiduciary Standards in Pension and Trust Fund Management* (Butterworth Legal Publishers) (to which Monks wrote the foreword), published in 1989. Says Monks: "The book was really key in giving us a scholarly source explaining the application of traditional trust law to the obligations of institutional fiduciaries with respect to ownership responsibilities of portfolio companies, especially under ERISA."

Establishing credibility as a force in Washington was also a priority. And therefore, Monks had to keep up his contacts with the Labor Department as well as the SEC and congressional committees that dealt with governance issues. Perhaps, he thought, ISS would work with the government and pension groups to establish voting guidelines for fiduciaries.

In late 1985, Monks and his small band of followers moved into new glass-enclosed quarters on Washington Harbor that was in walking distance of Monks' penthouse apartment in the Watergate. It was an understatement to say that the new space gave the budding enterprise room to grow. Only an optimist like Monks would put three people in a 6,500 square foot office. Ralph Whitworth, head of the United Shareholders' Association, Boone Pickens' advocacy group for individual shareholders formed in 1986, visited Monks and found him and two or three others working away in the huge office. "Bob was all effusive about ISS," recalls Whitworth. "He was showing us through the office, telling us what would be going here and there. I left shaking my head. I thought, he's going to get killed by the overhead."

The small ISS staff next drew up a nine-page set of corporate governance principles to guide them in furnishing proxy advice to clients. To begin with, the paper asserted that fundamental decisions about a company's existence including anything concerning its "ultimate destiny" should be made by shareholders, while management should run the day-to-day business. And so, ISS would condemn any attempt by management or directors to block shareholders' ability to make these decisions. That would include such measures as dual capitalization schemes in which a minority owner issues a second class of equity with fewer voting rights; restrictions on shareholder rights to call special meetings or amend the bylaws; cumulative voting, in some cases; golden parachutes; staggered board elections in which only some directors are up for reelection each year; and poison pills, including the sale of a company's crown jewels or changes in voting rights in the event of a change in control. "So long as shareholders have the opportunity to approve or reject a prepared defense, its existence is not *per se* objectionable to institutional shareholders," the document declared. However, it also noted that poison pills by their very nature were offensive to shareholders because they required that an acquirer negotiate with a company's board of directors.

The position against poison pills was problematic at the time given the Delaware Supreme Court's decision in November (1985) in the landmark *Moran v. Household International* case, in which the court supported management's poison pill even though it had not been approved by shareholders. Monks, as it happened, knew John Moran because they had both been on the board of John Dyson's Esterline Corporation, which Monks had invested in as a venture capitalist in the mid-1960s. And in fact, shortly after the Delaware court decision, Monks invited him to lunch at the Sky Club in Manhattan. At lunch were Berman, Moran, the chairman of what was now called the Dyson-Kissner-Moran Corp., and his attorney in the case, Stuart Shapiro of Skadden Arps Meagher & Flom. Monks really just wanted to know what was going on in the case; he expressed his support of any further efforts to overturn the Household poison pill. After the ruling, which was not overturned, companies rushed to adopt poison pills, and by the end of

1985, some 37 had adopted them. By the end of 1986, the number would surpass 300.

To Monks, this ruling—and others that upheld managements' ability to bypass shareholders—meant that "institutional investors will have to involve themselves effectively in the corporate governance process." One way that ISS's set of principles identified was for trustee investors to initiate proxy proposals to eliminate such offensive provisions as poison pills; although these proposals would not be binding on management, they would provide a new way for shareholders to express their disapproval. But, as Monks began to stress more and more, another tactic for dissident shareholders would have to be a direct attack on a company's directors: do not vote for directors who feel it their privilege to ignore the rights of a company's owners. As the governance movement grew and matured over the years, the spotlight on directors would grow much brighter.[7]

Late in 1985, Monks approached Nell Minow, then at the Justice Department, with a job offer. Janet Brown, a friend of Minow's, had suggested her to Monks as someone who could find ways the firm could pursue shareholder litigation on behalf of clients—say, during a proxy contest. Monks remembered meeting her when he was at the DOL and she at OMB, and, without even asking for her resume, said he would like her to join ISS in February. But Minow had just started a maternity leave, about to give birth in January to a second child. Monks didn't skip a beat. "In that case, we don't need you til September," he said with a grin. Recalls Minow: "I thought, here we've got a really interesting guy with no ego in his writing (she recalled from her previous work with him), so he'd be really easy to work with. And it seemed like an interesting issue—although very quixotic—on which I'd be on the right side. That was important. So I said OK. I had no idea what I was getting into. It was a complete shot in the dark. But I felt he was right, that he was a good person."

The cause Monks espoused was also important to her. "It was very hard for me to leave the government," she says. "I believe in working for public policy. I literally would not get out of bed in the morning unless I felt I was doing something beneficial to the public good. So I never would have come unless I believed there was a mission that was very positive. But I never thought anybody would pay attention. I thought it was a little pipe dreaming. Yeah, of course shareholders should play more of a role. But come on, I thought, who's going to let them do it? It's never going to happen. There are too many obstacles in the way. Nevertheless I thought it was a great thing to promote. As long as I feel I'm on the right side, I'm happy. . . . One of the great experiences of my life was when I worked for the state's attorney's office and I would write these briefs and I would say, 'The People.' The defendants argue such and such, but 'the people' argue this. I would love that. I loved being 'the people.' And the shareholders are the people."

At the end of 1985, Monks was thinking more and more like an activist. In a speech to a Boston group of security analysts, he proclaimed that 1986 will be "the year of the owner" in which "we will begin to witness the emergence of involved and effective trustee/owners—whether acting singly or in concert—because the continued derogation of beneficiary values is neither right nor legally tolerable."

At the time, he was doing his best to come up with a way to bring this about, by participating in the 1986 proxy season that spring, just a few months away. What Monks was groping for was an issue that institutional investors simply could not ignore. He was well aware of the experiences of such corporate activists as Saul Alinsky and Ralph Nader—a classmate of Monks at Harvard Law School. When they went to the shareholders to vote on social issues, they failed miserably. Alinsky at Eastman Kodak and Nader at GM never received more than 2 or 3 percent of the vote. The Gilbert brothers, who, starting in the 1940s, were more focused on issues of shareholder value, were viewed as mere gadflies.

Monks needed issues that investors would understand as owners. "I wanted something I could get 45 percent of the vote for, something that the institutions felt they *had* to do . . . , and would be understood by the investment community as being the equivalent of a vote of confidence in the management," he explains. "So, after having been in the Labor Department, where I said you must vote, the next step was to put something up that anybody who read it would say, if this passes I am losing value. And I'm a trustee and whatever the hell else I do I can't lose value." The first year, in 1986, the main issue Monks raised would be staggered boards; Monks pointed out that electing directors to staggered terms removed an investor's right to monitor and elect corporate directors. "We picked that because it seemed to be something that was plainly wrong. It was purely disenfranchising the shareholders with no correlative advantage."[8]

Actually, the very first proxy issue ISS confronted revolved around another management entrenchment tactic that also wrenched voting rights from shareholders. In November, long before the start of the official proxy season in the spring, Monks heard about something "so outrageous" that he could not resist launching his very first proxy campaign right there and then. The Potlatch Corp., a paper company in which the Weyerhauser family held a large stake, had called a special meeting of shareholders for December 12, 1985 to consider a major change in voting rights. The proposed changes would give existing holders four votes per share, while new holders would have only one vote until they had held the stock for four years. Such "time-phased" voting was meant to encourage long-term investing in the company, but in ISS's view it merely served to entrench management—in particular, the Weyerhauser family—especially given that the company was under the threat of a hostile takeover by the Belzberg family of Canada at the time it made the proposal. Even after Potlatch greenmailed the Belzbergs, it forged ahead with its proposed change.

Monks now took his first stab at writing a letter to the institutional shareholders of a major corporation, recommending that they vote against a management proposal. And so, ISS was taking the unusual role of not only offering advice to clients on how they should vote on governance issues, but going far beyond that by distributing the same advice to all identifiable shareholders and the directors of the target company, representing its clients' interest. It was one way to promote ISS's name; after all, the firm only had one client. Monks sent the draft to his old friend and sometimes lawyer Joshua Berman, opening himself to severe criticism from an expert at writing letters both for big investors like Fidelity Management & Research who were clients and for SEC approval. And severe it was. Berman threw the letter out and started over. Monks' version was full of his own view of reality (as Berman wrote in the margins: "This is your theoretical paper"): ERISA trustees who were shareholders of Potlatch had a duty to their plan participants to vote carefully in accordance with certain basic principles such as, "encouraging self-regulation by companies as a realistic alternative to government involvement" and "preserving the integrity of the system within which private enterprise flourishes," among others. As Berman scribbled on this draft: "Investment people are not looking for a point of view. There are always two points of view. They are looking for a rational middle of the road position that they can rationalize in terms of investment values!!! What they want is the story—facts, etc., to support a position in this particular instance. What happens to values—short term and long term!"[9]

So Berman did his friend the favor of redrafting the letter to tell the story behind Potlatch's proposal and urging institutional owners to "express their views against time-phased voting," which is "a way to cut back on the voting power of public shareholders." He didn't, however, leave Monks' philosophy out, but rather built up to it: "The Potlatch amendment, like other corporate governance issues, raises the question of who in the final analysis is responsible for preserving the integrity of our corporate system. It is appropriate to look to the directors, who in this case have not seen their duties as we see them. Ultimately, however, one must look to the shareholders. . . . " At ISS's office, the small staff worked together in an assembly line copying and collating the letter to get it out to shareholders on time. In the end, the company won the day, with 68 percent of the outstanding shares. Yet, Monks was pleased. "We were just beginning to establish the 'right' of god-fearing, nice trustees to vote against managements," he later said.

Early in 1986, Monks began dreaming of running an activist fund or alliance. He wrote Berman: "How can I structure a relationship with one or more institututional investors with respect to their holdings in a particular company pursuant to which we are paid a fee or a share of the profits?" Minow later persuaded him not to take any payment in such relationships, but as a concept such a collaboration would be quite effective. Alternatively, he also had a scheme to cash in one of his personal investments to establish the foundation of a leveraged investment pool that would buy into companies requiring changes in their corporate governance. That was his investment in Pargesa, the 36 percent owner of Drexel Burnham Lambert, the U.S. investment bank whose junk bonds were fueling many of the era's takeovers.

Monks' experience with Pargesa was yet another wild ride for him in the world of finance, and provided more evidence that he had a keen eye for poor corporate governance. He had been serving on the board of Pargesa's U.S. subsidiary Lambert Bruxelles Corp. since 1983 (though not officially during his DOL service), traveling to Paris or New York every couple of months for board meetings. He watched the stock go up up up as Drexel's powers and profits skyrocketed in the early 1980s. Along the way, he met junk bond guru Mike Milken and attended one of the firm's junk bond conferences, the so-called Predators' Ball, in Los Angeles. But almost from his first dealings with LBC in 1983, he began to perceive problems with the company's investment in Drexel that others were not seeing. Among those problems: Drexel was not sharing its new-found prosperity by passing along substantial dividends to its 36 percent owner; Drexel would not consider any joint business dealings with Pargesa; and Drexel's prosperity could be short-lived. He was beginning to wonder about the acuity of those running both Pargesa and Drexel. After a December 1983 board meeting, he wrote to Pargesa's Eskenazi about the "ballet à deux" that they were conducting with Drexel:

> God Bless Bobby Linton. [Robert Linton, Drexel's chairman] He is plain spoken. Question—do you want to consider a common strategy with LBC? No shilly shallying, no politeness, no small talk. Just no, NO, NO, A Thousand Times No. There really was no need for Bobby to go on and on and on telling us how despicable we were as partners. . . . They want LBC to sell back its DBL stock at their price. They act as if we were a little bit stupid not to understand that this is really all that we can do. Are they right? . . . . We must move on and make new friends. We should go out of our way to attempt to do investment banking business with firms other than DBL. We will need these contacts in the future, and, by going "outside" we will cause Wall Street talk that could be embarrassing to Bobby L. . . . . My whole object is to have Drexel more anxious to buy than we are to sell.
>
> . . . Obviously, the DBL situation is a bit of "Potemkin village" in light of the realities of Milken's contributions to the firm's consolidated earnings. Competitive conditions are always fickle. Right now, things are going well for DBL. Will they always? Clearly, DBL has made no structural changes like Merrill Lynch or Shearson to diversify. Brokerage earnings have always been highly cyclical. Now they have cash and confidence. For almost all of the thirty-five years that I have known Wall Street, there has been a shortage of capital, really draconian efforts to keep partners from taking their capital out of firms, and poor public opportunities to raise additional capital. Clearly operating costs are poorly controlled and the salesmen really own the "clients." Not really a good business for passive capital. My conclusions—we had better sell quickly. I mean really quickly as things have a way of changing extremely fast. Once the attitude changes, it is almost inconceivable how people ever thought otherwise. Right now, Linton thinks he has all the money in the world, Mike Milken will always be happy to give it to him, and we are an unneeded nuisance diluting his earnings without contributing anything needed for their generation. This is an unusual time—almost UNIQUE—it is important to understand its uniqueness to comprehend how essential it is that we move immediately.

Monks was confident, given his own experience years earlier cornering Royal Dutch Shell into buying C. H. Sprague's oil operations, that they could force Drexel to raise its price. But Eskenazi had no interest in selling out at this time. Indeed, he continued to believe firmly that Drexel would be the U.S. link in his vision of a federation of banks crossing two continents. For his part, Monks grew increasingly frustrated with Drexel and the Pargesa board's starry-eyed view of the firm. He saw no chance for fairly recent LBC investors like himself to realize substantial growth in their investment despite Drexel's stratospheric rise in earnings, since Drexel was not willing to offer dividends, do joint ventures, or do a public offering. In fact, at one point around the start of 1984 Drexel indicated a "commitment," Monks says, to do a public offering of shares but backed out of it because Milken didn't want his children to know how much money he was making.

A year after his first letter, Monks ran into Jim Balog, Drexel's lobbyist in Washington, who cockily confirmed that Drexel had no interest in any kind of joint venture with Lambert Bruxelles. Again, Monks wrote to Eskenazi recommending that LBC sell its Drexel stake. Monks even offered his services as the person who would shop the Drexel stake around, so he would be the fall guy if that effort failed. But still Eskenazi had no interest in selling out of the high-flying U.S. junk bond house.

Monks was not shy about making his feelings about the situation known when he saw his fellow board members at their regular meetings. A few times a year, they met in LBC's offices in the Chrysler Building in New York. All four corner offices of that floor were reserved for the use of the French officials of Pargesa, who might come twice a year. Otherwise, they were empty. At the board meetings, the directors would sit down to a splendid multi-course luncheon, and then Linton would with evident pride deliver his "message from Mike." Invariably, that consisted of a report of some phenomenal amount of profits. "The Gallic eyes literally would fall out of their sockets. The French just couldn't believe their good luck," Monks says. "They were consolidating 36 percent of the earnings. And 36 percent of Drexel's earnings was $340 million [in 1985. At one point it reached $500 million]. I thought these guys would go crazy." Monks asked questions. But, there were no answers, and no other questions. The reality was, Monks says, that Pargesa's companies as a whole were losing money, and the assumed rise in Drexel's stock (it was private stock) made the group look profitable.

During one meeting, Monks excused himself to visit the men's room and while there encountered fellow director Didier Pineau Vallencienne, CEO of the French engineering firm Schneider. The shareholder activist asked the Frenchman: "Why are we putting up with all this shit, Didier? What's going on?" Here is how Monks recollects Vallencienne's response: "If you can imagine a man of great dignity using the urinal and at the same time raising both of his hands in the universally recognized French expression of 'Je ne sais pas!,' you will appreciate why the incident remains in my mind."

After the board meetings, a number of directors lined up outside Eskenazi's office to talk with him about personal business matters. European relationship banking being what it was, they all had business to conduct. One day, Monks too got in line. When his turn came, he said, "Gérard, you must be sick of hearing my questions that nobody cares to answer. Wouldn't it be simpler if I were just to resign?"

"Oh no Bobby," Eskenazi exclaimed in heavily accented English. "It is our great pleasure to experience your questioning energy."

He did stay for a while. "I kept telling them to sell," he recounts. "The only way you make money like this is selling white powder to school kids. I was on the record all over the place. The day [in 1986] Morgan Stanley went public at 2.8 times book, I said it's time to be a seller. They just couldn't believe me."

At one point, Monks along with some other directors toured the Pargesa group companies in France, Luxembourg, Switzerland, the United Kingdom, and Belgium. While stopping at Belgian financier and Pargesa cofounder Albert Frère's house in Brussels, Monks told him point-blank that Pargesa's involvement with Drexel was "idiot!" Furious with this characterization, Frère strode up to Monks, reached up to plant a forefinger on his chest, and declared: "Monsieur, vous avez tort!" (Sir, you are full of it!) And Monks shot back: "On vera." (We'll see.)

By early 1986, Monks was convinced that Pargesa would not see much more in the way of earnings from Drexel's ascent. "It is difficult to imagine its earnings from Drexel ever being higher," he wrote Berman. He thought it would be a good time for his own exit. But also, he envisioned a transaction in which he would sell out not for cash but for equity in a new investment pool for corporate governance transactions that sounded a lot like the Lens Fund Monks would create with his own money in 1992. As he wrote Berman: "The purpose of the investment pool would be to go into situations like, arguably, Household where we would have institutional clients and an active involvement by ISS."

In a January 8, 1986, letter to Berman, he expressed his desire to use the pool in forming "ad hoc joint ventures with selective institutional investors . . . to take control of a particular corporation, although the form could vary from voting solicitation to stock tender to merger proposals." The target companies would be violators of ISS's corporate governance principles. He proposed Household International as the first target; the project would involve a group of investors, led by ISS, proposing an independent slate of directors at the May annual meeting. Monks hoped that his idea for creating an investment pool from the sale of his Pargesa stock would flower in time to spar with Household that year. He even went to Paris on February 3 to discuss the deal with Eskenazi and try to secure his approval. "Hopefully we could have at least sketchy legal papers that would permit us to proceed on February 6 or 7 to buy stock in Household," he wrote Berman. The plan was for Monks himself to contribute $11.5 million "counterbalanced" by $23 million from Pargesa, half in the form of equity and half in debt, and then some more from banks. But Eskenazi didn't go for it. "What I didn't realize at the time," Monks relates, "was that the idea of Eskenazi being hostile to anything would have been against his character." An attack on Household, therefore, did not materialize. And the idea of an activist fund would have to wait until some years later.

As an aside, in early 1987, a few months after Wall Street arbitrageur Ivan Boesky pleaded guilty to insider trading in a development that would one day bring Drexel to its knees, Monks sold his Pargesa stake for about $8.8 million, recording a 70 percent profit over his $5.2 million investment ($200,000 of which was from other Ram Trust Service clients). Pargesa's other investors did not make out nearly as well. Drexel spent the entire year fending off attacks on its junk bond activities, and things just got worse after the October 1987 market crash. Finally, Drexel declared bankruptcy in 1990. As a whole, Monks says, Pargesa lost some $500 million. "For me," he says, "it was confirmation that I really could understand reality, notwithstanding that everyone around me saw something else. This experience enhanced an already alive instinct to rely on my own judgment—very helpful when dealing with the CEOs of the great companies of America over the next decade."

ISS's staggered board contests began with Times Mirror early in 1986, with another letter to investors. Again, Berman helped Monks write the letter, urging the publisher's shareholders to vote against proposed anti-takeover measures at a special meeting called for February 12. The defenses that Times Mirror was trying to erect were eight in number, including a staggered board and the proposal to change the state of incorporation from

California to Delaware, which had been much friendlier to companies of late. In its letter, ISS remarked:

> We view it as ironic that a Board of Directors so concerned with free-
> dom of the press and the independence and integrity of the company's
> media operations should find it appropriate—by approving manage-
> ment's proposal and recommending its approval by shareholders—to
> abolish the freedoms of the Company's shareholders, including specifi-
> cally their freedom of assembly (through their ability to hold sharehold-
> ers' meetings), their freedom to be represented by directors of their
> choice (through an annual election of all directors and the power of re-
> moval), and their freedom to act on corporate matters by majority vote
> (without a minority veto). . . .
>
> The Times Mirror proposal, like other corporate governance issues,
> raises the question of who in the final analysis is responsible for preserv-
> ing the independence and integrity of our corporate system. It is appro-
> priate to look to the directors, who in this case have not seen their duties
> as we see them. Ultimately, however, one must look to the shareholders
> themselves. Corporations and state governments, as the sponsors of em-
> ployee benefit plans, and financial institutions have the greatest respon-
> sibility for preserving the integrity of our capital system. We believe
> they should oppose . . . measures that are detrimental to the system. We
> view the Times Mirror proposal as such a measure. Regardless of the
> seeming futility of a negative vote on the Times Mirror proposal, insti-
> tutional holders should begin to make their views known by expressing
> their opposition to this proposal and others like it.

Only 16 percent of Times Mirror's shares were voted against the proposal and another 1.1 percent abstained.

Monks soon wrote his staff and board a memo outlining future strategy. What follows was a first draft of that memo:

> Potlatch and Times Mirror will be seen as what the French call "succès
> d'estime." They are beautiful, but we did not win and nobody made any
> money. We have, however, made ourselves known and credible and are
> entitled to solicit involvement in future cases. Inevitably people are not
> going to be involved in governance fights unless they can make money.
> They cannot make money unless we accomplish two things: 1. The ini-
> tiating and coordinating work, and 2. Win. We should try and get some
> of our friends (Dean and maybe Ned [Johnson of Fidelity]) to scan the
> various value screens to search for good targets. A good target will have

the following characteristics: 1. A poor growth record. 2. A poor performance in the stock market. 3. A management and director group holding
only nominal shares of stock in the company. 4. Any anti-takeover governance proposal in 1986.[10]

All along, Monks and his staff had been developing and refining ISS's
mission, and clarifying the program on paper. By the start of the 1986 proxy
season, they had a clear statement prepared. ISS defined itself as a means for
institutional investors to efficiently and cost-effectively carry out their voting responsibilities. "Realistically, no single holder can undertake a program
on a scale great enough to be effective, regardless of how large his individual
fund might be," the statement read. "By acting in concert with other institutions, however, it is possible to have an impact." ISS would coordinate that
network of institutions. This is how it would do that work: (1) Monitor the
governance provisions adopted and proposed by the Fortune 1000 and place
those companies with measures contrary to shareholders' interest on a negative governance list; (2) urge its clients to vote against particularly harmful
proposals, and do the same for other big owners by drafting a letter to shareholders, submitting it to the SEC for approval, express mailing it to the
largest 150 or so institutional shareholders, and following up with phone
calls; (3) track individual directors' records in supporting negative governance provisions at all companies where they serve; and (4) identify companies that have a poor governance record and good conditions for a
successful proxy contest (namely high percentage of institutional ownership
and low percentage of insider ownership), draft shareholder resolutions requesting rescission of negative provisions, and wage a campaign to win votes.
At the Council of Institutional Investors annual meeting that April in Santa
Monica, Monks laid out this strategy to the crowd: "Those corporations
having 'negative governance profiles' should be identified. . . . A shareholder's resolution should be developed for each of the NGP companies requesting rescission of those provisions that unduly diminish owners' rights.
[He had counted 150 major companies so far.] A resolution should be cleared
through appropriate corporate and SEC procedures for inclusion on the
agenda of the 1987 annual meeting. All institutional owners should be solicited with reference to this item on the annual meeting agenda." This task
would occupy ISS later in 1986, as it began work on eliminating poison pills.
    But for now, the search was on for more ways to become involved in
the 1986 proxy season—more staggered board proposals. Monks scanned

the papers every morning for ideas; people he knew were calling with their own. On March 19, Joshua Berman called ISS to alert the staff to a piece in that day's *Wall Street Journal* reporting on the Chase Manhattan Corporation's proposal to introduce a staggered board at its April 15 annual meeting as a defense against a hostile takeover. As an ISS staffer noted to Monks: "Josh suggested we pull the institutional holders of CMB and then compare the holdings of its biggest owners, which are also banks. His theory was that banks are owned by other banks, and that the back-scratching syndrome would be at work here. You will see from the attached that he was correct in his guess."[11]

And so out went a letter to the large shareholders of Chase Manhattan: ". . . We have advised our clients that, in our view, the proposal to stagger the election of directors is contrary to the best interests of institutional shareholders, and we recommend that they vote against the proposal. We are writing to urge that, even if you have a voting policy generally in favor of staggered boards, you reconsider this issue in the context of the Chase proposal for the reasons set forth below." The letter went on to describe the investments Chase has in other financial institutions that manage pension funds that invest in Chase, as well as the investments Chase has in companies it also lends to or could potentially lend to. "In our view," the letter read, "each of these financial institutions (as a fiduciary) and each of these industrial corporations (as a sponsor of an employee benefit plan) can be viewed as having a conflict of interest as to the voting of Chase shares. We have advised our fiduciary clients that in these circumstances it is especially important to exercise their voting responsibility with the single purpose of acting in the best interests of trust beneficiaries." And the best interests of trust beneficiaries was not a staggered board that shielded a company from being taken over. "Given the power of directors of a Delaware corporation to act on these kinds of matters [instituting defenses against takeovers that would affect shareholder value] without shareholder approval, it becomes increasingly evident that the most fundamental voting right a stockholder has is the power to reelect or replace the Board of Directors"—made much more difficult with staggered elections.[12]

At the end of the letter, Monks clearly could not resist expounding his general philosophy of corporate ownership in the context of society as a whole, beginning with a quote from legal historian James Willard Hurst, who along with Brandeis and Monks' old Boston Company lawyer David Engel, had best expressed his own beliefs:

"[S]tockholder surveillance [is] the principal internal factor on which tradition relied to legitimate corporate power . . ." The continued willingness of our citizens to have privately chosen corporate leaders make decisions affecting production, employment and quality of life has been countenanced because of the accountability of these leaders to the corporate owners. In our view, the practical erosion of stockholders' voting power undermines the very structure of private enterprise upon which our national economy and political system are based.[13]

One response to ISS's letter was that of Edward Zinbarg, senior vice president at the Prudential Insurance Company of America. "After careful consideration, we have concluded that Prudential may vote its proxies in favor of staggered boards in appropriate circumstances. As you may know, Prudential has a staggered board itself [to meet New Jersey insurance code]." The letter went on: "It seems to us that continuity of management within financial institutions, especially those with broad fiduciary responsibilities, is important. Measures which help assure continuity can strengthen the institution." Oh well. At least, the man bothered to write. And Monks got some positive response as well. Only 52 percent of the shares outstanding voted for the classified board, what the *Wall Street Journal* called "a surprisingly narrow margin, a sign of growing shareholder unhappiness with such defenses."[14] One commentator noted: "This suggested more opposition to defenses which had previously been thought a piece of cake" and that the narrow victory might push more companies to adopt poison pills that, due to court rulings, could be adopted without shareholder approval.[15]

Monks chose the next target: the Whirlpool Corp., the maker of washers and dryers. As he remarked in an April 1 letter to Berman: "We have a possible candidate for an eloquent protest in the Whirlpool Corp. Whirlpool does not represent any novel atrocities; it is simply a trash pile of the worst available." For its April 22 meeting, the company, which had two-thirds institutional ownership, was proposing a series of antitakeover measures, including staggering the election of directors. And so out went the letter, dated April 17, essentially posing the same arguments as in the Chase letter. Calpers also solicited votes against Whirlpool management. Barely a majority, 51.5 percent, voted in the changes.

Yet another letter went out on May 14 addressing proposals by the Occidental Petroleum Corp. for its May 21 annual meeting to reincorporate from California to the more corporate-friendly Delaware and to institute several defensive measures. Those included a number of restrictions on share-holders' rights—such as calling special meetings or changing the number of directors—and staggered, three-year terms for the 14 directors. The latter was the most egregious violation of shareholder rights in Monks' view. As he put it: "An argument often given in support of staggering the election of di-rectors is that it assures continuity and stability in management." In the case of Occidental, he wrote, chairman Armand Hammer—who Monks knew from his Machiasport refinery days and loved to antagonize—was then 87 years old; the company had had four presidents in six years; and eight of the ten outside directors were over 70 years old. "We find the continuity and sta-bility arguments in this case particularly unpersuasive." He went on to say that there were other ways the company could protect shareholders from hos-tile takeover than by staggering the board, which would prevent shareholders from ever dismissing the majority of the board at any annual meeting for any reason, as well as prevent them from considering a non-negotiated takeover offer. "In our view," he wrote, "the free trading market for corporate con-trol and an annual election of all directors are the two basic means by which corporate management is held accountable to the corporate owners." In this letter, Monks made sure that readers knew that if they already had voted their proxies for management and wanted to change their mind, they could do so by simply sending in a new proxy.

Monks was further enraged by what he saw as Occidental's deceptive presentation of the issue to shareholders on the ballot itself. The ballot de-scribed the item to be voted as "the proposal to change state of incorpora-tion to Delaware." For a week, until the day before the annual meeting, Monks and his small staff doggedly called and wrote the SEC to object to this wording on the grounds that it did not reflect the other eight items sig-nificantly affecting corporate governance and shareholder rights. He wanted nothing less than an SEC review, a brand-new ballot with more explicit wording, and a rescheduled vote. To no avail. Not until June 3 did he hear from Linda Quinn, head of the SEC's department of corporate finance, that the staff had decided Occidental's proxy presentation was adequate. As it turned out, the anti-Oxy forces did not do too badly. Sixty-four percent of Oxy's shares outstanding voted for the reincorporation measure, including the eight provisions.

The campaign itself—the letter writing and phone calling—was excit-ing. Monks believed in what he was doing. But the hurry-up-and-wait of the process was excruciating. Berman, first of all, was indispensable to the effort, but he was extremely busy working for other clients. When Monks and his wife, Milly, took him to dinner one night at the Sky Club in the Pan Am Building, Berman appeared to his old friend as "literally close to death from overwork." But much worse than waiting for Berman was waiting for the SEC to deliver its verdict on the letters Berman was writing. Monks phoned and visited the SEC daily, waiting for a response. "You're sitting there wondering how often can you call the guy and not piss him off," Monks recalls. "These little guys at the SEC could stop you dead in your tracks. We were being tortured by the SEC. I'm not sure we even got all the letters out in time for people to vote." Only later did Monks learn that great Wall Street lawyers would send copies of their requests for SEC approval to every official level of government up through the commissioners to the senators on the oversight committees in an effort to move the SEC staff along. And when the SEC finally did respond, its nitpicking drove Monks crazy, with its insistence on an "in my opinion" here and a "no approval was sought for this" there. But, of course, he readily complied with these changes.

The delay was definitely a problem in at least one campaign. On May 20, Monks wrote to institutional shareholders of General Re Corp., the big reinsurance company, which was proposing a package of five defensive measures to be voted on at the annual meeting a week later. Again, ISS appealed to the SEC to review what the activist group considered a misleading proxy statement, given its lack of detail in describing major changes to corporate governance provisions that would result from the proposals. In this case, the SEC *did* require the company to distribute corrective material and give the shareholders the opportunity to change their votes. However, shareholders did not receive the revised material until late in the day on the Friday before the meeting, which was scheduled for Tuesday following the Memorial Day holiday weekend. Banks holding shares for customers simply did not have time to mail the material to them, and Monks received at least one report that a bank decided not to mail it. Still, opposition forces did well; only 53 percent of outstanding shares favored the package of defenses.

With these results in his rookie proxy season, Monks should have been walking on air. And he was. But he was also well aware that the distance from a narrow loss to a victory was a vast one. Corporate managements held all the essential cards; they controlled the proxy voting and tabulation process, they could, and reportedly did, apply pressure on institutions with whom they did business, and they could draw from enormous resources.

Once they saw the opposition mounting, they could surely repel it with a lift of a forefinger. In Monks' view, the only hope of success was to recruit more and more institutions, as well as individual investors, to the cause. The proxy campaigns had laid a foundation; from the letters and follow-up calls, hundreds of institutional investors across the nation now knew about ISS. At industry conferences, some investors came up to Monks to remark on the value of those letters. The payoff would not be long in coming as some of those, like Alliance, Calpers, and others signed up with ISS. At this moment in time, though, ISS still had only one client—Batterymarch. Not that Monks made this public information. An article published in the *Portland Press Herald* on March 20 that year read: "Most of Monks' clients are in this country, he says. One of them is Batterymarch Financial Management. . . . "

Part of Monks' strategy was to use his connections in government to repeatedly raise the issue of corporate governance. Therefore, throughout the proxy season, he kept in touch with people in power at the Labor Department, the SEC, and Congress. He testified at government hearings. Specifically, at the DOL, his wish was to inspire a continuation of his legacy. For instance, on April 24, he wrote to Labor Secretary William Brock, concerning the report that Senator Cohen's subcommittee on Oversight of Government Management had just issued on DOL enforcement of ERISA. Monks called attention to the subcommittee's recommendation for clear rules regarding fiduciary stockholders' obligation to vote. He wrote of his concern that "many" institutional shareholders succumb to pressure from corporate managements to vote for antitakeover defenses that hurt shareholder value. Monks surely must have been pleased to learn that a few days later in an address to the Association of Private Pension and Welfare Plans, Brock remarked: "With regard to corporate governance, plan fiduciaries cannot be passive shareholders. Specifically, proxy votes that may affect the economic value of plan investments unquestionably involve the exercise of fiduciary responsibility. Those votes must be cast in a way that the fiduciary believes will maximize the economic value of plan holdings."

At the end of the proxy season, the shareholder activist set up a lunch with SEC chairman John Shad (one of several meetings he'd had with him), for June 18, to discuss the roadblocks Monks had encountered in opposing management proposals and how the SEC might help remedy those. One way was for the agency to require that companies announce any unusual proxy proposals when they have decided to propose them and not wait until issuance of the proxy statement; that would give any shareholders opposed to an item the time to communicate with other shareholders regarding the proposal. Another suggestion: require that companies disclose voting results. Monks' company had had a tough time getting hold of the final tallies of the proxy votes it had followed. He also used the occasion of this lunch to gripe about what he felt was the SEC staff's sluggish and inadequate responses to ISS's concerns about misleading information issued to shareholders of Occidental Petroleum and General Re. This and other meetings with Shad produced no concrete results.[16]

Even more important to ISS than keeping up government contacts was planning future battles. And so, by June 1, Monks and his staff had drawn up a draft strategy for the 1987 season. For one thing, they began research that would help wage an attack against the New York Stock Exchange's decision that summer, as a response to rising competitive pressures from other marketplaces with easier listing requirements, (including the American Stock Exchange and the NASDAQ) to drop the one share/one vote requirement. If the SEC approved that decision, companies with two or more classes of stock, some with more votes than others, would be able to list on the Big Board; that would encourage other companies to create dual-class capitalizations, since putting a greater portion of votes in friendly hands was an effective takeover defense. In favoring one group of shareholders over another, Monks and others argued, multiple-class structures reduce the accountability of corporate leaders to shareholders. Monks saw the controversy as "the best game in town from the point of view of public interest for the next year."[17]

But neither ISS nor the governance movement, in Monks' view, would get anywhere without support from the nation's shareholders. In fact, he thought it essential for the future of both that ISS go beyond responding to management proposals and help institutions file their own proxy resolutions in a direct challenge to corporate managements. Therefore, ISS created a new service to do this. The strategy, as noted in an internal memo, would be to focus the effort on rescinding poison pills:

> ISS wants to make it clear that institutions have no interest in running a company and in being rivals to management. We therefore have chosen to focus on pills, a corporate development resulting from action by the directors. Our standard approach will be simply a request for the directors to reverse their earlier action. The rescission resolution is designed to establish the fact that management is accountable to owners. The fact that poison pills are adopted by directors without shareholder approval seems at least anomalous. By proposing a precatory agenda item for the

annual meeting, ISS is giving institutions the opportunity to indicate both disapproval over not being consulted earlier and distaste for the poison pill. This strategy further avoids a difficult problem we would encounter in trying to propose the rescission of governance provisions that are protected by 80% superstatutory provisions.

This new approach is what caught the attention of a number of institutions ISS was meeting at the time, most notably TIAA-CREF, the teachers' pension fund, which would one day become one of the country's leading shareholder activists. CREF signed up with ISS on July 1 as the year-old firm's second client. Back in 1985, at the pension investing hearings he sponsored at the Labor Department, Monks had met Roger Murray, then CREF's chief investment officer, who was quite outspoken about shareholder rights. By the time Monks came to CREF's New York office to talk about ISS, James Martin was the CIO. As Martin's successor Richard Schlefer recounts: "Bob came in to see Jim—and I was at the meeting—to suggest that, because of all the antitakeover provisions that companies had adopted, some with shareholder approval, some not, that CREF consider filing shareholder resolutions. And that was really the first time that we really thought seriously about doing that. We had a frank chat about it, and we went on to do it."

By early August, ISS had already developed a list of some 20 companies with ideal characteristics as targets for anti-poison pill resolutions: high institutional ownership, low insider ownership, and mediocre management trying to entrench itself. And it had chosen among those as targets for CREF's and Calpers' poison pill rescission resolutions. As more and more companies adopted pills—200 by mid-1986—and as that trend increasingly incensed investors, the press would become swept up with the rescission movement in the 1987 proxy season. But even in the summer of 1986, Monks could see that the fight would be a hard one. "It is as yet unclear whether our clientele will want to pay for the "full court press" that would be necessary to achieve numerical victory for our rescission resolutions," Monks wrote. "We may therefore have to define victory as something different, for example as 80 percent of the institutional vote."[18] They began preparing for the 1987 proxy season by beefing up the case against poison pills. ISS hired economist Richard Ruback of MIT to help produce a study that would persuade the SEC and ERISA plan trustees that "certain fundamental changes, such as the adoption of a multiclass capital structure (the end of one share/one vote) and the adoption of a poison pill, will decrease the value of [an] investment. It may not be necessary to prove the decrease in value; it might suffice simply to refute convincingly the work of those who urge the opposite."

Also that summer, armed with this new rescission campaign, Monks prepared to go on the road with ISS. He thought his job would be made easier because two other shareholder activist groups were already in existence: "Aside from lending certain credibility to the whole area, Pickens [who had founded the United Shareholders' Association] and the Council [by then 40 members with $175 billion] make us by no means the most suspected, distrusted shareholders rights group in existence."[19]

In advance letters he sent to prospective clients, on July 2, he described ISS's initial success; in those cases in which it was involved, "institutional opposition held the pro management vote to only 51 percent." (Actually, the ISS annual report specified this result was in ISS's last five cases with the exception of Occidental.) But, he noted that in all honesty, nothing more would happen unless institutional investors intensified their efforts, because corporate managements would surely intensify theirs, and they were at a keen advantage. "In the next 2–3 years," Monks wrote, "institutional owners must initiate proposals in order to gain lead time necessary for successful challenge. It is critical if owners are to secure the credibility and financial gains that their shareholdings merit."

ISS would help by being the coordinator of a joint effort in what it called the Ownership Agenda, in which it would plan and implement an activist strategy for those who wanted to pursue one. He offered ISS's services in distinct categories:

- *Management governance proposals.* Ranging from the basic monitoring of proxy materials and providing recommendations on how to vote proxies, to drafting letters opposing certain management proposals and mailing them to investors.
- *Owners' governance proposals.* Identifying egregious corporations with high institutional and low insider ownership and a poor five-year earnings record; drafting shareholder resolutions to rescind certain provisions, clearing the material with the SEC, and assessing the cost of a solicitation effort; Coordinating institutional owners' response to the NYSE decision to drop one share/one vote; Acting as a liaison and lobbyist to government agencies, Congress, and the press.

A Georgeson & Co. newsletter for the fourth quarter of 1986 noted that ISS had "a more concrete plan of action" than the Council of Institutional

Investors in building institutions' resistance to antitakeover measures. That plan, Georgeson noted, included drafting shareholder resolutions and leading proxy contests against certain companies.

Throughout August, Monks was traveling from fund to fund to introduce ISS. For someone who had been a bank chairman, corporate CEO, and government official, this sales tour was a uniquely humbling experience. Campaigning for the Senate—in effect selling himself—was harrowing, but at least people were cordial. The reactions he got whenever he hit the road to sell ISS, from 1985 on, ranged from incredulity to outright hostility. "Let me see if I understand," one potential customer said after Monks had finished his spiel. "Right now, I own shares of stock, I collect dividends, and I run the risk of the market with respect to their price. You are telling me to spend money on a new service. Is it going to make me any more money?" Would it? Yes, in some in-the-clouds theoretical sense that this money manager wasn't ready to accept. Occasionally, as Monks tells it, "Our offering a new product was viewed as an implied criticism of [their] management in not already having availed themselves of its equivalent."

Public pension funds made themselves available—on their own terms. Often, the person he was supposed to meet was either late or didn't show up at all. In follow-up meetings, he sometimes found that the person he had met with did not remember what was said or agreed to in the previous meeting. Almost universally, the public plan officials who were veterans in the job impressed Monks as arrogant. Certainly, most were not willing to admit they were doing a poor or even mediocre job at anything, including proxy voting.

Even those funds that Monks ended up working with showed a degree of insolence that alarmed him. Years later Monks recorded:

> One pension plan executive over half a dozen years never kept me waiting less than half an hour. An hour was more customary. This would be true whether we met in his office or in a bar or restaurant. Another official simply has never yet shown up for meetings which were scheduled. In the category of "fringe benefits" for public officials is the condoning of alcoholism. . . . For a salesman, the problem of alcoholic customers is a dreadful problem. I have traveled 3,000 miles for a dinner meeting only to wait on the sidewalk for an hour finally to have my customer literally fall out of the taxi cab as I vainly tried to keep some of him off of the sidewalk. I have had customers fall off of banquettes in restaurants. The most disconcerting experience is to try to figure exactly what

portions of a conversation a drunk customer remembers the morning after. You can never count on a drunk failing to hear and remember precisely what you would prefer they not notice. Some of the most insightful analyses of my character have emerged under these circumstances.[20]

The August 1986 sales trip was not the worst in Monks' experience, though it wasn't a raging success, either. Most people were genuinely interested in what he was doing; they just were not excited about signing on the dotted line. In Madison, Wisconsin, he had an upbeat meeting with Ken Codlin ("solid, midwestern, but shrewd," Monks wrote in a memo about the trip) and Pat Lipton of the State of Wisconsin Investment Board. They were bent on making their own proxy season splash with some sort of initiative, but, Monks noted in his memo, Lipton was "grateful for the "pill" as an organizing principle." The next day, in Columbus, Ohio, at the State Teachers Retirement Systems of Ohio, he found a "first class sample of decent, competent, professional attitude," but "generally leery of outside services." The following day, he was in Jefferson City, Missouri, to meet with the executive director of the Missouri State Employees Retirement System, and later that day flew to St. Paul to sit down with the executive director of the Minnesota State Board of Investment. (The executive informed Monks that one of the pension system board's ad hoc committees was devoted to the issue of management entrenchment.) The next day, Monks found himself in Boise, Idaho, with the head of the state's public employee pension fund, a 70-year-old ex-marine, "a good ally." A few days later, Monks met briefly with a money manager in San Francisco who blamed activism for a loss of clients several years back, and later had a more positive meeting with DeWitt Bowman, chief investment officer of the city's public pension fund. The next day, he went to Los Angeles to see another big money manager, whom he described in his notes as "50ish, overweight, smart, insecure. . . . He has no doubt of the ultimate importance of ISS, but raises questions as to our staying power in the meantime."

Given his mixed success as a salesperson, Monks began to have an uneasy feeling. Where was ISS heading? What was its purpose in life? The incipient advisory firm had established contact with upward of 200 institutions including universities, foundations, mutual funds, money managers, and labor unions, as well as pension funds. But it still had only two clients—Batterymarch and TIAA-CREF—for whom it offered its basic service of voting recommendations on the proxies of 1,200 companies, plus the letter writing, solicitation campaigns. Although the public pension systems of California and New Jersey and the Fidelity fund group had indicated their intentions to sign up as clients—at $50,000 a year—they had yet to do so. No one told the outside world about this pathetic situation. Indeed, the Georgeson newsletter cited ISS's Janet Brown in describing her company's client list as including corporate and public pension funds, university endowments, and all types of institutional money managers.[21]

The seven staff persons, including Monks and his assistant Barbara Sleasman, were swimming in the company's capacious, $230,000-a-year office space. And Monks was carrying most of the cost of the $660,000 annual budget (excluding his own salary, which was nonexistent). ISS had embarked on a number of diverse paths, each of which was relevant to the cause of better governance. But questions gnawed at Monks. Should they be doing more? Or less? Or something different? "In focusing on issues such as proxy contests," he wrote to his directors in an annual report, "we run the risk of using up our energy on subjects that are, in the end, only a minor part of our mission."

That mission was instilling the sense of ownership in every investor and then motivating investors to behave like owners. "ISS has determined," Monks wrote in a strategy memo, "that there is no market for the theory of ownership, and we must therefore start with the proxy issues that obtrude in an unignorable way at the present time." He also continued to hope that ISS could file some kind of litigation that would help further the mission, which was the reason Minow came on the staff. Some lawsuits could be filed in connection with proxy contests, perhaps concerning the fairness of the voting mechanics or the conflicts of interest of a bank that handles a company's employee benefit plans and votes the shares. Others could be minority shareholder suits brought by institutional investors who believe their rights have been violated. "ISS could involve itself with litigation in several different ways that might provide a good source of income," Monks wrote. He also wrote a quick, handwritten note to Berman: "I would like to get the "right" lawsuit started."[22]

Once people feel like owners, ISS could proceed with a "shareholders' agenda" that would include such issues as how directors set executive compensation as well as the need for both greater corporate compliance with the law and ongoing disclosure of any information affecting value. In this and other ways, Monks was both insightful and characteristically over-optimistic about the shape of things to come. As he wrote to Peter Drucker on

October 10: "Over time, they [pension plans] will forge continuing relationships with each corporation that they own, so as to make managements appropriately accountable for long-term performance. This accountability will in turn improve corporate competitiveness. As these fiduciary owners— acting severally at first, but increasingly in concert—become still more active and informed, they serve to liberate corporate managements from the burden of short-term performance. . . . The active involvement of powerful fiduciary owners enhances corporations' sensitivity to public concerns. It lessens the violence of hostile takeovers, and it improves the United States' global competitiveness." Monks was so excited about this prospect that he, with Minow's help, even obtained a ruling in the form of a letter from the Justice Department—finalized in the summer of 1987—that it would not violate antitrust rules if the pension plans of several large corporations got together to talk about issues raised by the proxies their pension funds vote. (In a debate some years later sponsored by *CEO* magazine, Walter Wriston told Minow that he had personal inside knowledge that ISS was in violation of antitrust law. "It was my great pleasure to inform him about the letter," she says.) In this scenario of radical change Monks had full confidence—and indeed by the mid-1990s, it had begun to take shape.

But in the summer of 1986, Monks had some doubts about ISS's ability to help bring about this utopian world, and felt he needed to turn to someone for advice. He knew that one of his own strengths could be a vulnerability; he was well aware that he had the personality of a rower, who could just keep going and going until exhaustion or a waterfall stopped him. Fortunately, another feature of his personality was his ability to take criticism. "I needed a reality check from people who knew me well enough to tell me," he recounts. And so he scheduled a meeting for late August, inviting Berman, Dubow, and Michael Christian, with whom he'd worked at The Boston Company. To prepare, he sent them all the 23-page annual report outlining the work ISS had done so far and its immediate goals. The report dated August 4 concluded with a section entitled, "Specific Request For Advice":

Is ISS a business? We have committed a significant amount of energy, ingenuity and resources to ISS. We need outside evaluation of what we have accomplished and what we are trying to do. ISS was organized as a business rather than a non-profit organization because of my conviction that we needed marketplace discipline for our ideas. If we can't get people to pay, our ideas probably do not have commercial value . . . We need a hard judgement on whether we have a basic business.

"On the assumption that we have a business, are we organized appropriately to develop it? While I am aware of our progress in certain areas, I am more aware of the high human cost of achieving it and of what we have not been able to do. I tentatively feel that if we do have a business, we probably ought to expand our staff significantly (by adding, for example, a competent institutional salesman) . . . to pursue leads that we have already developed."

In notes he took in preparation for the meeting, Monks already seemed to know that ISS needed an injection of creative ideas. "Present products," he wrote, "are only salable to companies with special characteristics: non-bureaucratic, reprisal proof, personal interest." There were very few who would qualify. "Either we have to develop new products that are perceived as cost effective for plan sponsors; or we have to change the surrounding circumstances that makes good governance today an expensive luxury." What new products could ISS put forward? Among the ideas he mentioned: "Advise New York, California, Wisconsin re 'divestiture'; governance rating service, analogous to credit rating."

At the meeting, the most incisive comment, and the one that stayed with Monks for years, came from Christian, who was then president of the Boston Safe Deposit and Trust Co. He told Monks: "I have never encountered a business based less on market considerations." What impressed Monks was not that someone recognized that ISS had a product people did not need. Indeed, he himself, as the salesman, knew how hard it was to explain to institutions why they needed ISS's services when they had been getting along so nicely without them. As Monks later explained, Christian "made me understand that what I was trying to do was going to be real hard and take a long time. Mike's remark sobered me to that."

He realized that ISS was not going to get lots of clients and lots of funding for some time. "Many people, possibly most, think that it [ISS] is a good idea, but only a very few feel justified in supporting it," he wrote in a mid-October memo, sounding dejected, resigned to taking a less prominent role for a while. Meantime, another problem surfaced. Economist Richard Ruback's work for ISS to determine a reduction in shareholder value resulting from the adoption of poison pills did not appear to establish a clear link. So, it was going to be hard for ISS to communicate to institutional investors the risks and opportunities of shareholder activism.

To survive without much funding and without a readily salable message and still be effective was a great challenge. Monks had to dismiss three staff members, including Janet Brown. It was awkward telling Brown about the downsizing because she had come with him from the Labor Department, and Monks found it hard to explain to her what he was doing. He was not exactly sure himself. What was left was a skeletal staff of himself and two part-time professionals, Minow and John Pound, who had just left the SEC and was working on his PhD at Yale. The projects they would work on would have to be high-leverage projects that got lots of bang for the buck.

That meant the small ISS staff would concentrate on establishing ISS as an authority on governance and an indispensible resource for investors or anyone interested in governance issues. So, it would do some behind-the-scenes work in the 1987 proxy season, writing anti-poison pill resolutions for CREF. By autumn, it had already begun this project in order to make all the deadlines for the 1987 proxy season. By October 30, CREF had submitted its resolutions to the SEC for approval.[23]

But, most important at the time, ISS planned to speak out about an issue it felt could be tied more clearly to value and would illustrate ISS's effectiveness in protecting value. It would try to be a leading voice in challenging the New York Stock Exchange's decision to eliminate the one share/one vote rule. The exchange had submitted the proposed rule change to the SEC for approval. But ISS, as well as some others like Boone Pickens, wanted the SEC to hold hearings on the matter, hoping not only that the SEC would block the rule change but also insist that one share/one vote hold for all exchanges, including the NASDAQ. Minow, newly arrived at ISS, was very excited about this project. "I'd spent eight years on regulatory stuff," she says. "I knew exactly what to do. It was unbelievably lucky that I arrived just as the first major regulatory issue in the history of corporate governance was happening. I was the one trick pony of all time, and Bob had asked me to do the one thing I knew how to do." And, the SEC did that fall decide to hold the hearings in December—only the second time it would hold hearings on an exchange's rulemaking.

Monks wanted to prod the government—whether the DOL, the SEC, or Congress—to pay attention to other proxy voting issues as well. He was hoping to draft SEC proposed regulations to require that fiduciaries like pension fund managers make their votes public. In his view at the time this, and not confidentiality, was the best solution to the conflict of interest dilemma. In fact, the previous spring, Monks went at it with Boone Pickens at an investors' seminar in Rochester, New York—Monks arguing for disclosure and Pickens for confidentiality. In addition to these efforts, Monks and Minow were publishing their thoughts in major newspapers and trade journals and their own newsletter, and making themselves readily available to the press.

As voting obligations became clearer, it was also rapidly becoming evident that ISS had to give the institutions something they needed: voting recommendations on an increasingly larger scale that would eventually cover all U.S. stocks. This service would take time to build. But in the end, it would prove to be ISS's core business.

7

Poison Pill

If you're trying to start a business, you just try everything. You spread your seed around as much as you can and see where it grows. What we were trying to do was something that captured the popular imagination. Staggered boards didn't do it. People were interested in that, but it wasn't too big a deal. What did do it ultimately were poison pills that were passed without shareholder approval. Where we previously said, "You've lost some of your vote," with the pills we said, "You've lost your ability to sell your stock." If Carl Icahn was going to bid for 52 percent of the stock, all these guys wanted to get in line to sell. The pill said, if he already had 20 percent, he couldn't buy any more. So the free ride was over. These guys could no longer sell their stock. That got people's attention.

Bob Monks

By the end of 1986 and start of 1987, ISS's work drafting resolutions and speaking out for shareholders had begun to pay off, in image if not in dollars. Its role as a proshareholder voice in defending the one share/one vote rule was important. In a collaborative effort, Minow, Ruback, Pound, and Monks submitted written commentary that SEC commissioners subsequently praised. Eventually, "The SEC wrote the rule, which was a revolutionary thing, really around what we filed," Minow later maintained. "I was very very proud of that." The SEC rule essentially prevented public corporations from issuing new classes of stock, with some exceptions, by prohibiting the stock exchanges and the NASDAQ from listing and trading stock of any company that issues new shares carrying more than one vote per share. When the Business Roundtable, the association of big business, challenged the rule, the courts threw it out. But later on, the New York Stock Exchange adopted what was essentially the same measure.

In 1987, Monks and ISS would largely become preoccupied with institutional investors' fight against poison pills, a battle that he had played a large role in creating. Corporate attorney Marty Lipton became corporate America's greatest ally when he invented the poison pill, which soon became the most popular method of fending off corporate raiders. Monks opposed the pill for two reasons. One, he felt that there were other ways to fend off hostile takeovers that didn't violate shareowners' rights. Also, many companies already had other antitakeover provisions in place. "What they really wanted to do was transfer control from the shareholders back to the directors," was Monks' position. But as much as he disliked the pills, Monks was even more disturbed by corporate managements' resolve to bypass shareholders in adopting them. He had to admit that in one or two cases, poison pills were actually beneficial to shareholders; but there was no defense for leaving shareholders out of the decision.

Several institutional investors, encouraged by Monks and others like the Council of Institutional Investors (CII), stepped forward in late 1986 to propose anti-poison pill resolutions to put before the shareholders at annual meetings. Monks' clever idea, which he passed along to a number of activists, was that rather than submit a shareholder resolution calling for rescission of the poison pill and opening up the debate on the substance of the issue, they would do better to write the resolution calling for a shareholder vote. Even fans of the pill would find it hard to oppose the right to approve it. The resolution that ISS helped TIAA-CREF write was worded as a request from shareholders that the company rescind its poison pill "unless shareholders are given the opportunity to affirm its adoption by a majority vote of outstanding shares." It went on to say: "This resolution does not prohibit management from resisting a tender offer. It merely signals management that shareholders insist on their right to vote on major changes in the company's governance structure which will affect the value of their shares."[1] Most of the 60 or so anti-pill resolutions filed with the SEC—a bit more than half of those actually got SEC approval to run in the proxy statements—were also written in this way. Also as Monks had advised, CREF and the California government employees' and teachers' funds chose to target companies that had high institutional ownership (in the range of 50 percent to 80 percent of total shares) since individual holders usually vote with management and the institutions had fiduciary reasons (thanks to Monks) to vote against management. When in the fall the funds filed these resolutions with the SEC, Jamie Heard, then with the IRRC and later to join USA and finally ISS, claimed they were the pension funds' "first concrete steps to play a much more active role in the corporate governance process."[2]

Monks had long been disturbed by the response some companies had to any challenge being mounted against their takeover defenses. Some CEOs would pressure their own pension fund managers. And now, they'd begun writing letters to other CEOs asking them to lobby their pension funds to vote for antitakeover measures and against the shareholder resolutions, and some of the recipients acknowledged following up on such pleas. These executives believed they needed to communicate their views to plan sponsors or else face possible acquisition by raiders. Poison pill inventor Lipton, swiftly picking up on the CEOs' action, wrote to all his clients, prodding them also to write to their fellow CEOs on these issues. In an ominous tone, he cited the creation of investor groups like CII and USA and the anti-poison pill resolutions as evidence that "institutional investors are supporting corporate raiders for the purpose of continuing the junk-bond bust-up takeover frenzy."

As Monks saw it, the letter-writing campaigns were just an overt manifestation of the conflict of interest inherent in the proxy voting system. Corporate executives were in his view making inappropriate efforts to influence the vote with no regard for the pension fund managers' fiduciary duties toward beneficiaries. The duty was to vote exclusively in the interest of beneficiaries, not in the interest of other companies' CEOs. Monks was particularly frustrated with his successor at the Labor Department, Dennis Kass, who he felt did not take a hard line against the CEOs in question. The Investor Responsibility Research Center, in its study of the proxy process that spring, backed up Monks' view, saying the department "has demonstrated little concern about the exercise of voting rights. So far it has declined to issue a policy statement on voting responsibilities. It has taken no enforcement action involving voting abuses brought to its attention. . . ."[3] (For his part, Kass had a number of other priorities and had launched a campaign to root out fiduciary abuses in all areas, including proxy voting.[4])

Monks did whatever he as one civilian could do to combat this development. While he could not compel the Labor Department to take definitive action, he continued to put out the message, in the press and in speeches— always identified as the former pensions administrator—that pension plan fiduciaries are "required by law . . . to demand full accountability from corporate management." In the interest of his larger vision, he added, "Shareholders have good reason (pension beneficiaries' interests) to put pressure on managements to maximize profits in ways that do not pollute the atmosphere, cause workplace injuries or harm customers."[5]

Also, although ISS wasn't itself sponsoring any resolutions, Monks added his voice to those of the resolutions' sponsors. On March 18, 1987, Monks authored a letter to more than 100 major institutional investors ("everybody we'd met") urging them to vote "yes" on the anti-poison pill resolutions. "I want to make sure that you understand the importance of the opportunity being offered to you over the next 10 weeks, as you are asked to vote on poison pill resolutions at over 60 companies," he began. The letter pointed out right up front that of the more than 300 poison pills adopted to date, none were submitted to shareholders for their approval. Given the chance, would shareholders have voted them in? Monks wrote that in light of the available evidence, they should not have. An SEC study released in October 1986 showed that "pill plans have a significant negative impact on share prices." (He did not point out that the study had been criticized for its short-term view—two days after the introduction of a pill.) But, he ended with, "the issue is not the advisability of poison pills, it is the legitimacy of action by corporate management that devalues the shares without submitting it for shareholder approval."

The test case in this campaign turned out to be one of TIAA-CREF's resolutions, at International Paper Company. The company had adopted the pill in December 1985, and CREF, which owned about 1.8 percent of the company's shares, filed the resolution with the SEC in the fall. There then ensued a months-long stream of letters from International Paper and CREF to the SEC over whether the resolution should appear on the proxy statement. CREF won that fight and began soliciting other institutions for their votes. International Paper's executives wrote to more than 300 of their fellow CEOs asking them to vote their pension plans' shares against the resolution. Apparently, the company did not have a lot to worry about. As Schlefer recalls, "I was amazed at how many people told me right out, 'Well, we always vote with management.'"

CREF made its final appeal at the annual meeting on April 14, 1987. Monks sent Minow to the event, which was at the Metropolitan Museum of Art on Manhattan's Fifth Avenue. She sat next to Schlefer, who rose to speak to the huge crowd on behalf of the big pension fund's first corporate governance resolution. It lost. But for a shareholder initiative opposed by management, it did very well, garnering about 27 percent of the votes cast (about 19 percent of shares outstanding). And the proposal probably would have done even better if the company hadn't been reporting such good earnings. At the annual meeting, the paper company reported that its first-quarter profits had tripled from the year earlier.

That begs the question: Why go after a company that was serving its shareholders so well on the bottom line? Monks, who was advising institutions on drafting the resolutions, was also making suggestions on the choice of target companies. And, as mentioned, the priority was to find companies with high institutional ownership and not necessarily poor performance. (International Paper had 59 percent institutional ownership.) The choice was the correct one at the time because it was the best way to launch the movement. As Monks explains today, "We needed to show that we could produce meaningful percentages of shareholder votes on given issues. History shows that only a handful of proxy contests for control had elicited more than 10 percent of shareholder votes on *anything* over half a century. I was fixed on the notion of getting over 50 percent of the vote on something. We didn't ever want to control; we wanted to create a presence that management could not ignore." Later, after the activists had established their presence by consistently producing material results, the strategy changed. "Ultimately," says Monks, "shareholder activism would be valuable only to the extent that it would be proven to add value."

As the 1987 proxy season entered its final stage, Monks and Minow used their newsletter to broadcast the shareholder activists' viewpoint in the ongoing poison pill melee to more than 100 investors and others. In the publication, which Monks viewed as "one of the best means of advertising available to us," ISS criticized corporate managements for making such a fuss over "a mild procedural resolution sponsored by shareholders" and posed the question: If these defenses really were meant to protect shareholders, why were companies "afraid" to ask shareholders to adopt them? Moreover, the upstart firm claimed that International Paper's move to ask shareholders to approve an increase in the number of authorized shares as part of another takeover defense "is close to an admission that the shareholders do have a right to decide whether a company should adopt a poison pill." (Shareholders approved that measure, though activists like CREF's Schlefer claimed that the item's true goal was so clouded in its presentation that shareholders didn't know what they were voting on.)

But as he saw shareholders losing what he had felt were well-orches-trated campaigns, Monks directed his anger not so much at corporate man-agements and their aggressive tactics as at the system that allowed these tactics. Back in 1986, when he was becoming more involved in proxy mat-ters, Monks had made it his business to educate himself about the proxy voting and solicitation process. That spring, he called John Wilcox, the head of the proxy solicitation firm Georgeson & Co., and asked him out to lunch. "He wanted to find out how the proxy system operated," Wilcox recalls. "Over the period of a couple of years we would meet regularly. I was explaining to him the inner workings of the proxy process. There's no place you can go to learn how the proxy system operates. There's no school, there are no courses. The inner workings of the proxy process are based on a structure that is a combination of federal law, SEC regulations, state laws, corporate charters, and then a whole lot of practical things that have built up around that, such as back office practices on Wall Street. So it's a jerry-built system. He wanted to understand the system, so he studied it. He's very thorough."

But Wilcox was surprised to see what Monks was really thinking of the proxy process a full year after they had first met. On April 17, a few days after the International Paper meeting—during which time shareholders at one other company, NCR, also voted down a poison pill resolution—Monks sat down at his computer and banged out a brief memorandum to Wilcox (who was the solicitor for International Paper) with his verdict so far on the operation of the proxy system. Although he was addressing someone who had spent his entire career in the proxy solicitation business, he had few kind words about the system. Wrote Monks: ". . . I have been wondering what, as a practical matter, would be required in order to assure a legitimate electoral process. Ultimately, nothing but grief will result from continuation of the present rather cynical dysfunctionality. It seems to me, therefore, in everybody's interest to try to assure an honest vote. . . ." It was clear to him, he wrote, that without use of a proxy soliciting firm, shareholders would not be able to do better than this initial, only fair performance. Among his chief complaints in the letter: "The number of processes that must be performed for the registered owners (e.g., custodian banks) to forward their proxy cards to those [money managers and other institutional investors] entitled to vote are patently unsusceptible of being performed within the requisite time. Obviously, proxy solicitors have worked out "short cuts." "Are they legal?" he asked, adding, "There is *no* verification process of the validity of the proxies." One idea, he said, would be for companies to appoint an independent entity to verify the voting procedures.

If this was a way to make friends in the solicitation business, Monks wasn't scoring well. Wilcox was annoyed by the criticisms of such a neophyte. He began his passionate reply: "I want to register my strenuous objection to the statements in your April 17 letter and accompanying memorandum . . . I am surprised to see you make unsubstantiated charges of dishonesty and broadside attacks on the proxy system. It is wrong of you to complain of poor results on shareholder proposals when you know that the proponents did not do the work necessary to achieve a better vote. It is wrong of you to fault the proxy system and to suggest that corporations are using illegal methods when you know that shareholder proponents made a conscious decision not to wage full-fledged proxy fights on behalf of their proposals, not to hire proxy solicitors, and not even to conduct a minimum solicitation to bring in additional votes. It is wrong of you to suggest that because corporate managements did make the commitment to aggressive proxy solicitation they have somehow crossed the line of fairness." Wilcox adamantly defended the system and his own firm as being fair and honest. He noted that institutional investors that have shares registered in bank and broker names should make sure their voting instructions are executed by those custodians, and that corporations and solicitors work hard to make sure investors receive materials. Furthermore, he called Monks' complaints "self serving" and pointed out that perhaps there was another reason the resolutions failed: a lot of people agree with management on the merits of poison pills. "You should not fall into the trap of concluding that people who disagree with you are all victims of coercion or illegal tactics."

That reproach hardly stopped Monks. He remained steadfast in his belief that the proxy process was basically unfair. During that proxy season, he wrote a few other letters to Wilcox, whom he had come to regard as a friend who liked to discuss the theory and workings of "shareholder democracy." In those letters and in others to congressional legislators, Monks laid out his concerns about the system; namely, that it was undemocratic, heavily weighted toward management in terms of the process and the resources, and reeling with the potential for conflicts of interest. He wasn't the only one complaining about the process. In late March, IRRC's Jamie Heard summed up the initial findings of a proxy study by saying the solicitation process "provides opportunity for outright fraud" and leaves "so many opportunities to alter the vote along the way."[6] Boone Pickens was also railing at the system, which he said allowed companies to place undue pressure on pension fund executives and money managers.

Monks was pleased to see that the conflict of interest issue finally began stirring interest at the Labor Department in 1987. David Walker, the Deputy Assistant Secretary of Labor in charge of the pension system, announced that the department was examining charges of executives improperly trying to influence proxy voting and was seeking a test case.[7] Also, Monks' trusted department ally, Morton Klevan, the Pension and Welfare Benefits Agency's director of policy development, was quoted saying: "If a plan sponsor feels strongly about proxy voting, it appears that the worst thing he could do, from a legal point of view, is direct the proxy voting of his investment manager."[8] That is because he could then be taking on liability for the pension fund manager's day-to-day investment decisions. Monks, of course, had been urging Walker, Klevan, and Lebowitz to get moving on proxy voting issues. "He was encouraging the department to issue some guidance on fiduciary duty," Walker says.

In another regulatory venue, Monks was on the front line. In June 1986, he was appointed as a member of the bipartisan California Senate Commission on Corporate Governance, Shareholder Rights and Securities Transactions. Created in large part by Senator Dan McQuorkadale and one of his advisers, Dick Damm, the group met periodically to discuss the effects of corporate takeovers on the state and whether any legislation was needed to dampen the impact. The 31 commissioners—among them McQuorkadale, chairman of the commission, state Treasurer Jesse Unruh, Assistant Treasurer Kathleen Brown, and leveraged buyout artist Jerome Kohlberg—convened at various University of California campuses and drafted a number of bills.

Monks used this opportunity to try to change the system single-handedly by following up on his conviction that full disclosure—rather than confidentiality—was the best remedy for institutional investors' inherent conflicts of interest in proxy voting. He drafted proposed legislation and got a state Senator, John Garamendi, to sponsor it. The bill gave owners of a company (such as pension funds and their beneficiaries) the right to know how trustees of their stock (money managers) voted the stock's proxies and why, and whether there were any conflicts of interests in the voting and any contacts made with boards of directors. Such disclosure, the theory went, would prevent money managers from voting in line with their own interests even when pressured by corporate CEOs. As he explained in ISS's May 1987 newsletter: "If the votes do not have to be revealed to the beneficial owners, the only ones who know how a trustee votes are the corporations who count the votes, and they have all kinds of opportunities to pressure the trustees to vote their way. If trustees must reveal their votes to the beneficial owners, they will have an unassailable reason to resist that pressure, and will be able to meet their obligation to manage the fund for the exclusive benefit of the true owners." The bill passed and in 1990 became law. Monks' hope was that other states would follow California's lead. But none did. And even in California, no one, to Monks' knowledge, ever actually used these new rights to demand disclosure.

It wasn't long before Monks reached the conclusion that Boone Pickens was right: confidentiality is the best way to avoid the conflict of interest. As he told me: "No level of government—elective, judicial, administrative—is going to enforce the conflict of interest provisions in the fiduciary laws. Thus, the big financial service conglomerates are free to ignore their transcendent obligation to beneficiaries in favor of accommodating the more immediate concerns of the corporate managements in whose gift is other important business. So, trustees need protection, and I became an equally committed believer in the protection of confidentiality."[9] Beginning in 1988, institutional investors would use the proxy machinery to help them get companies to agree to confidentiality.

At the end of the 1987 proxy season, Marty Lipton gleefully distributed a memo to Wachtell, Lipton clients entitled "Pill 31—Institutions 0, CalPERS and CREF Shut Out." He reported that on average the resolutions at the 31 companies where those two institutions sponsored resolutions won only 20 percent of the outstanding shares. The sponsors of the resolutions, meanwhile, were trumpeting victory. Stating results in terms of the votes cast, they garnered up to 41 percent in one case, while they had been shooting for 10 to 20 percent.

Still, Lipton felt it important to issue this warning: "The Council of Institutional Investors apparently is not giving up. Word on Wall Street is that they are soliciting contributions for the purpose of financing a renewal of the anti–pill campaign. The refusal of the activist institutions to accept the will of the overwhelming majority of shareholders is further proof that their objective is not corporate democracy, but promotion and encouragement of bust-up takeovers."

Years later, Lipton laid some of the blame for this short-term attitude squarely with Monks, as both regulator and activist: "I didn't agree with his position that they had to virtually automatically always go for the takeover premium. That was his position. . . . He's the quintessential shareholder activist seeking maximization of shareholder value in the short run."[10] And indeed, on the surface, Monks' active opposition to poison pills appeared to confirm this view that he was in favor of institutional investors taking the short-term profit and running. Yet, his beliefs were quite opposite, as he had repeated time and again since his service at the Labor Department. As long as a fiduciary has fully evaluated the long-term consequences for shareholders of a takeover versus continuation of current management, whatever choice he/she makes has met the legal requirements of ERISA.

But there is another element to consider as well. When a raider moves in on a company, the rising stock price that results is not necessarily a reflection of a short-term view. Indeed, it is common knowledge that a company's share price reflects the present value of future cash flows. As Monks' client, TIAA-CREF's Schlefer, explains: "One thing a lot of people don't focus on in the stock market when they talk about investors being short-term oriented is that the price of a share of stock is really meant to reflect the consensus about what the long-term prospects of the company are. So say all you're interested in is getting the stock up ten points or whatever. What you're really saying is you're interested in changing the future outlook for the company, which is then reflected in the stock price. If that happens right away, then you've really achieved your objective and you can sell out. But the price really reflects the expectations of what the company is going to do over the next five, ten, 15 years."

For years, the accusation of short-termism dogged Monks. A book published in 1986, *Takeover—The New Wall Street Warriors: The Men, The Money, The Impact* (Arbor House, New York) by Moira Johnston, attributed to Monks the view that pension fund fiduciaries should take short-term profits in takeover situations. After hearing from Monks and his lawyers, Johnston wrote him an apology: "That section of the book would have been enriched and balanced by including quotes from yourself. The fact that they were not is a reflection of the tight time frame in which I worked, rather than my lack of recognition of the significant role that you have played in the evolution of the institutional investor in the American economy." She indicated that any future printing of the book would more accurately reflect his views.[11]

At the same time, Monks advocated prudence and long-term thinking, however, he—a business owner himself—realized the corporate managers' dilemma. A raider arriving on the scene may not always offer a price that adequately represents a company's long-term value; but there may be little a management can do to get a better price, because, Monks says, investors in the real world are not as long-term oriented as they need to be. And, yes, fiduciary obligations may have something to do with that. "If I owned stock at 30 in the market, and somebody offers 40, and somebody else says I'm supposed to act prudently and figure out what the long-term best interest of my beneficiaries is, I've got to be a fool not to sell it," Monks says. Given this situation, Monks admitted that corporations had a problem—now. His view was that over time, in the ideal world, the corporations themselves could preclude hostile takeovers by insisting that their pension funds act as long-term owners of the companies in which they held stock, by forming ongoing relationships with managements. In the mid-1980's frenzy, there was hardly time for that situation to develop, and so he could easily understand how the poison pill gained such quick popularity.

So, while he immersed himself in the poison pill battle and the conflict-of-interest questions that it spawned, Monks continued to promulgate the broader message that a long-term relationship between shareholders and managers was the ideal. In a speech to corporate officials in May 1987, he addressed the negative effects that the lack of such a relationship, due to "shareholder inertia," had on corporations:

> One major reason for the recent spate of merger and acquisition activity is that as a result of board and shareholder inaction, assets become undermanaged and thus artificially lowly-valued in the marketplace. Takeovers correct this situation but come so late in the day that needed adjustment is well overdue and the whole process will predictably and needlessly be a very disruptive one. . . . Isn't there an intermediate point at which continuous shareholder involvement is competent to reduce the scope of artificially lowered values due to undermanagement? . . . In a *Newsweek* interview, Carl Icahn said, "if the rules were changed [to make management more accountable to the shareholders] you wouldn't need guys like me. I'm talking against my own business, but basically if you had answerability, if you had true corporate democracy, you wouldn't need people like me."[12]

How to change the rules? In Monks' view, the essential rule already stood in the form of ERISA, which establishes pension funds' fiduciary duty toward their beneficiaries. That law, properly enforced, was the stick that would guide institutional investors to behave like responsible owners.

Value—the carrot—had to exist as well. But in Monks' view, the value of working with management on long-term goals was intuitive.

ERISA, as he saw it, should force pension funds to abandon their short-term, trading mentality to become long-term investors. First of all, it helped create pension funds that would just keep growing and growing until they would be so large that it would not be economical for them to trade in and out of stocks. Just selling out of big positions could depress the market price that the seller would receive. In a speech to the CII at its first annual meeting in 1985, Monks made this additional observation:

> Public and private benefit plans may be the American equivalent of the so-called "permanent shareholders" in Japan. Plan holdings constitute such a large percentage of the total market that it is not possible for the ERISA system, taken as a whole, to sell out its holdings in the largest companies. . . . It is now possible for individual plans to get rid of specific market holdings. It is not possible for the benefit plan system as a whole to dispose of significant holdings. Who would be the buyer? As the law develops regarding the exact scope of trustees' obligation to act regarding certain corporate malfeasance, it is obvious that gridlock could occur. If the law regards a particular corporate action as so antithetical to the beneficiaries' interests as to require divestiture by one fiduciary, it would not be permissible for another plan to be the purchaser. For permanent shareholders, therefore, simply disposing of an offending investment is no longer a practical option.

Over time, he believed, ERISA would help steer most plans into funds that track an index, thereby cementing their status as "permanent" shareholders. His reasoning was that since index funds generally outperform actively managed funds over time, it is more prudent for pension plans to index their assets than to dole them out to active managers. In fact, he even went so far as to suggest a Labor Department regulation specifying that indexing equity assets would satisfy requirements for prudence in pension plan investing. "Such a regulation would . . . make short-term considerations irrelevant," he and Minow wrote in *Pensions & Investments Age*. And, they went on, funds would then begin to act collectively to protect the value of their assets.[13] Given the reluctance of institutional shareholders to expend resources for activism, organizations like ISS could provide a means for taking collective action. "I believe, in fact, that institutional investors have the obligation to develop suitable mechanisms for collective action," Monks said in his speech to the CII. Ultimately, though, the proxy system itself would have to change and ERISA be enforced with more vigor to give institutions a more level playing field with management.

Coincidentally, Monks had just become involved in a project that would index what would become a huge pool of assets. In December, he was named a trustee of the new Federal Employees' Retirement System, having been nominated by Senator Bob Dole and appointed by President Reagan. FERS was a giant government thrift plan—or defined contribution plan like a 401(k) in which the contribution amount is predetermined—that Monks liked to refer to as the largest defined contribution plan in the world. The goal was to include all federal employees over time, who would be able to save up to 10 percent of their pay tax-free until retirement, with a partial match by the government. Most intriguing to Monks was that federal employees would now be able to own stocks—through an index fund—where previously they could own only federal debt through the government's defined benefit pension plan. Along with that stock ownership came proxy votes, and Monks wanted to make sure that FERS found a way to fulfill its obligation to cast those votes. "By creating the largest institutional investor in the country, the federal retirement system could become a very important shareholder in many companies," Monks told *Pension World* magazine. "The Congress wanted to make sure there was no way by which this could result in the government or its employees exercising a powerful voice in the management of the private sector."[14]

What happened was that Wells Fargo bank became the manager of the equity assets, which were in an index fund, and also became responsible for voting the shares. In 1990, Wells Fargo engaged ISS to make recommendations on every proxy issue being considered at all the companies in its portfolio—essentially all publicly listed stocks in the world, some 6,000 companies. Wells Fargo "underwrote our expansion," Minow says. So, depending on how often Wells Fargo followed ISS's advice—and in most cases, ISS's clients have—the firm was determining how the FERS shares were voting. By 1990, Monks and FERS had gone their separate ways. Monks found that getting the FERS chairman to concentrate on defining board procedures and the board to agree on the statute's exact intentions was too frustrating, and he left after two years.

8

The Big Break

Because of his experience in business, he was able to explain to us the levers of power and to refine our focus. An invaluable adviser.

Jim Burton, CEO, Calpers

ISS spent the second half of 1987 preparing for the next proxy season, while continuing to seek out ways to enhance its image and create a market for its products, and in turn draw more clients. Around that time, Monks decided to sponsor a competition among college students as a way of getting ISS's ideas and themes into the academic world. He offered $10,000 of his own money for the best solution to corporations' potential runaway powers. As a side benefit, Monks thought that the project could help ISS solidify its relationships with the judges—among them Boone Pickens, Reuven Frank, Calpers' chief investment officer Greta Marshall, and Gordon Binns—and indeed, some of the organizations represented by the panel eventually became clients.

The contest presented a case study of a hypothetical corporation, Universal Products, Inc., that among other things produced vital defense products. The CEO recapitalized the company in such a way that insiders held control. He then moved the legal domicile of the company to Luxembourg where it could save $150 million in taxes and suffer little government interference in its operations. About 100 students and teams of students from various prestigious universities submitted essays both diagnosing the accountability problem and offering ways to solve it. Monks said he was disappointed that in the vast majority of cases increased government regulation was the favored prescription, rather than some means of increasing shareholders' restraint on management or board oversight. None of the essays were top-notch; in fact, when asked in 1998 which essay had won, Monks could not recall.

ISS's big break finally came in February 1988 when the Labor Department issued a landmark letter on proxy voting. The "Avon letter," released on February 23, was the result of an investigation into the practice of the cosmetic company's CEO to review money managers' votes *against* other companies' initiatives or *for* shareholder resolutions. The letter, written by Monks' old associate and friend Alan Lebowitz, who was now Deputy Assistant Secretary of Labor, marked the first time the agency had set down on paper what Monks had established in his first *Institutional Investor* speech: that the proxy vote is an asset of the pension plan and must be exercised for the exclusive benefit of plan participants. As Minow recalled: "We had a messenger bring it over. We were all so excited, we were reading it together to look for those magic words." The exact words were, "The decision as to how proxies should be voted with regard to the issues presented by the fact pattern are fiduciary acts of plan asset management." In a subsequent speech, David Walker, now the Assistant Secretary of Labor heading the pension agency, asserted that to meet this obligation, pension plan sponsors under ERISA must draw up detailed policies governing proxy voting and document all votes and the reasons behind them. This was the kind of guidance from the department that Monks had been encouraging his successors and the career bureaucrats to issue.

In the meantime, non-ERISA plans such as state pension systems, which became the driving force in the shareholder activism movement, were not really exempt from these rulings. To qualify to receive favorable tax treatment under the Internal Revenue Code, non-ERISA plans had to manage their assets for the exclusive benefit of the beneficiaries, which meant meeting the "prudent man rule" of labor law.

ISS was beautifully positioned to take advantage of this new regulatory climate. Monks quickly sat down to map out a brand-new business plan and marketing campaign. He summarized ISS's unique strengths in the emerging corporate governance field, which he referred to as the field of "fiduciary voting." They included: ISS's principals' prominence in the area among policymakers, in industry, and the press, and as advocates for clients in proxy and ownership matters; and the firm's development of databases. The plan was to help pension plans meet their newly established fiduciary obligations in a number of ways—from auditing voting policies and practices to recommending how to vote. At the same time, ISS would continue its consulting work assisting activist shareholders. Monks well understood that this advisory activity could stir up controversy for ISS. But, he noted, "There is a need to forcefully advance the entitlement of shareholders in order to add value in this type of business." In other words, he needed to continue to create the market for his services.

His hope was to find new financing (at least $1.35 million after taxes) by coaxing some financial institution to become a partner in the firm—now that a market for the products was much more discernible than in the past. This was particularly important at the time since Monks—the sole financier of ISS—was about to lose the $100,000 in annual income he had been earning from Shearson American Express (1981–1986). That money stemmed from his sale of The Boston Company to the brokerage firm and his agreement to serve as a consultant to the board.

A possible opportunity lay in Lambert Bruxelles Corp.'s interest at the time in taking a sizable stake in a U.S. commercial bank. CEO Gérard Eskenazi was intrigued with the idea of somehow exporting the continental notion of relationship banking to the United States. Monks offered to introduce him to his old school chum Frank Cahouet, chairman of Mellon Bank. In the event of a deal, Monks thought, he himself would be a good candidate to go on Mellon's board; then, he might convince Mellon to form a joint venture with ISS. But alas he was dreaming. He did take Eskenazi to Pittsburgh, but in the end Cahouet was not interested.

Literally as he was setting down his new business plan, new clients began to walk through ISS's door at Washington Harbor, most of them inspired—or prodded—by the Labor Department's new vigilance in the voting area. From ISS, they were getting recommendations on how to vote on specific, contested issues, to make sure they could demonstrate that they were being "prudent men" in their proxy voting. As Minow later recounted: "We had three clients. [The third was Fidelity.] Then, Labor issued the letter and within a month our client list had grown exponentially twice. We went from three clients to nine to twenty-seven within a month. All of a sudden, everybody needed some sort of 'deniability'—another Washington thought—on proxy voting. And they knew us because we'd been around, we'd been giving talks, we'd been writing, we'd been sending out free newsletters to everybody, and we were all there was." That summer, interest would increase as the Labor Department followed up the Avon letter with investigations of several companies' voting policies and practices. As Monks put it, this was "demand based on fear of liability."[1]

During this time, Monks was becoming much closer to one of ISS's new clients that he had been helping for some time: Calpers. The fund would prove to be pivotal both to Monks' work and to the shareholder activist movement. Since early 1986, Monks had been in touch with Calpers' chief investment officer Greta Marshall—who knew him from his days at The Boston Company—as well as investment officer Jose Arau, and others at the fund. He was a rich resource for them, "helpful on background information, and much more savvy at how to go about this" than they were at the time, Marshall says. But it wasn't until he met Richard Koppes, general counsel since May 1986, and then Dale Hanson, who became chief executive in April 1987, that he became an intimate adviser to the big pension system. Koppes had become increasingly interested in the fund's corporate gover-nance activities and took the initiative early in 1988 when he was in Wash-ington to introduce himself to Monks. As he tells it: "I kept reading about this Bob Monks. He really was a leading figure in corporate governance. I just called his office up and said I'd like to come see him. I went to his office on the Potomac, Washington Harbor. It was the most breathtaking office I'd ever been in. The Potomac looked like it flowed into his office and out the other side. There were only three people in the office. Bob spent over an hour with me. He is such an intellectual and such a leading force in his field. We just struck up a friendship. He and I would talk often, and I would always make a habit of having dinner with him when I was in Washington. It was a three-hour event. I always took a long list of issues to talk about with him and would come back with an equally long list of ideas. And I'd be ex-hausted. There was an idea every ten seconds it seemed like, and I was scrib-bling away. A great idea man, and I used him a lot for that."

It was also in 1988 that Monks was getting to know Koppes' colleague Hanson, whom he had met at one of the many conferences they both at-tended. He found the Calpers CEO to be full of energy and ideas. In fact, years later, Monks wrote, "Nothing would have happened without the in-volvement of the Public Employee Retirement System of California. More particularly, nothing would have happened without the involvement of Dale Hanson. It was Hanson who had the imagination, the energy, the charm, the courage, and the tenacity to meet with 65 CEOs and to communicate the re-sults of those meetings to the press."[2] And, at many of those companies the balance of power then shifted as investors pushed them to change.

Hanson did not start out as an activist when he took the helm at the big fund. He came from Wisconsin in 1987, where he had been chief operating officer of the state's employee trust funds. As he related in an interview in 1997 with the author, "Contrary to public belief, I knew absolutely zip about corporate governance. They didn't hire some wild-eyed flaming liberal to go after companies. I didn't even see corporate governance as being part of the equation. Calpers had already joined the Council of Institutional Investors. Two weeks after I started I went to a CII meeting. I remember that as I was leaving I thought to myself, 'This group will never survive.' The members were more interested in the politics—who was going to be vice chairman, etc.—than in how to present their agenda. The labor types viewed the agenda as pro labor." Toward the end of 1987, however, Hanson began to take much greater interest in Calpers' corporate governance program, largely because Koppes pointed out to him that it needed some direction. Together they started to examine what the program was trying to accomplish. Monks would prove invaluable to them in that effort, at first as an unpaid consultant and finally as a paid adviser later in 1988 when Calpers became an ISS client.

The 1988 proxy season proved to be a good advance on 1987 results and proof that ISS was gaining respect in the corporate governance arena. Two New England businessmen Monks knew well, Michael Dingman and Paul Montrone, chairman and president respectively of a conglomerate called Henley Group, asked him to solicit votes for them in favor of an anti–poison pill resolution at railroad operator Santa Fe Southern Pacific. The resolution actually was sponsored by a group of trainmen who worked at one of the company's two railroads and wanted their line to be sold to employees. Earlier, Henley, which owned some 16 percent of Santa Fe's stock, had threatened a proxy battle to take control of the company. It withdrew that challenge when a white knight investor, Canadian developer Olympia & York, was given two board seats, but it held onto its stake. When Dingman and Montrone became frustrated with Santa Fe's unwillingness to be acquired, an attitude firmly backed by the company's poison pill defense, they called their friend Monks.

ISS did not do the solicitation work officially on behalf of Henley; indeed, Dingman and Montrone did not want it known that they were soliciting votes. ISS simply did it on its own behalf and hired the solicitation firm Disston Associates of Greenwich, Connecticut, to assist in the campaign for votes. For the first time in the short history of the shareholder activist movement, the dissidents won—with 61 percent voting in favor of the resolution. "Our work was widely understood to be essential to the results obtained,"

Monks wrote his staff in August of that year. Although the resolution was advisory in nature, its passage put great pressure on management to give something to shareholders. In December of that year (1988), Santa Fe revised its poison pill to give shareholders a greater say in takeover bids.

Another significant fight that year for the activism movement and for ISS was at the Gillette Company. Coniston Partners, which held a 6.8 percent stake in Gillette, was trying to take control of the razor maker by running its own slate of directors at the April 21 annual meeting; the New York investment group hoped to put the company up for sale. Monks and Minow decided that Coniston's cause was one worth fighting for, in the interest of producing a major victory for shareholder value against a high-profile company that had once committed one of the most grievous violations of shareholder rights—paying greenmail. Nearly two years earlier, Gillette had paid $560 million in greenmail to get rid of another suitor, Revlon. On top of that, Gillette had a potent poison pill and recently had appointed new directors without shareholder approval. "It is the most important proxy contest since the beginning of modern shareholder activism," Monks told *Pensions & Investments Age* magazine on April 4, 1988. So he decided to go around to ISS clients to scare up votes for Coniston's slate.

ISS's case against Gillette only got better as the firm continued researching the company. The activists ran across a Gillette SEC filing relating that the company had paid Drexel Burnham Lambert so that it would not finance any company interested in acquiring Gillette for three years. Monks complained to Wilcox, who was working for Gillette in the Coniston fight, that this payment was a waste of shareholders' money, not to mention a tactic that could prevent shareholders from seeing greater returns on their investment. In turn, Wilcox brought the matter up with Gillette CEO Colman Mockler Jr. and convinced him to call Monks to discuss the issue. As it happened, Monks remembered Mockler from Harvard days; they had been in the same dorm. In the phone conversation, Monks recalls, "I asked Mockler how this expenditure of money could conceivably be in the interest of shareholders. And I said, 'How can you justify this cheating?' I was the preacher's son on this one. But he had nothing to say." As Monks tells it, Mockler fumbled over his words, remarking in essence that everybody does it. The shareholder activist also objected to Gillette's tactics, including running a full-page newspaper ad a few days before the meeting implying that one of Coniston's foreign investors, Tito Tettamanti, was the person behind the scenes who was really in control.

Coniston lost narrowly, but sued the company for running the ad and won a favorable ruling from a federal judge. Before the judge decided whether to hold a new election, however, Gillette settled the litigation with the group by agreeing to buy back some shares and releasing prospective buyers from agreements they had made not to make a run for the company. (Gillette remains an independent company.) Also at that year's Gillette annual meeting, an anti-greenmail resolution sponsored by Calpers won with 56 percent in favor, the first proposal of its kind to pass. It asked the company not to make such a payment again, and indeed, Gillette did not greenmail Coniston. The investment partnership walked away with about $40 million for its efforts.

ISS's services were also sought by Hollywood producer Burt Sugarman, who was stalking Media General, the family-controlled media company, with a $70 a share bid. Senator Timothy Wirth of Colorado called Minow at ISS. Sugarman was in his office, he told her, and needed help soliciting votes for his takeover offer. The bid failed in the end.

Another assignment later in the year was referred to ISS by Wilcox. While speaking at a seminar in September in Los Angeles, Monks met with Emil Martini, who, with his brother Robert, had founded and continued to control Bergen Brunswig, the New Jersey drug wholesaler. To assure a tranquil transition after their retirement, the Martinis were in the process of doing the reverse of what most corporate leaders were doing at the time: relinquishing control. The brothers were proposing to surrender their Class B stock, which had the right to elect the majority of directors, to the company in exchange for ordinary stock. And they wanted ISS to give a governance opinion to go along with Merrill Lynch's fairness opinion on the value the Martinis would get in the exchange—in time for the shareholders meeting scheduled for January 1989. Monks agreed to do so, and, as in all these cases, did not take a fee.

But ISS's and Monks' most significant accomplishment that year was its advisory work for Calpers. As he became better acquainted with Hanson and Koppes, Monks began contributing some guidance on Calpers' involvement as a nonvoting member of the equity holders' committee in the Texaco bankruptcy case. Texaco had filed for bankruptcy in late 1987. One of the biggest equity holders was corporate raider Carl Icahn, who held a 17 percent stake in the company. In the spring of 1988, Icahn was trying to acquire Texaco in bankruptcy by offering up his own reorganization plan. In fact, he asked Monks to testify in support of his plan, on the basis that the company's reorganization plan eliminated a number of good governance provisions. And Monks complied.

Texaco emerged from bankruptcy that April, under the company's reorganization plan. But shortly afterward, Icahn waged a proxy battle for 5 of Texaco's board seats. His goal: to get enough of his people on the board to support his $14.5 billion takeover bid. As the owner of a voting advisory firm, Monks now had considerable influence on the outcome of the Texaco-Icahn contest. His opinion of Texaco's president and CEO James Kinnear was greatly enhanced by the executive's promise that in return for Calpers' vote—and given a victory against Icahn—it would work with the fund to find a way to give shareholders a say in the selection of directors. Also, Minow was impressed with Kinnear's declaration at a gathering of major investors that all his money was invested in Texaco, proof that he was committed to the company's future. So, despite Monks' earlier testimony for Icahn, ISS recommended that its clients side with management on this one.

Monks penned a letter to several major clients outlining his reasoning. He was hardly complimentary toward Texaco management, pointing out that this was the same management that had wasted shareholders' money by paying greenmail to the Bass Brothers in 1983; acquiring Getty Oil in a way that led to a mega-lawsuit with Pennzoil (which claimed to have agreed to take over Getty first) and resulted in Texaco's bankruptcy filing; engaging in prolonged litigation with Pennzoil before settling for $3 billion; and devoting plentiful resources to fighting off Icahn. On the other hand, Monks wrote, the company faced a much more uncertain fate with an Icahn victory than under current management, given the split board that would result and the raider's vague financing plans for his offer. "So in the final analysis, it comes down to a matter of trust," Monks wrote. One of Monks' major reasons for "trusting" management was Kinnear's willingness to listen to and deal with shareholders. In fact, as a supplement to his letter, Monks sent along a draft of a letter he hoped investors would send to Kinnear, insisting that Texaco follow up on its pledge to provide shareholders with some way to nominate their own candidates to the board. Monks' letter, wrote *Pensions & Investments Age,* "which many institutional investors called thoughtful and convincing, persuaded some large institutional shareholders . . . to line up behind Texaco management." Icahn lost the contest 41 percent to 59 percent.

After management's victory, a meeting with Calpers was set up for August 24 to begin the discussion that Kinnear had promised. Monks went with Koppes, Dale Hanson, and Calpers board member (now CEO) Jim

Burton to the meeting at the company's headquarters in White Plains, New York. "He was great for formulating strategy," Koppes told me in an interview in 1998, explaining the reason for inviting Monks. "We were very new to the corporate world. But Bob had been in the corporate world. He's kind of a pariah. But he knew their mind-set."

But, Monks was too good at that meeting. When the four members of the Calpers contingent arrived at the executive floor reception area, Kinnear himself came in to greet them and lead them to his office—something that immediately impressed Monks. As so often happened in his career, Monks had a connection with Kinnear, because they had gone to the same school—St. Paul's. They exchanged a bit of small talk as they marched through acres of empty desks and past abandoned offices, evidence of the cutbacks brought about by the court penalty and bankruptcy, until finally reaching the corner office. There they met Joe Flom, the New York attorney (from Skadden Arps Meagher & Flom) who was then considered America's premier corporate lawyer. Seeing Flom, Hanson immediately concluded that they were not going to have an easy time selling their notion of greater shareholder participation on the board of directors. Indeed, the well-mannered Kinnear let Flom do much of the talking. The CEO blushed as Flom described him as an important executive who was "giving you his time." In a patronizing tone, the lawyer told the guests it was nice that people like Calpers wanted to be interested in big corporations. Throughout the session, Flom repeatedly dashed out of the room to rejoin, by phone, the board meeting of another client company, leaving the Calpers meeting in an uncomfortable silence for a minute or two.

Through all this, Monks was squirming in his seat, worried that Texaco was taking control of the meeting. Finally, since his then–potential client was not speaking up, Monks jumped in. Using his best salesman's tactics, he described what the huge pension plan wanted to explore with Texaco: to have institutional investors represented on the committee that nominates directors. Monks and Kinnear spoke for some time. By the end of the session, Monks felt that Kinnear was sincere in wanting to find the right answer. It seemed to be a good start.

(After the meeting, Monks was about to return to Portland when Koppes asked him to join them for dinner. He later found out why. When the check came, none of the Calpers folks budged; so he picked it up. As Monks reflected on this years later, after many such meals: "Much can be derived from this small reality: These were people who couldn't afford to buy lunch, but they could make other people very very rich.")

Rather than thanking Monks for asserting Calpers' position, Hanson snubbed him. He was clearly annoyed. "Bob is a terrific salesman. He dominated the meeting," Hanson said years later. "Since we were the shareholders and not Bob, we concluded that he ended up being more of a distraction. That was the last time we took Bob with us to a meeting with a CEO. In fact, that was the last time we took anyone outside Calpers to meet a CEO. We continued to use Bob for advice." Remarked Koppes about that day: "They both had good-sized egos, so it was hard to fit them both in the same room." Koppes phoned Monks to tell him Hanson was peeved, and Monks in turn called Hanson to apologize. Over the years, they became close allies. But Monks remained convinced that he did the right thing by speaking up. "The reason I talked was because Kinnear was talking and the Calpers people were saying absolutely nothing. I think I simply misjudged Dale's comfort level," Monks says.

Jim Burton, who has been Calpers' CEO since 1994, confirms Monks' version of events. "Bob brought his own portfolio and standing as former head of ERISA," Burton says. "It was clear Flom wanted to throw us out. Bob validated our being there. And he was very valuable in the comments he made."

Subsequent meetings that fall between Calpers and Kinnear did not go well. Texaco did not appear willing to give investors any real influence in the director selection process. Calpers needed to do something to get these talks moving. During a phone conversation with Koppes and Hanson that November, during which they were discussing their frustration with the lack of dialogue with Texaco, Monks invented a new type of shareholder resolution that would prove to be important to Calpers in dealing with Texaco and other companies in the future. The idea was to propose a resolution binding on management for an amendment to Texaco's bylaws authorizing a shareholders' advisory committee (SAC) to work with the board of directors. Monks had adapted the idea from the equity committee that Calpers had been on during Texaco's bankruptcy and reorganization. The proposed committee, consisting of representatives of the seven largest shareholders willing to serve, would provide another way for shareholders to express their views to management.

As Monks explains: "This resolution was a way of getting people's attention, putting in something that they couldn't ignore. The SAC had no legal power. It was something the shareholders would elect that would advise the board. It was just a way for shareholders to funnel their opinions." They could have proposed a resolution to repeal Texaco's poison pill; Carl

Icahn still held his position and remained a threat, and so challenging the poison pill could have had dramatic consequences. But Monks believed that that would be unfair to Kinnear. "I had to do something that a guy like Kinnear, who is a very good guy, honorable as hell, would understand was a reasonable resolution," Monks recounts. "Texaco was terrified because, Christ, they had Carl sitting there owning all that stock. The last thing Jim wanted was to have his poison pill go away. We could have gotten a lot of votes for an anti-poison pill resolution, because we could have gotten Carl's vote and some more." Instead, Monks thought up the SAC resolution right there on the phone, while he was sitting in his turret office looking out at the Potomac. And Hanson responded enthusiastically.

Once Monks conceived the resolution, Calpers retained David Martin of Washington law firm Hogan and Hartson to draft it and send it to the SEC for approval. ("Fortunately, PERS has good lawyers, etc. All I have to do is churn out the good ideas. Whoopee!" Monks wrote Dubow on December 5, 1988.) Martin got the resolution vetted by the SEC right before the deadline for Texaco's annual meeting. But, the shareholder group hoped that the resolution would never actually be voted on. The goal was to use the resolution to frighten management into talking seriously about shareholder participation on the board. And indeed, when Kinnear found out about it on December 21 ("a nice Christmas present for Jim Kinnear," Koppes wrote Monks), he phoned Hanson "all agog that we'd do something like this to them," Hanson later recalled. Shortly thereafter, Kinnear began talking more seriously than ever about cooperating with the giant fund. The company offered to nominate to its board someone from Calpers' list of 15 qualified director candidates, and it selected New York University President John Brademas. Monks advised Calpers to drop the SAC resolution and take this offer. The press treated the nomination as a triumph for newly activist institutions. As for Icahn, he sold his stock that June, reaping a $650 million profit on his investment.

To Monks, the settlement was bittersweet. He had begun to think about the shareholders' advisory committee in grand terms as a way for shareholders to monitor companies at no cost to themselves and to voice ongoing concerns. Another day, perhaps. But, even though Calpers negotiated away Monks' resolution, the fund did take a special liking to it. "It became one of our favorite resolutions to introduce to get management to sit down and talk with us," Hanson says. "The SAC resolution was one of the early efforts and one of the more successful things we did to get people to talk to us. No

CEOs would meet us before Kinnear. He became sort of a convert. After he stepped down, he took great pride in the fact that he was one of the first CEOs to meet with the so-called crazies. Texaco was one of our favorites, in that it was our first. Like a first girlfriend. Ultimately we prevailed. In order to be credible, we had to have some victories, and Texaco was the first. That helped build the larger than life reputation Calpers obtained."

By the fall of 1988, ISS was helping Calpers assemble a coherent corporate governance strategy. "We discussed what we thought were the most important corporate governance issues at that time—board independence, executive compensation, takeover defenses," recalls ISS's president and CEO Howard Sherman, who was then research chief. "We recommended both a policy position and an action plan. We recommended that they approach portfolio companies to express their concerns, and offered our assistance all the way from initial communications to the ultimate challenge—filing a shareholder proposal."

Monks was finally beginning to feel a sense of accomplishment, not only that ISS was attracting business but that corporate governance and shareholder activism were becoming accepted as part of the conventional business world. Six "governance centers" had been set up at various universities, and ISS's principals had been involved in some of them. Also, prominent academics and regulators were writing about the area, lending it the aura of legitimacy. "I have really come to the end of the beginning. When you can read Peter Drucker in the *Harvard Business Review* or Lester Thurow in the *Sloan School Report* at the same time as knowing that Chairman [David] Ruder of the SEC is speaking on the subject, one is entitled to believe that corporate governance has become part of the vocabulary and consciousness of business America," he wrote ISS chairman Dubow on October 20. "Indeed, seeing all of these articles reminds me of the feeling of running for office and seeing my bumper stickers on the cars of someone who is neither a relative, employee, or otherwise known to me."

For all its activities and impressive visibility in 1988, ISS was still not turning a dime of profit. It could claim to have some of the leading institutional investors as clients, including Calpers, General Motors, Fidelity, Alliance Capital, Wells Fargo, and TIAA-CREF. ("My best experience," Monks says, "was in the second call on David Williams of Alliance. He said that the materials we provided were helpful. I asked whether it might not be appropriate to pay for them. He said yes. Wow!") But the firm needed more business.

ISS was continuing its effort to become the preeminent resource for institutional investors on corporate governance, from its newsletter to its proxy issue judgments. In its advisory work, it was pushing its evaluations of proxy contests—estimated at about 40 a year—and of corporate and shareholder proposals. These confrontations also created opportunities for the firm to comment publicly on important governance issues such as director qualifications, executive compensation, management and directors' stock ownership, management entrenchment tactics, and shareholder rights. The firm was developing a data base of directors at U.S. companies complete with their performance in various governance areas. This was in line with Monks' conviction that shareholders must focus on directors, that is, hold directors accountable for companies' performance and certain basic issues including executive compensation, takeovers, and other questions of a company's fate, and even selected social issues, such as obedience toward criminal laws. The idea was to use the database internally as a research tool and eventually to offer clients ratings of directors. Corporate profiles and an executive compensation database were also in the works. As Minow observed in her strategy memo for ISS on August 22: "The great thing about dealing with institutional investors is that if information exists, they are virtually obligated to look at it, not just as a matter of competition, but as a matter of fiduciary responsibility. . . . The information we are talking about could change the world." For its best clients—CREF, Calpers, and Fidelity—ISS would continue to assist in choosing targets for shareholder resolutions and often drawing up the resolution itself, arranging meetings between management and shareholders, and advising on proxy voting policies.

But Minow emphasized the importance of ISS remaining objective, putting a rein on Monks' inclination to become more and more involved as a "player" in corporate battles and be paid as such. "There is no way that we can act as an advocate with one hand while we wrap ourselves in the flag of objectivity with the other," she wrote in the strategy memo. "With our record of pounding so hard on the conflicts of interest that impede market forces in the exercise of ownership, we have to be above suspicion. . . . If we are going to pursue advocacy or participation . . . , we could sell off the part of the business that provides services for institutional shareholders as soon as possible."

Besides, there was the concern that regulators would take notice. ISS was already vulnerable in a regulatory context. Back in the spring of 1988, as ISS's client list quickly lengthened and the firm began expanding its services, the small staff had faced a big potential problem. Up until that time, ISS had made sure to get any advisory letters it sent out to clients and investors approved by the SEC. But now, as it became clear that ISS was going to be reporting on proxy statement issues at an increasing number of companies, it would soon become impractical for the little firm to process hundreds of recommendations through the SEC, especially given the agency's torpid response time. Although it seemed logical to Monks and Minow that ISS should be exempt from the filing regulations, there was no clear language granting exemption to this type of proxy advisory service; ISS was the first of its kind.

So Minow, the regulation expert, took it upon herself to compose a polite letter to the office of chief counsel in the SEC division of corporate finance, explaining in detail why ISS believed it was not subject to the proxy statement filing requirements. Essentially, her argument was that ISS was neither the sponsor of shareholder resolutions or dissident slates of directors nor a paid agent of such a sponsor, to whom the regulations were meant to apply. "It is our understanding that firms who provide voting information but who are not the sponsor's agent—like brokerage houses and the Investor Responsibility Research Center—were meant to be exempt," she wrote. Ironically, it took another letter and several months for the SEC to respond, not with an answer but with some questions.

After Minow explained her position further, the agency's counsel wrote back the following: "I remain unable to conclude that the furnishing of proxy voting advice by the company would be exempt from the filing requirements of the Commission's proxy rules." At that point, Minow took the liberty of making an interpretation of that statement, and in turn taking some risk. In her view, the SEC's real concern was that if ISS were exempted, people receiving ISS material would still assume that the SEC had approved the firm's material. So, Minow and Monks decided—without informing the SEC—that ISS would not get SEC approval on most of its advisory letters and instead add a note to its proxy voting recommendations indicating that the contents were not approved by the SEC and reflect just ISS's views. The risk was that the SEC would find ISS in violation of the law, but in Minow's practiced eye, this was a low risk. So ISS went on with its business, filing with the SEC only in the case of a proxy contest.

If ISS were to become a paid principal in activist endeavors, though, the regulators might wake up to such infractions, staff members feared. In any case, Minow in her strategy memo to Monks encouraged him to continue doing what they had been doing as advisers: "Your discovery on viewing the pollution in the river in Maine was, in a way, like Newton's being hit on the head with the apple. I think you have been a true visionary in pointing out that something is wrong with the way that corporations make decisions, and that an unprecedented opportunity exists to do something about it. If what you want is to transform the American economy, minimize agency costs and externalities, and bring about true corporate democracy, . . . there is no greater contribution that we could make than providing a way for the shareholders to hold management accountable. And the best way for us to do that is to provide them with the analytic support and resources necessary to justify actions in their interest."

9

Power Base

He often described to me how he'd tried to do something and failed,
but that there's a need to take risks.

Robert Monks Jr.

L ate in 1988, it looked as if Monks' quest for a financial partner had
finally landed a real prospect. The firm in question was not one that
he had considered until its CEO knocked on his door.

Frank Baxter was the chief executive of Jefferies & Co., which was
Wall Street's second most maverick brokerage firm after Drexel Burnham
Lambert. Jefferies, a small firm with some 550 employees and $12.5 mil-
lion in profits, did such nonestablishment things as discreetly accumulate
and dispose of large blocks of stock after New York Stock Exchange trading
hours—often for some of the most notorious corporate raiders of the era.
Its reputation was besmirched in 1987 by the legal complications of its
founder, Boyd Jefferies. That year he admitted to parking stock for arbitrageur Ivan Boesky among other violations; in return for his cooperation
with ongoing investigations, the government pledged not to bring charges
against the firm. The sandy-haired Baxter took over as CEO.

After 1988's raucous proxy season, Baxter began thinking that the culmination of the big takeover movement of the 1980s was going to be that
the ultimate owners, the institutional investors, were going to start being
much more proactive. After all, they now had $2.2 trillion in assets and
owned 50 percent of the shares traded on the New York Stock Exchange and
65 percent of the Standard & Poor's 500 stocks.[1] Plus, throughout the 1980s
the institutional holders had sold out to LBO artists like Kohlberg, Kravis,
Roberts & Co., making a nice profit, but allowing the buyers to make much

more because they had acquired control—and the institutions were just beginning to realize what they had given up by selling out. If his theory was correct, Baxter reasoned, Jefferies was in a good position to take full advantage of this development. Since it did not have a well-established corporate finance department serving lots of big U.S. companies, it had little business to lose. The firm could afford to represent proactive institutional investors in helping to link them up with company managements who want to develop a stable, long-term relationship with their owners.

Just as Baxter was starting to consider this opportunity, the September 12, 1988, *Fortune* magazine landed on his desk, and one of the feature stories was about the new assertiveness of institutional investors. Along with the story ran a sidebar about ERISA, accompanied by a photo of Bob Monks. The text identified Monks' role at ISS and expressed his views that pension funds "have no business being anything but long-term holders of securities and that CEOs should demand that their own funds' investment managers meet that obligation." What that means, he was quoted saying, is "a cooperative long-term arrangement between managers and owners." At once, Baxter picked up the phone to call Monks. "I told him that it looked as though we could have a similar agenda," he recalls. "I went to Washington, we had lunch, and found we not only had similar agendas but in many ways similar values."

Monks was at that very moment working on a speech to the National Association of Corporate Directors that bemoaned institutional investors' willingness to relinquish the "control premium" or what he defined as "the value that accompanies control" of a corporation.[2] First, he said, they gave it to management who used it to increase their own pay beyond what they were worth or to entrench themselves through by-law and charter provisions such as poison pills, but not to increase the overall value of the corporation; and then they gave it up to entrepreneurial buyout artists—raiders or the managers themselves—who would buy the company using lots of debt and proceed to restructure it, raise the stock's value, and make a fortune. In the speech, which he delivered on October 25, Monks put forward the still radical notion that institutional investors as fiduciaries have a legal obligation to become more actively involved as controlling owners in overseeing their properties "in order to avoid losing money for their trust beneficiary." The reason they were not more involved, he said, was, one, their conflicts of interest (which Monks hoped the Labor Department's new enforcement efforts would begin to solve), and, two, the reality that an institutional investor who chooses to take action must shoulder the entire cost of that action, while any resulting gains are shared by all the other shareholders who take on no cost. There was, in other words, no effective means of taking collective action. But perhaps Jefferies offered one way. By working together, Jefferies could use ISS to help it get business from state pension funds by offering them ISS's services; ISS could then help the funds forge links with corporate managements.

To Monks, Baxter's call was one of the first concrete results of his and Minow's press strategy—which was, in essence, talk to any reporter who calls. "I think we return every phone call we ever get from a journalist; we realized that we would live and die on the financial press," he says. "The reason was that we were trying to do something new and we simply had to make ourselves known." Before too long, Baxter asked Monks to consider joining the Jefferies board. Monks was intrigued. After seven years out of the financial services industry, it was tempting to dive back in and familiarize himself with the new people, products, and language of the field. And he thought that Jefferies, as it developed a new business based on institutions' increasingly assertive role at corporations, would provide a conduit for him to reach institutions that was much more effective than his own Lone Ranger style.

He would not join Jefferies' board and invest in its stock until February 1989. But after meeting Baxter, he quickly formed a relationship and friendship with him. Over time, the connection with Jefferies proved to be vital in his and—as he saw it—the movement's evolution, although not in the way Baxter initially envisioned. Instead of providing a link to institutions, Jefferies introduced Monks to two individual investors—some might say corporate raiders—who found they could use someone like Monks at just the point he found he could use someone like them. The two men were the financiers Richard Rainwater and Harold Simmons.

That fall of 1988, Baxter invited Rainwater to speak at a Jefferies sales meeting in Dallas and asked Monks to come along as well. Rainwater had made a fortune crafting deals for the Bass Brothers of Fort Worth by buying into such operations as the Walt Disney Company, Prime Computer, and Texaco. (Ironically, the latter investment resulted in Texaco's payment of greenmail to the Bass Brothers, which led California Treasurer Jesse Unruh, with Monks' encouragement, to found the Council of Institutional Investors.) In 1985, Rainwater struck out on his own and began doing deals in the energy and health care industries with the likes of record producer

David Geffen, the Equitable Life Assurance Company and, for a while, the Basses. As he got to know Rainwater, Monks grew to like him and was taken with his energetic operating style: "You would be sitting there and the phone would ring and it would be Richard Rainwater and 23 other people on some call he had going, and he would want to talk to you about something. He collected people, ex-CEOs, whoever."

Over the ensuing weeks and months, Monks and Rainwater talked about combining forces, along with Jefferies, to provide "active shareholder services."[3] One possibility was to start small by choosing a company that Rainwater felt was, in his words, "poised" for change and whose management may be interested in working with a group of active shareholders. Then Monks would ask his biggest clients to get involved. Another option was to form an investment fund in which the participating pension funds and other institutions would invest in the interest of either one target at a time or several at once. To Monks, this vehicle would provide activists and other institutions with a means of taking "collective action at reasonable cost." ISS would gather the institutions; Rainwater would identify the targets and be the point man in dealings with management; Jefferies would provide marketing, administration, and other services. Unlike Lazard Frères & Co.'s just announced "white squire fund" meant to be friendly to corporations that were under or potentially under siege, this "collective shareholder" fund would represent the institutional owners, not the managements.[4] Monks' idea would someday become his own Lens fund—sans Rainwater and Jefferies. Monks had already discussed the legality of such an arrangement with his friends at the Labor Department, Mort Klevan and Alan Lebowitz. But for a long time, he hoped in some way to link such a new fund with other powerful forces.

At the time of his initial contacts with Rainwater, late 1988 into 1989, ISS had several other pots boiling. Monks had commenced discussions with proxy solicitors Georgeson and some trust banks on a different, less ambitious joint venture to sell two services. One, called the annual proxy audit, would review and evaluate a plan sponsor's proxy voting policies and practices to determine whether they met legal requirements. The other service, proxy support, would help clients implement a system allowing them to vote all their proxies and document those votes. In the interest of the latter program, Howard Sherman, who had joined ISS in April 1988 to oversee its research, and Minow were then hard at work on a proxy manual to be completed by year-end; it was to be a definitive compilation of past practice and ISS recommendations with respect to all subjects that had come up at annual meetings over the past decade. The manual would provide the basic information companies would need in voting their proxies, supplemented by the advice that ISS would provide on specific proxy contests and merger proposals. By 1998, the manual was in its fourth edition and included such features as a proprietary model that values executive compensation proposals.

Intensive marketing would soon begin involving mailings, telemarketing, and follow-up visits by ISS principals ("It has been our view that one cannot sell [the] product over the phone or by mail; human intervention will be necessary," Monks wrote Dubow). Their timing would be good, because the 1989 proxy season was imminent, and —as Monks learned from his contacts with DOL's pensions administrator, David Walker—the Labor Department would be issuing its enforcement report from the previous year's investigation of proxy voting practices of pension fund investment managers. The report revealed that many managers did not know who was responsible for casting the votes and were not sure if the proxies were being voted at all; it reiterated the DOL's previous pronouncement that fiduciaries need to vote the proxies, set policies and procedures for proxy voting, take no direction on votes from anyone, keep good records, and weigh the issues carefully. Monks and ISS planned to take full advantage of this situation; in fact, a telemarketing script drawn up for the firm specified, "We now want to stress his or her potential liability under the DOL's new announcement and get him or her to accept our basic package on a 30-day free trial basis."

Monks recognized that as dull and time consuming as this consulting/proxy analysis side of his work was (especially for an impatient man who had shown that he liked to move on to new career challenges, if not entirely new careers, every few years), it was essential as a basis for building credibility; it would, among other things, allow him eventually to operate some kind of an activist investment fund. Besides, the consulting work already had given ISS an immeasurable amount of clout in proxy contests—and in turn, as he saw it, in corporate America—simply by bringing a growing number of big institutions together in the same place. These institutions were not purposefully making a statement as a group. But, they might as well have been since, as ISS clients, they were all paying for voting recommendations based on a consistent policy. As Monks wrote his board members in a November 30, 1988, memo:

Through the relationships developed in marketing and providing consulting services, ISS, in fact, can have strong influence on substantial voting blocks. What is perhaps more important is that ISS is *perceived* as having greater power than it actually has. . . . ISS' ideological and business objective has been to demonstrate the increased value produced through the effective involvement of ownership and its capacity to hold management accountable. With the development of a "real" and an "apparent" capacity to "deliver" institutional votes, ISS has taken an important step forward towards achieving its objectives. To the extent that ISS can devise a structure for effectively marshalling ownership (i.e., an investment management fund), it will thereby be enhancing the value of the underlying stock. . . . While we are selling a needed proxy product, we are, thereby, putting ourselves into a position to provide one yet more valuable. Each client supplies us not only with a cash fee; they also provide unique access to votes respecting all the companies in their portfolios. We are paid for giving recommendations; we are gradually getting ourselves into a position to provide results. We have gotten to the point at which our clients *are, and are perceived to be, the dominant voting factor in most close corporate contests.*

To have such influence was a dream of Monks, a desire that certainly lay behind his quests to become a U.S. senator. Surely, at this stage he did have the kind of power he articulates here. Whether he had as much clout as he says is questionable, but he may well have. Many in the field have repeatedly credited Monks and ISS with having had an enormous impact on the corporate governance/shareholder activism movement, but often in a behind-the-scenes way. He himself says he made a point of not taking public credit for accomplishments in the field, especially high visibility situations like proxy contests—in part so as not to give any potential clients reasons to reject ISS out of hand. The firms' principals tended to give credit for resolution victories to the sponsoring public plan or the Council of Institutional Investors.[5] But ISS's visibility and power would inevitably grow. In 1997, two industry conferences—those of the American Bar Association and the National Association of Corporate Directors—featured panels entitled, "Does ISS have too much power?"

In late 1988, the firm was involved in making what it viewed as a pivotal recommendation in the Bergen Brunswig situation—the one in which the Martinis wanted to give up control. ISS came out in favor of management's plan to change from dual-class capitalization, in which a private, B class held by the Martinis possessed control, to single-class capitalization, in which all stock was common stock equivalent to the existing A stock. This would be accomplished through an exchange of the B shares for newly issued A, or common, shares. Monks was particularly enamored of this assignment, not only because he was such a fervent advocate of one share, one vote, but also because the value placed on the exchange was going to represent the actual value of corporate control. "It is this value that is the subject of hostile takeovers and that is lost by institutional inactivity," he wrote his directors at the end of December. "Now that we can place an exact number on it, we can be persuasive in costing inactivity." Many analysts and institutional shareholders had publicly come out against the proposal, saying the Martinis would be charging class A shareholders too high a price to acquire control, at 9.5 A shares for each B share. But ISS took the stand that given the outrageous sums that outsiders were paying to acquire control of companies, the class A shareholders were looking at a bargain. "I cannot recall another situation in which controlling shareholders gave up control, at any price!" (except by selling the entire company), Monks further explained his opinion.[6]

Monks and his staff actively solicited votes in favor of the Martinis' plan. They sent letters and then hit the phones, in some cases supplementing the calls the Martinis themselves had made to big investors. Some of the people Monks contacted were outspoken about their frustration regarding the proxy system itself—"how management has effective control over the voting process and the proxy machinery, and the 'joke' of the director nomination and election process," Monks related.

Given the heated disagreement over the Bergen-Brunswig matter, Monks wrote his directors, "A strong affirmative vote will strongly reinforce the perception of ISS' 'power.'"[7] And there was a strong affirmative vote—60 to 40 in favor of the Martinis' plan. Although it is difficult to draw absolute conclusions about the result's effect on the perception of ISS's power, there had to be some positive impact. As Monks reported to his board: "Many of our clients voted against our recommendation, but enough went along that our efforts are seen as the margin of victory."[8] One investor in particular, Roland Machold, director of the state of New Jersey's pension system, who voted against the Martinis' plan, confirmed the point about ISS's role when he told Monks, "You cost us money."

Again, as it had done with Coniston, ISS accepted no compensation from the Martinis for having done the work they requested—explaining that ISS only accepted payment from its institutional investor clientele. But Monks did, some time in 1989, ask Emil Martini if he would contribute to a governance center that was being set up at the University of California at

Berkeley. Martini, Monks says, "was very correct, acknowledged that he owed us something, and made a contribution."

By early 1989, Monks was engrossed in another matter that had surfaced early in December. Shearson Lehman Hutton (owned by American Express) had dreamed up a product that would involve offering shareholders three "unbundled stock units" in exchange for common stock, and four companies were eager to be the first ones on the block with these so-called USUs. Sara Lee Corp., Pfizer Inc., American Express Co., and Dow Chemical Co. were going to convert 6 percent to 20 percent of their stock into the new units. None of the USUs would contain the right to vote; that would simply vanish, along with any assumed value. In essence, shareholders would be asked to give up their proxy votes and thereby give up control. Needless to say, the whole idea was distasteful to Monks. And he phoned the author of the concept—Shearson banker Ron Gallatin—to tell him so. Apparently aware that Monks was a former director of Shearson American Express (after the sale of The Boston Company), Gallatin was more than cordial. Since Monks was coming to New York the next week for a sales appointment, Gallatin asked if he would like to discuss the matter on the way into town from the airport.

That day, Monks got up at 5 A.M. to catch the flight to New York. The Shearson managing director picked Monks up at LaGuardia Airport in a stretch limousine. The two men proceeded to disagree, politely, all the way into midtown. Gallatin impressed Monks as clearly ingenious but seemingly without any concern for the long-term consequences of his idea. He knew the banker was bewildered by him. "He couldn't figure me out. What did I want?" Monks later recounted. When the limo reached midtown, Monks thanked Gallatin and hurried in to meet his potential client, only to find that he had been stood up.

Monks planned to challenge Shearson on the USUs at the SEC, which was then reviewing both the prospective uses for the offerings and a NYSE proposal to exempt the newfangled securities from its one-share, one-vote rule that ISS had fought to preserve. Monks, always thinking of that money and mission double helix, had bigger plans as well that included an opportunity for ISS to make a buck. If this was such a good idea, as the market and some major corporations appeared to think, he could make it even better by curing the voting problem. He went to competing Wall Street firms with a proposal to redesign the concept so that it would incorporate the vote. If an investment bank could sell the idea to corporations, Monks reasoned, ISS would make a cut of the underwriting fee. Sounding as if ISS was a proud David to the mean old Shearson Goliath, Monks wrote his board at year-end 1988:

> In my view, Shearson has made the judgement that they can roll right over ISS on this offering; our strategy is, first, to cause them delay; second, the need to [have them] explain why they have eliminated the vote; and finally, the need to amend. In the meanwhile, we ought to be able to make arrangements with other underwriters. . . . We are trying to establish between our market (and government regulatory) power the ability to determine what securities are acceptable and which are not.

Within a couple of weeks, Monks had written detailed objections to the proposals to Shearson, ISS clients, SEC commissioners, Congressman William Clay, chairman of the Committee on Education and Labor, and the directors of the four companies involved. He followed up by arranging meetings with five SEC commissioners. Four of the five commissioners told him that they would like to see voting rights attached to the USUs. Picking up on the issue, ISS's most important client, Calpers, composed a letter to the SEC detailing the reasons for its opposition to the Shearson offering and also asked all of its fund management firms to state their position on the new securities. By February, Monks was being recognized in the national business media as the primary force opposing the USUs. "Our sense has been that we can demonstrate governance concerns relate directly to economic value; and ISS is the principal expert in the field of governance," Monks wrote his board. "ISS must lead in defining the new field of governance. (Indeed, it may be only an immodest overstatement to recognize that this activity was the essential factor in the *creation* of the field.)"

Before long, Shearson, in need of some heavyweight marketing support, convinced Goldman, Sachs & Co. to join as co-underwriter of the USU offerings and bring in more institutions to buy the product. Monks called his best contact at Goldman, Jun Makihara, Ben Makihara's son, who agreed that the voting problem should and could be worked out. In the end, however, the SEC refused to go along—because of both accounting and voting rights problems—and the USU, in any form, could not fly.

Monks had not lost sight of his original inspiration for getting into the corporate governance area: the moral problem posed by companies that harm society, whether by pollution or other means. In this vein, he and Minow in 1988 launched an effort to motivate shareholders to reduce corporate crime. Their position was that companies were getting away with major offenses such as defense procurement fraud or pollution because in most cases the costs were relatively low compared with the gains. Fines were affordable and executives rarely went to jail. But they also held that criminal activity hurt shareholders, who had to pay for both the defense and—as taxpayers—the prosecution; often suffered a loss in value if the crime affected the company's reputation and in turn its market share; and might face less potential gain if the company loses the goodwill of government and society.

The ISS solution was to develop shareholder resolutions—binding on management if passed—proposing that companies adopt the following by-law: any director who is convicted of a felony in connection with his or her service as a director, or any director serving at a time when the corporation is convicted of an "extraordinary" crime, should become ineligible for service on the board, unless that person had voted against the conduct leading to the conviction. The notion, as Monks stated in a letter about the idea to Exxon, was that "the directors take full responsibility, to assure that all constituencies know that from top to bottom people have their jobs on the line."[9] The proposed rules would provide incentives for directors—who, the assumption was, want to continue serving as directors—to create systems that would minimize or reduce criminal activity of any kind. In Monks' interpretation of pension fund fiduciary responsibility toward beneficiaries "who want to retire in a country that is among other things law abiding,"[10] the funds should vote for such a resolution; no doubt ISS would recommend they do so.

To help ISS draft a proposed by-law to "diseligibilize" directors, Monks hired attorney William Weld, whom he had met through Massachusetts Republican politics in the late 1970s. Weld had just resigned as chief of the criminal division of the Justice Department in protest of what he saw as Attorney General Edwin Meese's loose ethical standards. Later Weld became governor of Massachusetts. (Years later, Monks said of Weld, "He appears to have the same kind of priorities that I do, many of the same drives that occasionally end up in short term failure—his nomination to be Ambassador to Mexico and my various efforts to get elected." After Weld resigned as governor in 1997 to fight for his nomination and that nomination was blocked by Senator Jesse Helms in a dramatic standoff, Monks sent him a dozen roses and offered his services as "private sector career counselor" again.) For ISS, Weld drew up proposed by-laws for specific industries including defense, manufacturing, mining, food and drug, and automobile, as well as one addressing environmental dumping.

While publishing articles and communicating with Calpers and CREF on this issue during the fall of 1988, Monks sent letters forwarding the proposal to about 50 big companies. The idea was first to ask the companies to adopt the by-law and, if rejected, then develop the resolutions. In one missive to Exxon Corp.'s then CEO and Chairman, Lawrence G. Rawl, sent on October 26, 1988, Monks pointed out that ISS clients who held Exxon stock "have expressed serious concerns about your commitment to compliance with the law. . . . They are long-term investors; they would prefer not to sell out because of their concerns, especially since they believe that your poor record has depressed the stock. The alternative, then, is to work with you to improve value." The alternative Monks proposed was for the board to adopt the by-law. The reaction to the letters, he told ISS directors, was "sulphurous." [sic] In Exxon's case, the assistant treasurer, Alan Harrison, called Monks, challenging him to cite cases of Exxon's criminal conduct and where it had affected the stock. Irate, he went so far as to call Monks a "son of a bitch," Monks reported to his board. "Such would not seem to auger well for ISS sales in that direction. In the long run, we stand to establish great credibility for having asserted the determination of owners to require that their corporations conduct their affairs within the framework legislated by society."[11]

In response to the call from Harrison, a few months later Monks wrote back to make one citation—a $2 billion judgment against the oil company for overcharging customers for oil from a Texas field. The verdict and amount were upheld by the U.S. Supreme Court in early 1986. He never heard from Exxon on this topic again. But it was only a couple months later, in April 1989, that the Exxon tanker *Valdez* ran aground in Alaska and leaked 11 million gallons of oil into Prince William Sound. A federal court in Alaska ruled in 1994 that Exxon should pay $5.06 billion to fishermen and other Alaskans; appeals are ongoing. Shortly after the accident, New York City's pension fund asked Exxon to name an environmentalist to its board and set up a separate board committee to deal with public issues to prevent similar tragedies in the future, and Exxon complied. The following year, other funds also insisted that the company take steps to prevent another disaster.

In December, Monks' groundbreaking ideas began to get some publicity after he testified before the U.S. Sentencing Commission, which was holding hearings on developing mandatory guidelines for federal courts on sanctions for corporations convicted of federal crimes. Monks' suggestion of a bylaw amendment was well received by the panel, which asked him to draw up proposed formal guidelines based on the idea. With Weld's help, they did so. ISS's proposed guidelines instructed judges to consider the extent to which a company had adopted effective internal governance mechanisms, including the diseligibility bylaw, in deciding the severity of penalties. The notion that sentences be mitigated by a corporation's internal regulation was included in the Commission's final report—though there was nothing specifying diseligibilizing directors.

So Monks forged ahead with his plan. Calpers was interested in following up on his efforts by writing to 10 companies and asking them to adopt the bylaw. If that did not happen, then Calpers said it would sponsor resolutions in 1990. However, both the fund's and ISS's enthusiasm for the project petered out over the coming months as it became clear that investors, and crucially the press, just were not fired up by this challenge. "In many ways, we could [only] do things that the press picked up on," Monks explains. One problem, he says, was, "It sounded too much like a social and a moral concern," and for that reason the press was not interested. "I had to be careful I didn't get my messages confused. We said it's not a winner." And given ISS's limited resources, it could not afford to fight losing battles. As Monks later quipped: "It was one of those cases where the dog just didn't eat the dog food."[12]

As a postscript to this episode, however, there is little doubt that Monks' work on sentencing guidelines has influenced major cases—and in turn perhaps persuaded corporations to implement internal controls. Take the case of Louisiana Pacific Corp. In May 1998, the forest products company pleaded guilty to criminal violations of the Clean Air Act and agreed to pay $37 million in fines. Under the law, it could have been fined nearly triple that amount. But the federal judge in the case took into consideration that the company had "put in place numerous and meaningful measures addressing conduct at the company." Notably, though, five of the nine existing directors were on the board at the time of the violations.[13]

Busy as Monks was, he made himself busier by lunching with Washington power elite, taking on speaking engagements, writing articles, and giving testimony. Minow was also writing articles and going out on the speaking circuit. Keeping ISS's name visible to the press and the other powers that be was critical, Monks thought, to the success of its business and its cause. "Testifying and being published gives ISS a kind of credibility and near "official" status that is very valuable in dealings with government agencies," he wrote to Dubow. And that image was essential if ISS were to effectively pressure government agencies to continue clarifying the fiduciary duty that money managers as equity investors had to behave like owners of corporations. What that meant was that Monks spent some of his time taking Labor Department people out to lunch, and meeting with officials from other agencies that had jurisdiction over asset managers, pension funds, other institutional investors, and trustee banks, such as the SEC, the Office of the Comptroller of the Currency, and the IRS—all of which had either taken action to or expressed interest in taking action to enforce fiduciaries' voting obligations.

All along, Monks continued to toy with the notion of running a proactive investment fund. While continuing discussions with Jefferies, he also began mentioning the idea to others—in fact, anyone who showed a modicum of interest such as the brokerage firms Goldman Sachs and Lazard Frères, and even the New Jersey state pension system. In early December, Monks met with Roland Machold, head of the New Jersey pension system and one of the leaders of the Council of Institutional Investors, to sound him out about working together on an activist fund. "You are a good candidate," he wrote Machold on December 5 before meeting him, "because of owning over 5 percent in 21 different companies. How can you assure that the power of your ownership position is asserted in such a way as to enhance the value of the holding? If you believe, as do I, and apparently Graham and Dodd, that effective shareholder involvement is linearly connected with enhanced values, you must be concerned as to how to organize yourself to be effectively involved." Machold was intrigued. They agreed that Monks would meet with the fund's board that March to discuss the idea that he would be an investor in just those companies in which New Jersey's fund had at least a 4 percent interest. His compensation would be based on the value he could add to those investments. Nothing came of this initiative.

Meanwhile, Monks and Baxter sought the advice of former SEC Commissioner Al Sommer on the feasibility of jointly running a fund. For years, Monks and Sommer, then working as a lawyer, would meet on a regular basis to discuss their mutual interest in corporate governance issues. Sommer told them that he did not think they would run into any insuperable legal problems in pursuing the venture. "We all decided that it would be well to start off by working with a specific target company, identify its institutional investors, and attempt to get them to make common cause with us," Monks reported to his board at the end of December.

One day early in April 1989, while Monks was attending an investment conference, he got a call from Rainwater. "Come on down to Fort Worth. I want to talk to you about something," was all he said, Monks recounts. He flew to Texas and went to Rainwater's headquarters, where he was impressed by the openness in the design—the airy feeling created by glass walls separating the offices and the huge white blackboards that aided the process of continuous brainstorming. There he met with Rainwater and one of the many young gifted investors he was mentoring, Edward Lampert, a tough-minded former arbitrageur at Goldman Sachs & Co. who impressed Monks as "pure aggression." Lampert had met Rainwater, another Goldman alumnus, while vacationing on Nantucket and was inspired to leave Wall Street to start his own fund investing in undervalued stocks. So at the ripe old age of 26, Lampert was running North American Partners, and Rainwater and some of his friends—including record producer David Geffen—had invested in it. It turned out that NAP had a sizable investment of about $100 million in Honeywell, the Minneapolis-based maker of electronic control systems for buildings, industry, and aircraft. The company was not looking well, having sustained a $435 million loss in 1988, and that after four reorganizations in four years.[14]

Seeing itself suddenly vulnerable to a takeover, on March 23, Honeywell proposed two defenses—one to stagger the election of directors and so prevent its board from being replaced all at once, and the other to require that shareholder actions be taken only at shareholder meetings called by management and not by written consent. The company had already denied the shareholders' right to call a special meeting themselves. The proposals were to be voted on at the company's annual meeting on May 5. Lampert and Rainwater wanted to sink the proposals to keep the company feeling susceptible to takeover and demonstrate the unhappiness of its shareholders. They would then be able to get management to listen to their ideas for reorganizing the company. Since NAP held only about 3 percent of the stock and wasn't interested in buying control, they needed help. Monks' role would be to persuade the company's institutional shareholders, many of whom knew him and were clients, to vote against management's resolutions. If they could keep the vote below 50 percent of the outstanding shares, they would win.

Monks took the challenge—not because this was an issue so vital to shareholder rights and corporate governance, but because here was a battle that looked fairly easy to win. Honeywell was 70 percent institutionally owned and the activist ringleader, Rainwater, was a celebrated financier.

"What I needed to do was to up the visibility of shareholder activism and its efficacy," Monks recalls. Working behind the scenes for someone with the stellar reputation of Rainwater was made to order. "I couldn't work for most of those guys (corporate raiders) because they were basically thought of as being schmucks. What I was trying to do was to use the energy of other people's money as a way of escalating the awareness of ISS and of our cause. But I couldn't do it in such a way that it escalated the awareness of people who then said, 'Now I see it and I don't like it because of the people involved.' I had to be very careful." And given what he knew about Rainwater plus his confidence in Baxter who had introduced them, Monks felt that there was no danger and much to be gained in going with Rainwater and his cohorts. "I felt that Richard Rainwater was a first class guy, and I was willing to bet the business that he wasn't a schmuck. He is hugely creative. He is the outstanding entrepreneur of my acquaintance."

Minow was also taken with him. "We had a great meeting with him and his people in Washington," she relates. "They came into our office, and I can't tell you how thrilling it was to hear somebody speak our language. We'd been talking for such a long time in a world where no one seemed to hear a word we said. And somebody came in and said, 'Well, shareholders are important and managers shouldn't be allowed to get away with murder.' And we were just so thrilled. It was like a drop of water in the desert. We said, 'Yeah we know that, we know that, and we can do this for you and we can do that for you.'"

Rainwater was not directly involved in the effort. After having made the introductions, he let Lampert do the work; it was after all his fund. But in the press and in Monks' talks with investors, Rainwater was associated with the challenge to Honeywell throughout the episode. And in Monks' mind, Rainwater was the the man calling the shots, especially about ISS's involvement. Monks suspected that Lampert was trying to exclude him from the action; the shareholder activist would be participating in a meeting and figure out from what was being said that he hadn't been invited to a previous meeting. "Eddie kept trying to keep me out of the deal," Monks says. "He had nothing against me; he simply couldn't see involving anyone who wasn't doing him, personally, any good. Rainwater would periodically 'recreate' me as a participant."[15] Reportedly, it was Lampert's craving for control at NAP that led to his split with Rainwater the following year.[16]

Monks and Minow made sure that there would be no conflict of interest for ISS in taking on this assignment. After a great deal of discussion, they decided that ISS's key role was to work on behalf of its clients who owned stock in Honeywell. Therefore, they would accept no payment from the Rainwater-Lampert aggressors for work on their behalf. "The proposition of not being paid by Richard was important to us," Monks says. "To this day we have never been paid by anybody but the stockholders for anything."

From the start, Monks was determined to make Honeywell the shareholders' first absolute victory trouncing a proposed corporate antitakeover device—as opposed to a victory on a shareholder resolution urging but not requiring management to make a change. And in claiming this trophy, he knew that the shareholders would really be accomplishing much more; for their vote would serve to inform management that they did not support its business strategy. But how to win with so little time? First of all, he would do what Georgeson's Wilcox had pointed out that institutional investors generally had failed to do: make an all-out effort to win by hiring a major proxy solicitation firm. And so, Monks hired Georgeson to help ISS. "Most people wouldn't touch us because they didn't want to get on the wrong side of Honeywell, since they might get hired by Honeywell, and Honeywell was a better hirer than we were," Monks says. "But John said fine. He was willing to play with us whenever Georgeson didn't have a conflict of interest. And he was glad to get into this argument. So we actually had, for the first time, the ability to demonstrate what a professionally conducted proxy effort could do in opposition to management." Proxy solicitation firms do not really solicit votes in a contest; they assemble a profile of a company's shareholders, seek out those in charge of the voting, coordinate with the protagonists, and collect and count ballots. While these are major tasks, it still left Monks and Lampert to do most of the soliciting themselves. And they did not have much time.

At once, Monks began recruiting institutional backing. He approached two of his most supportive fund officials, Hanson of Calpers, owner of about 1 percent of Honeywell, and Abbott Leban, chief counsel to the Pennsylvania Public School Employees' Retirement System, with less than a 1 percent stake. Monks had met Leban at a number of investment conferences, and the two men agreed that it was time for his fund and others to begin working with managements for change. After making sure that Rainwater and Lampert were people they would want to be associated with, the two state funds publicly backed the effort. Not that their tiny portion of stock was going to win the day. But, later, as Monks went around to other institutions, he would be able to say that these two hulking, highly respected funds endorsed this aggressive campaign. And that is what he did. The two funds themselves did not have to lift a finger. "ISS's ability to marshall two state funds legitimated us and legitimated the Lampert/Rainwater effort," Monks explains. "This made it clear that not just a bunch of activists, nor a bunch of greedy bastards, but real institutions with real beneficiaries were concerned in this matter. This was a first. It was a hugely important step."

Moreover, now that they had assembled an impressive stockholder group—composed of NAP, ISS, and the two pension funds—Monks and Lampert could approach the company with a measure of bargaining clout. On April 9, a few days after Honeywell's proxy material announcing the proposals had been approved and released, Monks and Rainwater phoned company president and CEO Dr. James Renier. They expressed their concerns about the company's performance and asked him politely to drop the proposals and meet with them to discuss ways to improve the stock price. The answer was no. As the shareholders' response, Monks told his associate Howard Sherman to deliver the Lampert/ISS proxy material to the SEC for clearance. Their message in the material was as follows: "The stockholder group . . . believes that these measures may eliminate important rights to influence or change management currently available to the stockholders. We recommend a vote AGAINST these proposals." The battle was on.

Before the dissidents could start canvassing for votes, they needed the SEC's okay on the proxy material. While waiting, they compiled a list of contacts and phone numbers. Then they waited some more. Sherman tells this story: "At one point Bob was impatient with the commission; they weren't clearing our material as fast as he would have liked. So he told me to go down to the commission and get it cleared. I'm not a lawyer, so I didn't know whether this was appropriate or not. But he's my boss. Somehow I managed to convince the security guards that I had business on the 5th floor. I went up there, and I found the people who were clearing proxy filings, and I said, 'I'm here to see if I could accelerate clearing our proxy material.' And they looked at me like, 'Who are you? How did you get up here? Nobody comes up here. Get out of here.' I left. We got it cleared." The word came at 4 P.M. on Friday, April 28, only seven days before the meeting.

At 4:01 P.M., the fax machines at Georgeson were smoking as they transmitted the proxy material to many of Honeywell's institutional investors and a news release to the press. Trading volume in Honeywell's stock soared that day to double the normal 250,000 shares, and the stock shot up 2.3 percent. On Monday, Monks, Lampert, Sherman, and the Georgeson team hit the phones and began working their way down a list of 300-odd names. Many of those they contacted seemed friendly. That is because over the past several months, Monks had been collecting institutions' voting policies, written after the Labor Department, in its February 1988 Avon letter and subsequent statements, obligated funds to set down policies on how they generally would vote on specific governance issues. The institutions that opposed staggered boards landed on Monks' call list. To Monks, the calls had two purposes—ostensibly to get votes against Honeywell, but also to make more contacts in the investment world to help build ISS's business base.

The crucial first contacts were made by Monks and Lampert. Sherman spent the week in New York, working out of Georgeson's office as the liaison between Monks, Lampert, ISS, and the California and Pennsylvania pension funds. As Sherman relates: "I would be on the phone to tell Bob, 'We contacted 20 of the top 50 today. Five will go our way. I think you need to call others to follow up.'"

On the day of the annual meeting, Monks, Sherman, and Wilcox met in Minneapolis's Orchestra Hall. Lampert addressed the crowd of about 600, explaining his position on the proposals and denying any interest in taking over the company. Monks briefly spoke as well, directing his remarks to the board members. The vote was too close to call. After the meeting, Monks and Lampert stepped to the front of the hall to confront CEO Renier. "We looked the guy in the eye and said we thought he ought to contract the size of the company" to increase its share value, Monks recalls.

It wasn't until a week later that the company announced that the dissidents had won. Although the proposals won the support of more than half of the shares that were voted, they fell short when measured by shares outstanding—which was the official yardstick. The company only got 46.6 percent on the staggered board proposal and 43.4 percent on the elimination of shareholders' ability to act other than at company-called meetings. (Some 80 percent of outstanding shares were voted.) That day Honeywell's stock jumped more than 2 percent. The ISS staff was ecstatic. Says Monks: "They got more than we did. Only 29.5 percent of shares outstanding were voted against the staggered board and 32.6 percent against the other proposal. But you never saw that. You saw that they weren't successful, because we kept them from getting 50 percent." To Monks, and others, the victory set a clear precedent. "The paper said, "Insurgents Win." Insurgents only used to win through takeovers," Monks says. "But we were winning as the owners." As the press reported, what was intimidating to corporate America was the idea that individual investors owning just a fraction of a company's stock could wage a successful attack by joining forces with the powerful institutions.

Now the shareholders wanted Honeywell to make some dramatic changes. A week or so after the victory was announced, Rainwater invited Monks to Minneapolis to meet with Honeywell's management at a local business club, along with himself, Lampert, and Dale Hanson. Monks says that he planned to urge the company's management to sell off assets and buy back stock. The day of the meeting, he flew into town early so he could go to General Mills' headquarters for lunch with CEO Bruce Atwater, a prominent figure on the Business Roundtable and one of the most vocal corporate critics of shareholder activism. Atwater didn't show, but Monks had a long argument over the subject with the CEO's lawyer. When Monks arrived at the downtown club for the Honeywell session, he sat down to wait for the others. Soon, Rainwater appeared, only to inform him that he would be excluded from the meeting, by the request of the company's management. Later, at the airport, Monks learned that the meeting had gone fairly well. The investors issued their demands for focusing the company on its core controls operations. Management was defensive, insisting that they and not the shareholders had the right to run the business. But the shareholders were adamant in stating their view that this was their company and they should determine what business it should be in. Lampert soon increased his investment in Honeywell to about 5 percent.

On July 24, Renier announced a dramatic restructuring. Honeywell would spin off most of its defense businesses and sell an interest in a Japanese joint venture, and it would use the cash to buy back a load of stock, raise the dividend, and build up the core controls business. "Rather than batten down the hatches and do nothing, they found a way to create more value, which is the best takeover defense of all," Sherman says. "It was an educational experience for the market. A lot of what we were doing back then besides building a business was trying to prove a point: That good corporate governance creates value. A lot of people just didn't buy it; some people still don't." Honeywell's stock had increased some 10 percent from the time of the announcement of the Rainwater group's involvement to the defeat of the proposals, and 22 percent (from about $71 to nearly $90) by the time of the restructuring announcement. For Monks, Honeywell was the beginning of a whole new direction in his career, because it proved that shareholders did not have to wait for a corporate raider to acquire a company or put a company in play to reap value from it; rather, they possessed the clout to influence and work with existing management. "Strategic institutional involvement in corporate governance can make a difference," ISS later wrote its clients. "Shareholders should limit their involvement to issues like those at Honeywell, where management tried to reduce accountability. Once shareholders establish a structure that aligns their interests with management's, they can be assured that the corporation will be as productive and competitive as possible." The episode confirmed his feeling that an activist investment fund would work well because it could act as a private, Rainwater-like investor that brings along institutional support.

In the summer of 1989, Monks continued to firm up his relationship with Calpers by taking some of its top officers on a governance retreat, at Calpers' expense. As he had written his board to inform directors of the upcoming retreat: "We feel that we have been able to add value in a very dramatic way to their program; that they recognize this; and that they have adequate resources to be the "bell cow" for governance developments. I have been asked to meet with all of their top people for 36 hours in May or June to develop their strategic plan for the next three to five years." (A minor point of fact is that when he was meeting with Calpers' Koppes and other top officers in early February, Monks himself brought up the question of Calpers' strategic planning regarding governance and asked for a day and a half "in an isolated location" to help them with this.)[17] "Year one," Monks continued, "has been enormously successful. Calpers has energized all of the live bodies and even some who didn't know they were alive. Now Calpers should try to focus on particular objectives, the identification of its resources, their husbanding and focus."

They booked a conference room for two days at a resort in the wine country town of Sonoma to give Hanson, Koppes, and a few others an education in shareholder activism and corporate governance issues. Monks was impressed with Hanson's continuing enthusiasm for the subject and excitement about the impact he would have on the movement. "I cannot overstress the importance of Dale Hanson," he later said. "He was an energy, a traveler, a meeter, and a doer. He saw governance as the right thing for the beneficiaries of Calpers' plans—and for Dale Hanson." The two-day seminar in the wine country appealed to Hanson's private-sector-like predilection for strategic planning. And so, the top investment officers of the largest public pension plan in America sat with Monks, Minow, and Sherman, mulled the prevailing issues, and came up with a list of several things that Calpers—with ISS's assistance—could do in the corporate governance arena over the coming five years. (Another close confidant of the Calpers officers, New York attorney and trusted boardroom adviser Ira Millstein, would later convince Calpers to steer away from activist ventures designed merely to get votes—Monks' idea for building recognition for shareholder activism—and begin focusing *exclusively* on poorly performing companies.)[18]

One of the items on the list was the development of some type of coinvestment endeavor, perhaps even a proactive fund with Calpers as the initial investor. Given the public's recognition of Calpers as the foremost institutional shareholder activist, Monks began to see that there could be no better launching pad for his next project. And it seemed that such a deal with Calpers was virtually a sure thing. "While we have established the generic category of our relationship—investment management—and we know the fees paid to other "managers," we really cannot yet predict with accuracy the income from this activity. Nor is it yet clear whether we can interest other clients in this program. It does seem clear that the California program will provide us additional revenues to make ISS as presently constituted profitable."[19]

In the meantime, Monks was discussing a possible merger of ISS with Jefferies. A business combination was just one option he proposed for Jefferies while, as a director, helping the small brokerage house reestablish itself following Boyd Jefferies' conviction. "On the board he was very very proactive, asked challenging, provocative questions," says Baxter. Monks enthusiastically supported the idea of hiring bankers and traders from the now discredited Drexel—which meant a lot considering he had served on the Lambert Bruxelles board and knew quite a few of those bankers. "It seemed like a preposterous thing to do," Baxter recounts. "We were just recovering from our own scandal. I remember someone high up at Drexel said, 'Frank is either stupid or crazy to do this.' Bob was supportive though." It turned out to be a shrewd move.

In Monks' mind, the combination of his and Baxter's companies would help Jefferies serve institutional investor clients better and would help ISS fulfill its dreams of bringing shareholders and managers together to talk over impending issues and transactions such as acquisitions, and developing securities that meet investor approval. A November ISS business strategy memo read in part: "ISS' challenge is to conduct itself in such a way as to aid all participants in the new governance structure so as to advance the 1) principal and 2) practice of effective accountability. ISS, in essence, is the advocate and the incarnation of the new system." A merger would also, Monks told Baxter, enable Monks to recover what he had invested in ISS—some $3 million through mid-1989, plus estimated costs (til the deal's closing) of up to $1 million. That summer, however, Jefferies decided against a merger with ISS—though they continued to consider joint ventures.

By late July, though, the Calpers-ISS activist investment venture was looking quite real. Hanson and Koppes agreed to Monks' presentation of expenses. To Monks, it appeared that the two men had pretty much carte blanche to do what they wanted in this area. "They apparently have adequate authority from their board both as to the substance and the finance of what we propose, so they need only mention what they are doing," he reported to Dubow. They did, however, indicate some "internal political problems," though Hanson added that he did not view them "as being material to approval of our governance project." By October, the project continued to appear likely, Monks reported to his board. For some reason, however, the Calpers management was uncomfortable with the term "investment management," and so Monks called the assignment an "activist value enhancement program," aimed at improving returns from a select group of companies.[20] The scope of the relationship would be whatever the partners wanted it to be: filing anticriminal director eligibility by-law resolutions, proposing shareholders' committees at specific companies, publicly soliciting votes for an opposing slate of director candidates, and, perhaps, even suing companies.

At the time, Monks reported to his board, "The option was available for ISS to work as a principal—using its own and others' money, and the leverage conferred by its substantial client base, to create parallel value for itself and clients," which might include raising a fund to invest in targets. While he acknowledged the potential for conflicts of interest, he maintained that they could be managed. ISS would simply be "backing up its rhetoric with hard cash."[21] But Dwight Allison, who was an adviser to ISS's board, believed that in taking on this task, ISS's image was becoming blurred and confusing and was "probably a reflection of Bob Monks' personal ability to tolerate ambiguity." He was against ISS branching out to become a principal in proactive investing. Thoughts began to circle in Monks' head about splitting the company in two, so he could do what his heart craved—go after undervalued companies—and ISS, which now had about 40 clients for its proxy advisory service, could get on with its business.

At the end of October, Monks wrote that he had an agreement with Calpers with four objectives: to create a national registry of corporate directors, profiling current and potential directors, in line with Britain's Proned; to develop shareholders' committees at certain corporations, in 1990 Avon, Occidental Petroleum, and TRW (where Calpers did submit resolutions for such panels); "to coordinate shareholder litigation so as to reestablish management's duty of loyalty"; and to solicit proxies in support of shareholder resolutions. He would not, then, be an investor with Calpers or an investment manager for the pension fund. And he had also decided to reject an overture from Jefferies to invest jointly in companies targeted for activist shareholder involvement. But Monks continued to believe that advising a fund or creating some other kind of what he called "collective action product" was the way to go given his and ISS's growing set of relationships with big owners of American corporations. What he now had in mind was for ISS to identify target companies and get principal shareholders involved in bringing about change, and to organize the activities of any established shareholder advisory committee.

Early in 1990, Monks engaged in a series of meetings with U.S. Treasury Department officials. Treasury Secretary Nicholas Brady had become greatly concerned about U.S. business's ability to compete in an increasingly global business environment, and he assigned his deputies to investigate what was needed to make companies competitive. Viewing ISS as the nation's foremost expert on governance, which Undersecretary of Treasury for finance Robert Glauber noted to Monks, Treasury became intrigued by Monks' and Minow's idea that effective governance would improve corporate performance—in particular, governance by pension funds acting as long-term investors by indexing their equity holdings. The department invited Monks to explain these notions more fully. Monks took Calpers' Dale Hanson and Richard Koppes with him to the meeting. To Glauber, he explained his idea of an interagency coordinating group of the DOL, the SEC, and Treasury, to develop guidelines for fiduciary voting. And he suggested actually imposing some indexation on pension plans. One appealing aspect of that idea, he argued, was that its implementation would require no legislative action; another was that it was good politics to support owners and ownership responsibility. (In fact, he and Minow were just pulling together a proposal for Calpers, at Hanson's request, calling for the creation of a National Association of Indexed Funds, which never came to fruition.[22]) However, as Monks noted to Dubow in a January 5 letter,

"They [at Treasury] full well understand that our proposals would have the result of threatening several billion dollars worth of consulting and money management revenues." This could "infuriate and harm some of our clients." Even so, he encouraged the government's interest, even volunteering to organize a meeting with other institutional investors in February. Treasury, Monks wrote Dubow, "views this as one of their top priority items. This gives us the chance to make clear to our clients that the way to the Treasury lies through ISS."[23]

In speeches to both business and investor groups over the following months, Treasury officials often sounded like allies of Monks. Glauber told a group of treasurers: "I urge you to look at your investors as potential partners in achieving your strategic objectives, rather than [as] adversaries."[24] In the summer, Michael Jacobs, director of the Treasury Department's Office of Corporate Finance, remarked to a conference on institutions' fiduciary responsibility that the priority for a board of directors must be "maximizing the value of the corporation, because for any [other] goal to take precedence . . . would not only be a violation of the directors' fiduciary responsibility to shareholders, it would also undermine the competitiveness of our nation's economy." He also suggested that institutional investors have a duty to behave as owners rather than traders. "One idea," he said, "would be for institutional investors to allocate more of their money to investment managers who have the skills and resources needed to directly monitor the performance of boards. . . ."[25] Monks' dream fund. And in March, Brady remarked before the Senate Finance Committee: "Our country's pension funds are the ideal candidates to provide the committed capital our corporations need."

At the same time, Monks' abiding influence at the Labor Department was also coming to the surface. Toward the end of January, David Ball, then the government's pensions administrator, delivered a speech that rewarded Monks for all his persistent contacts with Labor Department powers that be, including Ball himself. In a presentation to the Financial Executives Institute, the Assistant Secretary of Labor suggested that pension funds are obligated to take action if they believe a company is poorly run. "I believe that as institutional shareholders own an ever greater portion of corporate America, it is inevitable that those responsible for the management of plan assets . . . will have to become more activist as shareholders," Ball said in his speech. Peg O'Hara, director of corporate governance at the IRRC, called the speech "a ringing endorsement of shareholder activism." At that time, and in presentations later that year, Ball referred to Monks' 1983 speech, "The Institutional Investor as Corporate Citizen," as "seminal," forming the policy basis for the department's continuing action on proxy voting.[26]

The same day as Ball's January speech, the department released a letter that reinforced the message, articulated by pensions administrators Monks, Walker and Ball, that pension trustees had an obligation to vote. In fact, the letter was in the form of a reply to a letter Monks had recently written to the pension agency in which he had pointed out that some investment managers had stated in their contracts with pension funds that they would not vote proxies. Who, then, had the responsibility to vote, Monks asked the department. When he saw his friends Klevan and Lebowitz in mid-January, they told him that the department would soon send along its reply, and release it as an official response known as the "Monks Letter." The two Labor officials considered this to be an excellent document containing fundamental guidance on governance matters. They insisted that managers who forgo voting are still responsible for that duty unless they specifically assign it to someone else.[27] "Everybody's ducking [the responsibility]," Monks complained to the *Wall Street Journal,* noting that a recent Labor Department study had found that many fund managers did not know who was voting proxies.

At least two people, however, resented that a former pensions administrator—from six years earlier no less—would be dictating policy. Two attorneys, Mayer Siegel, a partner at Fried, Frank, Harris, Shriver & Jacobson, and Carol Buckmann, a pension specialist with Sullivan & Cromwell, wrote their objections to the ruling in a *New York Law Journal* article. They maintained that the Labor Department's letter would "make investment managers more reluctant to assume responsibility for voting proxies. We believe that if an investment manager does not wish to assume this responsibility, it should be free not to." Moreover, they asserted that in both the letter and Ball's speech,

> the DOL has come perilously close to advising plan fiduciaries that they have a fiduciary responsibility to oppose the enactment of protective devices such as poison pills, staggered boards and similar devices. Many courts have approved the adoption and maintenance of such devices in appropriate circumstances as producing greater value for shareholders in the event a corporation is acquired in a hostile takeover. . . . The proper use of these devices and their limitations is the subject of much controversy. Certainly, plan fiduciaries should exercise their best judgment in deciding whether or not to vote for such provisions in particular

circumstances. However, we strongly object to the DOL raising to the level of a legal requirement the controversial views of a former administrator. . . .

It is disturbing to see the DOL so in the thrall of the ideology of a prior administrator. It is one thing for the DOL to set forth its views as to the procedures that plan fiduciaries should follow in exercising proxy voting responsibilities. It is quite another for the DOL to "suggest" to them how to vote. And this is what it appears to have done.

Both the speech and the letter were timed to prepare institutions for the upcoming proxy season. Corporate governance proxy resolutions that Monks had been the first to encourage on a broad scale were booming. For the spring of 1990, institutional investors had proposed more than 120 such proxy resolutions, up from 70 in 1989 and 28 in 1988. ISS itself was by then busy mapping out its own agenda for that year's round of annual meetings. It had received interested calls from parties involved in Campbell Soup and Cummins Engine, among others, and was considering which if any assignments to take. In the meantime, Monks became a key behind-the-scenes player in a very public drama at General Motors.

Earlier in the year, Calpers' Koppes and Hanson together with their adviser, Ira Millstein, had taken the initiative to bring the CEOs of corporations and the top officials of public pension funds together to talk. Champion International Corp. offered its woodsy Connecticut retreat called Tree Tops for the conclaves. Present were four CEOs of corporations—Bruce Atwater of General Mills, Andrew Sigler of Champion, James Kinnear of Texaco, and John Georgeson of International Paper—and four CEOs of public funds including Koppes and Hanson of Calpers, Harrison Goldin of New York City, Pat Lipton of Wisconsin, and Paul Quirk of Massachusetts. The first couple of meetings were marked by testiness on both sides. At the third meeting, in November, Koppes said to the group, "Is there one corporation we all could agree on that we as shareholders should be concerned about? That we have a right to be concerned about?" The response was unanimous: General Motors. The auto maker's domestic market share had been dropping, and its stock badly lagged the Standard & Poor's 500 stock index. Meanwhile, GM's Chairman and CEO Roger Smith had announced that he would be retiring that summer.

Acknowledging the presence of Millstein, who was a key adviser to GM's board, Koppes recalls, "Everyone kind of turned and looked his way.

And Ira said, 'Don't look at me. I'm not responsible for them. If you're so concerned, you should write a letter to the board.'" He added that as shareholders they had the right to ask the directors what they were doing to find Smith's successor and to demand that the board assess candidates other than just Smith's own preference.

On the flight back to Sacramento, Koppes decided he would like Calpers to take a crack at a letter and began composing it in his head. At one point, he leaned across the aisle to Hanson and said, "Would you let me write the letter? With your signature, of course."

"Sure, go for it," Hanson said.

Then Koppes added, "I'd like to consult with Bob Monks."[28]

Hanson readily concurred, and together at a meeting in Sacramento in December, they asked Monks to prepare a draft of the letter. Even though GM's pension fund was an ISS client, Monks agreed. (Still he passed the matter by Binns to make sure it was okay with him.)

Koppes was grateful for Monks' guidance. "Bob was so helpful in drafting that letter. It really was basically Bob's ideas. It was Bob's call on how to say it, what to say." In the letter, Calpers referred to itself, as Monks suggested, as a "permanent owner," since most of its more than 6 million shares were then being indexed. The "guts" of the letter, as Monks referred to it in the cover letter to Koppes accompanying his draft, was in asking the board to describe its policies governing its relationship with "permanent owners," and what standards of performance the board has established to evaluate GM's new management over 3-, 5-, and 10-year periods. The cover letter explains Monks' thinking in posing these questions:

This is "where we establish a tone of polite persistence. It is unlikely that GM has any "board level" policies either with respect to shareholder relations or performance standards to which they will hold the company to be publicly accountable. If they do, we should know them. If they do not, a respectful inquiry like this one, from a shareholder with a significant long-term investment, is likely to encourage them to develop some. Can any board of directors really tell one of its principal shareholders that there are [and will be] no policies for relationship with owners and no criteria for evaluating management's performance. (sic)

. . . The development of a relationship between shareholders and management will create a context for more substantive discussions that do not infringe on the Board's responsibility to establish the overall direction of the company. . . . [29]

At the same time, by sheer coincidence, Ned Regan, the New York State Comptroller and head of the state employees' retirement system, was writing to GM on the same topic. His deputies also asked for Monks' input. Monks made a few suggestions, some of which were used—the fund is a "permanent shareholder" of GM; "Selection of a CEO is the most important responsibility of a board"—and also supplied a list of GM's directors for the pension fund's mailing. Regan asked the GM board to detail how it planned to go about choosing a successor to Smith and whether it would prefer a candidate that would continue GM's policies or take a different path. So, because of his reputation and contacts, Monks had the opportunity to make his mark on both letters.

Smith did not immediately respond to the letters. Apparently, without consulting with the board, Smith phoned California governor George Deukmejian to complain about Calpers' demands and approved a press release stating that corporate governance, including the selection of officers, is the board's responsibility and not any business of shareholders. Several of GM's outside board members, however, supported Hanson's initiative. In March, Smith held meetings with both Hanson and Regan. At the meeting with Calpers, the fund demanded that GM's board discuss the criteria used to select and monitor the company's new CEO. The press gave the episode a great deal of attention, citing it as evidence of the growing assertiveness of institutional shareholders in corporate America.[30] Even so, Monks told his board, he "resisted the temptation to "blow our horn" about GM."

From then on, institutional investors began to play a much more vocal role at GM. And in 1994, GM's board adopted guidelines on "significant governance issues." They included discussion of policies that had concerned Monks such as the formal evaluation of the CEO and board interaction with institutional investors—specifying that individual directors may on occasion meet with investors and other constituencies, with management's knowledge.

In February 1990, Monks traveled to Dallas with Frank Baxter and other Jefferies directors for a board meeting and get-together with some of the brokerage firm's big customers. Baxter had asked Monks to make a presentation about shareholder activism, and during his talk one man in the room kept interrupting with questions. Monks suspected a hidden agenda. "I couldn't understand what the hell he was asking me," Monks recalls. Later, when he returned to his hotel room, the phone rang and it was the questioner from the meeting. "I'm Harold Simmons," he said. "I enjoyed talking to you today. Come on up and see me. I'd like to talk some more."

Simmons, the son of grade-school teachers, had accumulated a great deal of wealth in the stock market and through acquiring control of numerous companies. At the time he met Monks, he had either a controlling interest or 100 percent ownership of 17 companies, including NL Industries, a Houston-based chemical firm, Amalgamated Sugar Co., and Baroid Corp., an oil field services firm. *Forbes* pegged the 58-year-old Texan's worth at $1.9 billion.

Monks remembered that Simmons had been involved in a Labor Department enforcement case brought before his term as pensions administrator. The case charged Simmons with violating his fiduciary duty by using pension money from companies he controlled to help finance his takeover of Amalgamated Sugar. The DOL ordered that his companies' pension plans refrain for three years from purchasing stock in companies in which Simmons owned an interest of at least 2 percent.[31]

Simmons seemed intent on telling Monks how ridiculous the government was in bringing the case against him because all he had done was make everybody a lot of money. But now he really wanted to talk about another issue. Simmons, through NL Industries, had accumulated a 19 percent position in Lockheed, the Calabasas, California, defense/aerospace company (the country's sixth largest defense contractor), which had been performing poorly with declining profits and stock price. After Lockheed reported a plunge in profits for fiscal year 1989, Simmons met with CEO Daniel Tellup and asked to have some representation on Lockheed's board—6 of 15 seats. But he was swiftly rebuffed. Simmons now wanted Monks' help in executing an attack strategy aimed at wresting away control of Lockheed from management: a proxy contest.

After meeting Simmons, Monks called his longtime partner Dwight Allison. Allison had been a director of a shipping company called Sea–Land Corp. that Simmons had tried to take over. "Dwight is just absolutely incorruptible," Monks said, "and he thought that Harold was trying to get away with something at Sea–Land. He recounted to me vividly what dealing with Harold was like. So I felt that I had a little bit of a problem there, but I felt I could deal with Harold." Here was another situation, like Honeywell, where Monks thought the shareholder activist movement could ride on the coattails of a well-heeled raider. But the risk here was that the raider was not quite as respectable in investors' eyes as Rainwater had been.

Simmons had assembled a slate of 13 director candidates—among them, former Texas Senator John Tower, retired Admiral Elmo R. Zumwalt III, and himself—to run against the Lockheed slate at the annual meeting scheduled for mid-May. This was an ambitious undertaking. Since a company is not required to run information on opposition candidates in its proxy statement, Simmons needed to identify the Lockheed shareholders, prepare his own proxy material, and mail it out to the shareholders in time for them to vote. In fact, he had less time than he originally thought, since Lockheed chose to move up the date of its annual meeting from mid-May to March 29 in reaction to Simmons' challenge. Monks had enough experience to realize that Simmons, even with his large stake in the company, would spend a lot of money and probably lose.

Shortly after his initial meeting with Simmons, Monks returned to Dallas to meet the raider's whole team. That included his lawyer, who clashed with Monks. "He just couldn't believe me," Monks recounted. "He just was so angry that Harold was taking anybody else's advice. I told Harold what to do, and this guy just about went crazy. He just thought it was the dumbest idea. But Harold did exactly what I told him." And that was for Simmons to throw his support behind four already filed shareholder resolutions on governance issues to lure institutional votes for his slate. Monks also made Simmons see that by aiding a victory on corporate governance issues, he would be pressuring the company to get rid of defenses, putting it in a negotiating posture. "At that time I was really good at this because I knew what worked—the resolutions that I could get 30 or 40 percent of the vote on," Monks says. Simmons was impressed. "Bob Monks is on the right side of the issue," he says today. "One of the leaders in getting institutions to participate in stockholder rights battles." In February, Simmons backed four resolutions proposing a ban on greenmail payments, confidential voting, elimination of the company's poison pill defense, and a bylaw forcing Lockheed to opt out of antitakeover provisions under corporate law in Delaware, where the company was incorporated. (Monks had said that the effect of state legislatures' protection of corporations in takeover situations was to turn common stock into "junk stock.")

Monks was familiar with the resolutions being filed at Lockheed, because it was ISS's job to be well informed on all shareholder actions. In fact, ISS had helped bring Lockheed to the attention of resolution filers. Every year, the firm compiled an informal list of 10 companies that seemed to be performing badly and were therefore attractive for shareholder involvement. It shared the list with some clients, and the word would get around. Some activist funds and the Council of Institutional Investors put together their own target lists. Generally, TIAA-CREF and the state funds would sponsor the resolutions. But for some, ISS wrote the actual resolutions and the funds simply submitted them to the SEC for inclusion on the target companies' proxy statements. This year, Lockheed had appeared on a few of the target lists. All four of the resolutions were plain-vanilla—that is, they were resolutions that ISS and others had ushered through the SEC in past years so that by now they simply sailed right through, with very little expense carried by the filer.

Monks felt particularly proud of this accomplishment, but not only because ISS had overcome SEC objection on some of these issues. The way he saw it, resolutions addressing antitakeover defenses did not really get to the heart of the matter, which was how the target companies' boards were running the businesses themselves. Securities law barred shareholders from filing resolutions having to do with actual management of a company. To Monks' delight, however, the antitakeover defense resolutions took on a secondary, larger meaning. "They were taken as a vote of confidence in the management," Monks says. "We were successful in creating a new language. I have always regarded this as one of my own largest contributions, as I consciously started with the need to improve on my betters—Alinsky and Nader, who in the '60s had legitimacy and celebrity well beyond what I would ever have and yet only got 3 percent of the votes. By using simple symbolic votes, we made it relatively easy at any annual meeting to make managements be accountable. With the help of the financial press, there could be no way for a management to "lose" one of these votes and retain its credibility." Monks, with his feel for both Japanese culture and metaphor in general, came to call these plain-vanilla proposals "Kabuki resolutions" because they were so like the Kabuki theater in which mythical characters symbolically act out themes of current interest, carrying multiple layers of meaning. In any case, despite Lockheed's protests, the SEC approved the inclusion of all four resolutions on the company's proxy statement, and the fight was on.

Simmons then began calling on some of Lockheed's major institutional shareholders. Many of them liked the Texas tycoon's arguments that Lockheed was too broadly diversified away from its core aerospace and defense business, and were pleased by his surprising pro-shareholder stance. Calpers wanted a bit more, however—a panel of shareholders to advise Lockheed's board in the case of a Simmons victory. Simmons promised such a shareholders advisory committee, and Calpers promised its vote. Two days before the annual meeting, the fund announced it had voted for Simmons' candidates.

CEO Tellup was stunned by Calpers' announcement. It now seemed absolutely feasible that Simmons, with his 19 percent stake and powerful institutional backing, could take control of the company. And so, without skipping a beat, Tellup too began playing the corporate governance game, creating a virtual bidding war for institutional votes. Lockheed responded to the greenmail resolution with one of its own that contained even stricter provisions. Then, Tellup agreed to reserve up to three seats on the board for shareholder nominees. The way the press interpreted this move was that Lockheed's management, like many in the business community, viewed Calpers as the country's foremost shareholder activist whose lead others would follow. That image was due in great part to Monks' efforts in recent years.

At the annual meeting, held inside a Lockheed hangar in Burbank (which Monks did not attend), Tellup continued his appeal for votes. Addressing the crowd, he told of meeting with 70 institutions during the few weeks of the proxy contest and declared his intention to support substantial votes by shareholders on the governance initiatives. He also pledged to meet Simmons on a regular basis to discuss Lockheed's future. Lockheed won the board contest hands down, 60 percent to 40 percent. The four shareholder initiatives also passed. The bylaw amendment was binding. As for the other three nonbinding resolutions, Lockheed's response to their passage was a pledge to establish confidential voting, ban greenmail, and look into eliminating the poison pill. (Which it failed to do.)

Monks regarded this outcome as a resounding "victory," and many in the activist movement cited Lockheed as their greatest moment to date given the decisive role corporate governance issues played in a contest for corporate control. ISS itself could claim a large portion of the credit for the achievement. Most of those the firm solicited on behalf of Simmons' slate did vote for Simmons, according to a report to the ISS board. Meanwhile, in other confrontations that proxy season, Calpers succeeded in forming closer relationships with the managements of TRW and Occidental Petroleum in return for withdrawing its bids for shareholder advisory committees at those companies (it lost a vote on a SAC at Avon).

That spring, Monks received more press attention than he ever had. He was profiled in the *New York Times*[32] and the *Financial Times* ("he rowed in the winning Cambridge eight in the 1955 Boat Race"),[33] and appeared as an authority on governance on ABC's *Business World* program. On that broadcast, Monks' holistic view of corporate governance came into clear focus when he was asked by anchorman Sander Vanocur to what extent shareholders should control a company and not worry about the workers and the community. "I think that a proper company treats its workers correctly," Monks replied. "A proper company, after all, wants to be in existence for a long period of time. A proper company wants to have good employee relations, it wants to have good relations with its community. But the function of a company is the long-term enhancement of the value of the holding for the owners. They can take into account any manner of factor that loans [sic] itself to long-term value, but they can't get cut off from their roots and simply do whatever they want to do because it feels good."[34]

Meanwhile, to Monks' gratification, corporate governance/shareholder activism was being recognized as an increasingly powerful movement. Indeed, at that time, which was the start of a recession, institutional investors and the media were proclaiming that a closer relationship with corporate managements was essential to improve the competitiveness of U.S. business. "With more states enacting laws that inhibit hostile takeovers and many corporate raiders now busy running the industrial companies they have acquired, pension fund activism is increasingly seen as one of the few ways of keeping management on its toes," said the *New York Times* on February 23, 1990. And *Pensions & Investments'* April 16 issue reported: "Harvard University Business School Professor Jay Lorsch told the Council of Institutional Investors meeting April 2 that activist institutional investors are beginning to have an effect on corporate America." Of course, top company managers had another view: that the activists were meddling in corporate affairs and could hamper the fulfillment of long-term strategies.

After the Lockheed results came in, the SEC launched an investigation of ISS. Monks suspects that someone on the company's side complained to the SEC about perceived conflicts of interest in ISS's participation in the proxy contest. But anyone who knew about ISS's involvement may have wondered: How could the firm be advising America's biggest pension funds objectively on the Lockheed resolutions and board election while at the same time Monks was advising Harold Simmons on how to win?

Nell Minow, who had always worked at ISS only part time, got a call at home from an SEC staffer. "Are you the general counsel of ISS?" the man asked. When she answered that she was, he informed her that the firm was the subject of an SEC investigation.

Minow assumed that the SEC was looking into something ISS had just started on—making calls on behalf of Calpers to support their resolutions. "Is it that?" she asked.

"Oh no, we don't care about that," said the SEC staffer. "It concerns Lockheed." He did not go into more detail, even to say that the investigation focused on suspected conflict of interest, although that is what Minow and Monks assumed. Over the ensuing days and weeks, SEC investigators asked ISS to supply them with copies of all phone records and other information.

ISS had not done anything with Simmons that it had not done before with Rainwater or Coniston Partners or others. In fact, Minow and Monks had had a big argument over ISS's involvement with both Texans. Monks was inclined to take payment from Rainwater and Simmons for his role as an adviser and advocate. But Minow resisted. It wouldn't be right, she said, since their main business was giving objective advice to pension fund clients. Monks agreed. "Nell," he said, "is my canary in a coal mine." (Coal miners used to send a canary into the mine to test for dangerous gases.) But she was completely comfortable with ISS acting as an unpaid adviser. "We were working in furtherance of our own views," she says. But, "even though I had a good answer," Minow says, it was evident that mounting a defense against any SEC suit would be "hideously expensive," especially for what was then merely a breakeven operation.

And it was undeniable that the SEC was serious about pursuing this case. So, Monks and Minow knew what they had to do. They took quick action, first of all, to protect ISS. In a memo to all clients, Monks declared that the firm had been offered, but never taken, fees to promote certain causes "because we cannot guarantee the independence of our advice if we accept compensation from a party, even one we agree with." Furthermore, he reassured clients that all of ISS's projects were consistent with its policy of a commitment to shareholders and what is best for all of a company's shareholders.

Around this time, Monks was alarmed to hear that Georgeson's John Wilcox had remarked in a speech that ISS's work was "illegal." In fact, Wilcox had merely touched on the question of whether or not the type of advice being given by ISS was a solicitation under the proxy rules and should be clarified. But, without confronting Wilcox, an enraged Monks consulted an attorney, who drafted a lawsuit against his friend, Monks later told him. But then he just sat on it. About a year later, Wilcox, who had tried unsuccessfully to call Monks several times and then learned through an acquaintance that he had offended him, called him again to resolve the situation once and for all. "We arranged to have a meeting here in New York," Wilcox recounts. "He was on the advisory board of Mitsubishi and they had their meeting in their building. So I went up and we went into a meeting room, and he just absolutely laced into me about all of this. Anyway, we talked about it. I said, "That's a very extreme interpretation of what I said." The issue was not a new one. It had been raised by a number of people. I took complete blame for it and apologized and hoped that would be an end to it. And it was. We became friends again."[35]

By early June 1990, Dwight Allison somehow ascertained—even without yet knowing about the Lockheed investigation—that Monks was preparing to break away from ISS. As he wrote to Monks' son Robert: "I infer that RAGM may think his active involvement with ISS borders on being counterproductive; that his protean energies and ideas may be conflicting with ISS's needs to expand a well-defined business without the confusion of entrepreneurial chaos." In Allison's view, Monks had two choices: to start a fund or be a "one-man band" on corporate governance, speaking and writing about it, advising either side in proxy contests, and even linking up with others in proxy contests.[36]

By the end of that month, the ISS directors learned that Allison's sixth sense was correct. Monks had already decided that he was going to leave ISS and form a new company, called Institutional Shareholder Partners. "My constant pursuit of cause was beginning to risk the business of ISS," he says. "And in order to promote the agenda, I couldn't afford to spend any more time at ISS, because that was pretty well established and going okay." He knew that there would continue to be a perception of conflict of interest as long as ISS pursued activist causes, and at the same time he wanted to become more, not less, involved in activism. Indeed, he was hoping that Calpers would become the first investor in an ISS-sponsored proactive fund. As Monks noted to his directors: "ISS, in its present incarnation, is really the step child of RAGM's true ambition. Proxy analysis was a back door way of making corporate management accountable. The irony is that proxy analysis is the business that pays our bills; it is the core of our commercial enterprise." The only solution was to split up the company.[37] Over the next few months, that's what he did. He transferred all his stock in ISS—worth an investment of some $3 million—into an irrevocable trust and made his nephew Nicholas Higgins and his son Robert the trustees. In June 1995, that investment would cash in at about $11 million with the sale of ISS to Thompson Financial for

$12.5 million. (Monks used some of his $8 million profit to help finance his son's entry into the banking business, founding a community bank in Portland called Atlantic Bank. The bank was successful, but in 1997 many of its investors wanted to cash out; so Robert Monks Jr. sold the bank to regional player People's Heritage Bank based in Portland.)

But in September, 1990, Monks, at age 56, moved his office two floors down in the same building ISS occupied, taking with him his longtime assistant Barbara Sleasman. Minow, his trusted partner, stayed behind to run ISS—now with a client list numbering 80 institutional investors with more than $1.3 trillion in assets under management—with its new controlling shareholders, Robert Monks Jr. and Nicholas Higgins. In true form, Monks was already working on several different projects. He was writing a book with Minow on corporate governance (remarking to the *Financial Times* that the writing process was creating mood swings "of manic proportions" and a "great sense of self-loathing"). He was developing his fund concept, and talking to Calpers about becoming the first investor in what would be a $1 billion pool. At the same time, Monks was alert to Honeywell and Lockheed-like situations in which he could help powerful individuals link up with big institutional investors to take on a company—anticipating that, for now, institutions alone would not have the resources or the will to challenge big corporations. And he was scouting around for a target company to make his debut as a kind of gadfly corporate America had never seen before.

10

Taking on Sears

*Where do you begin? The place to begin is with the board. The way
in which you communicate the desire for some kind of change is
through effecting a change in the board.*

Monks strategy memo

Early morning Thursday, May 9, 1991. At the Palmer House hotel in
downtown Chicago, Monks awoke without the help of an alarm.
Milly, who had flown in the night before, was still dozing. He
showered, shaved, and put on his Sackville Street best, a conservative dark
blue suit and rep style tie. Today was a different kind of election day for
Monks. At the annual meeting of Sears, Roebuck and Company, he was
making a run for the board of directors.

As he was happy to point out to anyone willing to listen, the idea that
the shareholders were the ones who elected people to boards of directors at
U.S. corporations is a "sham." There are no truly independent directors, his
spiel went, because they are all selected by the CEO and only then put to
the shareholders for a vote. The so-called independent director, then, owes
his position to the CEO. "What right do owners and employees have to
participate in the process?" he asked. In truth, the emperor had no clothes,
and Monks was never shy about—indeed, thoroughly enjoyed—revealing
such nakedness to the world. This time, he would use real-life drama to
make a point, and put himself in the lead role. The idea was to propose
himself as a candidate for the board of a major company and then simply see
what ensued.

So far, media coverage of his race had been favorable, making him out
as an intrepid underdog. One reason that the contest was prominent in the

press was because 1991 was such a slow year for proxy fights. What had begun to happen that year in corporate America was behind-the-scenes, quiet negotiation with activist shareholders such as public pension funds; corporations were eager to reach compromises instead of suffering the expense and the exposure of fighting shareholder resolutions. Another reason was that once again Monks was on the cutting edge, introducing yet another new front in the shareholder activism movement.

Occasionally that morning, Monks felt a nervous twinge zip across his stomach with the thought that he would be attending a meeting where he was not only the star attraction but, to many people there, an inimical presence. As this was Sears' hometown, most of the attendees would be Sears employees or loyalists who would defend the company against any outsider unwelcome by management. Furthermore, Monks was naturally a bit jittery on what was really the fourth election day of his life. It had been some time—15 years—since that day he lost to Edmund Muskie in the general election. But, the backbone that allowed him to run against someone like Muskie in the first place was still intact. Any apprehension today was momentary.

At 7:30, Monks and Milly ate breakfast with a small group of associates in the hotel dining room. At 9:00, the couple excused themselves to depart for the proceedings. Outside, Chicago was bathed in a cool yellow light of early spring. They walked the short distance from the hotel across South Columbus Drive to the Art Institute of Chicago, where the meeting was to take place in the Rubloff Auditorium, starting promptly at 10 A.M. Hand in hand like young lovers, they made their way slowly along the flower-trimmed path to the entrance of the building. As Monks pushed open the door to the lobby, he found himself assaulted by photographers and TV cameramen. Milly, who while following her husband's work had a busy career of her own, was shocked at the level of attention being paid her husband. For his part, Monks was imagining the next day's headlines, joking to himself: "Lamb on the Way to the Slaughter" or "Don Quixote Meets the Windmill." But in his gut he expected something much more favorable.

There was a large crowd milling in the lobby. It was one of those occasions where he felt self-conscious of his height: at 6 feet 6 inches, he generally stood out like a Texan in Tokyo, and today he could feel everyone looking his way. His eyes groped for a friendly face, and found the familiar and not unfriendly visage of Marty Lipton, one of corporate America's most powerful weapons in a takeover fight, who had been working for Sears to help the company ward off Monks. Lipton was best known as the inventor of the poison pill, one of the prime targets of ISS's shareholder resolutions. He and Monks had known each other for years, having served together on numerous conference panels, representing opposite points of view, and they'd spoken on the phone a few times during the Sears drama. To Lipton, Monks was "the quintessential shareholder activist seeking maximization of shareholder value in the short run."[1] Monks, the rower and debater in school and the negotiator in business, who respects a strong rival, had always held Lipton in high regard.

Now, he stepped up to Lipton, noting to himself that the lawyer's glasses were so big (to accommodate thick lenses) that they made his face appear swollen. As he got closer, Monks spied beads of sweat on Lipton's face. He could see that the man was not enjoying himself, at least so far, and he decided to help make the morning even more pleasant.

"Hey, Marty," Monks boomed, arm extended. "These guys really owe you. If you hadn't shown them how to cheat by shrinking the board, I would have won!"

"I sure hope so," the counselor replied humorlessly.

While they made small talk, Monks let his eyes roam around the room. Strangers met his glance with recognition, then, embarrassed, turned away.

A Sears corporate aide interrupted the conversation to escort Bob and Milly into the auditorium itself. As he entered, Monks scanned the scene before him: the huge hall was already brimming with people. There were several thousand seats on two levels and an expansive stage. Above it, on a large screen, the name Sears, Roebuck and Company was emblazoned in huge white letters on a deep blue background. Two tiers of banquettes, draped with red velveteen, stretched across the stage. Cards bearing the names of the nine directors were displayed evenly spaced across the rear table, and the names of company officers and directors who were resigning that year appeared in the front, bisected by the podium from which chairman Edward Brennan would conduct the proceedings.

They walked down an aisle to their seats, near the front on the right. There they found the rest of their party already seated: Arthur Dubow, who would speak today to formally nominate Monks as a Sears director; David Martin, the lawyer who had guided Monks through the nomination and solicitation process; Kim McCarter, a willowy blonde who was Monks' assistant at his new organization Institutional Shareholder Partners. Beside them, in the aisle, stood their own lectern and microphone. In discussions that week between Martin and the company, Sears agreed to give Monks all the time he needed to speak his mind.

Brennan, in his late 50s with slicked back graying hair, small eyes, and a pale complexion, made his way over to the Monks party to greet the man who had cost him some sleep and his company more than a few dollars. Sears was not just another job for Brennan. His grandfather, father and uncle had all worked for the company, and he himself spent his 35-year career there, the last five as CEO. Brennan himself was one of the three other candidates nominated for election to the board that day—all three current directors who were nominated by the company itself, in fact by the board's nominating committee that was chaired by Brennan. If Brennan harbored any resentment toward Monks, he did not display it now. Instead, Brennan was as gracious and civil as the host of a dinner party. After gently shaking Milly's hand, he spirited Monks off to meet with the other directors, who were gathered in a room off stage having coffee. As Monks later recalled, "Nobody was rude, but there was a perceptible chill in the atmosphere." He failed to make eye contact with Don Rumsfeld, former CEO of G. D. Searle & Co., the health care products maker, and President Reagan's representative in the Middle East in 1983 and 1984, whom he'd met just a few days earlier when making his pitch to the trustees of the Sears employee benefit plans. But, Monks chatted amiably with Sybil Mobley, Dean of the Business School at Florida State, Nancy Reynolds of the PR firm Hill and Knowlton and Philip Purcell, CEO of the brokerage house Dean Witter Financial Services, which was now Sears' best performing division. In his campaign for the board, Monks had called for the Big Store to commission a study to explore spinning off all businesses that were not related to its core occupation of selling retail merchandise. Purcell joked that Monks might be able to do for him what he couldn't do for himself and force Sears to divest itself of Dean Witter.[2] Brennan broke in, as the meeting was about to begin. Monks returned to his seat and waited anxiously for the CEO's opening remarks.

Seeing the directors now seated all in a row, it occurred to Monks that they resembled a medieval rendering of the Last Supper. Milly, meanwhile, viewed them only a bit differently—as a "celestial jury," and she pictured them wearing choir robes and emanating a soft light.

When he left ISS in September 1990, Monks did not know precisely what he would do next. He had a vague notion that he wanted to go after one of the worst-run companies in America—and do so in a major way.

That could mean either running for the board or filing some kind of share-holder resolution. But resolutions were already old hat. He had been down that road before, and others had then taken the baton from him. Now, he longed to clear a new path for shareholders by becoming a candidate—the shareholders' candidate—for the board of a major corporation, and in doing so also demonstrate how corporate America and the regulatory system in which it operates makes such a campaign extremely difficult.

Actually, the idea of running for the board of a major company did not come from Monks. It came from his former business partner Allison. In July 1990, when Monks decided to create ISP, Allison asserted at a meeting and repeated in a subsequent letter to Monks that "ISP should now aim at the center of the target, namely, the election of directors who view them-selves as responsive representatives of the shareholders. The only way to bring about this result is by the nomination of directoral candidates by a coalition of institutional shareholders, specifically public pension plans, joined perhaps by certain mutual funds." But public pension funds and mu-tual funds would never stick their necks out in such a way. Neither would a corporate raider, who would fail to see money-making prospects in such a bid. Bob Monks, on the other hand, had plenty of motivation to put him-self on the ballot.

The Sears race was a big risk for Monks, who was always one to cal-culate the risk and reward of every step of his career as if time was an in-vestment in the truest sense of the word. If he got too small a vote, he could look like a fool. And in turn, his crusade for better corporate gov-ernance at U.S. companies could indeed appear as ridiculous as Don Quixote's. His credibility damaged, it would be hard for him to continue to be an effective voice for change. That possibility is what most troubled Monks as he prepared to go ahead with the fight, his first as protagonist. In all the other battles he had let others take the lead. This time had to be different. No one but himself had any interest in standing up against a major company to run for the board.

To many, Sears, Roebuck was synonymous with apple pie and baseball. In recent years, the 104-year-old retailer had diversified with great fanfare into financial services businesses. It bought the venerable Dean Witter Reynolds brokerage firm as well as the Allstate insurance company and Coldwell Banker, a real estate finance company. What did all these busi-nesses have in common? Their products were sold to retail customers: Sears could now sell stocks as well as socks. But in reality the synergy theory did not hold; the nonretail businesses were distracting management from the core retailing business, which was falling on hard times as the competition from specialty retailers intensified. Earnings from the U.S. retail operations came in at a paltry $37 million in 1990 compared with a peak $656 million in 1984.

Monks' choice of Sears was not immediate. After all, there were other poorly run companies out there. He contacted two of his most trusted colleagues in the investment arena and asked for their suggestions: Dean LeBaron and Fidelity Chairman Ned Johnson, both classmates at Harvard. LeBaron was a good friend and Johnson was a former roommate of Monks' longtime friend Dubow. Several companies met Monks' criteria, which included (1) being involved in a business in which he had some experience; (2) performing poorly; (3) having a vacancy on the board; (4) having a large defined benefit pension plan that would make him even more useful as a director; and (5) having a poor governance profile, that is, a set of directors who were not truly independent of management.

By the fall, he had before him a list of prime candidates including two defense contractors, Lockheed and Northrop; three oil companies, Exxon, Mobil, and Chevron; and Eastman Kodak and Sears. While he had more work to do to trim the list to one target, he knew that to meet SEC and corporate filing deadlines in preparation for the upcoming annual meeting season, he would have to begin the process now—with all the companies. But how to begin? Even though most of these companies had provisions in their bylaws for shareholders to nominate candidates for director, Monks assumed that any shareholder who was bold enough to step forward would not be welcome to such an exclusive club. Still, he figured that the proper way to go forward was by following the companies' stated processes. "I couldn't very well mount a hostile proxy contest if I hadn't taken the trouble to give the company the chance to place me on the board after going through the process that they announced publicly," Monks explains. So, in November, he took time out from his analytical work to send letters to the nominating committees at each of the seven companies to propose himself as a board candidate.

The letters were four single-spaced pages clipped to a resume formatted in small type to keep it to two pages. Monks was typically sweeping in making his appeal. "The continued profitable functioning of large American corporations is one of the essential elements in a healthy and peaceful world," he wrote, and that was only his opening sentence. He wanted the nominating committee to know the great importance he was placing on the role of boards of directors. Next, came his own qualifications—his work in law, energy, and financial service businesses and in government; his involvement with institutional investors; and his many stints as a director. The latter included Codex, Esterline, Westmoreland Coal, Sulpetro, The Boston Company, Jefferies & Co., Lambert Bruxelles and, from 1985 to the present, the diversified industrial concern Tyco Laboratories; also, since 1987, he had been serving on an advisory panel for Mitsubishi International Corporation. He gave several references, mostly CEOs. (Oddly, he stated that he served as the federal official in charge of the private pension system, ERISA, for "two" years, 1983–1985, when clearly he served in that capacity for only 13 months, January 1, 1984, through the end of January 1985. A bit of exaggeration to help his cause perhaps? He says he was referring to two calendar years.) Finally, he revealed his prime purpose in nominating himself as a director: "I have become convinced that one of the most important elements for the legitimacy of Boards of Directors is in demonstrating that membership is not self perpetuating and that there exists a functional process for outside nominations."

All but two of the responses were negative. Actually, Exxon and Chevron failed even to acknowledge Monks' letter. (Although Monks did not follow up with those two companies at the time, he struck back at Exxon the following year.) Kodak and Sears said they would consider the matter.

Sears' relatively cordial response, however, did not really figure into Monks' ultimate choice of the company as its target. By process of elimination, first of all, Lockheed was out, since Monks' past association with Harold Simmons would certainly taint his credibility as a director candidate. Northrop's poor performance had more to do with criminal proceedings against the company than misguided operations. The standoff in the Persian Gulf, about to explode into war, assured that Exxon, Mobil, and Chevron's shareholders would be content for a while.

It came down to Kodak and Sears. Sears' governance profile was particularly bad, in Monks' view a "monarchy." At the time, Brennan held the positions of chairman; CEO; chief executive of the largest division, the retail group; and trustee of the employee benefit plan. On the board, he headed the nominating committee. Monks liked to repeat Minow's remark that, "Brennan has five jobs on the *Titanic*. To whom was he accountable?" But the deciding factor was that Sears was clearly in worse shape than

Kodak, and the shareholders were beginning to complain loudly. When Monks saw in the January 1991 issue of *Fortune* that Sears ranked 287 out of 306 in a listing of America's Most Admired Companies, he had his target.

However, only about a third of Sears' outstanding stock was held by institutional investors, who were more likely to know Monks and to vote against management than were individuals. Meanwhile, some 23.5 percent of the stock was almost guaranteed to vote with management, as it was held in Sears' employee benefit plans, representing 230,000 of Sears' half million workers. These two factors did not bode well for Monks' fortunes at the ballot box. But, as chance would have it, the company was one of the few in the country to use a system of cumulative voting to elect its directors, which meant that a shareholder could cast all of his or her votes for one nominee. In the case of Sears, with 15 directors, five of whom were up for reelection in 1991 (the board held staggered elections, with one third on the ticket each year), this meant that a shareholder given five votes, representing five open board slots, could cast all five for one nominee. A candidate could be elected with the support of as little as 17 percent of the vote. Suddenly, winter seemed a lot warmer. At Sears, Monks would not only put on a good show, he actually had a chance to win.

At one point, Monks was in Boston and decided to drop in on Ned Johnson at Fidelity just to see what this owner of 550,000 Sears shares had to say about his plan. According to Monks, Johnson expressed unbridled enthusiasm for the idea. "Helluva good idea," the Fidelity chairman said. "I wish you'd do it. I'll support you fully."

Encouraged by Johnson and others, and hardly willing to wait until Sears issued its inevitable rejection of his proposed candidacy, Monks launched the campaign. He hired Washington-based lawyer David Martin, former executive assistant to SEC chairman John Shad, to guide him through the regulatory process. He knew Martin as someone who had worked closely with Calpers, and also as the nephew of one of his classmates at St. Paul's. (That classmate was Peter Ward, the pitcher in one high school game in which Monks hit a powerful triple that clinched the game. For years, Ward joked that Monks' hit that day drove him to take up tennis.) Monks already missed Minow's counsel and companionship, but for the sake of ISS's integrity, their ties had to be completely severed. By the end of January, he had bought 100 shares of Sears stock, spending some $3,200, and got his college buddy Dubow also to buy 100 shares and to formally nominate him. By coincidence, Dubow's grandparents had run a Chicago company that manufactured sporting goods for Sears and Montgomery Ward. Dubow sent the necessary papers by overnight mail to Sears from his home in Arizona. But right before the deadline for filing shareholder initiatives, February 1, Monks got a frenzied call from his friend. The whole nominating packet had been returned. Apparently, the by laws had been changed so that the deadline was not at least 90 days before last year's annual meeting, but now at least 60 days before that meeting and no more than 90 days before. Okay, try again. The Alice-in-Wonderland journey through the rules of the game had begun.

So, Sears did not yet know that Monks was fiercely determined to run for its board. The board's nominating committee met in mid-February to pen an official "no thank-you" card to Monks in reply to his November letter. But by then, Monks' campaign was in full gear. By the end of February, the shareholder activist was busily plotting strategy with his newly hired proxy solicitor, Georgeson & Co., and his public relations firm, Alan Towers and Associates, both in New York. He needed to decide how he would present his case to shareholders. "I want to take a Nixon in 1968 approach towards the substance of Sears' business problems—'I have a plan,'" he wrote Wilcox on February 28, referring to Nixon's convention speech on Vietnam that year, when Monks was a delegate for Nelson Rockefeller.

> My message is that Sears is publicly, unmistakably a troubled company. Troubled companies have a particular need for the questioning persistence of genuinely independent directors. As such, I would expect to raise questions in a variety of areas—governance questions and ones of business strategy. Should Sears deconglomerate? But I want my business utterances to be in the mode of questions appropriate for board considerations. . . . The campaign should be simple—Voting for Monks is the correct, legal, appropriate, prudent, necessary way for a fiduciary (or other) shareholder to express to management the desire for change.

What did all this have to do with Nixon's plan to end the Vietnam War? "It always fascinated me," Monks explains, "that Nixon was able to say simply, "I have a plan" and get away with it all during the primaries and general election, while Hubert Humphrey was endlessly badgered. I figured that this was a winning way to deal with an otherwise overwhelming problem of public relations."[3]

Dubow succeeded in filing the nomination on the second try, on February 27. The following day, Monks wrote to Sears' general counsel, David Shute, to make a formal request for a list of all Sears' 344,000 nonemployee shareholders so he could prepare to mail his proxy material (once it was approved by the SEC) out to each of them and then start making follow-up calls to the largest among them. He also wrote Brennan to request the list, and to ask that the company adopt confidential voting and give him the opportunity to meet with Sears' employee-shareholders—members of employee profit sharing and pension plans—in April so that he could present himself to them as a candidate and hand out his proxy material. In his view, the trustees of the Sears pension plan, who were either directors or management or both, had a conflict of interest, although he did not say so in so many words to Brennan. He simply wrote, "It is the trustees' responsibility to assure that employee voting rights be exercised in accordance with ERISA."

The lack of confidential voting at Sears, meanwhile, was a big problem for Monks. As he puts it: "There is virtually no institutional investor who does not have the prospect or the reality of an important business relationship with Sears." Who, then, would dare vote for him, against management's wishes, knowing that Sears would be aware of how they voted? By the early 1990s, shareholder activists had filed many resolutions at U.S. companies demanding confidential voting. Many top corporations including IBM, General Electric, and General Motors already guaranteed confidentiality. Many others guaranteed it before a vote, but not afterward. Sears was in neither group.

While he was writing the letters, Monks got a call from defense tactician Lipton. That is how he knew that Sears had got Dubow's nomination papers and was taking his candidacy seriously. Lipton was familiar with Monks' crusade. In fact, he had received an advance copy of the book Monks had written with Minow on corporate governance, *Power and Accountability,* which would be coming out that spring. In the phone call with Lipton, Monks spoke freely, as he wrote in his February 28 letter to Wilcox, "I made clear that the whole project would involve significant cost, but that that was part of the message that I wanted communicated to the SEC and the public." Lipton told Monks he would be conferring with his client on the matter for a few days.

Monks filed his preliminary proxy statement for the SEC to review on March 1, knowing that it could take several weeks to clear. The proxy explained his reasons for running and how one could vote for him. Until the SEC gave the document its stamp of approval, and Monks distributed it to shareholders, he would not be able to solicit votes or even discuss his candidacy with investors. According to the law as it then stood, anyone involved in any sort of proxy contest—such as running for the board, attempting a takeover, or campaigning for a proxy resolution—could not actually speak to shareholders until those shareholders had received the person's SEC-approved proxy statement. Talking to the press, therefore, was also verboten.

This "quiet period" was just one of Monks' frustrations with the SEC during the month of March. He also ran into a brick wall when arguing for the ability to list some of the company's nominees as well as himself on his own proxy card—so that shareholders would have more of a choice than either casting all their votes for Monks or for the company's entire slate. At the time the Sears drama was unfolding, the SEC was considering major changes in the proxy rules, including this so-called bona fide nominee rule that kept candidates from listing other candidates on their proxy cards, and the rules restricting shareholder communications in proxy contests. Pension funds, most prominently Calpers, and other investors had written the SEC arguing that as in public elections, proxy contests should involve free give-and-take among shareholders. In fact, Calpers' adviser on this issue was David Martin. His work, including a letter listing some 50 proposed reforms so impressed Monks that the shareholder activist recruited him for the Sears campaign.

In time, by late 1992, the SEC—in part as a result of Monks' frustrations in the Sears matter—would repeal the bona fide nominee rule and also decide that a preliminary proxy statement is a public filing, hence allowing immediate public comment by the filer. The most important regulatory revision for the shareholder activist movement allowed more than 10 institutional shareholders to communicate on a contested proxy matter. But Monks was operating under the old, more restrictive regime.

On March 5, Monks heard from Lipton again with this none-too-startling news: "They are not receptive to your being on the board." Since Monks was determined to go ahead, Lipton suggested a one-on-one meeting with Brennan in Chicago. The purpose of such a get-together was to discuss Monks' motivations, and he jumped at the chance for personal contact. The meeting was set for Monday, March 11. Monks' advisers urged him to take someone with him, just to have a witness who would confirm his account of the meeting if it should ever be disputed. But he opted to go alone, since the meeting was supposed to be one-on-one; it was a decision he would later regret.

That day, Monks woke at sunrise at his winter home in Palm Beach, Florida, and caught an early flight to Chicago. He was greeted in the lobby of the Sears Tower by CFO Jim Denny. They stepped into an elevator and began the long ride to the 78th floor, engulfed in a throbbing silence. As the elevator doors opened, Denny remarked, "This is the first time bad news has gotten above the 77th floor."

Brennan showed up in shirtsleeves, looking a bit worn, having just come from a grueling interview with security analysts. The meeting began, and to Monks' surprise, Denny did not excuse himself. Monks was tempted to ask Denny to leave, but also viewed this two-against-one situation as a challenge his ego could not resist. He jotted down notes during the 45-minute session and retyped them later in narrative form. As Monks summed up: "The meeting was cordial to begin, deteriorating slightly over 40 minutes to being correct." Brennan made it clear that his preference would be for Monks to not run for the board.

"You've got a great record running for Senate, working for Reagan," Brennan said. "You've done more than any of us. But we feel good about our financial services business. Retail is where we're getting killed, and we just don't see how your qualifications will help us in the area in which we need it. I am CEO. I have to set priorities. We are taking a lot of hits right now from the press. I feel that we have great prospects of coming out on the other side, but for now we just have to hunker down, persevere and take our licking, knowing that we will ultimately prevail . . . . Your interests in governance are not our main concern. I am not sure that I would associate with them if I had the luxury of time and energy to think about them, but for sure they're only a distraction right now."

Monks listened closely, occasionally nodding, poised to reply. When Brennan was finished, Monks began. As he tells it: "I told them how I had come to choose Sears, that I reviewed the great companies of America, that I personally had a great deal of experience as a director of companies, that I had unfailingly been a positive force and contributed to those companies, that I looked for companies where there were vacancies and it was apparent to me that Mr. Telling [former chairman and CEO Edward R. Telling] would be at an age when normally he wouldn't run again for reelection, and I looked to companies where I could make a contribution. We talked briefly about the entry of Sears into the financial services business in 1981, which was substantially the same time when we were working with The Boston Company and merging it into . . . American Express with very much the same kind of thinking that Sears had had at the same time.

"I explained how I had made myself known to the nominating committee and the history of my dealings with them. I think that Brennan bought the "story" that I had selected Sears. There was no intimation that I was simply a gadfly. I explicitly spoke to the point that I had never met anybody on the nominating committee (in the context of saying that I didn't take their rejection of my candidacy personally). I spoke of the opportunities for Sears to take the lead in competitiveness, governance, stockholder relations." He briefly mentioned his and Minow's upcoming book on governance. "They did not pick up on this," he noted (Monks was wrong there).

"At this point, Ed became a little bit shorter as if, god dammit, the problem was retail and everything I was talking about simply couldn't be relevant until or unless retail was solved."

Monks' response was, "I am not a candidate to be a line officer in the company." He added that Telling's departure as director "would presumably also involve the chairmanship of the trustees of the Employees Profit Sharing Trust, that there could be real gain to the company in picking up directoral energy in [the pensions] area. Brennan did not pick this up." At least Monks thought at the time that Brennan did not pick it up. He would learn differently later.

Sensing that the meeting was nearing an end, Monks said something he had rehearsed in his mind. Looking Brennan straight in the eye, he said, "Ed, I respect your stewardship of Sears, Roebuck and Company, and I want you to acknowledge that there is no disrespect in my candidacy."

Brennan hesitated. "All right," he acquiesced.

Monks continued. "I want to conduct a campaign so that in two months' time we can gather in this room and in the same spirit, irrespective of the result, look back on what we had done as being constructive. By the way," Monks added, "losing is overrated as an educational experience."

At that, Brennan smiled. "Winning is the only thing," he asserted.

Monks' judgment was that Brennan and the other directors simply could not accept anyone as a candidate who hadn't been invited by them. As he noted the next day in a summary of the session he sent to Wilcox:

> I think in his own mind the action of the nominating committee of disposing of my candidacy because I didn't have a retailing background was absolutely correct. I don't think he would permit himself to recognize that it is a simple knee jerk reaction to an outside generated candidacy. The notion that a director needs particular sectoral experience not only has no basis in law and practice, but also is at variance with the

qualification of his existing "independent" directors. . . . All of this is in aid of the conclusion that Brennan sees his board as a staff competency and what he needs now is retailing. He has all the help he needs in financial service, thus making my candidacy redundant.

Monks was only half right about Brennan's thinking. Yes it was a knee jerk reaction, but not to just any "outside generated candidacy." It was a reaction to Bob Monks. "We did not want Bob Monks on the board," Brennan relates today. "We felt he'd be disruptive. We did some homework. Asked around. Heard how he'd acted in other venues [although not on other boards. Ed.]. We had a strategy, and we were working toward a plan to enhance shareholder value. The process dated back to the hostile takeover era in the late 1980s. We had to understand how our assets were valued, and we were looking at it month by month." In other words, Monks was a shareholder activist and they didn't want a shareholder activist on their board. The way Brennan remembers it, the March 11 get-together did nothing to change his impression of Monks as activist: "Monks said he was interested in getting corporations more active in voting their pension and profit-sharing shares in the companies they're invested in. He knew Ed Telling who was the chairman of the profit-sharing fund was retiring at age 72, and Monks said he'd like that seat. He thought he could take the profit-sharing position. He never said one word about company performance. He didn't level with us."[4]

The next day, Tuesday March 12, Monks faxed his account of the meeting to his proxy solicitor Wilcox, concluding with now a more developed strategic plan for approaching investors, once the SEC approved his proxy statement:

The most sensible way of communicating our message is to talk to the permanent shareholders. These are the index funds and other large funds that as a practical matter will always own some Sears Roebuck. The message is when you are a shareholder of a company whose performance is not to your liking, consider your choice. You want to continue to be a shareholder, you think the franchise is good, you don't want to sell the stock, you don't want to take the trouble yourself to try to cause a takeover of the company, you don't want to cause a proxy contest. Where do you begin? The place to begin is with the board. The way in which you communicate the desire for some kind of change is through effecting a change in the board. My candidacy permits a new technique for registering this sentiment. In the past, people have withheld votes from directors to indicate disapproval. [There is no way to vote "no" on a candidate or slate of candidates.] My candidacy gives you the opportunity actually to select a single director without thereby raising any risk of disruption in the board or takeover of the company, but on the other hand giving an unmistakable message of shareholders' determination that there be change.

Later that day, Monks received a call from Lipton. The lawyer wanted to know whether the meeting with Brennan had changed Monks' mind about running for the board. The call surprised Monks; he thought he had made himself more than clear the day before. No, he assured Lipton, nothing had changed. He was still very much a candidate. What Lipton did not tell him was that he and his law firm associates were already gathering munitions for the battle against him. Apparently, he just wanted to know for sure that now was the time to roll them out.

On hanging up, Monks decided to go for a long bicycle ride to clear his head about the upcoming campaign. He cycled for a few hours, riding about 20 miles from his house across the bridge into West Palm Beach, then south along the ocean before finally turning around to head home. But he had gone too far, and, after a while, he grew fatigued. A couple blocks from his house, a chauffeur-driven Bentley pulled out suddenly from behind a hedge and Monks could not avoid it. The collision dented the Bentley's door and left Monks with two broken ribs and a cracked hip bone. Somehow he made his way home, but later that evening he developed a fever and Milly had to drive him to the emergency room—where she talked the doctor out of performing surgery on his hip. For the next two days, he rested in bed, taking drugs to ease the pain. A week later, they flew home to Washington with Monks confined to a wheelchair during the flight.

Brennan's declaration to Monks a day earlier that "winning is the only thing" was no idle remark. On Wednesday, March 13, Monks, still in a stupor from his accident, learned that Sears was bringing out heavy artillery to fight him. That day, the company filed suit against him in New York State Supreme Court (Sears was incorporated in New York), claiming that his request for a list of shareholders was improper because Monks "does not have a purpose in seeking Sears' shareholder list other than self-promotion. . . . Monks' interest lies in the advancement of his career as a professional publicist, author and consultant on proxy fights and other corporate governance matters. . . . Monks has timed these efforts to coincide with the pre-publication sales campaign for a forthcoming book he has written entitled *Power and Accountability,* which extols his views about proxy fights and corporate governance matters." To support these claims, the suit even quoted from advance promotional material for the book: "*Power and Accountability* catches corporate chieftains in its cross-hairs. Chieftains that have been protected profitably for so long. . . . Monks and Minow were witness to the rise of the institutional investor, and played a part in investors' increasing involvement in determining corporate direction." The suit went on to invalidate Monks' request by pointing out that he did not, as required under state law, own Sears' stock for six months before making the demand for the stockholder list—although a court would likely forgive this transgression if a defendant produced a compelling reason for wanting the list.

It would only be expected that a company try to keep an aggressor from getting hold of a list of its shareholders. But, Sears was being unusually forceful. Normally, a company writes a cordial letter to the supplicant stating that because he or she does not have a proper purpose for having the list, the company will not grant it. Then, the supplicant sues the company in state court. In this case, though, Sears decided to show its teeth by taking Monks to court, asking the judge to deny him the list and charge him Sears' legal fees and other costs. As David Martin puts it: "It stopped the insurgent dead in his tracks and shifted the burden to him having to come forward and defend himself, as opposed to the company being on the defensive."[5] What it also did was put Monks on guard that this company was likely to sue him for just about anything he tried to do. And Monks did not have the resources or the time to defend a series of lawsuits.

Equally bad for Monks, the same day he got sued, Sears announced that it was shrinking the size of its board from 15 to 10, asking four directors who were Sears executives to step aside. (In addition, former Sears chairman Telling was retiring.) Sears explained to the press that it was merely trying to give outside, independent directors a greater voice on the board, as its board had long discussed doing, in keeping with a growing trend at the time in corporate America; Brennan would be the only insider left on the board. But there was no question that this action also crippled Monks' election effort. With the number of directors up for election now down to three from five, Monks, under Sears' cumulative voting system, now needed 26 percent of outstanding shares to win a seat on the board compared with only 17 percent before. Indeed, Sears' executives did admit that they had accelerated their decision to shrink the board in order to block Monks' attempt to win a directorship. Monks was dumbfounded.

That a major American corporation would so drastically restructure its board in response to his candidacy was incomprehensible to him. After all, he was not a raider attempting a hostile takeover. As a board member, he would not even be able to second his own motions.

He got his first calls from the press. Sears' general counsel, David Shute, had told the *Wall Street Journal* that in Monks' meeting with Brennan he "indicated . . . that he wants to influence the investment policies of Sears's pension fund and profit sharing plans" and did not even criticize Sears' performance.[6] Shute added that the nominating committee had rejected Monks' request for nomination because Monks would "attempt to put into effect his ideas of corporate governance reform at a time when the company needs to focus on improvement in financial performance." Surely Monks would have had lots to say to refute this distorted version of the meeting with Brennan. Yes, he was using Sears to promote his theories on corporate governance. But his theories included the importance of getting shareholder representation on boards of directors, especially at troubled companies. And that was what he was trying to do here. Corporate governance reform at Sears is precisely what would focus management on improving performance.

But because the SEC had not yet moved on his proxy statement, Monks could only issue a lame "no comment" to the press. Having filed his preliminary proxy statement on March 1, Monks had received the SEC's comments on March 15 and sent back revisions a few days later. His lawyer advised him to keep his mouth shut until his proxy statement got all the necessary approvals, or risk being sued by the SEC or Sears, who had shown it would leap at any opportunity to file suit.

Confined to his bed in Palm Beach, heavily drugged with painkillers, feeling battered both physically and mentally, Monks hit a low point. What had he got himself into? He had wanted to put on display for the world how difficult it was for shareholders to have a say in corporate governance. But he did not really know just how difficult it would be. When he decided to play hardball with a major corporation, it decided to play hardball back using the full force of its vast resources. He despaired that there was no way he could be elected as a director of Sears, Roebuck and Company and that now he was in danger of just making a fool of himself. Earlier in his career he had taken on two almost legendary incumbent senators and, predictably, lost. In retrospect, those races seemed to him somewhat foolhardy. But that could be chalked up to youthful enthusiasm.

Now a loss would only be humiliating. From his bed, he placed a call to his PR maven, Alan Towers.

Towers got the message when he phoned into his office from a Circle K parking lot in Phoenix, where he was on vacation. He called his client right away. As he updated Towers on the recent events, Monks sounded uncharacteristically weary. As Towers describes Monks on that day: "He had this moment of rationality, and rationality is not good for a visionary."

But in Towers' worldview, what Monks had just told him was good news. "Bob, you can't lose," he reassured his client.

"What do you mean? They've stacked the board against me."

"I'm just telling you that from a public relations standpoint, it's impossible for you to lose," Towers said, explaining that the press is always with the underdog, and the more Sears beat him up, the better he looked. "If you just finish the fight, you have to win. You may not win the board seat. But you'll change the way companies are run."

Before long, Monks was himself again: back in a fighting mood. He even held out hope that somehow despite all the obstacles, he could still win.

While he was waiting to hear back from the SEC on his proxy statement, Monks was, among other things, working on assuring that alternate victory: positive press. Towers had by the beginning of March developed a long strategy memo entitled, "X Candidacy Program"—X because, as with any client, he didn't want to let the news get out. The job at hand, as the memo stated, went far beyond just getting Monks elected to the Sears board. The PR program would aim to achieve two goals: "(1) To educate the professional/investment/academic communities about the restrictive director nomination process and its contribution to America's declining competitiveness, and (2) to enlighten the general public, Main Street, about the impact of the process on their standard of living." Before getting an SEC-approved proxy statement, the plan was to prime the pump by beginning to arrange interviews with Monks regarding the board nominating process and the impact of poor governance on America's declining standard of living and competitiveness. The "Main Street" discussion would emphasize lower rates of job creation, higher unemployment, and lower wage growth in the 1980s versus the 1970s. It would also demonstrate that the United States had recently had lower productivity growth than other major countries, declining global market share in some key industries, and higher rates of CEO compensation.

Towers also wanted Monks to prepare for the announcement day by writing a piece entitled, "Why I'm Running for a Seat on Sears' Board," that would be sent to the Chicago press. In addition, he hoped to find a freelancer to write a story about "Profiting in a shareholder-responsive company," demonstrating that effective governance, including giving shareholders a voice, can create strong financial performance. During the campaigning phase, the media plan included contacting *USA Today* for a story on the Main Street angle; interviews with journalists in cities with large Sears' operations such as Dallas, Los Angeles, and Columbus, Ohio; and interviews with organizations of individual investors.

As the Sears proxy statement got distributed to shareholders in late March, the press picked up on it. In that document, the company acknowledged that Monks' decision to run for the board on his own "was a factor in the timing of the current change" in the structure of the board. "Since the Company has cumulative voting, the decrease in Board size to 10 directors and the resulting decrease in the size of each class (that is, the portion of the board up for election each year) will make it more difficult for Mr. Monks to be elected," the proxy statement read. Also in the proxy, Sears revealed the enormous amount of resources it would be devoting to defeating Monks. It had recruited an army to solicit votes from shareholders. To begin with, Sears hired D. F. King & Co., a leading proxy solicitation firm, for a fee of $850,000 plus expenses to put 150 people on the case; the proxy statement indicated that D. F. King would actually be hiring people just to work on this one project. For $500,000, Sears also enlisted four staffers at Goldman, Sachs & Co., the company's financial adviser, to approach stockholders. Finally, Sears assigned some of its own people to make sure the job got done: "Officers and assistant officers . . . along with no more than 30 specially-designated employees, may solicit proxies by personal interview, telephone and telegram, in addition to the use of the mails," the proxy statement read. It also specified that Sears would spend an estimated $5,550,000 on that year's solicitation *over* what it would spend in an ordinary, uncontested election of directors—dwarfing Monks' $250,000.

With news of this formidable defense force coming so soon after Sears' other aggressive measures, Monks found himself suddenly and uncharacteristically afraid. As he later recalled his thoughts at the time: "For $5.5 million you could buy the best in leg breakers. (Was that Bentley just a coincidence?) You could write me a whole new biography; and you could keep all the juniors in a law firm busy concocting new and ingenious suits to bring against me—which while spurious would be bankrupting to defend." In his panic, he decided to transfer all his personal property into a new trust that would keep his assets out of the reach of anyone who might sue him. He phoned his nephew in Portland, John Higgins, who was also his partner in many ventures, and asked that he make the arrangements through the family's lawyer, David Wakelin. The revocable trust would limit Monks' personal liability on any account, thereby making him judgment proof. (That status holds unless it can be proven that the transfer was a fraudulent effort to avoid creditors.) "They can bring spurious suits against me forever, but I cannot defend myself and they cannot collect," Monks explains.

If he had not been so unnerved, Monks might have considered Sears' dramatic reaction to his candidacy to be a compliment. It was a mark of his success in his years of striving for better corporate governance—from the Labor Department to Honeywell and Lockheed—that a company the size of Sears would feel so threatened by him.

Given Sears' determination to keep Monks off the board, it did not make much sense for him to plunge into the long and costly legal mire of fighting to get access to Sears' shareholder list. It was apparent that Sears would stop at nothing to defeat his attempt at a board seat. So even if he succeeded in winning the lawsuit and the list, Sears would find other modes of attack. And they might prove devastating to his energy and reputation if not his wallet. In the end, Monks' gut feeling was that if he did not challenge the lawsuit, Lipton would spare him his most brutal tactics. So he let it lie. (The suit was later settled and dismissed.)

Instead, he would go in through the back door. His proxy solicitor Georgeson could find out who many of the shareholders were and make contact with them. Any investment manager who handles more than $100 million must report its holdings quarterly to the SEC. It's not hard for proxy solicitors to get their hands on those public filings. Hence, Georgeson was able to cobble together a list of big Sears shareholders. The solicitor would mail Monks' proxy material to those holders, and the candidate himself would then visit or call the largest among them. Georgeson was also able to reach individual Sears shareholders by sending proxy information to the brokers and banks that held shares for them; in turn those custodians delivered the information to the actual shareholders.

But what about the biggest group of shareholders—Sears employees? Monks had never received a reply to his February 28 letter to Brennan in which he asked for a chance to meet with Sears' employee-shareholders to present his case to them personally. So, he wrote another one on March 22 asking that his own proxy material (once it was approved) be distributed to employees. A few days later he heard back from Shute, who informed him dryly that since Sears had already begun its own mailing to employees, Monks' material would have to be mailed separately at a cost of $300,000 to Monks. Never mind that Sears had ignored his earlier request; Shute did not mention it. Monks' prompt, curt reply was the following: "Frankly, I had hoped in writing to Ed Brennan on February 28, that I could timely be afforded the opportunity to distribute my materials to employees in an effective and economical way." The $300,000 was not an expense that Monks was willing to bear. He had gone into the campaign with the notion that he would spend $250,000 and no more. If he could be assured of winning a good portion of that 23.5 percent chunk of Sears' shares by shelling out another $300,000 for access to this group of shareholders, he would have done it. But that was unlikely, since employees were generally loyal to management and those who were not would be scared off by the lack of confidential voting. Anyway, he hoped he would be able to reach the employee shareholders in other ways.

Finally, on April 2 Monks had his own proxy statement approved. He could now approach big institutional investors and answer questions from the press. In the statement, he made his message clear: "It is time for shareholders to ask for a new voice on the board to raise difficult questions about the company's strategic objectives." It was also time, he noted, for someone to challenge Sears on governance questions, including, independence of directors, the separation of the titles of CEO and chairman, and confidential voting. What did not appear in the final proxy statement was Monks' account of his March 11 meeting with Brennan. The SEC did not allow it since Monks, having attended the meeting alone, could not corroborate his story.

The same day the SEC cleared his proxy statement, Georgeson sent Monks the list it had compiled of 116 of the company's largest investors complete with contact names, addresses, phone numbers, and number of shares held. Now the real work would begin.

As luck would have it, the first stop was the Council of Institutional Investors' (CII) annual meeting two days later, on April 4. If he had not received SEC approval, he would not have been able to make this appearance. But, armed with boxes of his proxy statements, he went over to the Washington Court Hotel to be the featured speaker before an audience of major investors and major media. This was a crucial moment for Monks. He had no complete shareholder list and therefore no guide whatsoever to Sears' individual investors; he had no way of presenting his case to employees. And together, those investors accounted for some 67 percent of outstanding shares. If Monks had any chance of winning this election, he had to win over Sears' institutional investors. While he knew many of the larger investors personally, that hardly guaranteed their support. As he later put it to the *Boston Globe,* the likelihood he would succeed could be compared with "the second coming of Christ." Monks was not saying he would lose. He was just being the smart politician: setting up low expectations so that even a loss, if not too devastating, could seem like a victory for the crusade.

Because SEC rules require that anyone who is to be solicited first receive approved proxy material, Monks made sure that his proxy statement was placed on every seat in the room before he began his remarks. And then he made doubly sure he was within the law—and was sufficiently ridiculing it—by announcing, "Anyone who doesn't have a proxy statement will have to leave unless they permit this young lady"—he handed a stack to California Treasurer Kathleen Brown—"to give them one."

Even after the proxy statement got the SEC's nod, Monks could by law talk only about what was in that document and nothing else. Indeed, he even had to get his speech to the CII vetted by the SEC. "The proxy statement was a fairly dry piece of advocacy," his attorney Martin says, "in part because we tried to be more colorful, but the SEC gave us a ton of comments and it was reduced—not because we agreed so much but because we were so eager to get it out on time."

Even so, at the CII meeting, Monks managed to be true to his colorful reputation. Directing much of his speech to Brown herself as if he were merely talking to a friend, he started out by delineating the big picture of the corporate governance movement that would form the context of his Sears race. "This is an important occasion," he began. "It marks the end of the beginning of the first phase of modern corporate governance" (painfully convoluted, but still had the ring of something momentous) "during which it has become widely known that great corporations really have owners; that these owners are capable of watchfulness and of understanding their own long-term interest; and that these owners could use the machinery of corporate governance to express their wishes. . . . Institutional owners have acted with restraint—they have asked, not demanded; they have been willing to talk, rather than force confrontation."

"We are now ready to begin the next phase—that of knowledgeable participation by shareholders. In focusing attention on those companies that indisputably are 'poor performers,' institutional investors should initiate binding resolutions when managements will not participate in constructive discussion. The most important focal point is the process of selection for the board of directors." That is where Sears came in. Monks wanted to depict his contest for a seat on Sears' board as one element in the transition of the movement to the next, essential stage. First, he defined the word "independent," as in independent director. The word does not apply in a situation in which a nominating committee, headed by the chairman and CEO—Ed Brennan—"invites" people to join a board. "So long as an individual owes his membership on a board uniquely to personal selection by the chief executive officer, he cannot be considered to be independent." And when, as in most cases, a number of invitees are placed on a ballot to run for the same number of board slots—hence, uncontested—this is hardly an election in the true sense of the word.

Monks then ticked off the list of obstacles he'd encountered so far in his run for the board. He made the most of Sears' commitment of $5.5 million to fight him—well aware of investors' keen interest in unusual expenditures by any company, especially poor performers. "Respectfully, I ask Ed Brennan and the members of the Sears' board—"how can you justify the expenditure of over $5.5 million of company funds to defeat a board candidate whose worst failing is 'independence' at the same time as literally tens of thousands of Sears' employees are being laid off?" And he used this first opportunity since clearance of his proxy statement to rebut Sears' claims that he was waging this contest for personal gain alone. "My interest lies in obtaining a seat on the board of directors of Sears, Roebuck and Company. My purpose is to help an American company that has fallen on hard times. My hope is that through my hard work, inquisitive and independent attitude and talents I can put a valuable oar in the water. I am not interested in promoting myself as a publicist, author or consultant."

But he also freely admitted that improving Sears was not the only reason for his candidacy. He stated that he was running to show that the accepted system in which boards of directors are self-perpetuating and shareholders have no real choice or representation was wrong. That system, he said, should be questioned especially at companies like Sears whose performance has been disappointing. Monks further explained that his candidacy would provide shareholders with a new "mechanism through which shareholders can indicate to management their desire for change."

As to what steps he believed Sears needed to take to address its problems, Monks listed five—and all five would end up reappearing throughout the drama with Sears. The first four: Brennan step down from one of his duties as chairman and CEO; the nominating committee be comprised of only nonmanagement directors; the company develop a list of potential board candidates; and Sears interact more freely with its investors. The fifth suggestion, and the one that attracted the greatest amount of press attention, was the only one that struck directly at Sears' financial performance. "The company has consistently set a target of a 15 percent return on equity, which it has failed to achieve in recent years. [The company had failed to achieve that return for a decade. ROE was at 6.8 percent in 1990.] The board must insist either that these targets be achieved within a reasonable time or that the company be restructured." This was the stuff that those in the audience were waiting to hear. How exactly would Monks change Sears' business to beef up the bottom line? He did not say. He did not talk about divesting nonretail businesses, or "deconglomeration," as he had in his memos to his proxy solicitor, Wilcox. He did not talk about a plan for Sears and how that plan would boost earnings and the stock price.

In the end, he pleaded for votes: "I believe that I am acting in your interest in an unequal struggle." The applause was long and loud. Out of the corner of his eye, Monks could see Kathleen Brown applauding and smiling approvingly. He felt he was among friends, triumphant.[7] But that elation didn't last long. Always analyzing his own performance, he realized where he had fallen short. He knew that he had failed to give the voters what they most wanted: a tangible, "total return" reason to vote for him and against management, who publicly maintained that Monks, with his governance agenda, would merely distract management from the strategy it was undertaking to improve retail profitability. It was not enough for him to say that as a director he would ask the difficult questions and in doing so compel the other directors to demand answers as well. As he later put it: "I fed them the wrong meat. I didn't feed them enough dollars and cents."[8] This was squarely against Monks' operating philosophy of a double helix in corporate governance with one strand standing for mission and the other for profits.

Furthermore, he felt a bit foolish at trying to depict himself as the underdog. As he later wrote: "How can you feel sympathy for a 6'6" Harvard Phi Beta Kappa rich WASP who is happily married to Andrew Carnegie II's granddaughter?"[9] Good question. But, his opponent—lumbering, unresponsive, defensive to extreme excess—helped him there. Despite his doubts, the Council speech had been a dramatic launch for his campaign and impressed many of the attendees. In the coming weeks, he would sharpen his message to point more forcefully to the bottom line.

From Washington, Monks flew to Chicago for his first meetings with the press in Sears' hometown. At the weekly business bible, *Crain's Chicago Business,* the editors had already written their editorial for the next issue, and it was about Monks and Sears. Monks met with Lisa Collins, a *Crain's* reporter—"attractive smile, hard worker, well informed," he wrote later that day in notes to himself. She showed him the editorial *Crain's* was about to run. What he saw upset him. The editorial asserted that, though his cause was a good one, he was not the ideal candidate because of his governance fixation. Monks successfully persuaded the writer that he was not so single-minded, and the editorial was altered to something a bit more acceptable: "Mr. Monks, who isn't directly affiliated with any large stockholder, may not be the ideal standard bearer for restive investors. But why doesn't Mr. Brennan let his record speak for itself? Then again, maybe that's what he's afraid of."[10]

"This was a long and good session," Monks jotted down after the meeting with *Crain's.* "They were openly partisan against Sears. I began to characterize the Brennan/Shute/Sears [view that] Monks is a governance nut [with] no real relevance to the corporation's real needs as The Big Lie. [Sears] could easily have informed themselves of my capacity to help!"

Not quite as satisfying was another interview he had that day with a *Forbes* reporter, Marcia Berss, whom he describes in his notes as "Laide, jolie" (ugly, pretty). "She was plainly (i) well prepared, (ii) very dubious about governance. All business!" She had interviewed Brennan subsequent (sic) to my visit, so I went through the whole "Big Lie" routine. What could I do? What would I change? Business agenda? Business competency? Hard? Provocative. I made a conscious effort to relax and try charm." That Monday, April 8, Monks got good coverage in the *Chicago Sun-Times,* and two days later, he was featured in a front page business section story in the *Washington Post. Forbes* did not write a story. If the press was going to be the only way he could reach many Sears shareholders, he was doing a good job so far.

A frustrating moment in the solicitation season occurred when a producer of the *Tonight Show* called to ask Monks to come on the show in April. Monks, of course, was eager to appear before such a mass audience. As he later remarked: "It would provide a rare opportunity to inform a general audience about the realities of 'corporate democracy'" (hopefully with a sense of humor befitting the occasion). It came down to a trade-off of risk and reward. The reward would be the number of Sears shareholders who had proxy cards and hadn't filed their votes yet who would be watching the show and then run to their post office the next morning and vote their proxy cards for Monks. David Martin's bet was not a whole lot. "Measure that against the clear and present danger that the *Tonight Show* was going to be such exposure, so high profile and so clearly incendiary with Sears that it would run the risk of triggering some sort of legal action by the SEC or Sears," he says. Enough said. Monks did not argue with his attorney's viewpoint.

For its part, Sears' repeated charges in the press and to big investors were that Monks was a "one-issue activist" and "wants to use this company as a classroom ("an experiment" "a crusade") for his theories of corporate governance." Still, management at the giant retailer-cum-conglomerate was nervous. The company could see that it was not dealing with just another gadfly. Monks had a solid background in business and government and knew many of Sears' institutional investors well. No, he did not have a background in retailing. But he did know financial services and he did know how to be a director; it was hard for Sears to argue that it had to have a director who was experienced in retail. It was, then, in the realm of possibility that Monks could win. But why not just let him run on the merits of his experience? Because Brennan and other directors seriously thought that Bob Monks, once on the Sears board, would be disruptive and, when he did not get his way, run to the press.[11] And who could blame them given Monks' confrontational background as a shareholder activist and Lipton's assessment of him as a prime influence on investors to be short-term in their investing?

Sears already had engaged most of the artillery in its arsenal, but was still doing everything else it could think of. General Counsel Shute wrote Georgeson a threatening letter on April 10 because 10 months earlier the proxy firm had done some work for the Big Store: a fairly routine analysis of the composition of Sears' shareholders. As Shute wrote: "We are now shocked to discover that you are engaged by Robert Monks to assist his campaign to be elected to the Sears Board over the objection of management and the Board of Directors. The information that we shared with you in confidence, and which you obtained from other sources as our agent, could now be used for your new client against us." Shute made three demands: that Georgeson assure Sears in writing that it would not use in the Monks proxy contest any of the information it acquired in doing the previous study; that Georgeson assure Sears in writing that no one who worked on the Sears analysis was also working on the Monks matter; and that

Georgeson pack up all the documents it possessed pertaining to Sears' share-holders that it had acquired in doing the study for Sears and send it to the company. Wilcox readily complied with all these demands without making any sacrifices for his current client. With its extensive resources and con-tacts, Georgeson did not need to borrow from its previous work on Sears.

The task of persuading investors to vote for Monks was the candidate's job. The detailed work of checking up on investors' commitments to see if they were carried out and of tracking down custodians to see that the votes were actually cast was Georgeson's. The firm also made clear to the New York Stock Exchange that, given the contested nature of the Sears annual meeting, its broker members had to make sure that beneficial owners actu-ally voted their stock. Through those brokers, Monks sent his materials to more than 1,000 large shareholders.

Monks spent his days in mid-April getting on and off airplanes and trains to visit key people at financial institutions. He personally paid visits to the top 10 shareholders—mostly money managers and banks. For the most part, it was hard going.

Whether these people said so or not, Monks knew that they were com-peting for corporate America's financial business. Would they take the risk of alienating one of the country's largest companies? At a trust bank in New York, he met with the trust committee and was pleased with his reception. A few days later he got a call from one of those present, an old friend. "Bob," he said, "we're going to give you all our votes . . ." At that Monks interrupted with a vulgar phrase of disbelief. The friend continued, ". . . as soon as your deposits rise to the level of Sears.' " Now that he could believe.

He had some unpleasant encounters. One Texas money manager was so bothered by Monks' call and his spiel about the virtues of collective action by the shareholders that he began to shout: "Who do you think you are? Your shit smells, too." Monks hung up, and, startled at what he had just heard, spent several minutes gazing at the Potomac out the window of his office.[12]

The decision reached by the Wisconsin Investment Board bewildered the Monks team. Pat Lipton, then the pension system's executive director, knew Monks well from ISS and supported his governance notions. It turned out that Wisconsin had voting guidelines that placed him in the category of proposals unfavorable to management. For the fund to vote for him, he had to meet two criteria: first that the company is performing badly (so far so good) and second that he, as the outsider, had a credible business plan for the company. He did not have that, and therefore would lose Wisconsin's

1.4 million shares. To Lipton's assistant, Monks argued that he was not either running for a management position or trying to take over the company; he was running to be a director. As a candidate for director, it was inappropriate for him to have a detailed business plan. It was no use. The night before the annual meeting, Monks received a letter from Lipton explaining why she was voting for the management slate:

> . . . When a company has not been meeting its long-run goals, SWIB's guideline requires that an opposition candidate, or slate of candidates, have a focused business plan for remedying the company's problems and have the ability to implement that plan successfully in order to get our vote . . .

And then, somewhat inexplicably, given the makeup of Sears' nominating committee, the letter went on:

> . . . SWIB's proxy voting guidelines support use by corporations of nominating committees composed of independent directors to establish a process for selection of new director candidates. . . . SWIB's guidelines favor use of such independent nominating committees over proxy contests to select directors at underperforming companies where the candidates have not put forth a focused business plan aimed at realistically addressing company problems.
>
> I have no doubts that you would be an excellent member of the Sears Board. Your professional reputation and your concern over working in the interests of shareholders make you a fine candidate. However, I feel that it is vitally important to remain true to the underlying principles upon which our proxy voting guidelines are based.

But some important votes started coming in. On April 15, Calpers issued a press release announcing that it would cast its 2.3 million shares of Sears stock in support of Monks. While that was not too surprising, given Calpers' symbiotic relationship with Monks, it did represent a sort of break with Sears. In January, Calpers' Hanson and Koppes had met with Brennan and agreed to withdraw a proxy resolution it had already filed for a shareholder advisory committee—Monks' invention—in return for a pledge from the company to meet with the fund twice that year.

The Colorado and Pennsylvania state employees' pension funds also backed Monks. Jack Bogle, chairman of the Vanguard Group of mutual funds, phoned Monks to pledge his firm's support and later endorsed him publicly. Monks began calling Fidelity to make sure Ned Johnson followed up on his earlier pledge of support, but he did not get a call back until about a week before the annual meeting. On that call, Monks remembers, Johnson backpedaled, essentially saying that he could not promise Fidelity's vote, since voting decisions are made by individual fund managers. He did say, however, that he would vote the Sears shares in his personal accounts in Monks' favor and even offered to take out and sign an ad for the dissident candidate.[13] On April 29, a grateful Monks sent Johnson this letter:

Dear Ned,

You were kind enough to mention taking out an advertisement to help my effort with Sears. There follows a piece that will be printed in the *New York Times* this Sunday, May 5. Ideally, I would like to run some portion or all of this in an ad in the *Chicago Tribune* and/or the *Wall Street Journal* on the day before the meeting—Wednesday, May 8. Is this something that you could do?

He never heard from Johnson, and no ad ever appeared. In fact, he never spoke to Johnson again.

Meanwhile, Sears began finding that its oversized campaign against Monks was to some extent working against it. Stanley Rich, a New York CPA who was a trustee for an account with 1,000 shares of Sears stock, took the trouble of writing to the Sears public affairs department to put his disgust with the company on record:

I have received management's proxy, which I have discarded and am voting the Trusts' shares in favor of the dissident, Mr. Monks. In my opinion, any expenditure of the Company's funds for this purpose, let alone an amount of this magnitude, is not in the best interests of the shareholders, and indeed makes me question the overall competence of the Company's management and policy direction.

I might add that I have sat and do sit on the Boards of companies whose names you would recognize and after thirty years of experience, I believe I know the difference between valid company business and self-serving interests. Very truly yours, Stanley Rich.[14]

On April 18, Sears issued a letter to shareholders, from chairman Brennan, to re-emphasize and expand on points made in its proxy statement against Monks. The letter was mailed along with first quarter earnings, which were up from the year earlier, and reached shareholders at precisely the time they would have to make up their minds about voting. Among the assertions in the letter was that "Mr. Monks is using your high profile company as a vehicle to promote his personal philosophy on corporate governance." It also stated that when Sears met with Monks "he showed little knowledge of or interest in the operating or financial performance of the Company. Instead, he talked about his desire to become a director of a company having large pension and profit sharing funds that he could use to test his investment philosophy."

This letter, representing Sears' unlimited resources and its ability as a powerful corporate name to get its message across, enraged Monks. He asked his attorney Martin to write to the SEC to plead for relief. Under SEC rules, Sears was able to write such a letter because it had already distributed its proxy materials to all shareholders. Monks wanted the SEC to require Sears to correct its misleading statements with yet another letter to all shareholders. Martin drafted the request to the SEC, although he predicted that the agency would not respond. "Statements such as those appearing in the Letter regarding Mr. Monks' personal agenda amount to 'the big lie' of this election," Martin wrote on April 26. Regarding Sears' account of the meeting between Brennan and Monks, he wrote, "It is outrageous that Mr. Brennan is now permitted to get away with such a misleading characterization of the meeting." They never heard back from the SEC.

Late in the month, Monks started to consider publicly promoting what he had privately thought: that Sears should be split apart, its various businesses spun off to leave only the retailing core. Many of the shareholders he had met had expressed this view, as had some analysts. One caller that particularly impressed him was Guy Wyser-Pratt, a well-known Wall Street arbitrageur (investing in potential takeover candidates), who called out of the blue to voice his concern that Monks had not yet articulated a value investor's perspective: Sears should be broken up into pieces that would be much more valuable than the whole. The advice he got from Georgeson was to speak out for an independent investment bank's evaluation of deconglomeration and other strategies. So, finally, although late in the game, Monks would address the dollars-and-cents issue directly, proposing the consideration of new structures for the company—each of which could now be valued by analysts. "This should push some people back on the fence, and pull others over to your side, as they will more clearly connect the benefits of your candidacy to their pocketbook," wrote Georgeson's Ron Schneider. With interviews scheduled with PBS, CNN, CNBC, CBS and others, Monks would have ample opportunity to get this message out.

One person who was following Monks' campaign with particular interest was Harold Simmons. On April 30, Monks's former ally in the Lockheed fight wrote him a letter offering support:

> I've been following your effort to secure election to the Sears' board with interest in the business press. The Sears board would benefit from someone with your talent and perspective. I understand you are financing the Sears proxy contest on your own. I'd be pleased to contribute $25,000 to the campaign if that would be appropriate. Let me know. In any event, best of luck.

Monks thanked him, but declined the offer of monetary support: "I hope that you will understand that I am not declining to accept. I am only deferring it in the hope that it will stimulate a project on which we can work together."

As he continued visiting institutional holders, Monks also kept badgering Sears to let him communicate with employees. Some Sears staffers already had called his office to express their support. One contacted the *Sun-Times* to say that he and several fellow workers wanted more information about Monks and his candidacy but that Sears management would not give them any. "There are a lot of us who don't feel Brennan is running things right, and we want to see what this Monks guy has to say," the employee told the newspaper.[15]

That is when Monks began drafting a letter to the trustees of the Sears savings and profit sharing fund and ESOP. Now he took on the role and the tone of Robert A. G. Monks, former federal pensions administrator, who knew a lot about the law and violations of the law. No more Mr. Nice Guy. He laid out the facts: You are trustees of this plan, you have a responsiblity to vote in this matter, and the beneficiaries are entitled to tell you how to vote. Since he had not been given the opportunity in a practical way (that is, without spending $300,000 on a mailing) to present his case to employees, he wrote, it is probable

> that your beneficiaries will be . . . instructing you as to their choice of directors without knowledge of my qualification or candidacy. While all this presents me with a very serious problem in my efforts to get elected

a director, it also presents a very serious problem for the plan fiduciaries. [the trustees he was addressing] There can be no argument but that
the discretion as to (sic) whom to vote for director, when there is a
choice, is a "plan asset" within the Department of Labor's jurispru-
dence. [He should know. He made it that way.] "Is it legally appropriate
for you to accept and act on instructions when you know these instructions are based on impoverished information? . . . The question is not,
as the company's decision seems to imply, whether I can be forced to
pay an amount substantially in excess of the costs of distribution if the
company chose to cooperate, the question is how to assure that beneficiaries are informed so as to be able to make a legally effective choice as
to directors."

Monks copied the letter to the Labor Department.

Support for his position soon came from some influential Allstate insurance agents, who got in touch with Monks early in April to express
their desire to meet. The National Neighborhood Office Agents Club
(NNOAC), representing some 1,000 agents, had been fighting with Sears
and Allstate on several fronts and would have liked to have seen an employee on Sears' board. But they certainly were delighted with anyone who
might challenge the company. On April 16, one agent sympathetic to
Monks' cause faxed him a letter he'd just received from the insurance division's chief executive, Wayne Hedein, a profit-sharing plan trustee. "Dear
Fellow Profit Sharing Member," it began. "As you may know, Robert
Monks, who reportedly owns 100 shares of Sears common stock purchased
in January, has begun a proxy contest to win a seat for himself on the Sears
Board of Directors. In my opinion, he is pursuing a personal agenda and
has selected Sears, a high-profile company, as his platform. . . . Your vote
in favor of the slate of nominees proposed by the Board of Directors will
serve the best interest of all Sears shareholders." This was the first that
these employees had heard anything from the company about Monks' run
for the board. And even if they had wanted to support him, they did not
know how to do it; employees had received proxy cards that failed to provide a way for them to indicate a preference for the challenger and, of
course, they had not received Monks' proxy cards.

Three days later, several agents representing the leadership of the
NNOAC walked into Monks' Washington office. Monks gave them his
spiel, and described to them how the Sears profit-sharing plan trustees had
not given him a fair shake. The agents were impressed with the man and

what he had to say, but they were frustrated that they had no means of voting for him. Monks suggested that they take their frustration straight to the Labor Department. And they did. As they reported in a press release announcing their desire to "consider his candidacy" and describing their dilemma: "There is currently no method for Sears' Pension and Profit Sharing Fund members to vote their shares for other than the board nominated candidates. Therefore, we are asking Assistant Secretary of Labor David G. Ball to take appropriate steps to assure that Sears' employees are not deprived of the right to a meaningful vote at the 1991 annual meeting." A letter went out to Ball on April 23.

Monks also asked Ball to intervene in the matter. Sears and its Chicago attorneys continued to contend that they did not have to pay to distribute Monks' material; Monks responded that who paid was not the issue. Ball apparently took Monks' side. On April 30, Monks got a call and then a letter from the trustees of the Sears pension fund, indicating their desire to meet with him as well as the three nominees on the management slate (two of whom were plan trustees). However, this session was not called to enable trustees to better inform their beneficiaries on how to vote. The hour had by then grown too late for distributing any new material to employees; Monks argued that in that case the trustees had not properly done their job and the employees' votes should not be counted. But the trustees had their own solution to the time constraint. They decided that to meet ERISA's requirement to protect the interests of plan participants who could not make voting decisions on a fully informed basis, they themselves would assume full responsibility for voting on behalf of plan members—that is, not taking *any* instructions from the beneficiaries. The situation reeked with irony. To properly exercise their discretion in voting, the trustees had to hear from all candidates. Hence, the meeting with Monks was set up and could not be expected to be anything but a kangaroo court. So it was a Pyrrhic victory for Monks.

The interview was to take place on May 7, at 5:30 P.M., which gave the trustees exactly one day to make up their minds on how to vote 23.5 percent of the stock. The day before the session, Monks stopped in at the Labor Department to make a last-minute pitch to Ball to invalidate the profit-sharing plan votes, given the participants' lack of proper information. The Labor Department took no further action.

The next day he went to the Union League Club in downtown Chicago, where, in a private dining room, he met with all plan trustees except Brennan and another trustee, who were on the company slate and had excused themselves. Monks' reception there was chilly, to say the least. Indeed, one trustee, Don Rumsfeld, made it clear that he was annoyed at Monks for the dissident's op-ed in the *New York Times* two days earlier on May 5th entitled, "The Oxymoron in the Boardroom," which repeated the argument he had been making all along that independent directors are a myth and that shareholders are not welcome to nominate directors. Apparently Rumsfeld resented any implication that he was not independent.

The session lasted 90 minutes, enough time for Monks to state his case and answer a few curt questions. Monks explained his belief in the importance of Sears knowing and working with its shareholders, and that this relationship was especially worthwhile since quite a few of the company's institutional investors were indexed, "permanent" shareholders. "I went into my ultimate theories about the use of pension funds for refinancing industrial companies," he recorded later. Rumsfeld, who began the meeting with a scowl, appeared more at ease toward the end of Monks' talk. On leaving the room, Monks felt he'd done a good job of presenting himself as a credible candidate. Still, he was hardly surprised when he learned later on that the trustees had cast the votes of 23.5 percent of Sears shares for the management slate.

There was some suspense May 7th when the news came out that two Sears shareholders had filed suit in Philadelphia against the company attempting to delay the annual meeting. In the suit, the plaintiffs claimed that management breached its fiduciary duties in the proxy process by not properly informing shareholders of another, 1988 lawsuit that accused management of entrenching itself in a restructuring that year, at the height of the takeover era, and by management's extraordinary efforts to oppose Monks' bid for the board.

The next day, new disclosures regarding that 1988 suit raised more uncomfortable issues for Sears. The suit had already charged that the company, backed by directors, hastily beefed up its employee benefit plan holdings and took other measures to keep raiders away. It seemed to be an entrenchment move since, according to papers that the plaintiffs filed on May 7, Goldman Sachs had advised management that a "raider" could achieve a 37 percent to 69 percent premium over the stock's current value compared with only 23 percent to 38 percent for the Sears' plan. (Brennan later said the report was false.) In Philadelphia, meanwhile, a judge ruled that the annual meeting would go on.[16]

After breakfast that morning, Monks canceled interviews with several news organizations so he could spend the entire day on the phone, stumping for last minute votes. The last call of the day, his fiftieth, at 5 P.M., was to Jack Hoffman, the person in charge of the Sears accounts at Merrill Lynch. By then, Monks was hoarse and tired. And Hoffman's challenge to him on his motivations for running was the last straw. Why did not anyone seem to understand or believe his assertion that he was just a smart guy who as a director would stand up for the shareholders? The call quickly turned into a heated exchange.

"You should pay me for doing this!" Monks thundered into the phone.

"This conversation has concluded, Mr. Monks," Hoffman replied, and hung up.[17]

That evening, he welcomed Milly and a few advisers, who had just arrived in Chicago, and they all had dinner together.

Brennan rose to speak. Curiously, to Monks, the CEO spoke with absolute confidence, even when relating his disappointment with Sears' results. He acknowledged that Sears' performance—earnings off by 40 percent in 1990—had been "unacceptable," though he added that other service businesses were also doing poorly and indeed the whole country was in a recession. First quarter earnings, he noted, were up impressively from the year earlier. And then he went on to describe the status of each operating unit and plans for improving overall performance.

Question from the floor: When? Brennan: Work is ongoing, and "in somewhat less than five years, we'll get to acceptable return on investment," that is, from the 6.8 percent of 1990 to the 15 percent goal. Another question: Why is it that employees, who own 23.4 percent of the stock, do not have board representation? Brennan: "I am the employee on the Board." Why spend $5.5 million to oppose Monks? Brennan: Sears spent only $2.8 million, which was "still far too much." Why had Sears lost its position as the nation's preeminent retailer to Wal-Mart Stores? Brennan: Because Sears had been focused on its financial services operations. On the question of Sears' decision to shrink the size of its board, Brennan told shareholders that management was developing criteria for the appointment of new, outside directors and had already consulted with a top adviser to pension funds: one Institutional Shareholder Services.

For the first time, Monks came to understand why Brennan had found him—and the independence he represented—so threatening. Brennan was the king of this castle, and no one had ever challenged his authority.[18]

Then came the part of the meeting for the election of three directors. Finally, Monks would have his moment. First, his friend Arthur Dubow rose to nominate him with a short speech that boomed over the mike:

> Bob is an American success story in the classic mold. He believes deeply in the principles on which our nation was formulated and his professional and business accomplishments were always accompanied by public service in the communities in which he lived as well as on the national level. . . . His great skill as a director is to require management to ask itself the right questions and to justify their answers. . . . If the directors of Sears had asked the right questions, and management could not provide the right answers, then perhaps the directors would have exercised their most important prerogative and changed the management. . . . I strongly believe the election of Bob Monks to the Sears board will benefit the Sears shareholders and will be a first step to restoring Sears to its position as a highly profitable and well regarded company whose stock price will reflect its success.[19]

And then, to scattered applause, Monks rose to address the crowd.

"I am proud to be with you on this historic occasion," he began. "This is the first time in American economic history that an independent qualified individual has solicited proxies for election to the board of a major corporation in opposition to management's incumbent slate."

The speech was not long. But Monks delivered it slowly, often glancing up to catch Brennan's and the other directors' reactions. All he could decipher from their faces was grim hostility. But what else could he expect, he thought to himself. Naturally they would not appreciate being lectured to in public about how they have failed in their duties. Embarrassment, he thought, could be his most effective weapon yet in pressuring this company's board and management to change their ways. "Of one thing I can assure you, whatever else happens here today—Sears, Roebuck and Company has changed. There can be no turning back."

His main goal, he said, was to get on the board so he could ask tough questions. "But if I can't have that," he said, beginning to put his spin on an anticipated loss, "my second choice is to demonstrate the way that our system prevents those questions from being asked, and to get you, the shareholders, to ask some of your own." He himself posed five. The first addressed the strategy issue: "If management cannot find a way to add value to the enterprise as a whole, doesn't it make more sense to spin the individual business units off to the shareholders? . . . Will people buy stocks where they buy socks? If not, aren't we better off using that store space for more socks? . . . As a director I would move to engage a truly independent investment banker to consider this vital question." So far this was shaping up as the speech he should have been giving all along.

"Next question: Can a company year after year for over a decade fail to achieve its own criteria of earning 15 percent on equity without somebody insisting that something be done about it?" He would be that person. Third, Monks pointed out that the board was not doing its job if it allowed Brennan to hold three jobs—Chairman, CEO, and head of the retail operation—and to chair the board's nominating committee, allowing him "to pick his own bosses."

Fourth, he took the governance question head-on. Was Monks and his governance message merely a distraction for Sears, as Brennan and Shute were fond of saying? "Perhaps it is a distraction Sears could use more of." To whom was management accountable, he asked, when it budgeted $5.5 million to fight him? And was it fair that Sears does not give shareholders a fundamental right to vote in confidence, or that it did not give its workers information about how to cast a vote for him? "Sears, like a lot of other companies, has a system for shareholder nomination of director candidates. Apparently this is a fine system, from their perspective, as long as no one tries to use it."

Finally, and Bob Monks would not be Bob Monks if he didn't address this issue, he spoke about the Sears profit-sharing and pension plans. "These plans have now grown to enormous size. They are substantial owners of other American enterprises. . . . Sears and other plan sponsors must turn their attention and managerial energies to their responsibilities as owners of themselves and each other. Just because the merchandising division is in trouble and needs primary focus is not an acceptable excuse for failure to organize to deal with the requirements of the employee benefit plans."

He then summed up his qualifications for director. And then: "Voting for Bob Monks on the Blue Card may be the last chance that you have for some time to vote for a genuinely independent candidate for director—at least until next year's annual meeting, if I am not successful at this one."[20]

There was great applause. The speech was a good one. Every point was right on target. David Martin was greatly impressed and pleased. But at the same time, he says, he felt discouraged. "You knew that no matter how good it was, it didn't make any difference. Most of the people there at the meeting had already voted. And there were a lot of employees who were loyal to the company. We were going through the motions—and doing it well. That was very much a part of the strategy—that Bob be presented as a leader of corporate governance."

At a press conference afterward, when Brennan was asked what he thought of Monks' statement that Sears had changed as a result of his candidacy, the CEO's response was swift and to the point: "Baloney."

11

Checking Out at the Store

Mr. Robert Monks, leader of the battle to reform American corporate governance, has lost his bid for a seat on the board of Sears, Roebuck.
Financial Times

Dissident shareholder Robert A.G. Monks today failed in his unorthodox campaign to win a seat on the board of Sears, Roebuck & Co., but seemed to unlock considerable shareholder discontent with the performance of the struggling retailing and financial services giant.
Washington Post

Robert A.G. Monks, the eloquent institutional investor [sic] whose pointed criticism of Sears, Roebuck & Company made him a symbol of the activist shareholder, today lost his campaign to become a Sears director. . . . Although Mr. Brennan tried to dismiss Mr. Monks as an irritant during his campaign, it was clear that in defeat Mr. Monks, who said he planned to run again next year, had made a difference at the troubled retailing giant.
New York Times

"In a mathematical sense, Brennan and the board won, but in a real sense, they couldn't and didn't win," said Bob Figliozzi, director of research at Jesup Josephthal & Co. "They are now subject to the glass-house theory, and everyone will be watching their every move to try to turn things around."
Crain's Chicago Business

253

For a loser, Monks was looking real good: "I'm doing a jig," he told the *Chicago Tribune*. He may have failed to win a board seat, but the press had proclaimed him a winner in two other important ways. What he had won was, first of all, enough of a following to influence change at a major corporation. Officially, that following amounted to some 13 percent of the voting shareholders, which, while not a stunning result was impressive for a dissident who was attempting something no one had ever attempted and in doing so faced monumental odds. A significant number of Sears' employee shareholders, meanwhile, who had not received information about Monks or a ballot with his name on it, chose to use the management ballot they did receive to express their discontent with management. Some 23 percent of those workers who voted did not use all three of their votes because they did not cast a vote for chairman and CEO Brennan.

So far the scope of Monks' influence could not be gauged; the changes he could breathe into Sears were now measured only in terms of potential. But speculation was rife that the company would in some way have to respond to the voiced discontent of some shareholders. And, ironically, because of Monks' candidacy, Sears' board was now almost completely made up of outside directors whose every movement or lack thereof was under a national microscope.

Perhaps his greatest personal victory, however, was an even more ephemeral one: the recognition he had gained as the "leader of the battle to reform American corporate governance." Though it might be fleeting, this was an image he had been coveting for years. That image was burnished in no small way by the publication in 1991 of *Power and Accountability* (Harper-Collins). The book was the culmination of several years of Monks' private writing about corporate governance, beginning with the 100-page agenda he composed from his home in Maine in the summer of 1981. In the end, the book was a collaboration between himself and Minow, with Monks writing the first draft, and Minow using that to write a final draft.

In the book, they explore the problems of the modern corporation and create a case for their solution: the institutional investor acting as owner. "The aspects of the system designed to help the corporation preserve itself have worked, but the aspects of the system designed to make sure that this self-preservation was consistent with the public interest have not," they wrote. "State government, local government, boards of directors, and even the marketplace itself have all been unable to keep the interests of the corporation aligned with those of the community." Business has tried to maximize profit by "externalizing costs, placing the costs of unsafe working conditions on their employees and the costs of unsafe products on the consumers." When government stepped in, corporations found ways around regulation or decided to let shareholders pay for any offenses, they wrote. What is more, a gap developed between the true value of a corporation and the lower market value, which Monks and Minow explain as the difference between shareholders having control and not having control over a company's fate. In great part, they argued, all of this has been the result of the failure of the corporate governance system and a lack of any real relationship between owners and managers.

The solution, of course, was in the growing power and responsibility of institutional investors. "What seems . . . to be a beginning point," they wrote, "is to require that institutional owners act as such; that those with long term interests be required to be long term investors; that we stop regulating institutional fiduciaries in the interest of service providers and that we elevate the interests of the beneficiaries, who constitute an adequate proxy for the national interest." Meanwhile, on the corporate side, they wrote, directors and managers should consider shareholders to be their first priority. Other stakeholders should benefit in turn. "Directors who fail to consider the interests of customers, employees, suppliers, and the community fail in their duty to shareholders," they insisted. "A company that neglects those interests will surely decline."

Power and Accountability revealed the broader philosophy of Monks, who had been primarily known as a shareholder activist. The man who was so focused on battling poison pills and staggered boards was doing so in the interest of a vision for society. He truly believed that informed, activist trustees of pension funds, as long-term owners of much of corporate America, could become owners with the power to hold corporations accountable and cure some of the ills of the world. "Their beneficiaries have definable interests that are substantially congruent with those of society as a whole," the authors wrote. "They don't just want to retire with a comfortable income; they want to retire into a world where they can breathe the air and drink the water, where the economy is stable, the streets are safe, and criminals go to jail. In exercising their fiduciary responsibilities of ownership, pension fund trustees can restore accountability and global competitiveness to American business."

The book was received with generally enthusiastic reviews. One dubbed it "the textbook" on corporate governance and another termed it "a bible for the movement." The authors did suffer some criticisms, though, such as what the May 23, 1991, *Financial Times* called their "over-optimistic view of the hereafter," referring to the idea that accountability to pension funds could eventually solve societal problems. Economist Lester Thurow writing in *Fortune* (June 17, 1991) liked the case Monks and Minow make, but found the organization of the book "tough going." The *Economist* (June 22, 1991) thought the book naïve in praising the state of institutional activism in Britain. And in retrospect, the book's positive view of the Japanese and German systems—in which major lenders, or stakeholders like customers or suppliers, own much of the stock and therefore act as vigilant owners—seems extremely dated today. Indeed, Monks acknowledges that he overlooked the lack of independence on those companies' boards.

Given his reputable persona after the Sears fight, Monks hoped that the SEC would pay attention to what he had done—having dramatized the difficulty of making an independent run for a board of directors—and take it into consideration in its deliberations on proxy reform. In late summer 1991, he would write a letter to the SEC stressing the need for a number of changes. Moreover, his newly heightened reputation would prove useful in future contests. If he had driven Sears' management to distraction, imagine what he could do at other companies. Indeed, he began making concrete plans to launch his own fund, the Lens Fund.

But for now, Monks believed his main role was to keep on sticking it to Sears, until his presence did lead to concrete changes. He knew that meant another full year devoted largely to Sears. But what distinguished Monks in the community of shareholder activists was his willingness to stay with a battle for a long time; if he failed at first to strike his target, he would charge again. Such was the case with his run for the Senate in 1972. He lost, but did well enough to get up and run again. And even though he lost his second bid, his challenge came so close that he earned enough political stripes to get appointments in Washington later on. At Sears, too, he had lost, but turned in a good enough performance on which to build a second campaign.

How he was going to attack Sears this time was an open question. It was safe for the moment to declare that he would be back to make another run for the board. He would probably also file some shareholder resolutions or at least help others file them. He had time to figure it all out because he did not have to make any filings with the SEC for the 1992 annual meeting until late in the year. And maybe, in the interim, Brennan would surprise everyone with some dramatic strategic shift in direction. Certainly, with Monks hanging around on the sidelines, the pressure was on, and growing. After all, there was no doubt that Monks could pull off a real victory in 1992. Having established a base of support, he could conceivably expand that base; and if the Labor Department took his side, he could also win much greater support from employee shareholders.

Even Georgeson, which had agreed to take a much lower fee for representing Monks in the proxy battle than it would have taken from a larger client, was looking forward to a second heat with Sears. "There is no question that this was a special pioneering effort that we expect will have long-term benefits to our firm either directly through publicity, or indirectly through greater use of the proxy process," Wilcox wrote in a letter to his client on June 19. "I am sure you share our sense of frustration at attempting to wage a proxy fight with two hands tied behind our backs. Timing, legal roadblocks, financial constraints and Sears' strategy of barring us from soliciting significant portions of the ownership base prevented us from achieving the kind of results we would normally expect. Needless to say, we hope to have a second bite at the apple."

Before launching this second campaign—whatever it was going to be— Monks hoped to maintain some momentum from his election "victory." He spent considerable time that summer trying to construct a lawsuit against Sears charging it with unfairness in its tactics against him in the 1991 race. There must be some way, he reasoned, for him to leverage the blatantly outrageous measures Sears had used against him into some tactical advantage for himself. He contacted Michael Klein, a partner at the DC firm of Wilmer, Cutler & Pickering, who encouraged him to go ahead, confident that "communicating unfairness regarding the 1991 Sears election should be achievable without too much trouble. . . . The manner in which Sears and the incumbents reacted was unusually excessive and manipulative."[1] Given Sears' demonstrated willingness to use virtually unlimited resources against him, however, Monks began a search for well-heeled, committed allies who would not only help him finance a lawsuit that he reckoned could cost up to $2 million but also would lend the case a greater aura of legitimacy.

An obvious prospect was the group of discontented Allstate agents. In July, at the annual convention of the National Neighborhood Office Agents' Club in Las Vegas, Monks was the keynote speaker. There, before some 50 Allstate (i.e., Sears) employees, he elicited the ways in which he could help them. "What can I do for you?" he asked. He listed a few things, such as challenging Sears' actions against him that year and helping them as shareholders file resolutions on voting confidentiality, employee representation on the board, or other issues. "What can you do for me? Participate with me in trying to put right the stolen 1991 election. Stolen from me. Stolen from you. Be willing to be plaintiffs. Be willing to prepare and give me a statement outlining your efforts to indicate support for me on the proxy card."

In the end, however, the Allstate agents were not willing to help him finance a suit. Neither were any of the proactive institutional investors (public funds) he approached that summer. Richard Rainwater said he would only get involved in such a case if he was given an option to buy 500,000 shares of Sears stock by one or more institutional investors committed to this fight; that way, he would participate in any increase in the stock that might result from the lawsuit. That was unrealistic. And so, reluctantly, Monks abandoned the idea of filing a lawsuit.[2]

Instead, he decided to turn over the materials he had developed with Michael Klein to the attorneys representing shareholders in the class action suit filed in Pennsylvania just before the annual meeting. That suit charged Sears with breach of fiduciary duty in not coming forward with information on a pending Chicago class action lawsuit filed in 1988 and in not dealing fairly with Monks in his race for the board. Monks thought the new information might help them in their ongoing negotiations for a settlement.

In the meantime, Monks began plotting a second run for the board. In September, when he learned of the pending departure of one Sears director, he wrote to Brennan as head of the nominating committee. ". . . My understanding is that the trustees of the Sears' Profit Sharing Trust independently have considered my qualifications. In light of the foregoing and what I trust you will agree was my constructive candidacy for election at last year's annual meeting, and my achievement of substantial shareholders' support, I respectfully request the Nominating Committee consider me as a replacement director. . . . "

While awaiting the response—the expected rejection notice came on December 30—Monks had plenty to do. He began working on some draft resolutions for Sears' 1992 annual meeting to be held in the spring, and conferred with some potential proponents about planned resolutions on confidential voting and breaking up the company. But his most ambitious project was a resolution on a new kind of shareholder advisory committee that would have more power than the shareholders' committee he had helped Calpers develop years before, which the big pension fund had proposed at a number of companies to good effect. This new committee, authorized by a bylaw amendment, would consist of three paid representatives elected by the company's largest institutional shareholders; it would be funded with a penny a share (in Sears' case, up to $3.44 million) by the company itself; and have a right to meet with the company, propose candidates for director, and publish its views annually in the proxy statement. Although the new panel would not be able to order management around, it would be an effective way for long-term shareholders to keep an eye on things in good times and bad, and let their interest in corporate matters be known. As Monks describes the panel's theoretical impact: "A company that has an effective monitoring shareholder is worth more than one without one." The concept was a radical one in that it gave shareholders a much more direct and ongoing involvement in corporate governance than they had ever known. Even years later, Monks' face would brighten when he spoke about it. "It was probably the best governance thing I've ever done," he says. "It was the only real governance initiative put up ever because it confers real rights on shareholders. It creates, at the instigation of large long-term shareholders, a competency to inform themselves about company affairs and communicate with shareholders without economic consequences."

Monks developed the idea with his attorney, Joshua Berman, and decided to file it at Exxon as well as at Sears. At Sears, he needed to find a sponsor other than himself for the resolution. "I thought that being a sponsor of a governance resolution—a squishy soft governance resolution—would give credence to the very effective characterization Sears had made of me that I was an ideological shareholder activist with no notion of the business," Monks explains. "But I wanted this raised at Sears." And so, he gave it to the plaintiffs' lawyers in the ongoing Philadelphia case. His assumption was that they would file the resolution and then use it as a bargaining chip on Monks' behalf; that is, in settling the case, get something for him in return for not running the resolution at the annual meeting. "They were in a better position to use the chip immediately than I was," Monks says.

Monks himself filed the resolution at Exxon Corp. But why Exxon? The oil giant was at the time performing very well. Privately, Monks wanted to exact some revenge for Exxon's failure to answer his letter a year earlier to the nominating committee, suggesting that the company nominate him as a candidate for the board. And in fact when Exxon's assistant secretary called on December 4 to try to talk him out of filing the resolution, Monks told him that "the company's arrogance in dealing with my directoral nomination was one of the critical factors" in the decision to file the resolution.[3] Publicly, Monks acknowledged that Exxon was a well-run company, but pointed out that it was important for all companies, good and bad, to have good governance including a way for shareholders to monitor the company on an ongoing basis. Besides, he said, Exxon had been generally unresponsive to shareholders and to his own past inquiries concerning the board's handling of environmental as well as related director liability issues. He was referring to the two letters written to Exxon in 1988 and 1989 when ISS was wrestling with the relationship of corporate governance and investment policy to corporate crime.

The members of the proposed Exxon shareholder advisory panel would receive a $20,000 annual fee—half of the average fee paid to directors—be reimbursed for travel and other expenses, and be covered by directors and officers insurance. Exxon would spend up to a penny per share (about $12 million a year) for whatever the committee might need to perform its job, from sponsoring a proxy contest to elect a board nominee to retaining an investment bank or accounting firm to provide needed professional advice. Nominations for members of the committee could be submitted by investors who had owned at least $10 million in Exxon stock for at least three years; at Exxon, there were probably 100 such shareholders out of 709,000. The three committee members would have staggered terms, to track the pattern of the Exxon board of directors. Certainly, it was a bold and controversial proposal. On top of that, unlike most past resolutions, this one was binding, requiring that the company adopt it if approved by the shareholders. For what it was worth, ISS recommended that its clients vote for the proposal. To no one's surprise, then, Exxon began lobbying the SEC to keep the proposal off the proxy statement for its annual meeting scheduled for April 29, 1992.

In the meantime, Monks had begun settlement talks with Sears. Early in October, he bumped into Lipton at a conference in Washington, where they were both featured speakers. The attorney voiced Sears' desire to get Monks out of its life—in every way, including his legal claims, planned rerun for the board, and shareholder resolutions—by negotiating some kind of settlement with him. Always open to talking with any target company, Monks immediately agreed to meet. Though always on his guard, he had every reason to be confident. Not only did he now have Sears begging for a settlement, but this year he also had a key asset: Nell Minow. That fall Minow had joined Monks at ISP, leaving ISS in the hands of a new CEO, Jamie Heard. ISS was still losing money, but under Heard it would finally become profitable in 1994. As it grew, ISS became highly influential with both investors and corporations, many of which checked with the firm while designing their executive compensation plans and governance policies to make sure they would get the firm's nod.[4] In 1996, Heard says, ISS had about $10 million in revenues and $2.6 million in profits, up from $1.5 million in revenues and a half-a-million-dollar loss in 1991.

The first meeting with Lipton and Joshua Berman in Monks' Washington office that fall of 1991 led nowhere. The Sears representatives offered to negotiate a monetary settlement, set up meetings with the board or Brennan, and give Monks an opportunity to suggest nominees for the board. But the only way Monks would agree to settle anything was if Sears, as he wrote to Berman, "publicly gives credit to me for having been responsible for shareholder enhancing action."[5] A simple enough request on the surface, but one that would prove to be hateful for some reason to Sears as the discussions continued through March 1992.

Except for a few issues, including charges of breach of fiduciary duty in the way Sears responded to Monks' candidacy, the Philadelphia and Chicago lawsuits were settled together in late October with the following concessions by the company: (1) A new policy of confidential voting, in which votes are kept secret until all votes are counted, if the shareholder requests confidentiality, except in certain circumstances such as a proxy contest, and (2) a new policy for the composition of the nominating committee, requiring that it be led by a nonemployee director and be composed mostly of nonemployee directors. Although both of these policies were adopted at the August board of directors meeting, the settlement stated, "Sears acknowledges that the pendency of the Action and the plaintiffs' having previously raised such issue in the settlement discussions in connection with the Action were contributing factors in this action being taken." There was also (3) a new requirement that no officer or director may serve as a trustee for employee benefit plans that hold Sears shares and therefore may not determine how to vote those shares; (4) the addition of independent directors by the 1994 annual meeting; and (5) that 75 percent of the board consist of independent directors.

Monks shrugged off these concessions as unimpressive. Independence on the nominating committee and for employee benefit plan trustees? Bah, humbug. While these may sound good, Monks was skeptical that this was much of a change since the members of these groups would still be chosen by the CEO or the CEO's pals on the board. And, while Brennan would step down as chairman of the nominating committee, he would remain a member. The confidentiality policy, in particular, was hardly worthy of the name. "Imagine having a policy entitled 'confidential,' when the fine print stipulates it to be inoperative in the case of a proxy contest," he later wrote. "It's like a raincoat that works *except* when it rains."[6] And even without a contest, the confidentiality held only before the voting.

But his greatest disappointment came when he learned that the lawyers traded away his SAC shareholder resolution in return for an agreement by Sears not to contest their claim for legal fees in the settlement. "Apparently, without even making the effort to contact you or me, they agreed with Sears to withdraw the resolution," Monks wrote to Berman on December 11. "[Attorney] Greenfield said that 'our issues' were still on the table in the Philadelphia litigation. I said—'Big deal! Can you give me any justification for not calling Berman or me before undoing our work?' Silence." Fortunately, for the sake of the resolution, Monks had already submitted the same proposal at Exxon, which at the time was tangling with him at the SEC in an effort to keep the matter off the proxy statement.

That fall, pressures on Sears began to mount. Monks kept his candidacy very much alive, in part to drive Sears to settle with him and in part because there was some possibility he would run again, although he pretty much knew that he did not want to spend the money and the time for another contest. Also, Sears released disappointing third quarter earnings in the midst of a stubbornly weak economy. What is more, the press began reporting on the resolutions that were being filed at the SEC in preparation for Sears' 1992 annual meeting scheduled for May 14. One article credited Monks with helping an individual shareholder draft a resolution urging the board to appoint an investment bank (other than Goldman Sachs, which was Sears' traditional bank) to study the ramifications of spinning off Sears' financial businesses. That individual was an Allstate agent, Hazard Bentley. The activist and his attorney Berman became much more involved behind the scenes in helping to write a resolution asking for a bylaw amendment establishing confidential voting. The sponsor was an individual investor and member of the United Shareholders' Association, T. Boone Pickens' group representing individual investors. Monks' game plan was to endorse these and other proposals, perhaps even as he made his run for the board.

Those two proposals were not the only ones shareholders wanted to submit that year. Monks' campaign for the board was inspirational to a number of shareholders, big and small. The New York City Employees' Retirement System, under city comptroller Elizabeth Holtzman, called on Sears to keep Brennan from serving as both CEO and Chairman of the board. "The concentration of power in the hands of one person at the company could be stifling new initiatives and impeding the board of directors from independently evaluating the performance of top executives," Holtzman noted in a letter to the company in late November 1991. In addition, the United Shareholders' Association was proposing an end to Sears' staggered board. Yet another resolution favored a requirement that directors own a minimum 2,000 shares of stock.

In the first two months of 1992, Exxon was still arguing with the SEC over Monks' shareholder committee proposal. After lots of back-and-forth, the SEC ruled in February that Exxon must include Monks' resolution in its proxy statement for the April 29 annual meeting—rejecting Exxon's position that such a panel would interfere with the conduct of the company's day-to-day operations. It was a big victory for Monks.

The resolution appeared in the proxy statement along with Exxon's recommendation to reject it—that such a panel would duplicate and interfere with duties of the investor relations department, the board, and management; be "needlessly cumbersome and expensive"; discriminate against smaller shareholders; and have a budget of $12 million, "without any clear specification, other than fees and expenses for members, of how the money would be spent." Monks also got his chance to argue for the resolution in the proxy statement and in a letter to shareholders stating that:

Positive shareholder involvement means intelligently evaluating what the directors do and interacting constructively with the board. . . . Institutional investors don't have the resources to play an active, informed shareholder role in their various portfolio companies. My proposal would establish a three-person committee to take on the role of active, informed shareholder representatives. . . .

However, he was not able to speak on behalf of his proposal at the annual meeting April 29 because of a disabling case of the flu. A volunteer from the United Shareholders' Association spoke in his stead, guided by a memo from Monks.

The resolution did not do well. Less than 10 percent of Exxon's voting shares, including Calpers, favored it. "Everybody hated it. It was much too tough," Monks says today. "That was my finest, our finest hour. But it was a failure because I got caught up in the grandeur of it. It was such a first class idea, that I confused that with accomplishing a useful objective. It was, 'Bob Monks is a little too far out there.' And I hurt myself."

In retrospect, Exxon was probably performing too well for shareholders to make such a bold move against management. Monks has no regrets about the choice of a target. What was most important to him about this resolution was the idea itself. "It is the state of the art," he says. "It allows large long-term shareholders as a matter of right to solicit votes, to have expenses paid and to communicate through the company proxy statement. Today, people remember it because it is Exxon. A great name for a great idea."

The other major project Monks was working on early in 1992 was the establishment of the Lens Fund, which would "focus" on only a few poorly performing companies at a time. In December 1991, he launched a campaign to raise an ambitious $1 billion to seed the new fund—enough to allow him to take significant positions in his target corporations. His marketing plan for the new fund was simple: start with a big commitment from his friends at Calpers, and then go to others. Indeed, Monks had been discussing this kind of vehicle on and off with Dale Hanson for a few years already and pestering the Calpers CEO to bring the idea to the system's board of trustees. Finally, in mid-1991, Hanson agreed to do so, and Monks began several months of negotiations with Hanson and the Calpers trustees for a major commitment.

But in the spring of 1992, the main drama in his life was still Sears. In March, Monks and Minow continued the effort begun in October of trying to negotiate some kind of a settlement with the company. On March 6, while they were attending the same conference in New Orleans, Minow, Shute, and another Sears lawyer met to talk over the matter. The Sears people offered a hodgepodge of items, including their use of an independent vetting system for choosing new, independent directors. As Minow recalls: "I called Bob, and he kept saying to me, 'You're dreaming. They're just trying to distract us with this.' And there was no substance to what they were offering." Finally she presented Monks' final offer of the day: "Hire any investment bank of your choice, other than Goldman Sachs. Have them report to the board on the possible benefits of a breakup of the company. And we will go away forever. We will withdraw all five resolutions." The Sears folks did not ask her exactly how Monks would manage to do that when he wasn't sponsoring or even involved in all five resolutions. Says Minow: "If they had, I would have said, 'We are very persuasive.' But they just said no."

A week later, just days ahead of that year's deadline for filing to run for the board, Monks made a final stab at a settlement with Sears, conferring for a total of four hours with Shute in the courtyard of the Brazilian Court Hotel in Palm Beach, where Monks was staying. Monks pressed for the opportunity for Berman, Bob Holmes—a coinvestor and future Lens partner whom he had met when they were both serving on the advisory board to Mitsubishi International—and himself to meet with Goldman Sachs personnel to review their recommendations that the present corporate structure yielded the greatest shareholder value. If they ended up disagreeing with Goldman, the three men would be allowed to present their reasoning in a confidential session with the board. Monks' feeling was that the board would be compelled by their fiduciary obligations to take their analysis seriously. "I figured that we would be able to take exception to what Goldman said with sufficient clarity that they would in fact have to do differently," Monks explains. Shute rejected the idea. Sears' top management did not want to deal directly with Monks.[7] As he wrote to his friends and fellow activists Ralph Whitworth and Wilcox shortly after that meeting (March 16): "Ultimately, they were willing to contribute money and lip service, but they were not willing to make any substantive concession of any kind." Exasperated, Monks threatened to use the press against management and to use brokerage house analyses of breaking up Sears—which Shute had denounced as inaccurate—to solicit votes for the resolutions against management. Monks did find, however, that Shute seemed unusually receptive, in his own understated way, to some of his views. Monks wrote in the same letters to Wilcox and Whitworth, "He had no quarrel with my focus on Dean Witter as a place where Sears really had no synergy. And, Shute seemed to feel that my 1991 candidacy had quite a bit to do with the rise in Sears' stock. But Sears will never do a deal with me, period. The resentment, the loss of face and the absence of perception that they have to make a deal means that I—the messenger—am a larger problem than the message." Whitworth wrote back a few days later: "They really have no choice [but to divest their financial service businesses]. But it must be *their* idea. . . . Of course you have our unequivocal endorsement. There is a tremendous amount to be done."

The meeting with Shute helped Monks to weigh the pros and cons of running for the board. The pros were compelling. On the one hand, Sears did agree to give him a complete list of shareholders if he paid for printing and postage. And the company also said it would distribute his proxy materials to employees—again, at his cost—if he made it available by the end of the month. On the other hand, as Shute told him in Palm Beach, his presence on the board was "clearly not wanted" and he could not win because, "we have set the bar too high for you." Added to that hurdle was enormous cost compared with 1991. A preliminary analysis by Georgeson indicated that to have a reasonable chance at success, a campaign would likely cost up to $2 million, when considering everything from litigation to advertising, the broader distribution of materials, travel, and solicitation fees. At the same time, Monks would need to win just as many votes. Four members were up for reelection, and one of them was resigning. But Sears could not find someone new to run on its slate; so it decided to reduce the size of the board to nine members and run a slate of three candidates like the year before, which meant that Monks would again need 25 percent of the voting shares to win a seat. (Actually, Shute told Monks that the board tried to fill that vacancy, but four candidates turned Sears down because they did not want to be in a proxy contest with Monks.) Even more important to him, though, was the public perception of a second loss. "Our luck in 'winning by losing' couldn't last forever," he later wrote.

In the end, Monks decided that the negatives of running overshadowed the positives. Instead, he would devote his attention to the issues, by doing a full-scale proxy solicitation to support the shareholder proposals that would be on Sears' proxy card. These included deconglomeration, confidential voting, separation of chairman and CEO, elimination of the staggered board, and minimum investment by directors. One big advantage he saw in his more backstage role would be that the focus this year would be entirely on the issues, not on a personal battle between Bob Monks and the Sears board.

His major concern in pulling out of the race was how the press would react. "I WON last year," he wrote Berman, "largely because one paper— The New York Times—gave me good location, a good picture and used words like "eloquent." One can lose by just as slender margins." He would let his PR expert, Alan Towers, handle that one. "I have great confidence in his ability: A. To put the right spin on our announcement; B. To get the right journalists into the story the right way; and C. To handle follow up calls to maximum advantage. I have come to believe that "public relations" is a matter where one had best use professionals."

Curiously, in light of that statement, Monks issued his own press release on Monday, March 23, listing himself as the press contact. He had decided that using a PR firm contact in this case would weaken the image he had constructed of David versus Goliath. The release was entitled: "Robert Monks withdraws as candidate for Sears board: 'Honey, they shrunk the board—again.'" That, he said, was the major reason for his decision not to run. With only nine members on the board and three vacant slots, his candidacy would be, he wrote, "mathematically inachievable." He then announced his intention to solicit votes for specific shareholder resolutions including one, he said, to evaluate "spinning off to shareholders non-merchandising financial businesses that may be worth a great deal more if they weren't supporting a struggling retailer." That study would become the centerpiece of his solicitation efforts. The release said Monks would retain a proxy solicitor, Georgeson, to help him push for that breakup proposal and for the other resolutions as well. The market reacted to Monks' announcement by knocking Sears' stock down ¾ of a point to 46½.

Georgeson had already plotted the strategy. Again, they would run a limited campaign, sending off a letter to the largest group of holders and following up with some on the phone. In addition, Wilcox suggested in an April 9 letter that Monks run a newspaper ad "urging Sears employees to vote in favor of the shareholder proposals. . . . As we discussed on the telephone, the text of an ad might be built on the theme of: General Motors' Board has finally awakened. Sears' Board should wake up too." What Wilcox was referring to was a dramatic move early in April 1992 by outside directors of the car maker, partly in response to shareholder criticism of the company's performance. They demoted two top executives and took direct control of the board's executive committee from CEO Robert Stempel.

Monks did begin thinking about an ad, to run later in the campaign. But first, he immersed himself in drafting the letter to shareholders. On April 9, Monks sent out an 11-page letter to the 250 largest Sears shareholders in support of the five proposals. One by one, he explained in exhaustive detail his reasons for supporting those resolutions. In advocating a study of divestiture, he wrote:

If the only way you could purchase a $70 DieHard automotive battery, a $60 Villager woman's dress, and a $75 Craftsman electric sabre saw was in a unit consisting of these three items, would you expect to sell many units at $205? Clearly, in my opinion, absent other factors, the Sears business groups would trade at higher aggregate market values if traded separately than they would if combined in a single trading unit as they are today. . . . Sears claims its management and board of directors do . . . ongoing analysis of all business segments of the company to determine whether the current structure enhances shareholder value. Hence, Sears argues, there is no need for further study. This, I believe, should not satisfy Sears shareholders. In my experience, corporate managements and boards of directors like the power and prestige of managing bigger rather than smaller companies. Hence, I believe there is a need for an independent evaluation of the advantages and disadvantages of deconglomeration.

On April 30, Calpers, Monks' longtime associates in the shareholder activist/corporate governance movement, declared that it would withhold its votes for the Sears slate of directors at the annual meeting and back four of the shareholder resolutions—eliminating the staggered board, studying a breakup, splitting up the positions of CEO and chairman, and strengthening of confidential voting.[8] Given its recently announced 36 percent earnings advance in the first quarter on top of the 40 percent jump in 1991, plus meetings it had had with the fund's leaders, the company was dismayed at this development. However, Sears stock continued to trade at a level that was far below its 1980s' peak and the breakup value estimated by analysts.

Monks, meanwhile, was deep into the planning of a full-page ad that would run in the *Wall Street Journal* on May 6. Although the ad was on one level a plea for votes in favor of the resolutions, on another level it was Monks' means of addressing the board of directors, which he had been unable to do because he and Sears could not agree on a settlement. And perhaps on yet another level, the ad was Monks' revenge for Sears' refusal to give him what he wanted in a settlement.

Although intended for the eyes of Sears' shareholders and directors, the ad caught the interest of many other readers and become one of the most memorable ads in the history of proxy fights. "It was going to an extreme," Minow later explained when appearing on a televised debate about corporate governance. "We wouldn't have done that if we hadn't tried every other avenue we'd thought of. If we were persuaded of this strategy and that the board was focused on it, or that the directors were independent enough, or if any of them were willing to meet with us, perhaps it would not have been necessary. But under the SEC rules at the time, that was the only way to communicate with the shareholders."[9]

To design the ad, Monks hired C. Landon Parvin, an advertising copy-writer and political speechwriter. Initially, Minow advised Monks against taking out an ad. "I was dead wrong," she says. "I thought it would be a support our resolution type of ad. But when he and Landon came up with the concept of showing the directors I was all for it."

The idea behind the ad was to draw attention to the company's directors as the ultimate guardians of Sears' value. Parvin, Monks, Minow, and Towers decided to picture a silhouette of the Sears board members, based on their photos in the last annual report. Parvin faxed Monks three different headlines on May 1. "I tried and tried but the connection between an activist board and shareholder value is simply too complex for a main headline, because it's really two messages," he wrote. The choices were "Frozen Assets," "Sears' Largest Passive Loss: Its Board," and "Non-Performing Assets." Choice three was the winner. Towers suggested printing the name of each director inside their individual silhouette. But even for Monks that was going too far; instead, they put all the names of the directors, along with their chief affiliations, in small type below the group.

The text was written as a letter from Monks to the directors. After noting Sears' decline as a retailer and a stock, he got right to the point. "Regrettably, in my opinion, the reputation of the Sears Board of Directors also has fallen, due largely to its lack of energy and interest in making management accountable to shareholders. . . . We ask the Sears Board to give shareholders and the investment community a sign that it . . . understands its priorities. We ask the Board to take a modest step toward independence by reconsidering its blanket opposition to five shareholder proposals." The ad then explained the proposals, and cited studies showing that activist boards and shareholders increase stock values. Finally, the ad asked for shareholders to vote for the resolutions. There was some question as to who would sign the ad. Would it be Monks or just Institutional Shareholder Partners? Towers insisted that having Monks sign the letter would make it a lot more powerful because then the message would be personal, from Monks to Sears' directors. Not to mention that Bob Monks was by then well known to many readers. And so the ad was signed, "Bob Monks, Sears shareholder and president, Institutional Shareholder Partners."

As Monks later wrote: In the ad,

We were speaking beyond the board members. We were speaking to their friends, their families, their professional associates. Anyone seeing the ad would read it. Anyone reading it would understand it. Anyone understanding it would feel free to ask questions of any board member they encountered. . . . While it cannot be entirely clear to [directors] exactly what it is of value that they contribute in exchange for the very generous hourly fees (in 1991, Sears nonmanagement directors received an average of about $70,000 in fees) and the superb fringe benefits— private jets, foreign travel with spouses, insurance, pensions, free stock, free company products, and so forth—one thing at least is clear: They are not volunteering to be made a public spectacle of. . . . We hoped that the ad would incline Sears directors to find within themselves the energy for confronting Ed Brennan and management.[10]

The ad did at least part of its job: it got a reaction. Many individual shareholders called in to Georgeson to ask how to change their votes. One Dean Witter broker in San Jose phoned in this message, recorded by a Georgeson employee: "Concerned about anonymity, but wants to vote for shareholder proposals. Holds Sears through Sears 401(k) plan. Says 50 percent of Dean Witter brokers in his office feel the same way, but are being subtly pressured to vote for management, unlike Allstate agents, who have banded together." Another Dean Witter employee told Georgeson, "I voted for management, but would like to find out if I could change my vote in agreement with Mr. Monks. I hope this is confidential. I work for and want to continue working for DW." Another caller was described as "an Allstate employee; disillusioned with Sears."

Meanwhile, inside the company, Brennan was furious at Monks for placing the ad. (The *Chicago Tribune* did Sears the disfavor of reproducing the ad as the art to go along with a story about the Sears meeting.) "What he did was very disruptive internally," he recalls. "There was no purpose in doing that. A very unprofessional thing to do. When 350,000 employees see a picture [and ad] criticizing the ability of their board of directors, they are confused and offended, . . . and people tend to believe what they read in the newspapers. It caused a lot of conversation. To the directors, it was unfair and embarrassing."[11]

Whatever the effect of the ad inside Sears, it appears to have had a far-reaching effect on other directors throughout corporate America—which was what really made the ad worth its $116,000 cost. For years afterward, people would come up to Monks and mention the ad. Minow tells a story of attending the CII annual meeting in the spring of 1995 and listening to a presentation by the Campbell Soup Corp.'s CEO. He slogged through a slide show of people eating Campbell's Soup in different countries all over the world. The last slide was the Sears ad, and his commentary was, "This is what keeps me honest. I would hate for this to happen to me." Minow was thrilled and when she went up to him afterward, "he told me how brilliant he thought the ad was," she says. She began taking the ad with her wherever she went, including her visits with newspaper and magazine editors, who were placing increasing emphasis in their corporate coverage on company directors.

On May 7, the huge College Retirement Equities Fund, a holder of 3.3 million Sears shares, announced that, like Calpers, it would withhold its votes for management's slate of candidates. Its reason: Sears' continued poor performance "as well as a real concern about direction and timeliness of change in the future." Fund officers had reached their decision after a meeting with Sears' top executives failed to convince them that Sears was taking the steps needed for long-term success. It was the first time the fund would withhold its vote because of concern about a company's performance.

Next in line was Fidelity. On May 8, the giant fund manager, holder of 8 million Sears shares, announced that it would vote against management on at least two of the shareholder proposals—confidential voting and destaggering the board.

Still, the prevailing opinion among Wall Street analysts and others was that the resolutions would not yield an impressive vote. A telephone survey of 37 Sears institutional shareholders in early May by *Pensions & Investments* had the antimanagement side getting only 15 percent to 20 percent of the votes. "With Sears' stock price up significantly from last year," the publication hypothesized, "some of the edge has been taken off the battle." But some of the investors the publication interviewed were still dissatisfied, given the poor performance of Sears' core retailing operation. Sears management, said one, has "just been asleep at the wheel. They refuse to accept the fact that they're no longer a power." For his part, Monks began once again to turn likely defeat into victory by setting up low expectations: He declared that if three of the proposals got an average of at least 20 percent support, he would run for the board in 1993.

This year, the Sears annual meeting was a much less dramatic affair than the year before. It took place in a low-ceilinged hall at a Marriott hotel in Lenox, Georgia, outside Atlanta. Naturally, given the location, the crowd was much smaller. Yet there was a feeling of tension in the air, like the humidity before a storm. When Monks arrived for the meeting, a woman from the United Shareholders Association came up to him to complain that the company would not let her distribute fliers in support of the confidentiality resolution. Monks asked Shute to remedy the situation, and he did. Monks' entourage was also smaller this year, consisting of Alan Towers and "Kit" Bingham, a research assistant at ISP. Bingham was a friend of Monks' godson Jesse Norman from the United Kingdom, and Monks hired him in late 1991 because he needed a job. "We had to convince the immigration authorities that I was an expert in corporate governance," Bingham says. But as he learned more about Monks and ISP, he was quickly becoming one. Once a week, he and his boss would sit down for a 20-minute chat, and, says Bingham, "I'd come out feeling that we were saving the world. It was very clear to me that he took a very wide view of the whole question—protecting the environment, job creation. He made that clear to me. A large part of the credibility of the movement was that it was rigorously focused on the economic, what could be measured. Monks knew that what he cared about most would not play in the press."

Monks warned him that the Sears meeting would probably be tedious, slick on presentation, and low on content. But he was wrong.

The three of them found seats on the right side of the room, midway back. After Brennan's spiel about that year's results in which he painted a scenario of continuing improvement and predicted that the company would reach its stated 15 percent return on equity goal by 1994, comments were opened to the floor. A great deal of venom was spilled that day. A former employee spoke movingly about the sense of loss of family in her being terminated by Sears. An elderly lady, a former Sears employee and customer, told Brennan at the end of a lengthy harangue that "your retail stores are lousy" and suggested "a total overhaul." The crowd applauded. An individual investor pointed at the seated directors and scolded them: "You, the directors, sit idly by while one of America's crown jewels is crumbling."

Paul Farago spoke in support of his confidentiality proposal, and Monks briefly seconded the motion. The other sponsors also rose to move for adoption of their resolutions. The boldest presentation was that of Hazard Bentley, the sponsor of the resolution to study breaking up the company and an Allstate employee for over 25 years. Previously, he had told Monks, "I might as well deal with this up front, because if things continue the way they are, there won't be a business to employ me anyway." Obviously nervous about confronting his bosses, and no doubt risking his job, Bentley made himself clear: "There is a failing today on the part of management at all levels to adhere to the principles this company was founded on. I believe the weak management attitudes are now bleeding from the parent company into healthy entities within the Sears network."[12]

This year, voting results were announced at the meeting itself. Two of the proposals—for protecting confidentiality of shareholder votes and for electing directors annually—won a stunning 41 percent of the vote, and the resolution to separate the positions of chairman and CEO won 27 percent. Bentley's proposal got a respectable 23 percent vote while the fifth proposal, to require directors to own a minimum 2,000 shares, won almost 20 percent. Shareholders withheld a record 5.8 percent of votes for the management slate of directors. *USA Today* proclaimed "Shareholders revolt at Sears" (and, incidentally, listed every member of Sears' board). And the *Wall Street Journal* reported "Stockholders Send Message to Sears Board—Surprisingly strong support for 5 proposals indicates frustration over results." As corporate governance academic John Pound put it, "Phenomenal. It really shows what a tremendously mainstream set of issues these are becoming. A few years ago, that kind of support would have been unheard of."[13]

At the same time, however, Brennan interpreted the vote result as what it actually was: a victory for Sears. It was, he said, "in no way a defeat. I can't conceive why people would think that." But most corporate governance experts agreed that the Sears board would not be able to ignore such a loud reprimand from shareholders. And even Shute told the *Journal:* "We'll take this seriously."

Monks wasn't shy about proclaiming the day a victory. "Forty percent of the shareholders voted to repudiate the board. It's hard to imagine a clearer message that came out of the meeting today. If this were the House of Commons, the cry would be to resign." Yet, the vote caught Monks himself by surprise. Asked if he would now run for the board again, he blurted that it would probably still be "mathematically impossible" for him to win.

In the cab on the way to the Atlanta airport, Monks was very excited. Alan Towers turned to his friend and client and remarked, "Nothing can't happen." To Monks, the reason that statement was true was that the Sears directors were not about to let Brennan put them through such an ordeal yet a third time.

The following month, something did happen. The board made some modest governance changes in direct response to the shareholder vote. "The vote caused significant negative publicity," Brennan relates. "In response to institutional investors' requests, we went to complete confidential voting. And we put in a requirement that directors own 1,000 shares." But they kept the staggered board and did not separate the chairman and CEO positions. Whether accurate or not, Monks took some credit for these limited changes. "It meant that I was getting through to at least one or two of the directors." There was also a sign that the board might move to break up the company or at least study such a notion. According to the Investor Responsibility Research Center's *Corporate Governance Bulletin* of September/October 1992, at that June board meeting, the Sears directors asked its banker, Goldman Sachs, and another bank, Morgan Stanley, to study the possibility of divestiture. That was an incredible move. In the months leading up to the annual meeting the company line had been hold together. In January, Brennan told *The New York Times* (January 11), "We have no plans to break up the company. We think the company is stronger together than it would be apart." On April 1, the *Journal* reported, "David Shute said Sears believes such a study is unnecessary because management and the company's investment banker, Goldman Sachs & Co., are already studying the company's configuration and making frequent presentations to the board. At a board meeting in February, he noted, there was 'an absolutely clear consensus' that the company should not be broken up." In the April 1992 proxy statement, the company noted:

> Management has concluded, and the Board concurs, that the businesses owned by the company are more valuable to the shareholders when operating as segments of a single company than they would be if divested and operated as separate businesses. This is due to a number of complex factors, including the strength of the Sears name, advantages in raising and allocating capital, mutually beneficial business arrangements among the various segments, and significant operational economies of scale.

Given these statements, it would not be unreasonable to conclude that when Sears did finally decide to restructure—at the very end of September 1992—the shareholder vote and subsequent pressure from shareholders like Calpers had something to do with it. The decision—made after four Sears board meetings that summer including a daylong session on September 30—was to reorganize the business "by creating separate, publicly traded companies enabling shareholders and other investors to participate directly in Sears' successful financial services franchises," the company announced

(Sears stock rose 3 3/8 points to 44 3/4, adding $1 billion in value, while the rest of the market edged down). Yet, Brennan maintained that there was no surprising reversal on the part of the board. "We have consistently said that our board periodically reviews the structure of Sears to ensure that we are enhancing shareholder value," he said. "Our action is a result of intensive study."

Long after he had left Sears, Brennan continued to assert that all along, month by month, the Sears board was looking at ideas for creating shareholder value, including divestiture. "We'd been looking at alternatives, including the disposition of assets and the breakup of the company, since 1988," he says. "We did a preliminary restructuring in 1988. In fact, when Monks spoke at the [1991] annual meeting, we were way down the road. We were considering everything from a disposition of more assets to a breakup via spinoffs. There's no way you could make such a huge [strategic] move in a matter of months. Monks even wrote me a letter after we announced the restructuring saying we'd gone far beyond what he envisioned." Without Monks running for the board, Brennan says, "The restructuring would have happened the same way." What about all those public statements—including the one on the proxy statement—that Sears' board and management had decided the company was best left alone as is?

This is how Brennan explains it. A couple years before the restructuring, he formed a group of three executives, including himself, to mull ways to improve the stock price and reduce Sears' growing debt load. "We brought in Hank Paulson from Goldman Sachs and swore him [and the firm] to absolute secrecy," Brennan recounts. "We didn't bring the board in until we'd put together a series of 12 alternatives, from asset dispositions to total breakup." Not until the final decision was made did Brennan want to reveal management's thinking to outsiders. "If you haven't yet made a decision, you cannot say what you're doing," he maintains. "It would be disruptive to the market and to employees. You want to lay it all out on the table, and I did."

However, the company was already in a state of uncertainty, given the price of the stock and the loud complaints to the shareholders—including some employees like the Allstate veteran who sponsored a resolution. Perhaps a statement from the management that it was seriously considering a major change and in the process of studying the best change to make would have had a calming effect.

In any case, the shareholder uproar probably did accelerate the inevitable restructuring.

Brennan concedes that "Monks and the governance movement made us much more aware of our institutional shareholders." In the effort to defeat Monks, he says, "I spent a lot more time out visiting with major institutional investors" such as Fidelity, Texas Teachers, and the New York State Employees' fund. "Yes," says Brennan, "you have to give him some credit."

The national press gave him a lot of credit. On October 12, 1992, the editors of *Pensions & Investments* wrote:

> Shareholders should find new energy and strength in the breakup of Sears, Roebuck & Co., even though every activist proposition over the past two years of the intense corporate governance battle with Sears management failed to achieve even a vote close to majority. The lesson: Shareholders don't need a majority to attain their objectives. . . . Much of the credit for the Sears breakup should go to Robert A.G. Monks, the Washington-based activist in corporate governance, who unsuccessfully sought a seat on the company's board; the United Shareholders Association . . . and the activist public pension funds that supported the effort to change Sears. Mr. Monks and the USA—along with some securities analysts—suggested Sears could improve shareholder value by divesting its financial services units and focusing on retailing. Sears essentially agreed. . . . The breakup of Sears also shows that while the takeover era of the 1980s has ended, necessary corporate restructurings still continue through other means, namely, the corporate governance movement.

Monks himself immediately got some prime media space on the *Wall Street Journal*'s Op-Ed page (October 1), and he used that opportunity to proclaim, "This is an extraordinary milestone in the history of shareholder activism."

But Monks wasn't yet through with Sears. Despite the company's momentous announcement, he, like some Wall Street analysts, was skeptical that management would actually follow through with the plan. So, in November, he submitted, in his own name, the shareholder advisory committee resolution that he had run at Exxon the previous spring. "It seemed to me important to maintain our position of 'creative tension' with the Sears management," Monks later wrote. After receiving notice of the resolution, Brennan called to ask Monks to come to Chicago for what would be their second meeting in this two-year drama. This is how Monks—who was then running the Lens Fund—described the December 14 meeting in a memorandum he wrote shortly afterward:

> The conversation was intense and civil. He is very confident that Sears will be able to effect the full reorganization announced at the end of September. He recognizes that Wall Street is very doubtful about management (that is to say Ed Brennan's) capacity to implement the plan. He feels that he is well on the way to providing solid rebuttal to this suspicion.
>
> What he wants from us is relief from confrontation so as to be able to devote energy more fully to the reorganization. I told him how much stock Lens owned and said that our interest was entirely in the side of achieving potential stock values. I passed the question of whether we would agree to withdraw our resolution until the end of the conversation. Third, I directly asked him whether our involvement with him had produced value for the shareholders in Sears. It is on this subject that the preponderance of the time and intensity was devoted. It is clear that he finds the prospect of continued adversarity [*sic*] with Lens a very unattractive one. I suggested to him that he should rise above personal pique and recognize that the additional focus required had accelerated the reorganization. At this point, Ed becomes a little hard to follow. One has to think of him as having been a child of a classic Catholic upbringing, thus he can harmonize absolute belief in Sears as one company; absolute belief that the financial service values had maximized; and absolute belief that the divestiture outlined in September is now appropriate. Somewhere, there is a grudging recognition that our energies were in aid of a value enhancing strategy.
>
> . . . We want Sears to take the lead in creating a structure for continued effective ownership involvement. To make a long story short— and it was a long story—Brennan agreed subsequent to the annual meeting to consider in good faith a proposal for an ownership committee. It seemed to me intelligent to leave the discussion at this point, because clearly we are not going to get any consideration until the reorganization is complete. In short, we will not publicly harass Brennan . . . and he will agree in good faith to consider a modern structure for shareholder involvement in governance. I don't rate the probability of Sears' acceptance very highly, but I believe being able to recite their involvement in the process will significantly advance our cause.

At the end of the meeting, he agreed to withdraw his resolution on a shareholder advisory committee. Shute's hands appeared to be shaking as he quickly compiled an authorizing letter and passed Monks a pen for signature. A few days later, Monks mailed the following handwritten note to Shute: "Dear David, This confirms my oral advice and your letter of 14 December to withdraw my proposed shareholder resolution. Congratulations to all at Sears for pulling off such a bold refinancing and restructuring. Bravo for you. Your friend, Bob Monks."

Sears did accomplish its divestitures—with great fanfare and great success. The stock soared. In 1995, after the spin-off of Allstate completed the divestitures, Brennan retired and Arthur Martinez succeeded him as CEO. Under Martinez, the Sears retailing operation came back with a vengeance. Monks kept his original 100 shares and owns the stock to this day. His profit? He had bought the shares for $3,200 and spent some $675,000 on the two proxy campaigns. By December 31, 1992, the shares were worth $4,550. Still, Monks held onto them for sentimental reasons and holds them til this day. As of August 26, 1998, those 100 shares, including the value of the spunoff businesses, Allstate and Morgan Stanley Dean Witter, was $17,400. Obviously, that doesn't come close to making up for the expenses of the proxy fights. But Monks maintains that his willingness to spend that kind of money on Sears is what gave him and his fund credibility in battles to come.

How can you measure the impact of the Sears drama on the rest of the corporate world? You get a sense of it by talking to people working in corporate governance as advisers, investors, and directors. "Corporate governance is evolutionary," begins David Martin. "This may not be a watershed event. In movements, events become watersheds if they are the most momentous events of the time. Sears propelled the movement forward. This and other events. It takes its place as part of the parade. Those were heady times. Sears was at the peak of the movement. Issues were new then. Now, there's a sense of it's old hat. But boards of directors at a much lower level ponder governance issues much more than they were 20 years ago. Maybe we don't have to have any headlines."

Ed Brennan himself, having served on several boards, had this to say in an interview with the author in 1997: "In terms of corporate governance and the movement to make boards and managements more receptive, I think they—all corporate governance interest groups—have had an effect. Monks was one of the people at the head of the pack. I don't think there's any question that corporate governance has changed. Boards today ask more questions and are more active." As to his experience restructuring Sears, he later said, "If there's any wisdom to be passed on, [it is] the importance of being much, much closer to the large institutional investors earlier in the game."

When Monks looks back on the Sears experience, he sees it as a great accomplishment in his career and for corporate governance. By engaging in this battle, he helped change SEC rules on shareholder activities in proxy contests, enlightened shareholders and managements as to the true need for confidential voting, illustrated the extremes to which management would go to cling to power even when not confronted by a threatened takeover, illustrated the weaknesses of laws that assure pension plan and employee shareholders' participation in the governance process, made it indisputably clear that shareholders are not welcome to elect directors to the board, and placed new emphasis on the role of directors on U.S. corporate boards. "Sears was where I got tired in the battle, but revived in the war," he says. "I felt exalted by the effort. I had fought the fight and had created a changed perception of the possibilities for shareholder activism."

12

Money Where His Mouth Is

These companies get into a shape where not only does nobody own them from an economic point of view, but nobody owns them from a moral and psychological point of view. Ownership in the larger sense. And therefore, everybody's trying to accommodate so many different constituencies that nobody really takes hold and does what someone with a holistic viewpoint would understand has to be done. A company that nobody owns flounders. Ownership comes out of a very moral, personal feeling about yourself. You have to own yourself. You've got to be responsible for yourself; you've got to be responsible for your things. What in a situation like this we can do is act like a lens and focus the ownership energies, and thereby make it possible for managements to confront issues they couldn't otherwise confront.

Bob Monks

In 1992, while continuing to goad Sears, Monks finally managed to give life to the Lens Fund. He contributed $10 million of his own and set out to raise $1 billion, a moon shot for a newcomer to the money management business. In the meantime, Monks put his own money to work. His partners in this enterprise—who would not immediately contribute significant assets—were Minow, his nephew John Higgins, and Bob Holmes, a former partner at the boutique brokerage firm Lazard Frères & Co. and a top executive at several other financial companies.

280

Monks' son-in-law drew up a logo of stars filtering through a lens. They were ready to begin.

Over the following weeks, Lens developed a "screen" to help identify target companies, largely through the efforts of Dean LeBaron's Battery-march—the same investment management firm that had been ISS's first client. The strategy was to find large companies Monks called "promiscuous conglomerates" or "misconglomerates" because they had made significant and unrewarding investments outside their core businesses. In selecting its targets, Lens would need to know which companies had "a governance gap," that is, would most likely be affected by shareholder pressures. And so, the fund would examine the board structure and composition, as well as man-agement's responsiveness in crisis situations. The chosen "focus" companies would have to have low insider ownership and high institutional owner-ship—and in the latter group, relatively high ownership by activist share-holders—and could not be in a heavily regulated industry. Lens would take a close look at the financial reports, invest in the focus companies, to become a significant shareholder, and construe a turnaround strategy for each of them. The fund would also identify weaknesses on the board such as staggered elec-tions, few independent directors, and directors that did not invest enough money or time in the company; then it would propose changes. "If there is a bad board," Minow says, "then you know that whatever the right answers are, the right questions are not being asked."

The partners would then introduce themselves to the CEO and CFO, and lay out Lens's suggested strategy. If the management assented to the fund's suggestions, Lens partners would sit back and wait for the stock to rise. If not, and the Lens partners remained unconvinced by management's defense of its own strategy, they would do what they do best: meet with management again, propose shareholder resolutions, contact outside (non-management) directors, and—most effective of all—go to the press. (Increas-ingly, it became Minow's role to deal with the press, "Bob doesn't trust himself with the press," she says. "I usually handle it. He's had a few lulus. One time, we agreed on a particular investment and worked out how we'd orchestrate the public announcement. The plan was to keep it private for a couple of months. Monks told the next reporter he talked to.") They would do whatever it took to convert management to its way of thinking, or, if nec-essary, eject management altogether.

One day, the four partners sat down together at an office in Boston to discuss their initial prospects. One company that kept popping up in the screens was the Digital Equipment Corp. "We decided that there was no way on earth we could get rid of the CEO. He was the founder, and he seemed so entrenched. And we didn't feel we understood the industry well enough," Minow says. Shortly afterward, the CEO, Ken Olsen, left the company.

In July 1992, Lens divided up its $10 million into four equal parts to invest in the first four focus companies: Eastman Kodak, Westinghouse, American Express, and Sears. Except for Sears, which Monks was already handling on his own, Lens launched its activist campaigns, writing letters to each of the companies' CEOs outlining its view of the companies' problems and suggesting a meeting to talk about solutions.

Late that summer, Monks got together with James Robinson III, CEO of American Express, whom he knew from The Boston Company sale and liked very much. The company was having a great deal of trouble, and Robinson was taking the blame. Just prior to the meeting with Monks, the American Express board asked Robinson to retire and set up a search committee—that included Robinson—to find his successor.[1]

In the meeting with Monks, Robinson was cordial, though the activist was frank with him. They talked about the difficulty of maintaining momentum at a large organization, and Monks bemoaned the company's efforts at synergy. The company had acquired a controlling stake in the brokerage house Shearson in 1981 and bought the rest in 1990, but had not been able to fulfill the vision of selling stock to credit card holders. The trust culture of a credit card company just did not fit the sales culture of a brokerage house, and Shearson had a number of problems of its own. Monks recommended divesting the Shearson business.

That fall, Calpers targeted American Express as a company with poor performance, and Hanson and Koppes met with the company. At one point, New York real estate tycoon Disque Deane, a shareholder of American Express, invited Monks and a couple large shareholders to lunch, where he urged them to point their activist guns at Robinson. Alarmed by the hostility in the air, Monks phoned Robinson and offered to provide his support and that of others he knew.

On January 25, 1993, the board approved the search committee's recommendation to appoint Robinson's choice Harvey Golub as CEO, keep Robinson as chairman, and allow him also to head Shearson. The stock reacted with a sharp drop, as some institutional investors sold out. Some big shareholders expressed their consternation over the board's decision at meetings with Golub. Again, Monks offered Robinson his support. But, on January 29, with the stock off 13 percent and shareholders clamoring for a change in management, Robinson resigned. In subsequent months, the board engineered a complete restructuring, which included among other things the sale of Shearson, a spin-off of Lehman Brothers, and the sale of The Boston Company. In the process, American Express shed half of its assets, but was now able to focus on its core businesses. In retrospect, Monks says, his offer of support "was the wrong thing, and it was too late. Most shareholders saw Jim as the problem. I should have recognized that." The stock went up, and Lens sold out at a profit.

It took a while for Lens to arrange meetings with the remaining two CEOs. On Friday, October 22, 1992, Monks, Higgins, and Holmes, traveled to Pittsburgh to meet Westinghouse CEO Paul Lego on the top floor of the headquarters. The company's financial results had been weak and were getting weaker. It had recorded a $1.1 billion loss in 1991 and was going to lose money again in 1992. That previous Monday, after the company announced a charge related to its bleeding real estate finance subsidiary, the stock had crashed and Lego found himself refuting rumors that Westinghouse was filing for bankruptcy. These woes would soon prompt several activist U.S. pension funds to follow Monks in complaining personally to Lego and to file shareholder resolutions to be taken up at the annual meeting in the spring of 1993.

For the first half-hour of his meeting with Lens, Lego gave his version of how Westinghouse had wound up in critical condition, emphasizing that he had nothing at all to do with it. Then, insisting he was eager to hear Lens's strategic plan, Lego allowed Lens strategist Holmes to speak, though interrupting him frequently. The problem, as Lens saw it, was that Westinghouse had unwisely broken away from its traditional electrical manufacturing business, entering such new fields as real estate finance, furniture, and broadcasting. Not only did the company lose its focus by diversifying, but in the process it burdened itself with an enormous amount of debt. As the losses mounted, Westinghouse regularly took special charges accounting for losses in its various businesses. Hence, the management, which had been painting rosy scenarios for some time, had lost all credibility, Holmes said. The bulk of the Lens plan was to write off Westinghouse's finance company, spruce up the furniture division for sale in three years, and do a public offering of at least half of the broadcasting group, or, alternatively, half of the environment products group, spin off the rest of the broadcasting group to shareholders, and refocus on the core electronic systems, environmental, and industry and power systems. Lego said he agreed with all of this except he preferred to sell environment products rather than broadcasting.

The Lens team wanted Lego to understand how poor the market's perception of the company and its management was. Monks used the word "criminal" in describing common views of management, noting that credibility had to be restored with a dramatic restructuring plan. As Monks later noted in a memo: "We continued to stress—seven times between Bob and myself, after I started to keep count—the essentiality of doing something now, today, before the end of the year." Lego acknowledged that his remark that he himself couldn't last more than a "couple more quarters like this one" was an overstatement and that he literally had run out of time. One move the Lens partners indicated was necessary was a complete write-off of the finance subsidiary as soon as possible—although they insisted that the company should not accept a pending offer from GE Capital, which they figured was too cheap. Lego appeared to agree.

He asked for his guests' help in not going to the press with the news of an upcoming major write-off and that they furnish him with a copy of the Lens strategic plan for Westinghouse. Monks was only too pleased to do the latter, since he figured Lego might use it for leverage with his board and, as the ever PR-conscious Monks wrote in his memo, "We can use the plan and covering letter—'We are glad to forward, at your request, a copy . . .'—to establish Lens in the press as the (A) brilliant; (B) timely, and (C) welcome provider of value enhancing information to corporate managements. This is just the slot we are looking for. If we can establish it in 1992, we will have done a lot—hostile effectiveness with Sears, cooperative effectiveness with Westinghouse."

As for governance matters, Monks objected to the company's confidential voting policy, which allowed for secret balloting except in the case of a proxy contest. Lego appeared to acknowledge the Kafkaesque quality of the provision (it was later changed on the advice of the board's counsel, Ira Millstein). When Lego defended the company's staggered board, Monks seemed to persuade him of its inappropriateness in a world devoid of hostile takeovers. At one point, Lego remarked that his board members perhaps were not so much to blame for the company's performance given they had so many other directorships. Monks cut him short. "Crap! The market has passed judgment on the Westinghouse board, and it failed," he said.[2]

After the meeting, the Lens partners agreed that Lego seemed capable of handling the job of CEO in the short term, but he probably was not going to last. As Monks noted in his memo: "When somewhat philosophical or conceptual questions like—'What is the core business of Westinghouse?' were raised, Paul was more comfortable with the practical requirements—whatever the hell we have to keep in order to show $1.2 billion EBIT [earnings before interest and taxes] which we need for a $25 stock." Monks did send the strategic plan plus a governance plan calling for genuine confidential voting, a destaggered board, nominating committee of independent directors, separation of chairman and CEO, greatly enhanced disclosure of executive compensation, and an advisory body of shareholders. In making these suggestions, Monks cited recommendations from several sources—including poison pill inventor Lipton—for improved relations between directors of U.S. companies and institutional shareholders in the interest of greater competitiveness and access to capital.

There were other meetings with Lego. But, nothing much ensued. So the Lens partners took their gripes to the board by sending all the members its strategy letter. In late January 1993, the board pushed Lego out, replacing him with a temporary CEO.

On April 28, 1993, Monks and his associate Kit Bingham attended the Westinghouse annual meeting in Minneapolis. The temporary chief executive assured everyone that the restructuring was on track and that management was "evaluating opportunities and considering alternative strategies," which provided a "powerful springboard for future business." Then Monks rose to speak. Addressing his remarks to the board members, he pointed out that he owned more stock than the entire board of directors put together and expressed his disgust at the way his property was being handled. "This is a $22 stock hiding in a $15 price," he said. He asserted that Westinghouse was in a grave financial crisis with an inability to raise capital, and "management was not taking steps fast enough" to avoid disaster. "Your progress does not reflect the overwhelming need for urgency," Monks scolded. "This board is part of the problem, unwilling to invest and unable to provide single-minded focus." The directors should resign, he said, if they can't make the tough decisions and demonstrate their commitment with real time and real investments. His remarks echoed his own Op-Ed appearing in the *Wall Street Journal* the day before, entitled, "To Change the Company, Change the Board." In that piece, he noted that Westinghouse's outside directors "do not have strong backgrounds in finance or business," and some of them serve on too many boards to be effective. In his talk, Monks announced that he would refuse to vote Lens's 132,000 shares for the four directors running for reelection. He sat down to a round of applause, and a man sitting nearby shook his fist in approval.

At the end of June, the Westinghouse board hired Michael Jordan, a partner at business consultant McKinsey & Co. and former president of Pepsi-Cola, as the new CEO. During 1993, the Lens team met twice with Jordan to urge him to follow their blueprint and do so quickly, but here Monks had met his match. Jordan listened politely and then remarked, "That's interesting."

"Michael," Monks said, "'That's interesting, yes,' 'That's interesting, no.'"

"That's interesting," Jordan said. "I'm not going to let you bully me."

At the end of both meetings, Jordan said the same thing: "Gentlemen, this is very interesting. We'll read your reports with great care and we will talk again." But he did nothing.[3]

Minow heard him speak at the CII meeting that year and then suggested he consider paying his directors in stock as an incentive. "You're absolutely right," Minow recalls his words. "And we're going to get around to that real soon." But there was never any evidence that he did so.

Toward the end of 1993, Lens submitted a shareholder resolution for Westinghouse's annual meeting to be held in the spring of 1994. The resolution called for the separation of the positions of chairman and CEO, and the election of a chairman from among the outside independent directors of the board. These steps, Monks wrote in a supporting statement, would avoid the inherent conflict of interest in a senior manager acting as his own monitor. "The combination of the chairman and CEO duties is a common practice and can sometimes be justified by a company's performance and responsiveness to its owners," Monks wrote. "Westinghouse, however, has reached a crucial point in its history and will need to make a new compact with its owners. As it forges a new direction for the difficult years ahead, the company must demonstrate that a rigorous system of management accountability is in place." After receiving news of the filing, Jordan agreed to meet with Monks in February. They discussed Jordan's strategy, and Monks, who had been hearing from all kinds of sources that "Jordan is very capable," agreed to withdraw the resolution.

With the board solidly on his side, Jordan was able to carry out his vision for the company, albeit slowly. It was a different vision than Lens had. Lens viewed the sale of the broadcasting operation as the best course, since it would supply cash to reduce debt and allow for an improved credit rating and future financings to strengthen the industrial operations. Jordan took the opposite route, selling industrial and building up broadcasting with the acquisition of CBS. Results continued to drag in 1994, but as Jordan proceeded with his strategy, the stock went up and Lens sold out at a modest profit in the summer of 1995. "It was clear what Jordan wanted to do," Higgins says. "We felt we'd done all we could."

The actions of the Westinghouse and American Express boards were two of several prominent examples of a new quality of independence on the boards of U.S. corporations that had littered former CEOs across the corporate landscape. It had been driven largely by institutional investors' concerns about corporate profitability as well as the sour stock market. Certainly, Monks played a role in inspiring this independent attitude. Most recently, it was he who in 1991 and 1992 illustrated that the independent directors at Sears were oxymorons on the board, publicly embarrassing them. In late 1992, the General Motors board, in a move led by outside directors, ousted CEO Robert Stempel. At IBM, the board forced CEO John Akers out the door. Noting these events, articles were being written about the powerful new "concentration of ownership" by pension funds, which Monks had recognized a decade earlier. The CEO departures, said *USA Today,* offer "powerful evidence that the movement to reform the way U.S. companies are managed and monitored is gathering steam. In theory, this is the way companies are supposed to work: Stockholders own the company. They elect a board of directors to look out for their best interests. The board hires a chief executive to run things."

By the fall of 1992, the funds had some new weapons to wield in the battle. The SEC now allowed them to solicit broad support for shareholder actions without first asking for the agency's approval. Previously, a shareholder could not even discuss an investment with more than 10 shareholders. In addition, the SEC required a complete accounting of executive pay in the proxy statement. Shareholders were becoming more and more annoyed with CEOs who awarded themselves huge pay increases, particularly when the company did poorly or laid off lower-level employees. Increasingly, Monks and Minow were outspoken about *undeservedly* high executive pay packages. But they stressed that there was nothing wrong with million-dollar salaries and bonuses if they had been earned. What is more, they consistently complained about option structures that rewarded executives on the upside but did not punish them when the stock fell.

The third company Lens approached was Eastman Kodak, which had been doing poorly in both its core photographic business and its diversified areas of medicine, information (printers/copiers/microfilm), and chemicals. Its $5.1 billion acquisition of Sterling Drug in 1987 had burdened the company with debt, now at $10.3 billion, and was not delivering the expected profits. In the autumn of 1992, for consideration at the upcoming annual meeting, Lens submitted Monks' "Exxon resolution" asking for the establishment of a company-financed committee of major shareholders that would monitor management, based on the belief that Kodak's board was not adequately exerting pressure on management to make changes.

On November 16, 1992, Monks, Holmes, and Higgins flew to Rochester to have a conversation with Kay Whitmore, a 35-year veteran of Kodak who had been CEO for two years. Confronted with the cubic Kodak tower, planted amidst a barren patch on the edge of the downtown district, Monks immediately saw the scene as symbolic of the company management's insularity and inability to respond to industry developments. "It looks like a 1930s temple in the middle of an urban renewal area that never got rebuilt," he later recorded. In the hushed atmosphere of the executive offices, the men spent an hour talking about the company's problems and strategic options.

It was evident during the meeting that Whitmore, who was trained as a scientist, was perplexed about why the Lens people were in the room. At one point, the CEO turned to Monks. "Bob, do you mind if I ask you a question? Why are you here? Why did you pick on me?"

A bit surprised that the answer wasn't self-evident, Monks responded politely. "We went through a list of the companies with the worst total rate of return, and you were on it."

"You mean to say," Whitmore said, "that if our stock price were higher, you wouldn't be here?"

"Right," Monks replied. "There would be more promising objects for our initiative."

"I can never get you people straight. Some years ago, some people came in here and said, 'We want you to have minorities on your board,' and we put minorities on our board. They didn't ask us to make an efficient board. Now you're in here about the stock price. I don't know what running a company's all about now."

Monks was not one to support a rainbow coalition approach to assembling a board of directors. As he told one interviewer at the end of 1993: "A board is not a place in which to demonstrate a social conscience. This is not the purpose of a board."[4] To him, the board's function was to assure the preservation of shareholder value. But to Whitmore, the idea of being ruthlessly judged by the market did not compute.

The Lens trio emphasized the need for Kodak to sell and/or spin off some divisions, and slash costs in order to pay down debt and give management the flexibility to reestablish a competitive position in its imaging technology business. They criticized Kodak for not speedily selling off 10 pieces of its money-losing information division, as the company had announced it would do. Whitmore indicated that this would get done. They also discussed the need to sell the medical and/or chemicals groups to help pay down Kodak's crushing debt. Whitmore preferred selling chemicals over medical, which he believed would in time benefit from Kodak's core technology. Kodak's soaring R&D and administrative costs were another subject of the discussion. "There is no sense of urgency," Monks later wrote of this meeting. "There is no feeling that a year or so makes any particular long run difference to the ongoing nature of EK. There is a presumption that the enterprise will survive largely in its present form." Lens planned to spend 1993 "creating a legitimate position, framing the issues and entitling ourselves within the parameters of management's pace of change to raising real definitional questions in 1994."[5]

However, the situation evolved at a much faster pace than expected. In December, Lens sent a 17-page letter to Whitmore critiquing management's operational and financial strategies and outlining Lens's suggested recovery program, essentially more detail on what they had already discussed, and detailing a "governance plan" similar to the one it had sent Westinghouse. Soon afterward, Whitmore announced a new executive compensation plan requiring the top 40 managers to buy stock and the appointment of a new committee of independent directors to place greater emphasis on achieving shareholder value. At the same time, Kodak hired a new CFO, Christopher Steffen, who had helped engineer turnarounds at both Chrysler and Honeywell. He was the highest ranking outsider Kodak had brought in since 1912. Steffen publicly stated that Kodak's debt was way too high and that he intended to slash the debt-to-capital ratio from 59 percent to 30–40 percent, if necessary by selling off assets.

In April, Monks, who had met Steffen when the latter was serving as CFO at Honeywell during the Rainwater-Lampert-Monks proxy contest and found him appreciative of the value of good governance, met him again to talk about Lens's strategic plan for Kodak. At that meeting in Rochester, Steffen was clearly frustrated by an inability to take the action that he believed needed to be taken to restore Kodak's bottom line.[6] That same day, Monks also met again with Whitmore and concluded from both meetings that while Whitmore was receptive to investors' ideas, he probably was not capable of taking Kodak entirely through the restructuring process.

Toward the end of February, Lens's shareholder committee resolution, SEC-approved and bound for the proxy statement, suffered a fatal blow. To Monks' and Minow's utter dismay, Calpers, emerging pretty much out of nowhere in this situation, publicly struck a deal with Kodak to support management. "We withdrew our resolution almost at the last minute, ostensibly because we got some concessions from them," Minow says. "but in reality because without Calpers it was going to be tough to get a respectable showing."

Steffen lasted only a few months, dismissed on April 28, the day Monks was attending the Westinghouse annual meeting. On May 3, a week before Kodak's annual meeting, Monks wrote to Whitmore expressing his distress on hearing the news. Other investors had called, he wrote, and "wanted to hear from me whether I think it means that Kodak has stepped back from the sense of urgency that [Steffen] brought to addressing the company's underperformance, and what I can do (and what I recommend they do) if that is the case." A subtle threat? He recommended a meeting or conference call with major shareholders, but none took place.

But even after the annual meeting, Kodak wanted Lens's support. Minow met with Kodak's general counsel and made the same offer she had made to Sears the year before: Hire any investment bank to provide a report to the board on the possible benefits of a breakup of the company, and we will leave you alone. Where Sears had said no, Kodak agreed. Lens filed no resolutions for the following year's annual meeting.

As a result of Whitmore's failure to take an aggressive approach to solve Kodak's problems, the board took action in August by forcing his resignation. His dismissal was in part at the insistence of a major shareholder, Fidelity Management, but certainly Lens had played a part in applying new pressures to both Whitmore and the board. Says Monks: "We were the people who called a spade a spade and said Kodak was a company that people ought to pay attention to. That was our function." In October, the board hired George Fisher, chairman of Motorola, who appeared to be the right man for the job. Happy with that choice, Lens sold out. "They never acknowledged it," Holmes says. "But they [Fisher] took exactly the five steps Lens had outlined." In July, a company spokesman told *CFO Magazine,* "Our interaction with Monks and Lens has been helpful and constructive."

The fund-raising for Lens, meanwhile, was not going well in 1993. For years, Monks had pressed his friend Dale Hanson to get the Calpers board to consider making an investment in an activist fund. At first, Hanson demurred. "I'd told Bob a long time before, when he talked to me about the concept of a corporate governance fund, 'I think it's too early,'" Hanson remembers. "A few years later he came back to me and said, 'You were right. It was too early. I waited, and now I'm ready.' But I still thought it was too early." Even so, Monks believed the time was right and wanted an answer. So Hanson went ahead and broached the subject with the fund trustees.

That was the fall of 1991. Monks the politician and salesman knew exactly how to proceed. The first thing he did was go to Dean LeBaron of Batterymarch to forge a joint venture of sorts. LeBaron recruited one of his people, Jim Pannell, to help Monks develop the Lens screening process and then assist him with initial marketing. Together, they took a few trips on LeBaron's Gulfstream jet to visit public pension funds, including Calpers. Early on, they suspected that some Calpers trustees were reticent. Jim Burton, then a Calpers executive, cautioned Monks that being a valued governance adviser did not qualify him to be an acceptable money manager for Calpers.[7]

In the summer of 1992, Monks was upset on learning that the Calpers trustees nearly dropped its consideration of Lens. He was attending a dinner Hanson put on to honor corporate chieftains who had excelled at governance, when he learned that earlier in the day the trustees had voted on a motion to reject Lens. It was rescued, Monks says, by Olena Berg, who as chief deputy treasurer was Treasurer Kathleen Brown's representative on the board. Shortly after Berg joined the Calpers board in early 1991, she got a call from Monks, who wanted to introduce himself and his notions of corporate governance to her. Not yet current with Calpers' work in that field, she did not know what he was referring to; to her, corporate governance was no more than a concept she had encountered in business school. But Monks came to her office and gave her a basic education in the movement. In 1993, she would go to Washington to sit in the same office Monks once occupied as the DOL's pensions administrator. In the 1992 Calpers trustees' meeting, Berg effectively defended the position that Lens should get some further study. After Monks learned about this close call, he decided that he was not being properly informed about the board's work on his solicitation. So, he hired Dick Damm, the legislative aide he had met while serving on the California governance commission, to look out for Lens's interests. The cost: $4,000 a month.

Also that summer, Monks determined that Lens was ready to hire a full-time salesperson. Pannell was having such a good time working with Monks that he volunteered to do the job starting September 1. The tab: a two-year contract at $200,000 a year (with $60,000 deferred to be either converted into equity in Lens or used as a termination fee). Everything was on schedule for Pannell's job switch when his wife went into premature labor with their first child. Charlie Pannell was born five weeks early and was rushed into the intensive care unit on a ventilator. When Monks found out what happened, he called the hospital in Boston and got Pannell on the phone.

"Do you want me to come sit with you?" he asked.

"I'm okay. Please don't go out of your way," Pannell said, assuming Monks was in Boston.

"I'll be down in two hours," Monks replied. And he got into his car, drove from Portland to Boston, kept Pannell company in the hospital, and took him out to dinner.

Pannell and Monks agreed to split up the selling job. Monks would concentrate on securing an assignment from Calpers, and Pannell would work on getting business from other funds. "The idea was like *Field of Dreams:* if we got Calpers in, everyone else would come," Pannell says. Over the following year, Monks made several trips to Sacramento, sometimes with Pannell, sitting down with Calpers trustees and staff, and paid a few visits to the fund's consulting firms. Meanwhile Pannell toured the country, visiting the managers at some 60 pension funds and consulting firms, often with Monks at his side. Their sales pitch: Lens is the ultimate value fund, taking the dogs of the dogs and helping to groom them. Funds were impressed by the access Monks was getting at companies like Kodak, Westinghouse, and American Express. About half a dozen funds showed "serious interest" in following Calpers into Lens—indicating they would make total commitments of $300 to $400 million in assets on top of whatever Calpers itself might contribute. Meantime, Hanson and Calpers trustees were upbeat.

Then it got tougher. "It seemed like Consultant of the Week," says Pannell, recalling Calpers' use of one consultant after another to scrutinize Lens. First came Wilshire Associates, the fund's traditional consultant. Then, Lilli Gordon and John Pound, corporate governance experts, who gave Lens a positive review in January 1993. Their study indicated that Lens's activist approach would deliver excellent returns, better than that of other, friendlier "relationship" investors. But still Calpers delayed making a decision. The entrepreneur in Monks did not have the patience to bear the painfully slow decision-making process of a large government organization. For a while he understood the fund's position. This was a new idea, and Calpers needed time to digest it. But before long, Monks became impatient. There were numerous meetings, which did not seem to lead anywhere. Most of the trustees wanted to go with Lens, but a couple remained skeptical of corporate governance. So the process dragged on.

As the summer of 1993 approached, there was still no verdict from Calpers. But Monks had a deadline of sorts. He had to decide whether to keep Pannell or pay him a $60,000 fee that would cancel the second year of the contract and save himself a much larger sum of money. Certainly, if Calpers signed on by July, he would keep Pannell to help Lens secure other investors. If the fund continued to drag its feet, Monks knew he would be unlikely to get the business he had hired Pannell to get. "I was in a game I couldn't afford," he says. "I couldn't afford to keep Jim forever without some business coming in the door." So Monks pushed Hanson to accelerate the decision-making process.

In visiting with the third consulting firm, Hamilton, Lane, Monks, Pannell, Minow, and Holmes got the distinct feeling that the consultants thought Lens was controversial. They suspected that Hamilton, Lane would not recommend Lens to Calpers, but got the fund's promise to give Lens a chance to respond to the report in person. On the morning in July that the trustees heard this consulting firm's presentation, Monks waited nervously outside the board room, along with Pannell and Hanson, who also remained outside, pacing the floor. Hours later, at lunchtime, Burton came out and told Monks that the trustees had changed their mind. They would not let him speak on his own behalf. They had taken a vote and decided not to hire Lens.

"What was the issue?" Monks, visibly angry, demanded.

"Want the truth?" Burton asked.

"Of course."

" It was you."[8]

Monks was simply too hot to touch. Having come from so far away and waited so long and hoped so hard, Monks was livid. He tore into Burton and his associate, Chuck Valdez. In his rage, he hurled profanities at them. "He also called us stupid, petty bureaucrats," Burton recalls. "He got real pissed off. He was very upset. Shortly afterward, we patched it up. I care about what he's doing. He's a change agent."

To be sure, Monks' controversial image was not the only problem Calpers had with Lens. The trustees were reluctant to engage a money manager who did not have a proven track record. Although Monks had been an investor for many years, more often than not as an activist board member, he had not been investing in the exact style that he was then doing with Lens and therefore could not cite a long-term performance record tied to that strategy. Short-term, Lens was doing well, with a 26 percent return from July 1992 to July 1993, triple the Standard & Poor's 500 Stock Index. He was trying to sell the fund based on his demonstrated capacity to bring large institutional investors together on specific issues. But that was not enough for pension funds that routinely measured a manager's past performance against the market and other money managers in selecting their investment advisers.

A related problem was that Calpers believed it was already activist enough on its own and did not need to invest in an activist fund. But most important, Calpers was afraid of the controversy. The fund already had earned the scorn of many major corporations for its shareholder activism. Hiring Monks would arouse even greater ire in the corporate community and, as he invested the Calpers money and began playing the activist role, the fund would be the one to get heat from companies and their advocates. The decision was not unanimous. Several trustees liked the idea, defending it as an investment that would produce superior returns. For those trustees who decided against Monks, Hanson explains, it was "an issue of the personality. They were nervous about Bob out representing Pers. They wanted to represent Calpers' program/agenda themselves. Bob is too much go-for-the-jugular." At the same time, Burton says, in the final discussion, everyone gave Monks great credit for the help he'd given Calpers.

Monks sprang back from this disappointment with his usual agility. He decided to take another tack. Back in February, while he and Milly were at their house in Florida, they got a visit from one of their son's childhood friends, Charles Woodworth, who lived nearby. Woodworth felt close to the Monks family and held Bob Sr. in high regard. When he was 19, he had a pushcart outside Faneuil Hall in Boston from which he sold a cheese and cracker holder he had designed and made himself. When sales took off, he went to the nearby Boston Company offices to share the news with Monks. As he launched excitedly into his story, he noticed that Monks was writing something down. Without reacting to the story, the bank chairman then asked him, "Do you have an accountant?" A bit startled, Woodworth replied that he did not. Monks handed him the paper. "Call this fella. Then come back and talk to me." Woodworth was delighted with this response. Here was someone who was taking him seriously as an entrepreneur.

Some 15 years later, Woodworth, who was in the business of raising funds for investment managers, would return the favor with some advice for Monks. Aware that fund-raising for Lens had not been going well, he said, "I think you need to go to a different group of investors." Other than public pension funds, that is.

"Prove it to me," Monks challenged him.

Woodworth arranged meetings for Monks with wealthy individuals, investment fund managers, and family office managers. After the Calpers rejection, Monks took him on full-time. They worked through the rest of 1993—attending the CII annual meeting and calling on West Coast consultants—and well into 1994 before they got their first sight of money. Woodworth finally succeeded in securing a lunch meeting with two officers of Soros Fund Management. This group of funds was run by George Soros, the world-renowned investor who in 1970, when he was a mere research analyst, helped Monks become a millionaire. "Bob blew them away," Woodworth says. "He can weave for an audience how it works for them." When he arrived in his office the next day, Woodworth found a message that Soros had called. He wanted to meet and was available "anytime." The following week, they had lunch at his office. On meeting Monks again after 24 years, Soros remembered the Westmoreland investment well. They talked, and by the time coffee was served, Soros made a $25 million commitment to Lens, which later became $50 million. If he could not get Calpers, Soros was a promising alternative.

The arrangement they made with Soros was that once they agreed on a target investment, Lens and Soros would both invest, each would talk separately to the corporate executives about strategy, and Lens would organize other shareholders. The $50 million would be invested in Lens's other target companies. Later, Lens got more individual investors and a couple more institutional clients, including the State of Wisconsin Investment Board (SWIB) and Hermes, the manager of the U.K. post office and telecommunications workers' pension funds. Today, there is $50 million invested in Lens's second fund, Lens II. But, when affiliated funds are included—Ram Trust Services, which handles the extended Monks family funds, the Soros Fund's separate account of some $80 million, and other separate accounts worth about $5 million—the Lens group has some $300 million under management. Also, a new joint venture with Hermes in the United Kingdom will start off with between $250 million and $350 million under management.

"By 1995, Lens had three years of history and they'd put some good numbers on the scoreboard," says James Severance, SWIB's investment director. "Bob has visited with us over the years. He cuts a big figure, both physically and otherwise. Brokering reform at companies takes a diplomat who can, when the moment calls for it, bare his teeth." In mid-1997, Lens celebrated its fifth birthday with a compounded annual return of 26 percent, outflanking the Standard & Poor's 500. Still, people were hardly knocking down Lens's door. One morning in June 1997, for instance, Monks and Minow made their presentation at a fund in Baltimore, where the listeners appeared so bored—one even fell asleep while Minow was talking—that it was obvious they had made their decision before the meeting began.

A key issue with Soros was how Lens would be paid. Again, this was where Minow and Monks parted company. Monks wanted a percentage of what Soros would make on any investment they worked on together; Minow wanted to avoid being a gun for hire and have Soros just pay a management fee on all the investing Lens did for him, like any other client. "This has come up in many different contexts where I have perceived a conflict of interest," she says. "And I think that Bob will tell you that if he didn't know I was going to say no, he wouldn't have brought it up. He always says, 'Nell is my canary in a coal mine. Let's just make Nell a little uncomfortable. If we make her a lot uncomfortable then we know we're in trouble.' We had a big argument at ISS. He wanted to take money from Harold Simmons to be an advocate, and also with Honeywell. It's a good thing I was there. We can only lose our virginity once. Let's do it with the right person. He was going to go to Soros and ask to be paid. I said 'No . . . No No No No.'" In fact, she refused to sign papers that were necessary to enroll a brand-new institutional client for Lens until they resolved the matter to her satisfaction. Monks told her that they would proceed with Soros only if she was happy, and if having Soros pay a management fee to Lens was what made her happy, so be it. And so it was.

By the end of 1993, Lens had sold out of Sears, Kodak, and American Express. One of its new investments was in Borden, the dairy products company, which in retrospect was not a good choice for Lens.[9] "We didn't realize that it was too late to save it," Holmes says.

Borden had unsuccessfully branched into regional brands, a high-cost strategy given the inability to do national advertising and marketing. The milk business had become less profitable as derivative dairy products, which Borden did not have a strong presence in, gained in profitability. Results were dragging. The only thing that was increasing was the level of debt. In September 1993, Holmes, Monks, Minow, and Higgins met in New York with Borden chief Anthony D'Amato, who had been CEO for two years. As Monks describes the experience: "The CEO came in and six people came after him, in chain lockstep, gedump, gedump, gedump, gedump. And only he talked. And boy was he hostile." At one point, D'Amato glared at Monks and asked him, "How did you get so rich, anyway?"

Monks gave him a grin. "Well, I'll tell you. I inherited it, and I married it." D'Amato shook his head and under his breath said, "I knew it."

"Oh, Bob, come on," Minow chided, adding, "He made a lot more on his own than he got any other way."

Toward the end of the meeting, Monks asked how Lens could best be of help to Borden. D'Amato's response was that what he really wanted was to have them leave. They were distracting him from the job he needed to do.

Even after getting such an unfriendly reception, Minow was under the impression that there was one good thing to say about Borden: its executive compensation program as stated in the most recent proxy statement was quite reasonable. Top managers had not received any bonuses because results had not hit the required target, and their stock options were under water due to the sinking price of the stock. So, when it was her turn to speak at the meeting, Minow started out by commending them on their pay plan.

But as soon as she returned to her office in Washington, Minow received a call from an investment manager who told her about a new compensation deal the company entered into after the proxy statement came out.

Minow was stunned. "Oh really?"

The new pay plan, disclosed in an SEC filing, was to be presented to shareholders for approval at the upcoming annual meeting. When Minow saw it, she was aghast.

"It was by far the worst compensation plan I'd ever seen," she says. D'Amato had a five-year contract that would hold even if he left earlier. And both of his residences, plus the taxes on them, would be paid for by the company on the theory that he needed them both to do his job. "As opposed to the rest of us who keep ours for the fun of it," Minow quips.

"It's reprehensible that the people who are the wealthiest are the ones who get out of these day-to-day expenses." Also, the plan gave the CEO 100,000 new options at a strike price to be named later. (Normally, the price is the stock price on the day the plan takes effect or a premium.) If the shareholders voted down the stock option award, the company would make up the difference in cash.

Over the next several months, Lens communicated to D'Amato its suggested strategy, which included reducing debt, divesting, liquidating, or downsizing lower margin businesses, and providing justification for retained divisions. The fund principals also asked the company to set up a nominating committee on its board and remove the company's former CEO as a director. Not much got done, and Lens let the press know its feeling that D'Amato was not doing a good job. In that vein, Minow also took the liberty of sending the CEO's proposed five-year contract to a newspaper reporter she knew.

At one point, D'Amato called her, furious. "Nell handed me the phone," Monks says. "I told him plainly that he was the wrong guy to run the company."

That spring, the board ousted D'Amato and replaced him with a temporary CEO. It also set up a nominating committee and replaced the former CEO (D'Amato's predecessor) as a director. Minow and Holmes went to the annual meeting. "We saw the company was drifting, deteriorating fast," Holmes says. Minow stood up to describe D'Amato's compensation contract and stock option plan (The option portion of it was not approved; the cash portion of the contract held). While she spoke, she received, to her surprise, three rounds of applause. In her remarks, she asked the head of the board's compensation committee to apologize, which he did not do. When she then asked him to promise never to enter into such an agreement again, his attorney advised him not to respond.

Lens met with new top management, including CEO Ervin Shames and CFO James Van Meter, in July 1994. "We communicated the perspective of ownership—a sense of urgency, a willingness to 'write off' the dairy unit and to recast the balance of the company into two divisions, the need for new directors," read Lens's 1994 annual report. But things only got worse. In September, Kohlberg, Kravis, Roberts & Co., the buyout firm, announced that it would acquire all the shares of Borden in exchange for $14.25 of the common stock of RJR Nabisco. Lens took a small loss on the investment, but Monks maintains that it could have been much worse.

"KKR bailed us out," says Monks. "There wasn't any there there. You can repair something that's malfunctioning, but you can't create something that doesn't exist. There was no core business. No real business."

A lesson learned? Says Holmes: "If we'd done even more basic research, spent more time digging into it," maybe Lens would not have invested at all. However, the experience also points to the one great weakness in Lens's strategy. As an outsider, it has to rely only on publicly available information. Hence, its analysis is incomplete. The partners hope that its research will allow it at least to ask the right questions when meeting a CEO and thereby get a much better feel for a company. And the more involved Lens gets, the more of a real sense it gets of who is running the place and how they are running it.

They had plenty of time to get to know Stone & Webster. The engineering company was the smallest target Lens had picked to date, and the first one that was not a conglomerate. But at the time Lens invested, buying 90,000 shares in 1993 for a 1 percent stake, the company had a heaping portion of problems. Stone & Webster had a stellar reputation as a builder of nuclear power plants, but was not coping well as that industry declined. For one thing, it had not effectively made the leap abroad to take advantage of the burgeoning demand for electricity in developing nations. Moreover, the company continued to carry burdensome overhead despite a shift from cost-plus to fixed-price contracts, and also appeared to be carrying excess capital in the form of Treasury bonds and stock holdings.

It was evident to Monks and his cohorts that major obstacles prevented the company's leadership from even trying to find, never mind execute, solutions. Operational losses were masked in net results by earnings stemming from a big surplus in the pension fund and various real estate and stock investments; while the company recorded a $2 million net profit in 1993, it also benefited from a $14 million credit stemming from the pension fund surplus that was not itemized in the income statement (which was perfectly in line with accounting standards). Logically, without this information, shareholders and analysts would believe that results were better than they actually were and would not be as motivated to pressure management and the board to be accountable—although the stock had been performing much worse than that of peers, perhaps partly for this reason. Another obstacle to change was that 37 percent of the stock was held by the employee stock ownership plan (ESOP), giving the board and management a large friendly stockholder to bolster their actions—or inaction. Finally, the board included such management-sympathetic types as the company's lawyer and consultant and the former vice chairman of the ESOP's trustee, Chase Manhattan Bank. Meanwhile, the 80-year-old Peter Grace, chairman of W. R. Grace, who had served as a Stone & Webster director for some 50 years, was the only board member with significant investment in the stock, indicating to Monks one reason that the board as a whole lacked an owner's natural zeal to get the company moving.

On September 21, some of the Lens partners met with Chairman and CEO William Allen Jr., Chief Operating Officer Bruce Coles, and CFO William Egan at Stone & Webster's New York headquarters. They talked about the company's financial blight, possible asset sales, and growth plans. Monks pointed out that assets such as a sizable stake in Tenneco Corp. were tying up capital that could either be invested in the company or distributed to shareholders. The company's officers, offended by the questions Monks and his partners were firing at them, were unwilling to consider asset sales at the time, insisting that the capital was needed as a reserve for possible future construction jobs.

Monks followed up with a letter to Coles in October in which he blatantly proposed that Stone & Webster either privatize by allowing the ESOP to buy out all other investors or concentrate on improving shareholder value for the public shareholders. "If a company cannot offer shareholders a competitive rate of return, it seems to me the company must determine whether it can justify having public shareholders at all," he wrote. On the issue of excess capital, he asked, "Have any outside advisors provided the company with guidelines relating to levels of assets prudently required to meet satisfactory bonding and working capital needs?" He enclosed Lens's calculations of the realizable values of the company's assets, noting that they totaled about twice the market value of Stone & Webster's stock. Moreover, he wrote "our review has led to the conclusion that the [pension] surplus has been an obstacle to the company's growth, because it has removed the pressure to perform."

Coles did not reply to Monks' letter until late December—too late for Lens to file a shareholder resolution for the spring 1994 annual meeting. As it turned out, Coles' reply was "nonresponsive and naïve," Monks later wrote. Although he had hoped to avoid confrontation, he was beginning to realize that this might not be possible. In January, Monks wrote back to the company, proposing himself and Joseph Blasi, an expert in the area of ESOPs whom Monks had contacted, as nominees for the board. A letter from the head of the board's newly formed nominating committee indicated that it was not willing to make the time to give Monks and Blasi full consideration as candidates for the slate. Monks penned a letter to CEO Allen on February 22, asking to sit down and talk.

On the morning of March 15, 1994, Monks, Minow, and Holmes returned to the company to meet with Allen, who was in his mid-70s and would retire as CEO at the May annual meeting but continue as chairman, and Coles, who would replace him as CEO. (Later, Lens took some credit for Allen's decision to step down. In their first meeting, Minow asserts, "That company was about as resistant to change of any kind as any I've ever seen. Allen was making no plans to leave, and [previously] made no mention of leaving.") They spoke for two hours. Allen listened patiently to the investors' views, taking copious notes on a yellow pad. Monks and his partners thought it advisable to liquidate certain assets unrelated to the core engineering business, distribute at least some of the proceeds as a dividend to investors, and invest the rest in the business. Those assets included Tampa real estate, a holding of 700,000 shares ($35 million) of Tenneco stock, and a huge pension fund surplus. "The whole example of what they said about the Tenneco stock really tells you everything about that company," Minow says. "We said to them, 'Tell us why you have Tenneco stock as an asset of the company.' And they said, 'It didn't cost us anything. We got it years ago in a transaction.' [Note: It was a portion of fees received years earlier when Stone & Webster had a financial services business.] That gives you some idea of their complete failure to understand the concept of asset allocation. We said, 'It cost you whatever was on the other side of the transaction, and you still haven't explained why you have it now. What is it doing for you now? Why is S&W a holding company for Tenneco stock?'" Coles seemed reluctant to sell anything. As Monks wrote in a memo about the meeting, "Coles is terrified at the notion of distributing assets to the shareholders. 'We may need them.' He has no conception that the principal virtue of a public company is the rapid access to competitively priced capital."

Among the reasons Coles gave for the company's poor financial results were: Stone & Webster was in a transition phase in its move from 85 percent of revenues from the energy business to 50 percent in that field; it still needed to hire staff in the new areas; and there had been delays in the start of awarded government contracts. Moreover, Allen and Coles held that it was difficult to win bids when competitors were willing to take business at low margins. In January, Stone & Webster management had retained

Goldman Sachs to explore international investment opportunities and help the company present itself better to investors (as then executive vice president Jim White told *CFO Magazine*).[10]

To the Lens partners, there seemed to be no philosophy or mission guiding the company, beyond a desire to liquidate some unrelated assets and reserve the cash for a time when demand increased. In his memo about the meeting, Monks noted, "Coles is two levels too high; not acceptable as CEO of a NYSE-listed company." As for the board of directors, the Lens partners maintained it was "docile." Coles and Allen were "genuinely amused" by that characterization, Monks wrote. At one point, Monks found himself saying, "You are not bad people," prompting his hosts to break into laughter. Monks added: "You are prisoners of a system that does not require you to respond to 'creative tension'" (because 37% of the stock was in friendly hands).

The management was not so amused to learn the following month that Lens had filed a suit against the company, its directors, and Chase Manhattan, the ESOP trustee, in Federal District Court for the District of Massachusetts. Lens claimed that Stone & Webster had committed fraud by failing to disclose that its engineering division had been operating at a loss and to identify its source of reported net profits as the pension plan surplus. In that regard, Lens feared a "needless dissipation of shareholder assets," said the suit, which also mentioned the continuing increases in top executives' pay in the face of declining profits. "We've spent the past eight months asking Stone & Webster to conduct its affairs like a publicly owned company," Monks said in a press statement. "It prefers to enjoy the benefits of the public market, but without the responsibility of full or accurate disclosure. The company's recent announcement that it expects a large loss in the first quarter and a loss in 1994 means the deception is finally ending. [Though it had not yet restated past earnings.] With management and its agent Chase controlling 37 percent, we've turned to the court to help before it's too late."

The lawsuit was a creative tactic—and a risky one in three respects. Monks had decided not to file the suit in Delaware because he believed the courts there to be biased toward corporate management; not to use one of the usual shareholder plaintiff attorneys because they were not people Lens felt acted solely in shareholders' interest; and not to ask for damages. By not asking for damages it might seem that Lens was saying there was no damage done; but Lens gambled that it would give them credibility as plaintiffs, since shareholder lawsuits had routinely asked for so much in damages. Instead, Lens asked the court to order the company to provide accurate financial disclosure and to postpone its May 12 annual meeting to permit a proxy contest or solicitation for "no" votes for the board. Moreover, the suit sought the removal of Chase as the ESOP trustee because it had failed to "vote its controlling interest in Stone & Webster for the exclusive benefit of the employee members." The evidence it cited was that Chase had voted in favor of management on every proposal. Under labor laws as they then stood and as Monks himself had helped establish, Lens charged that Chase was obligated as a trustee for employees to try to right the foundering Stone & Webster ship. There was no question that the lawsuit was a shot in the dark. Its premise was bold and new and unlikely to succeed. But it served a purpose for Lens in that it made news, thereby intensifying the spotlight on Stone & Webster's drab performance, and it was just one more way to badger the management. "We sued in order to have a public airing of the company's practices," Monks later said. "We wanted the management to understand that we would "go public" consistently until they dealt with us."

The annual meeting May 12 was disappointing for Lens. Even before the meeting began, things were not going right. While chatting with Monks and another shareholder near the doorway of the building where the meeting was to be held, Minow remarked politely to an elderly man, "If you're looking for the Stone & Webster annual meeting, it's that way." The man glared at her, then barked, "Why aren't you down there, then?" Taken aback, Minow said she was talking to some friends. In response, the man started yelling at her: "You have friends! You'd better be thankful you have friends!" and then marched off. "That," Monks said, "was Peter Grace."[11]

For the first time ever, the Lens fund partners had planned to vote their shares at the meeting itself rather than beforehand. They mistakenly thought that simply bringing their proxies to the meeting would suffice. But they soon found out that they needed to bring documents from their custodian bank confirming that they were the holders of the shares they were voting. "It was a bit embarrassing," says Georgeson's Wilcox, who was working as the company's proxy solicitor. "I remember the people at Stone & Webster laughing at that." As a result, Lens was not able to vote on the shareholder resolutions, including one on confidential voting, and withhold its votes for the four board members standing for re-election in Stone & Webster's staggered election system. Even so, the fund went ahead and announced in a press release that it had withheld its votes on its 172,000 shares, representing it as a vote of no confidence in the management. "This board needs a message that shareholders will not support a board that hides negative earnings in the pension surplus, a board that fails to respond to five years of unacceptable performance," Minow said in the release. Lens also noted that another new investor was accumulating a large stake in the company: Frank Cilluffo, a private investor from Portsmouth, New Hampshire. The very day after the meeting, Lens urged Stone & Webster to appoint Cilluffo to the board (which it did in January 1995).

In July 1994, Lens lost its case in court when the judge threw it out, and the company hailed the decision as a victory over "frivolous" charges. But it subsequently won a fight over whether it could examine company records. And in September, *CFO Magazine* published an article about Stone & Webster entitled, "True Lies: How GAAP Conceals the Real Story at Stone & Webster," that related the saga of the company's mismanagement. "We circulated the article among all the institutional investor holders, thus enhancing our own reputations and drawing attention to the real problem," Monks says. The following year, Stone & Webster restated its numbers precisely as Lens had asked. Meanwhile, things were just getting worse at the company. In 1994, it lost money on a net basis for the first time in six decades and laid off 1,000 of its 6,000 employees.

Planning for Lens's involvement at the 1995 shareholders' meeting seemed in retrospect as shoddy as the previous year's work. Each shareholder at a company is allowed to sponsor only one resolution. In this case, 10 resolutions were submitted by shareholders with obvious ties to Monks such as his nephews John Higgins and George Monks, Jr., and other relatives—and the SEC did not allow them. The fund's hope was that the slew of resolutions (on everything from destaggering the board to requiring directors to make a minimum investment in the stock to retaining an independent investment banking firm that would evaluate options for divestment of assets) would be approved by the SEC and then become bargaining chips for the partners to negotiate changes with the company. Although Lens knew it was taking a calculated risk with the 10 proposals, it did not expect the SEC to reject all 10 of them. Surely, the agency would preserve at least one. And it did not expect Stone & Webster to put up a big fight. In a SEC filing the size of a telephone book, Stone & Webster objected that in reality, these proposals were from a single proponent and therefore should not be allowed on the proxy statement. The company supported its case with other arguments as well. As Minow recounts, "In one of the resolutions, I referred to the fact that Peter Grace had been on the board for half a century. They objected. It wasn't true at the time I wrote it. But it would have been true at the time it would be voted on." Wilcox, for one, was surprised by Lens's misstep in filing the 10 proposals: "That was an error," he says, "and that error was compounded by the fact that they hadn't designated which proposal should survive if the SEC ruled there was a single proponent. So they were all thrown out. They didn't get any proposals in."

As a result, Lens had to piggyback on someone else's proposal. And luckily, the resolution it cared about most—that the company hire an investment bank to consider asset dispositions—had also been proposed by a friend, Alan Kahn. It was really more than luck. Kahn, an investor who had been known to use litigation against corporations, met Monks several years earlier. "One of the first things I heard from Bob Monks was a lie," he says. "He told me that he tends to speak in hyperboles. That's a lie. I don't think he speaks in hyperbole. I think that he speaks with extraordinarily strong conviction and a sense of complete moral rectitude. Somebody who speaks from that platform sounds like he's using hyperbole because of the dramatic nature of the context of what is being discussed." In 1989, ISS—and most directly Minow—had worked to help Kahn in his case against Occidental Petroleum (again, Monks' nemesis Armand Hammer), which was financing the construction of the Armand Hammer museum of art. As Kahn explains: "It turned out at the time the largest shareholder in Occidental was Calpers. Nell knew all the people at Calpers. Through Nell I asked Calpers to be a co-plaintiff in the case. They said they couldn't do it. Occidental is based in California, the museum was in California, and Armand Hammer was a very high profile guy. This was too political. But they said they'd give me a strong affidavit in support of my case. Nell got that affidavit from Calpers for me." In preparing the case, Kahn learned that some of the art in Hammer's collection was bought with company funds. "After I showed the checks to Calpers and told them what I'd learned in discovery, Calpers said enough is enough, they would agree to come in as co-plaintiff. So at that point we had the assistance of the California attorney general's office." But the challenge failed and the museum got built. Later, Kahn acted as a consultant to Lens in the use of litigation as a weapon in the corporate governance movement.

By sheer coincidence, Kahn had long had an investment in Stone & Webster and had long been frustrated with its undervalued stock. Aware that at least some of Lens's 10 proposed resolutions would likely be rejected by the SEC, Monks wanted to make sure that the most important one—the hiring of an investment banking firm—had a backup. So he recruited Kahn. "They needed a stockholder to do a proposal," Kahn recounts. "I volunteered. That's how that shareholder proposal got on the proxy statement. I was glad to help." Minow actually wrote the resolution for him to prepare it for filing at the SEC.

Monks admits making mistakes in planning for the annual meeting. He blames Lens's decision to use a law firm that was not sophisticated enough to deal with the surprising hardball tactics Stone & Webster and its lawyers used. However, he did persuade the company to let him speak at the meeting on the subjects of the other proposals. He would do so at the points on the agenda when shareholders turned to address the election of directors and approval of stock options plans. So, when Monks arrived at the stately Hotel Dupont in Wilmington, Delaware, he put on his usual confident air although he was apprehensive. He and some of the other Lens partners hosted several friends and two reporters for lunch in the hotel's vast formal dining room. Then, it was upstairs for the meeting.

This would be the last meeting Allen would run, for he was about to retire as Chairman. He yielded the podium first to Coles. What the CEO had to say indicated that shareholders, most probably Lens, had had an impact on the company—though he certainly didn't give them all the credit.

> Myself and a number of directors have visited a number of you. We are listening. We will continue to strive for dialogue. The theme is change. Over the past 106 years, Stone & Webster has always changed with the changing times. The past year . . . in July the board resolved to sell all investment securities, including the Tenneco stock [which was sold]. Also in July, the board resolved to buy back up to 1 million shares. . . . In August, the office park was put on the market. Our engineering division has a new head and has reorganized into four business units. There's been a reduction in the work force and the addition of two new directors. The reduction in personnel has resulted in $55 million in savings. We have new incentive compensation, a new CFO, and our Cherry Hill facility is on the market. We have brought our cost structure into line with revenues. The first quarter we have recorded a profit of 32 cents a share. In the first quarter of 1994 we had a loss of 86 cents a share. Some would say we've been adverse to change. I say we've embraced change.

He went on to point out improvements in total backlog, international business commitments, and investment in developing projects and new technologies. "Stone & Webster has refocused its business—cut revenues in the process, which generated working capital. We now will put that to work." Coles gave great credit for the changes to Goldman Sachs, which had reviewed the company's capital requirements and noncore assets, "which led to the asset dispositions and buybacks."

The next item on the agenda was the election of directors. From the back of the room, Monks raised his hand. His unsuccessful effort to take the podium at the front to speak to the three board nominees was recounted at the start of this book. Finally, he situated himself at the front but all the way to the side of the room. He was allowed to ask presubmitted questions, but, awkwardly, only through Allen. "Thank you for the summary," he addressed Coles. "And thank you for the sale of the Tenneco stock. I'd like to ask the members of the board to consider Mr. Cilluffo as board chairman, an owner as chairman and a chairman who is different from the CEO." Turning to Coles, he asked, "What are the benchmarks with which [the directors can] measure your performance in 1995?"

Allen interrupted. "Mr. Coles has given his summary. The question is out of order. You're directing your questions to me. I am the chairman of this meeting, and I am going to control this meeting."

Monks took a step toward Allen, and, alarmed, Allen raised a hand to stop him. "Why don't you stand back there before we get too close together?"

Monks, inwardly pleased at the reaction he was inadvertently provoking, obediently stepped back. "The Tenneco stock is being sold, but is not something to be proud of," he said. "Cash flow is a negative $40 million . . ."

Coles interjected that that figure was wrong.

"What are we electing?" Monks continued. "Three directors. What are they committed to?" In advance of the meeting, Monks had submitted several questions he wished to direct to all three nominees. Among them: Would they consider full confidential voting? Would they disclose any relationships they have with the company other than that of director? Would they instruct management to meet periodically with significant shareholders and direct the nominating committee to consider nominations proffered by shareholders? Would they adopt a policy to evaluate its own performance and that of the CEO? Would they support sale of certain assets (some assets had been on the market for a long time), and a discontinuation of expenses related to the holding company? His goal was nothing less than to expose the nominees to the light of public scrutiny right there and then. In doing so, he was trying out Minow's long-held theory that Heisenberg's principle—observation changes what is being observed—applied to directors as well. They behave differently—more responsibly—when they are being watched. Indeed, Lens itself operated largely on that theory.

"I will determine whether the directors wish to respond," Allen asserted. At once, Cilluffo offered to respond first.

"Yes, unquestionably yes," was his answer to the question of whether he'd support full confidentiality. "I've received letters from shareholders who fear reprisal." He also gave his sanction to all of Monks' other questions.

The next nominee, J. Angus McKee, was more evasive. "I believe in confidentiality as laid out by the SEC."

Monks: "The SEC says nothing about confidentiality."

Allen: "Confidentiality is in effect."

The questioning resumed. McKee said, "It is not up to me to direct the nominating committee to do anything. I advise the nominating committee, and I believe we do evaluate our own performance."

Monks: "Give me an example. What is the evaluation?"

Allen broke in. "You've added a question you did not submit in advance!"

In the middle of the room, a voice rang out. "I am a shareholder with 140,000 shares. And I want an answer to the question. Are you allowed to answer a question that hasn't been pre-screened?"

Monks was permitted to ask his question. "Share with us your evaluation of the board's performance," he said.

"I've been associated with this company for 50 years," McKee said. "I think the management here is doing an excellent job, and I give it my full support."

The third nominee, Meredith Spangler, was in agreement with Monks on all points.

Next, Minow spoke in opposing the company's stock option plan for directors. "The outside directors do not consider Stone & Webster stock a worthwhile investment," she began. "They want us to give them 2,000 options. Why should we give them stock if they're not willing to buy it?"

Finally, it was Alan Kahn's turn to speak on behalf of his resolution to hire an investment bank. Kahn rose and announced that he would bequeath his allotted time to Monks. Standing at his seat this time, Monks spoke briefly in defense of the proposal. He held that the company had not tried selling lots of assets that were unrelated to the core business and yielding an inadequate return for the company. Goldman Sachs, he maintained, had been retained for very limited work that management would not detail at Lens's request. "Use Goldman Sachs," he said. "But ask them the right questions. . . . We need to have a measure of accountability. Do we want to be in the engineering and construction business, or do we want to be in the real estate and cold storage warehouse business? Voting for Alan Kahn's resolution is the only way we can articulate our concern for the company."

Kahn's resolution won 35.6 percent of outstanding shares—certainly impressive considering the ESOP's 37 percent holding. Nearly 30 percent of shares were voted against the stock option plans. As they left the hotel, Monks and Minow were smiling broadly like two kids who had just been to the fair.

After the meeting, Coles adamantly defended himself to news reporters. He asserted that the board agreed the company should be in engineering and construction and that management has done a lot of work to improve that business while disposing of unrelated operations and assets. "We're doing a lot of the things Lens wants," he maintained. He and the CFO, Jeremiah Cronin, objected that Monks charged the company with "hiding" the pension credit by not including it on the income statement. "That's an out and out lie," Cronin complained. As for hiring an investment bank, Coles continued to insist that given Goldman Sachs' assignment, another adviser would be redundant.

That may have been true, but no one could be sure. "Our big thing was we wanted to see a list of questions they'd asked Goldman Sachs to answer," Minow says. "Our view was they were not asking the big question of now what do we do, or what's the best way to optimize our assets. They were asking a series of smaller questions. Investment bankers are in business, and they will give the answer the client wants." Whether or not a second bank would have been unnecessary, the vote for the resolution was a vote of no confidence in the management.

In an interview with the *Boston Globe* July 24, 1995 the CEO spared no words in dismissing Monks as a "self-proclaimed gadfly" who would "jump on both sides of an issue very very quickly, . . . tends to use facts to his benefit . . . and to change facts to his benefit" and "appears to be looking for a short-term return." Barely a month after that interview, Coles up and left the company for what he called personal reasons. He moved to a privately owned company in the south, where he said he wanted to live. The Lens investors were shocked by the announcement. But they continued to be disappointed by the company's torpor in selling off assets it had pledged to sell.

What could they do? That summer, Lens initiated discussions with the Fluor Corp., another engineering company, about possibly making an offer to buy Stone & Webster. Lens even indicated its willingness to buy some of the Stone & Webster assets so that Fluor would only be acquiring those assets directly related to engineering. Fluor decided against an acquisition, but Lens then moved on to a second possible purchaser: defense contractor Raytheon Corp. "I knew that Raytheon would not do a hostile," Monks says, "but I wanted to create pressure that would obligate the company to recognize that values were not being achieved. We were trying to create an atmosphere in which the directors would realize that they could not indefinitely ignore the marketplace. Our continuing effort was to force the management to take steps to unlock the values." Monks says he convinced Raytheon's acquisition manager to place a call to Stone & Webster's Chairman, Kent Hansen. Apparently, Monks says, Hansen told him the company was not for sale. On September 1, Lens issued a press release entitled, "Lens tells Stone & Webster board to sell the company." In a letter sent to the board that day, Monks said, "We must conclude that the only way to realize full value of assets and save jobs of skilled professionals is to sell or merge the company," a statement repeated in the release. It continued: "We're now past the point of studying the divestiture of assets. This company needs to put itself on the market as the best chance to realize full value for shareholders." In the end, Raytheon opted not to mount an offensive for this prize.

In light of these comments and the rumors that resulted about Stone & Webster being in play, the board engaged Goldman Sachs that September 1995 to study strategic alternatives and possible purchasers or merger partners. In essence, the directors asked Goldman to value the company. According to Kerner Smith, the man who would take over as CEO in 1996, Goldman found that the value of the company was above where the stock was trading. And so, yes, the company would be in danger of being taken over.

Once Goldman presented its findings to the independent directors in October, the board announced that it decided to maintain the course it had previously plotted. Lens continued to demand "a thorough and unshackled review of the company's strategic options by an investment banker." As Monks had remarked in a September 12, 1995, letter to the company, "We have no idea what it is you asked Goldman, Sachs & Co. If you had asked

them for a plan for maximization of shareholder value, with full license to
consider disposition of corporate assets, that would be one thing. If on the
other hand, they were asked to approve a management plan (the elements of
which we are in ignorance), that would be another."

Lens and the board did have a constructive meeting in November. As a
result of Lens's suggestions, the board decided to begin paying members a
fixed number of shares of stock per year. It also included Lens's guidance in
the criteria it was using for recruitment of directors and a permanent CEO.
In urging the company to assemble a first-class board, Minow took a tough
stance. "Bob and I are willing to be on your board. You don't have to put
us on your board but you have to put someone better than us on the board.
And right now the people you have are not better than we are. We are establishing the floor for qualifications to be on your board. If you run the
same people again we'll run against them, and we will win because we're
more qualified than they are." Today she says that, "This has become my
favorite thing to do. But now I use other people as the floor. I've raised the
standard a lot higher than Bob and me."[12]

By February 1996, Stone & Webster had a new chief, H. Kerner Smith,
a veteran of the energy and industrial industries. Smith knew the company
well and was aware it needed strategic changes. While he assumed investors
were upset that the stock had fallen from the 40s into the 20s, he had little
notion of investors' disenchantment with the direction the company had
taken. He would soon find out. His first day on the job, he called all the
major shareholders and asked to meet with them, which, he found out later,
effectively reversed an unofficial policy not to talk to anyone—whether
shareholders, press, or analysts. "Prior to 1994, the company didn't even reveal their revenues, just reporting service revenues," he still marvels. His second day on the job, he called engineering analysts on Wall Street and asked
why they were not following Stone & Webster. Their answer was that they
had tried but no one at the company would talk with them. Smith began to
court both investors and analysts in an effort to energize the stock.[13]

Minow and Holmes visited Smith at the company and heard him outline the methodology he would follow to revive the company. The listeners
said the game plan sounded good and they would be watching to see if he
carried through. From the start, Smith says, "We assumed there was no
strategy at the company, and we were pretty much right." While the board
had previously requested the development of a strategic plan, he found that
only a modest business plan had been formulated and only for the four core

engineering businesses. Smith saw that what was needed—as unbeknownst to him Lens had articulated so many times—was a review of the company's capitalization, "the outline of a plan for the disposition and reallocation of assets," and he appointed a special board committee to draw one up. By January 1997, management finally had a good handle on what the company with its new strategy was worth—$55–$56 a share. Under Smith, Stone & Webster sold off assets and replaced 25 percent of the top 75 people.[14] The stock jumped to the mid-50s, though it fell back into the 40s with the onset of the Asian crisis.

"Lens keeps us on our toes," Smith says. "I receive calls from them, sometimes to compliment us on a move." He was pleased when at the 1997 annual meeting Monks stood up to commend his management on its progress. Lens doubled its stockholding in Stone & Webster that year. Finally, they had a CEO they could get along with. Hansen and Smith even invited Minow to give a presentation to the board at a retreat on corporate governance.

Today, Lens claims to have been the catalyst that brought about some 25 changes at Stone & Webster in a three-year span, including two CEOs, one CFO, 8 out of 11 board members, confidential voting, sale of various unrelated assets, closure of holding company offices in New York City, and a revised method of accounting for the pension fund surplus. Smith says that Lens certainly deserves some credit. "You can't manage a company from the outside," the CEO says. "But if you know the company has got jewels, you can help shine them up by providing some pressure." Monks insists, "What we effectively accomplish is to get the attention of the management and to have them understand that we are not going to go away." He calls Stone & Webster "the finest example of the governance process and shareholder activism adding value." Lens sold out, reaping an 85% return on its investment.

As usual, Monks had more than one item on his agenda. In 1994, he continued efforts to fill what he saw as a need for promoting an academic discipline in corporate governance by coauthoring a textbook with Minow. Released in 1995, it was called simply *Corporate Governance,*[15] and it was the soup-to-nuts treatment of the subject. The book also included several appendixes of relevant articles written by such other governance experts as Ira Millstein, Delaware Court Chancellor William Allen, and management consultant Hugh Parker. Minow spread the word about the book in visits to two dozen colleges, and many courses picked it up.

During 1995, Monks and Minow adapted the textbook to a general audience, coming out with *Watching the Watchers*[16] in 1996. There were two new chapters as well. The book covers some of the same ground as *Power and Accountability,* but goes beyond in its attention to how boards operate and relate to management, its search for the right balance among parties in governance, and its discussion of the changing international scene. It goes into great detail, for example, about an event that infuriated Monks and that he often holds up as an example of the ability of U.S. business to "coopt" government. That was the huge business lobbying effort that convinced Congress to kill the Financial Accounting Standards Board's desire to require accounting for stock option grants to top executives. *Watchers* also presents the notion of "pension fund capitalism," in which pension funds are motivated to become "ownership shareholders." Each corporation would be monitored by one or more shareholders under a structure to be determined, such as a shareholder advisory committee.

13

Strike Three

It's an opportunity I can't turn down.
Monks in an interview, spring 1996.

Even though Monks had been out of politics for many years, the political bug remained dormant inside him. In the spring of 1993, Governor John McKernan—whom Monks had helped reelect in 1990—asked Monks to think about running for governor in 1994. After serious consideration, Monks decided in December to decline. "So I thought okay he's through with politics," says Milly Monks.

But then, early in 1996, the political sirens resumed their song. Monks and his wife had just stepped out of their house in Florida, bags in hand, to return to Maine. On turning the key to lock the door, Monks heard the phone ring. He hesitated, casting a questioning glance at Milly, but then opened the door to grab the phone. On the other end was Senator Cohen's chief of staff who simply said, "Senator Cohen." Cohen then got on and said, "In five minutes, I am going to tell a press conference that I will not run for reelection. I think that you ought to think about running. I'll talk to you later." On the flight home, Monks and his wife talked about whether this would be a good opportunity for their son Robert Jr. to launch a political career. From his seat, Monks phoned his son and made the proposal. Before the plane landed, his son had called back and urged his father to run. Then others in the Maine political establishment chimed in, and once again Monks, his competitive spirit revived, began to like the sound of "Senator Monks."

He thought that finally here was a race he could win. The highly popular Cohen was a close friend. And after all these years, no one could doubt that Monks was a devoted Mainer—though he had been out of the state a great deal, partly for business, partly for the winter in Florida, and partly because his house had burned down in early 1993. The opportunity seemed to come at a propitious juncture in Monks' crusade. He had accomplished a great deal through regulation, ISS, and Lens. But he had not been able to make a dent in the conflict-of-interest dilemma, which stood as an insidious obstacle in his path. He already had reached the conclusion that the only solution would be a government decree that pension fiduciaries are to be held accountable to their beneficiaries, reached via Senate hearings. Here was his chance to get on the banking committee and sponsor hearings on the conflict of interest questions of ERISA fiduciaries that impede shareholder activism. "The opportunity to raise governance issues in the U.S. Senate is timely and so exciting," he said, "it's an opportunity I can't turn down."[1]

Monks was soon to discover that politics had changed in the 20 years he had been on the side lines. "We were incredibly naïve going into it," Milly reflects. "The Christian Right, that was a newcomer. That was probably the worst." The Republican Party in Maine was now divided between the prolife conservatives, supported by the Christian Right and others, and the moderates. But this was hardly the only new element in the game. Monks was soon to learn, once and for all, that he did not have what it takes to be a modern politician.

There was not much time to get organized. Monks decided that he would rent a Winnebago that would be sort of a traveling campaign headquarters and became known in the race as the Monksmobile. In April 1996, he and Milly, with a driver, began motoring around the state, often sleeping in the RV after nighttime engagements or when traveling overnight. In countless small towns, the Winnebago would barrel in, and Monks would emerge from it. He shook hundreds of hands at small gatherings. ("We campaigned in front of factories and stores, but less than in previous campaigns," he says. "How many people going into a paper mill at 6 A.M. vote in Republican primaries?") And he engaged in debates with his two opponents, Susan Collins, a former top aide to Senator Cohen, and state Senator W. John Hathaway. "He almost went to the debate in his sneakers, but I caught him," Milly said after one debate. "He's like an absent-minded professor."

One of his top advisers was Sharon Miller, the campaign manager for Governor McKernan's tough 1990 race. She remembered Monks fondly from that squeaker, because he kept raising and re-raising her spirits. He and Bob Jr. also raised a good deal of cash for that race—around $100,000—and helped prepare McKernan for his debates. Having served two terms already, McKernan was running in a recession and started the race 27 points down in the polls closing the gap to 11 points a couple weeks before election day. "The press and others had written us off," Miller recounts. "Bob called almost every day and told me, 'You're doing a great job. You and I are the only ones left who have faith.' There was absolutely nothing in it for him to do that. On election day he sent me an enormous bouquet of flowers." Later that day, Monks sat with her and watched the returns until victory was declared.

In his campaign, Monks presented a platform that applied his corporate governance expertise and vision to government. He was the candidate who would be able to make the government "more accountable" to the citizenry by (1) supporting campaign finance reform that would do away with political action committees and corporate welfare, and (2) cutting out congressional perks and undeserved advantages. Beyond that, his priorities were to reduce the federal deficit and debt, and eliminate the Departments of Energy, Education, and Commerce. With his program and easygoing one-on-one style, Monks won over many voters. "Maine is a family," said Cindy Faulkner, a fund-raiser who once served on Senator Cohen's staff. "He remembers everyone's name and who their relatives are." She recalled seeing Monks periodically in Washington when he would come to pick Senator Cohen up for lunch. "Unlike others who came by, he'd start talking to me about Maine and my family," she said.

He had a tough opponent in Susan Collins, who was the losing candidate in the 1994 governor's race that Monks had decided not to compete in. He endorsed the other, winning candidate. In 1996, she charged that Monks was being disingenuous in claiming credit for helping to shut Synfuels down, citing his testimony in the hearings that Synfuels was a good idea with a productive purpose. Monks angrily terms her Synfuels charges "utterly without merit. Anybody who knew anything knew that I was committed to getting Synfuels shut down. The power problems, the governance problems, the problems of incompetent officials were compelling." Collins' claims appeared in the *Bangor Daily News,* her hometown paper, but the paper chose not to carry Monks' written response, he says.[2] During the campaign, she also accused Monks of being sexist and objected that his wealth allowed him an unfair competitive advantage.[3] He wasn't taking money from political action committees (PACs); he had plenty of his own funds. But, he was still known as the Cape Elizabeth Millionaire, and in Maine at least, wealth was a competitive *dis*advantage.

Both Collins and Hathaway played up the fact that Monks was out of town for the previous two elections and did not vote, and that when he had been asked to name a Cape Elizabeth town councilor or his representative in the Maine legislature, he came up short. The reason Monks had missed some elections was that his house had burned down in February 1993, and while they designed and built a new, glassed-in home, he and Milly spent months residing in Florida. They could not move into the new home until Christmas 1995. (The story of that fire is amusing—in retrospect. Monks and his wife had left Washington in November 1992 to live full-time in Maine. February was a very cold month, and one night, demands on the heating system became so great that electric heating wires fused, sparking the fire at 3 A.M. Milly was the only one home and awoke to the sound of glass breaking; one of the plate-glass doors on the ground floor had been shattered by the heat. Smelling smoke, she grabbed the dog and ran down stairs, holding her breath through the cloud of smoke. She ran out the door and through the snow in her nightgown and slippers to her sister-in-law's house nearby. At the very moment the fire began, Monks happened to be in Los Angeles, boarding a flight to Sydney, where he was scheduled to meet the other members of the Tyco Laboratories board. The directors were going to visit Tyco's new Australian subsidiary, which established the company's position as the worldwide leader in—unbelievably—sprinkler systems.)

Twenty years after his last race, Monks still had three things going against him: he was from out of state and spent a great deal of his time away, he was rich, and he was an intellectual. One of his staff members, coaching him on the answer to the question, "Why do you want to be Senator?" advised him to say, "Three words: The national debt." Instead, Monks chose another, more characteristic answer: "The Greeks gave us philosophy, the Romans gave us law, and the U.S. has given us self-law, democracy. It's still young, only 200 years old, and still an experiment. I want to be part of the experiment." This was just too conceptual for many listeners to grasp.[4] Often, his speeches seemed forced, not from the heart. It was as if he were saying things he had been told to say, not what he really wanted to say. Even one-on-one, Monks sometimes seemed out of touch with regular folks and their everyday concerns, at times talking over their heads and using sophisticated words they did not understand. He readily admits that he never had the feel for politics that he does for business and law. The message he was required to deliver for the 1996 Republican primary had to go beyond his personal desires to reform Congress, business, and politics to include such party favorites as a balanced budget amendment, tax reduction, and a smaller government—which he also believed in but were not issues about which he felt passionately.[5]

However, for a while that spring Monks was in the lead. Then Collins' TV ads strengthened her standing. At the start of May, Monks and Collins were neck and neck, with nearly 40 percent of the vote apiece. Trailing them was Hathaway, the conservative, prolife candidate who was emphasizing family values. A native of Maine, Hathaway, a real estate developer, had spent a decade in Alabama. Very little was known about him. One of Monks' close friends and advisors called a friend in Alabama to ask about Hathaway, and learned of a rumor that six years earlier Hathaway had had sex with his children's 12-year-old babysitter. "In political terms, you've hit a gold mine," that advisor says. He urged Monks to hire a private investigator to check out the rumor, and Monks decided—against the advice of some of his campaign staff—to hire the Washington-based investigative firm Investigative Group Inc.,[6] run by Terry Lenzner. The investigator spoke to the girl's father and the district attorney. No charges had been filed against Hathaway. As the former Alabama Attorney General later told the *Boston Globe*, (which reported the story after it was broken by the *Portland Press Herald* late in the campaign) "The allegations were very, very serious and involved a minor. At the request of the family, and based on the recommendations of psychological professionals, the case was not pursued for fear of further traumatizing the minor. Had it not been for the recommendation of those professionals and the grief of the family, the case would have been actively and aggressively pursued." Hathaway denied the accusations at the time.[7]

"We were virtually certain it was true, but we had no proof," says Goldenfarb. "Proof would be the girl told us or Hathaway admitted it. The problem was, what do you do with the information if you don't have proof? Bob was adamant, you can't do anything without proof."[8] They tried but could not get the Republican state and national committees interested in pursuing the research. So, they dropped the matter, deciding not to call the press. The investigator did tell Monks that two newspapers, the *Press Herald* and the *Boston Globe,* were also fishing around in Alabama. (Editor's note: To this day, no proof has been unearthed to establish as fact that an improper relationship occurred.)

During May, Collins took the lead, and Monks ran a series of ads criticizing her. The ads did trim her lead but backfired because many people looked down on negative campaigning. Monks dropped in the polls, and Hathaway began rising, so they ended up about even behind Collins.

At the state GOP convention, ten days before the June 10 election, Monks gathered support. His ability to talk to individuals on their level seemed to have improved markedly. At a luncheon for Republican women, one attendee said that he changed her vote "as soon as he walked in the room. He went around to talk to every woman and later he went around again! He really listened." At his hospitality suite in the evening, he hired a Dixieland jazz band and workers to man an old-fashioned popcorn popping machine and a table of strawberry shortcake, and he ringed the room with geraniums from his nursery to give out to callers. Voters lined up to meet Monks, shake his hand, and talk for a few minutes. "Mr. Monks," one woman began. "Call me Bob," he said with his usual broad grin. "I'll never get elected if you call me Mr. Monks." He talked to them about schools, disabled children, fishing, shipping ports, often asking his visitors for their suggestions on how to solve the problems they saw.

But by the end of the convention, while the three candidates were close, Hathaway had risen in the polls, Collins had drifted back, and Monks was on her heels. Still, Monks was about to get the endorsement of Gov. Angus King, whom he had endorsed in the governor's race.

Miller received a call apparently from someone linked to Collins' campaign asking whether they were going to "let the goods out" on Hathaway in some new negative ads now that he had pulled ahead. The answer was no, they had no proof. The news came out in the *Press Herald* a couple days later, and soon other papers picked it up. Hathaway said publicly that there were allegations and he was interviewed by a state official about them, but that they were untrue. He said that the girl was "troubled" and had been treated for mental illness. Then he apparently tried to shift the attention away from himself by declaring Monks had hired an investigator to uncover dirt about him and had then leaked the matter to the press. The reporter himself told him this, he said. The Hathaway campaign began running ads with the claims about Monks, branding him a liar.

A radio reporter asked Monks directly whether Hathaway's claim was true. Had he hired an investigator? Monks responded that he had paid $10,000 for an investigator, but he had not leaked anything to the press. That was confirmed when the reporter who had broken the story called into the last televised debate, a few days before the election, to clarify to the moderator that he had never told Hathaway that Monks was his source. When pressed, Hathaway admitted that the reporter never did tell him that. Even after the debate, say Monks staffers, Hathaway continued to run the ads, and Monks ran ads defending himself.[9] Still, the phone calls coming into Monks' campaign office were devastating. Supporters called saying they would never vote for him now. "But they were shooting the messenger," Goldenfarb says. So-called opposition research is a well-used tactic in campaigns—the other candidates had done it—but somehow Mainers found it appalling. By now, Hathaway's campaign had lost its momentum, Collins pulled ahead, but Monks remained in third place. Monks phoned Gov. King and told him not to waste his endorsement.

In a televised interview the day before the primary, Monks conceded defeat. It was a stunningly bad political move. Even his own campaign staff was floored by the statement. Why give up with just one day to go—even if things look bad? Later, Monks' advisers explained that he was just telling it like it was. "He's never pretended to be a regular politician," his campaign manager, Willis Lyford, told the Press Herald. Monks' attitude was he had one more day of press attention and he wanted to use it not to get votes but to show the world what Hathaway was doing—that he was simply spouting a fabrication about Monks in the final days of the campaign to try to eke out a last-minute victory. Monks says that to prove to the press that he was not just out to get more votes but was sincere in his desire to reveal "the big lie," he first had to admit that he was going to lose the race. "I was trying to use the leverage of public attention on election day to get what I considered the right question aired," he explains. "I wanted them [the press] to pay attention to what had really happened."[10] The strategy failed. Instead, he was ridiculed for conceding defeat and continued to take blame for hiring an investigator and spreading the dirt on Hathaway. For a while, Monks considered suing Hathaway for libel, but did not want to stretch the matter out any longer.

The election loss was a huge disappointment to both Monks and his wife. The Press Herald dubbed it, "the most embarrassing defeat in recent Maine history" because the $2.1 million ($1.8 million of his own) he spent elicited just 12,851 votes, 13 percent of the vote. Hathaway, whose moral conduct was in question, managed to get 31 percent. "Afterward, walking in the streets, I felt totally ashamed," Milly admits. "And Bobby said, you've done nothing to be ashamed of. You haven't done anything." Two days after the election, Monks wrote his supporters in thanks. After a brief description of the previous 10 days, he wrote: "Our campaign experience is rather analogous to the question purportedly asked of Mrs. Abraham Lincoln—'Aside from that, Mrs. Lincoln, how did you enjoy the play?'"

Monks went away to be by himself for a week and then appeared to bounce back almost completely, throwing himself into a Lens Fund investment that had been developing quickly during the campaign: WMX Technologies, the world's largest waste management company. He took some comfort in what was written about him in *An Insider's Guide to Maine Politics, 1946–1996,* by Christian P. Potholm: "It would be too bad if all people remembered were his three losses instead of what he did to make modern Republican politics better. . . . It is difficult to see how the post-1972 Republican party would have had the winners it did in the succeeding two decades without his involvement."[11] Even so, some of Monks' closest friends believe that he has never fully recovered from the blow to his ego.

Many of Monks' friends insist that he would have made a good senator because he would have shaken up the establishment and their tired ways of thinking. Perhaps so. But politicians have to get elected. And to do so, they have to be attuned to answering people's immediate concerns and communicate on their level. Monks may have been too much of a visionary for his own good.

14

The Right Formula

It's a large job to take this on as a venture, but it'll be fun. It may well end up with a proxy contest for the board or a takeover.

Monks, from an interview, August 7, 1996

In their first lunch with George Soros back in 1994, Monks and Woodworth suggested going after WMX Technologies Inc., the troubled waste management company. Soros demurred. "Once a glamour stock, never again," the wise man of investing told his guests.[1]

Lens went ahead on its own, investing in WMX in the summer of 1995. At that time, Minow mentioned WMX to Albert Dunlap, the turnaround manager known as Chainsaw Al for his ruthless job cuts, who had just sold Scott Paper Company (a Lens investment) for a mint and was looking for a new job. Dunlap had asked her for ideas, and in a letter she threw out the names WMX, Westinghouse, RJR Nabisco, Aetna, Woolworth, Toys "R" Us, Dole, Tenneco, Time-Warner, and even AT&T (she failed to mention Sunbeam, where he ended up going in November 1996). In early 1996, someone from the Soros Fund called Lens to inform the fund that Soros was now building a position in WMX, and therefore they would now be working together on the same turnaround. Early on, a Soros group manager asked Minow if she thought Al Dunlap would make a good CEO for WMX, and she showed him her letter to Dunlap from the previous summer. Already, they were thinking alike.

Starting small, Lens had built an investment in WMX of some $25 million by the spring of 1996. By the time Soros called, Lens had yet to contact management. During the fall and winter of 1995–1996, some of the partners had begun discussions with WMX shareholders, trying to arouse interest in taking an activist stance. But, the Lens team was still too busy with Stone & Webster to involve itself fully in another big project.

Now, Soros and Lens would be advancing on WMX at the same time. As they had previously agreed, Soros contributed $50 million to the Lens fund to be invested anywhere but WMX. Soros Fund Management accumulated shares until by May it owned more than 5 percent of the stock at a cost of about $750 million.

This was almost an ideal situation for Lens. Having a lead investor like Soros was a powerful weapon. Meanwhile, WMX had a particularly large contingent of institutional investors, and many of them had sizable investments in the company. While Soros met with management separately, Lens would do its usual job of presenting a strategy to management and keeping investors informed. If the activist engine stalled along the way, the investors could fairly easily be rounded up for a proxy fight. "The connecting link is a leadership organization backed up by credible, mainstream institutions," says Monks. It was the right formula for bringing about that sense of ownership that he had been working so long to inspire in the institutional investors.

Founded in 1968 as Waste Management by Dean Buntrock and multiple-empire builder Wayne Huizenga (who would go on to build Blockbuster Entertainment and Republic Industries), WMX Technologies was the world's biggest trash hauler. Based in Oak Brook, Illinois, the company had grown like Topsy via stock-financed acquisitions of other waste companies. Then, in the early 1990s, as growth of the core collection business slowed, WMX began branching out into related fields, including hazardous waste disposal, incineration and landfills (both via a 58% investment in Wheelabrator Technologies), international waste hauling, water treatment, and air pollution control. By 1996, the diversification was not working out well. Earnings became highly erratic, with special charges taken in almost every one of the previous seven years.

Lens wrote its first letter to Chairman and CEO Buntrock on April 15. At that point, no one but Lens knew of the Soros Fund's growing position in the company. In her missive introducing Lens, Minow pointed out the stock's poor performance, a negative 3 percent average annual total return over the previous five years compared with 14.6 percent for the S&P 500. Having peaked at $46 in 1992, it then plunged into the low 30s. Among the reasons: Profitability had declined and debt had increased fourfold over six years, while net worth had grown only 80 percent. "We are concerned by reports of an accelerated acquisitions program," she wrote. "Your shareholders have no basis for believing that such a use of corporate assets will be any more productive than in the past." She pointed to a byzantine corporate structure that cried out for simplification. "If your corporate strategies have not worked, as appears to be the case, you owe it to the shareholders to change strategy," she went on. "We believe more aggressive action needs to be taken quickly, in the areas of finance, strategy, and corporate governance." The board's sluggishness in the face of the disappointing results appeared, in Lens's view, to stem from its lack of independent directors. Most of the members seemed to be friends of Buntrock's.

Greatly disturbed by Minow's letter, Buntrock phoned at once to schedule a meeting with Lens. On May 6, John Higgins and Bob Holmes (Monks was then riding around Maine in a Winnebago on the campaign trail) flew to Oak Brook, where they had a tense session with Buntrock, President Phillip Rooney, CFO James Koenig, and general counsel Herbert Getz. As the two Lens partners later recorded in a memo: "All were defensive, insecure, angry, challenged, unfriendly, and argumentative." The founder, Buntrock, was clearly in charge. The two activists deemed him "a powerful, dogmatic, not overly intelligent tycoon" and Rooney friendly and intimate with the business but an "order-taker." Koenig, who appeared to be the main architect of the company's complex financial structure—involving several partially owned businesses—and of the diversification strategy, impressed them as "aggressive, argumentative and generally unpleasant." Getz was the only one among the executives who showed he understood why Lens was in the room.

In explaining the company's sorrowful numbers, Buntrock blamed abrupt, unforeseen changes in industry conditions. "The synergies of expansion of services did not work out as we had hoped," he remarked in a vast understatement. Among the problems that had developed: the industry focus shifted from landfill to recycling, creating great landfill overcapacity; the hazardous waste business stagnated; customers began to focus on minimizing waste, competition increased, and environmental issues slid to the back burner on the public agenda. A strategic plan formulated in 1993 was not carried out because management was too busy. Another one devised by Arthur Andersen in 1994 and including a simplification of the corporate structure and a reduction in capital spending was then in progress. When the Lens partners inquired on the prospects of selling or spinning off their 56 percent of Waste Management International, "They were insulted by our lack of understanding, and their comments gave no hint of plans to cure international business," Higgins and Holmes wrote.

Plans going out were to increase prices. "Asked how they expect increases to be successful in the face of what they admit is serious and toughening competition, they had no believable answer," read the Lens memo. Management also aimed for $300 million of annual cost savings by the year 2000. Higgins' and Holmes' tentative conclusion in their memo was, "This company desperately needs a nearly complete management housecleaning. Buntrock is old and tired. His and Koenig's strategies have not worked. They were far, far too slow in reacting to changing industry conditions, and they continue to drag their heels in making changes to improve profitability. . . . The balance sheet is too heavily leveraged, and financial operations are reported aggressively. In many ways, management seems to treat WMX more as an investment portfolio than as an operating business. Their portfolio has losses, which they are loath to take."

Shortly thereafter, WMX had its annual meeting, which Minow attended. She planned to speak in favor of the shareholder resolutions that would be on the proxy (sponsored by others) for destaggering the board and barring directors from paid consulting jobs with the company, and generally on what she thought the company ought to be doing, including preparing a succession plan for Buntrock, who was then 64. The meeting took place near the headquarters, at the Drury Lane Theater, whose thick red carpets and gleaming chandeliers lent gravity to the atmosphere. Minow entered to find lots of employees and had the feeling that she'd mistakenly wandered into a pep rally. Before she had a chance to deliver her short speech, Buntrock announced that he was going to resign as CEO in June, though not as chairman, and let Rooney take the reins. Moreover, he said the board would accept both shareholder resolutions; it would propose both in the following year's proxy statement for a shareholder vote. Later on, Minow stood up and simply thanked him and followed up with a letter, suggesting a few other governance changes. They included adding a committee of independent directors to oversee CEO and board evaluation, the requirement that directors serve on no more than three other boards, the appointment of a lead outside director as a contact for shareholders and ombudsman for the outside directors, and payment of directors in stock or stock options. (The following year, the proposal to destagger the board did not pass.)

The investment by Soros Fund Management did not become public knowledge until late May, when its stake broke the 5 percent mark, requiring disclosure. Fund officials immediately commenced meetings with WMX management. Within a few weeks, WMX announced a previously planned strategy to begin swinging the ax, with $1 billion in asset sales over the coming two years. In July, Lens sent its "restructuring plan" to Rooney. It included the spin-offs to shareholders of the Wheelabrator majority stake and of the international component of WMX. In Lens's view, the stock could shoot up 50 percent as a result of these moves.

Lens did not meet with management again until early October. This time, Monks was back full-time on the team (and in a renewed Lens partnership agreement, had full authority), and went with Higgins and Holmes to Oak Brook. Again, their hosts were Buntrock, Rooney, Koenig, and Getz, but this time Rooney led the meeting and Monks made an effort at the start to set a friendly tone. They spent two hours together discussing WMX's progress on divestitures, which was slow, and the company's opinion of the Lens restructuring plan, which was not good. Management was bound and determined to keep both international and Wheelabrator as core businesses. However, the company officials did acknowledge the problem of unpredictable earnings.

During the meeting, Getz remarked, "You know, we are listening to shareholders all the time. Some of them tell us to go left, some of them tell us to go right." What he was really saying was, you shareholders do not really know what you want to do, and we, the management have to make the tough decisions. To the Lens partners, it seemed to be a divide-and-conquer strategy.

"That's a very interesting point," Monks replied. "If you're correct, the shareholders are doing a disservice. I don't have total information on this, but I think you're wrong. If a significant portion of your shareholders thought what you were doing was wrong, or you weren't doing it fast enough, would that be something you'd pay attention to?"

"Absolutely," Getz agreed.

After the meeting, Monks began working on proving his point. He called some big WMX shareholders to organize a meeting for them with management. All the while, he was in close touch with the people from Soros who had been talking with management independently.

In a follow-up letter to Rooney, Monks thanked him and clarified that Lens was not insisting that WMX follow the suggested strategy but at least should come up with something that would be as good for shareholders—and do so quickly. Then he reemphasized the value of Lens's arguments, saying, for example, "The international operations are admittedly marginal. This appears to tell the market that WMX management will not take decisive and appropriate action either to shore up or to terminate its international commitments and will leave them to wallow. These questions are plain. So long as there is no clear response, the company will not be supported by the investing public." At the end of the letter, Monks indicated that he was continuing to round up major shareholders and wanted to arrange a time for them to meet with WMX management.

In the meantime, on November 9, Minow met with the head of the WMX board's nominating committee, former Secretary of Commerce Alexander Trowbridge, in Washington. They began politely, he by insisting that the company had made a lot of progress thanks in part to Lens's pushing, and she by congratulating him on improved corporate governance policies and on Rooney's cooperation and performance thus far. Minow suggested several names of candidates to replace the four directors the company wanted to put up for reelection.

Then they each pulled out their agendas. Trowbridge went first, objecting to any plans for Lens to submit a shareholder resolution. Minow's response: "It has been our sad experience—though I am sure this would not be the case at WMX—that people are more responsive when we have a pending resolution." Asked what the resolution might be, Minow responded, as she recorded in her memo about the meeting, that "it depended on whether we wanted to do something related to the merits of our concerns or something to get a big vote." She told him it would not be about how many boards the directors were on (Trowbridge was on 10) or meager ownership of stock by the board members.

On Minow's agenda were two items: Get rid of Buntrock and Koenig. She leaped right into it. "Now, I am going to say something and I just want you to listen. I don't want you to feel you have to respond, because we are not going to resolve this today. Item one is this: in my ten years in this field, I have never seen the hostility and animosity from the people on the street toward any one member of a management team that I hear about Koenig. Simply put, he has to go right away." She blamed Buntrock for Waste Management's complicated structure and insisted that though he had relinquished the CEO job, he had continued to be far too domineering, creating a huge obstacle for Rooney.[2]

Once Monks was ready with a lineup of investors, he placed a call to Rooney. "I've got 30 percent of your stock who would like to meet with you in New York," Monks declared. Rooney agreed to a meeting, but the next day he called back and said he'd reconsidered. Now he said he'd meet only with Lens, but not until after November 22. However, by then, it would be too late for Lens to file a shareholder resolution for the upcoming annual meeting.

So Lens took out its planned shareholder resolution, on hiring an investment bank to review potential asset sales and, before filing it with the SEC, sent it over to the company in the hope of getting a reaction. "For some reason, this was like a magic wand," says Monks. "The guy called me back and said, 'Well you've broken the rules. We're being civil, we're talking. Why are you filing resolutions?'"

Monks pointed out to Rooney that he was not willing to meet until it was too late to file a resolution. "We've got to file," Monks said. "We can withdraw, but we've got to file." After much back and forth, Rooney agreed to meet in New York on Thursday November 21. (Lens still filed the resolution with the SEC, with the understanding that the fund would withdraw it if its view of management improved.)

That morning, Rooney first met with the Soros Fund's chief investment officer Stanley Druckenmiller and other Soros associates. Minow called to find out what transpired, but could not reach any of the participants. So, Lens had to fly blind. At 2 P.M., Monks, Minow, and Higgins arrived at Rooney's suite at the Plaza Hotel, where they found the CEO accompanied by Koenig, Getz, and another officer. Monks had asked his partner, Minow, to speak for Lens.

This was the first time Minow had met Rooney, and she started out by saying she had heard great things about him—he and her father were serving on a corporate board together—and that he had their support. "But we don't think you can do [the job right] with Buntrock as chairman," she said, adding that Lens would like to see him retire. Next she turned to face Koenig: "Mr. Koenig, I'm sorry to say this, but you really have to go." Later she learned that the Soros people had also demanded Koenig's resignation, and that Rooney indicated he would be reassigned. He made no such suggestion to Lens; in fact, he had no response at all. Later in the session, however, he did say that there would be changes in senior management.

They talked about the revised Lens plan, to divide WMX into two companies—good company and bad company. The good company was the domestic waste management business and the bad company the acquisitions made in the past several years. The idea was to get rid of the bad businesses and run the good business. While the company had been selling off assets, Lens and other investors asserted that that was not enough. They needed to sell more faster. In the process, management would simplify the corporate structure by eliminating any partial stakes in operations. Monks got the impression that management was favorably inclined toward these views, although Rooney still held that the international business might have great potential for growth. He said that WMX would announce a schedule of asset sales and other changes before year-end. Throughout the meeting, the CEO repeated the phrase, "You will be happy with the results."

The company's plan for the spring 1997 annual meeting was to run a slate of only four directors for reelection, plus the management resolution to destagger. The four who were up for reelection included Buntrock, who Lens wanted replaced, and two outside lawyers who provided services to the company and were over 70 years old. "Frankly" in that case, Monks told the WMX officers, "we're probably going to have to run four people against you." Overall, though, the meeting seemed to be a positive one. Afterward, Minow, Higgins, and Monks sat down at the Plaza coffee shop to discuss the meeting and make sure that they each had come away with the same interpretation of what had transpired.[3]

The next morning, Friday November 22, the Lens team held a conference call with 30 shareholders accounting for roughly a third of the stock, to fill them in on the latest. Monks gave them the lowdown on the meeting, including the news that WMX would announce a schedule of asset sales and other changes before year-end, which surely would give the stock a boost. The shareholders on the line were quite pleased. Indeed, Monks later learned that a few of them talked to Rooney themselves that day and also were favorably impressed.

When he got off the conference call, Monks changed into workout clothes and went to the health club at his hotel, where he got on a stationary bicycle. He tuned the TV to a business network and, as he pedaled, watched the stock prices sliding across the screen. "As I'm sitting there practically every transaction going over the tape was WMX, WMX. It was quite a weird feeling. The stock moved from 33 to 36, like an escalator." When Monks returned to his hotel room, the phone rang. It was Rooney, and he was furious. "What are you telling people? What are you doing?" he demanded. "You're making things very hard for me."

"What do you mean?" Monks asked, plainly astounded.

"Whatever you're telling people it's making things hard for me," Rooney said.

"Wait a minute," Monks objected, "I have a script that three of us compiled immediately after meeting with you." He fished it out of his briefcase and read it over the phone. But Rooney, beginning to sound weary, just kept repeating, "You're making things hard for me. You're just making things hard for me."

"I'm not going to let you go," Monks said. "What is one thing that I've said that doesn't accurately reflect what you said? And what is anything that you'd like me to go back and tell people that perhaps is unclear here or misrepresented?"

"You're just making things hard for me," Rooney repeated.

"Just tell me one thing I've said that's inaccurate," Monks tried again.

"You're making it hard for me."

Finally, Monks ended the conversation. "Look. I'll count on you to let me know if there's any way in which what I've written here, the entire script, is not a fair statement of what you intend or a fair statement of what you said. If you change your mind tell me."[4]

That Monday, Minow faxed Rooney a note. Thanking him for such a constructive meeting, she then wrote: "I regret deeply the discomfort we caused you with our conference call to the major shareholders. We thought we were very clear with you that we had been and would continue to stay in close touch with the other shareholders. And we were concerned that if we then told you that we would be speaking with many of them the next morning, it would sound as though we were trying to be much more heavy-handed than we wanted to appear, or, in reality, to be."

Two weeks went by and Monks got a call from an analyst at Goldman Sachs. The analyst said that at a conference of waste industry companies and analysts that day, Rooney went out of his way to say, "We made no undertakings to the shareholders. We have not committed ourselves to a timetable. We are being misrepresented." Monks' reaction to this news was the following: "You know I've been in public life and I understand that people can take away different understandings of what's said. All I can do is tell you I have a script the three of us took down afterward, and I'll send you a copy of the script." Soon, a half dozen or so WMX investors called Lens about the same Goldman meeting. Monks was fuming. To confirm that investors remembered the events he had presented them in the conference call, Monks contacted the investors who were on the Lens Internet Code accessed link—the private electronic communication network that Lens had set up for WMX investors. It supplemented the daily updates on Lens's own Web site and was made possible by the SEC's 1992 change in the proxy rules that allowed an unlimited number of investors to discuss a strategy without first filing documents with the agency.

"Rooney essentially denied any of the commitments he'd made," Monks remarked to the author a few days later. "But of the people we had on the conference call, five or six of them had seen him themselves." Monks dashed off a letter to Rooney, expressing "disappointment" at his comments at the Goldman meeting and specifying that shareholders were asking Lens to "send a stronger message. I would very much appreciate your assurance that this is not necessary. Your owners want and are entitled to know from you when you will disclose the company's strategic plans and its notions for new directors and for top management positions."

In December, Lens—backed by Soros—began preparing for a proxy fight in the spring involving both the resolution calling for hiring an investment bank and a contest for directors. At its own expense, the firm hired attorneys and proxy solicitor Georgeson to assist in the contest. It also, for the first time ever, retained a headhunting firm, the reputable Spencer Stuart, to find four candidates for a shareholders' slate of director nominees. "This is a huge change," Monks said in an interview at the time. "In times gone by, you never would have gotten someone like Spencer Stuart to associate themselves with a hostile effort." Moreover, it was an important step for activism because instead of pitting an activist against a company, as in Monks versus Sears, a respected headhunter would choose the candidates for the proxy contest. To show that it was still willing to work with management, Lens passed along some proposed candidates to the WMX nominating committee as alternate nominees for the company's own slate. These suggestions got no replies.

In addition, Lens contacted each WMX director by mail to explain its position. Moreover, it began planning to run a full-page ad in the mold of the celebrated Sears "Non-Performing Assets" ad run in 1992, with the intent of embarrassing the board into action just prior to the annual meeting. Like that ad, this one would depict a silhouette of the company's board of directors. But, this time the headline would be "Long-Term Liabilities." For its part, the Soros Fund filed a statement with the SEC indicating that it was "frustrated by the lack of progress" by WMX and intended to continue discussions with management on how to improve shareholder value, including suggestions for changes in management, operations, and capital structure.

Management's position weakened when on December 17, a federal judge in Tennessee confirmed a lower court's ruling against the company's Chemical Waste Management subsidiary for breach of contract and fined the company $91 million. The charges were that WMX had defrauded its partners, developers of the nation's largest hazardous waste dump, by cheating them out of royalties.[5] This ruling gave Lens another spitball to throw at management in its proxy contest, especially since three of the four directors running for reelection were also directors of that subsidiary.

WMX investors were excited by the developments, and for good reason. They seemed to have the firepower to win a proxy vote. As Monks points out, besides having Soros with them, WMX had lots of big institutional shareholders. "There's no big strong block anywhere," he says. "Soros owns 5 percent. But Capital Guardian owns 5 percent, and Fidelity owns 5 percent. A lot of people own 3 or 4. But the first 50 people own 70 percent of the stock. And they aren't schmucks. They're all J. P. Morgan and Alliance Capital. We've never had "the good people" rising up and saying, 'We don't like this company.' I think it is a unique shareholder event. Everybody's always said, 'We're going to get to a point where 50 to 100 institutions own everything.'" If the shareholders got four directors on the board, they'd have a strong voice there and the possibility of taking control the next year.

On December 23, 1996, the press reported that the Soros group had in an SEC filing expressed its wish to have WMX's chairman, CEO, and CFO replaced. Druckenmiller submitted the filing for Soros because he had grown impatient with management and in particular was disappointed that CFO Koenig was still in his job. So now it was out in the open. A few days later, the Soros Fund, Lens, and other investors were amazed to discover, in exhibits to a WMX SEC filing, that in his employment contract signed in June, Rooney had been awarded a 25 percent raise and a big sack of stock options. And in his August contract, Koenig got a 16 percent raise. Lens invited the board members to meet with large shareholders, but got no response.

In an update to WMX investors on January 10, Lens mentioned the company's plan to make some kind of an announcement after the release of fourth quarter results in early February. "We will know that they are just trying to buy time with more of the same if the announcement stresses: (1) massive layoffs, (2) cost-cutting, (3) incremental structural changes. Any of these items are warning signals. This management and this board have not earned the credibility necessary for this to be considered adequate." These types of changes had appeared in past reorganization plans, but no real improvement had ensued. At the end of January, anticipating the company's announcement, a Goldman Sachs analyst's report on WMX stated that shareholder pressures were likely to produce good results.

On February 4, WMX announced its restructuring plan. It included layoffs, another $1.5 billion in sales of noncore assets, a large share repurchase program, changing the company name back to Waste Management, and—finally—the replacement of Koenig. Moreover, the company announced the addition of a new director, Paul Montrone, a founder and director of Wheelabrator, which WMX controlled. Monks knew Montrone well; they had worked together in 1988 when ISS successfully solicited votes for Montrone's and Michael Dingman's company Henley Group in favor of an anti-poison-pill resolution filed at Santa Fe Southern Pacific. Monks was the one who had given Montrone's name to Minow to pass along to the company's nominating committee. There were, undeniably, some positive elements to this restructuring. But it was not enough for the activist shareholders, who were disappointed that WMX did not define a cohesive mission, did not divest itself of international and other activities not related to its domestic, basic waste handling operation, and did not really get rid of Koenig, since he was reassigned to another high-level job within the company, as an executive vice president. And it was not enough for credit rating agency Moody's Investors Service, which questioned the wisdom of a major share buyback at a time when the company was restructuring, carrying too much debt, and experiencing continuing earnings problems. Most important, it was not enough for the market, which also had to digest the announcement of a big fourth quarter net loss and an unexciting forecast for 1997. The stock dropped like a stone.

Steve Miller, who would arrive at WMX the following month, first as a director and later as CEO, says he never understood why investors were unhappy with the restructuring plan itself. But, he adds, "they just wanted a change in leadership. There was a lack of confidence that the management could execute anything."

After hearing the announcement and seeing the market's initial reaction, Monks made a date to meet with the Soros people the next day in New York to discuss shareholder strategy. Within a few hours, Monks was on a plane to New York. Late that night, Rooney reached Monks at the Palace Hotel to tell him that he was coming to New York early in the morning and wanted to have breakfast. In attendance at the Palace Hotel's gleaming breakfast area just off the lobby were Monks and Minow, Rooney, the new chief operating officer Joseph Holsten, and the new CFO John Sanford. The two activists were blunt. They told Rooney that the market's reaction was showing him the door. His job was now on the line. Minow felt uncomfortable. She had been supporting Rooney, even though the Soros group had not. "I was nervous about not being solid with the Soros people," Minow says, "but then I felt it would help us, if anyone ever complained that we were working too closely together and hadn't filed properly, that we had different ideas." Now, she and Monks were pretty much siding with Soros.

After breakfast, Monks and Minow went to confer with the Soros people. Together, the two investment teams decided that Lens would approach WMX with a proposal: that the board immediately elect two new members suggested by Lens and Soros. The two were to be Brian Corvese, a Soros managing director, and Herbert Lanese, former president of McDonnell Douglas Aerospace. Monks transmitted the message that very afternoon.

The next day, February 6, Buntrock called Monks, who was back in Maine, to tell him that he and WMX management would be meeting with some investors—Monks knew they were talking about Soros—that morning in New York, and wanted to fly to Portland to see him in the afternoon, apparently regarding Lens's new proposal. Monks quickly agreed and called Higgins to join them.

At the meeting with Soros partners Druckenmiller, Corvese, and Robert Jermain, Buntrock reported that the board would agree only to hire an executive search firm to find two candidates to stand for election as directors at the upcoming annual meeting. Moreover, he said that while Lanese would be a suitable candidate, Corvese would not since, in the board's view, a candidate recommended by a shareholder could not be considered independent and capable of representing all shareholders. The Soros group disagreed.

The meeting in Portland took place at the fixed base carrier at the Portland airport. Arriving first, Monks arranged to use the pilots' lounge for the session and dragged in a few office chairs. Buntrock, Rooney, and general counsel Getz soon arrived on a company plane and filed in. Half an hour later, John Higgins arrived, and Trowbridge flew in on another Waste Management jet from Washington. Buntrock got right to the point, stating the company's offer to "consider your suggestions through the nominating committee," which would then put up candidates for the board at the annual meeting. Hardly pleased with this, Monks responded that the company had suffered great damage since their last meeting in November, including the loss of the lawsuit and the "mishandled announcement" on the restructuring earlier in the week. He told the assembled executives: "We have managed to pull together a really effective solution: the willingness of your largest shareholder to surrender transferability rights [i.e., not to sell out in the short run] by putting one of his partners on the board; and the identity of Lanese—the best available senior corporate executive according to Spencer Stuart." For some reason, Buntrock then went against what he had told the Soros group earlier in the day and remarked that Lanese might not be sufficiently independent from the Soros group.

During the meeting, Monks made a few inflammatory remarks intended to increase the level of pressure on the management and directors. He warned that WMX would not be able to recruit new director candidates with the looming threat of a proxy contest, which Lens and Soros were plotting. He also referred to the lawsuit that WMX's Chemical Waste Management subsidiary had lost in December—a case where the judge said in his decision that the unit's management was operating within "a culture" of "fraud, misrepresentation and dishonesty." Since one of Monks' goals was to let management know the extent to which rumors about their activities were swirling around, he repeated a rumor about Rooney's children's business relationship with WMX. Rooney did not react to it, neither acknowledging its veracity nor denying it. Rooney's attorney has denied the accuracy of Monk's statements.

In a phone conversation with Buntrock on Sunday February 9, Druckenmiller said that the Soros-Lens proposal had been modified. Both now officially wanted Rooney out. Buntrock responded by agreeing to allow the three Soros representatives to meet with directors on Tuesday. On Monday, the Soros group formally nominated a slate of four directors. At a meeting with the majority of board members at Waste Management headquarters, the Soros partners explained their proposal and why they were unhappy with Rooney. The directors defended the CEO and would not discuss firing him. In addition, they told the Soros group that they had submitted their board nominations too late for consideration at the May 9 annual meeting.[7]

Buntrock and Rooney were fed up. That same day, they fired off a letter to Monks that illustrates both Monks' tactics and the effect they were having on the top managers:

Dear Mr. Monks:

You have stated in your promotional materials that you use the press as a weapon. And for the past week you have been threatening to run an ad critical of the Company in The Wall Street Journal, as well as undertake other initiatives, if we didn't meet your demands. But we will not allow our shareholders to be shortchanged over the long-term in order to save ourselves the discomfort of negative publicity.

During our two meetings with you last week it became increasingly clear that you were less interested in understanding the rationale behind our newly focused business strategy—much of which you have been advocating for some time—and more interested in using threats as leverage to get us to agree to your suggestions for two Board seats. . . .

Monks was quick to reply on February 14:

Dear Dean and Phil:

I am sorry to receive your letter of February 11, because it introduces elements of mischaracterization and personal attack previously absent in our communications. I have been glad of the ability to speak directly and honestly with you, despite our differences. Your letter marks a different course of "spinning" for the record.

After several months of intensive consideration, WMX management came up with a proposed solution to the company's admittedly very serious problems that involved the addition of not one new person at a senior level. (Paul Montrone, notwithstanding his outstanding ability, can hardly be considered an outsider.) The market has responded with a clear rejection of your plan. That is the source of the negative publicity.

In a company with a performance record like that of WMX, the market (and the press) can be expected to be skeptical when a company so thoroughly insulates itself from any outside perspective. The pattern at WMX, from the history of insiders, former insiders, and service providers on the board to the "confidential voting" policy that is more loophole than substance, supports these concerns.

After the company announced that Soros was a day late in submitting nominees for the annual meeting, CFO John Sanford phoned some big shareholders. One recalls his comments to the CFO: "I let him know, as a shareholder, that I thought I was going to get to vote on the company's restructuring plan [by voting for one slate of director nominees or another]. I hadn't yet decided how I'd vote. But now, because of a technicality, the company wouldn't allow me to vote. So, I told him, the company was violating its fiduciary duty to me. I expected a defensive response, but I didn't get that. He said he'd heard from a lot of shareholders who were not happy with the February 4 plan. The stock fell. People were voting with their feet."

On February 18, Rooney surprised everybody. Although his board supported him, he resigned. The growing outcry from investors for his ouster had just become too much for him. He said he did not want that issue to distract management from running the company and fulfilling the restructuring plan. "I am not prepared to let personal attacks distract this company," he was quoted saying in the *New York Times* the following day. The press treated the resignation as a win for shareholder activists—pointing in particular to shareholders' growing use of the 1992 SEC rule that allowed them to speak to each other about corporations. The activists were called "the raiders of the '90s," working in the interest of shareholders.

The activist investors in Waste Management were now faced with a new situation. "Rooney's resignation changed the whole thing," says Monks. "Rather than going to an annual meeting to try to get sympathetic directors to change the management, the management changed." Yes, Buntrock, the chairman, was still ruling over his kingdom; he became acting CEO while the board looked for a new one. But the directors pledged to Druckenmiller, who represented Soros, that they would bring new blood to the board—two new directors to replace two that were resigning—and hire an executive search firm to help with that and with finding a new CEO who would be, unlike Rooney, from outside the company. Pleased with this and Rooney's resignation, Druckenmiller dropped the proxy fight.

The other sizable shareholders who had been following Soros' lead were dazed. Some were even angry. But none were about to take the reins. When asked if he would ever lead such a fight, one of the largest institutional shareholders in Waste Management told the author, "No. We have a huge pension management business. A sensitive situation."

Remaining in the vanguard was Lens. And the other investors were happy about that. "I think they are absolutely top drawer people, in terms of standard of ethics, operations, and experience," remarked one in an interview. Lens still wanted to get rid of Buntrock and began plotting. One way would be to forge ahead with its shareholder resolution on hiring an investment bank, to get a vote of no confidence in Waste Management leadership. But it could also use the resolution as a bargaining chip, as it often did in these situations. Monks wrote Buntrock and director Montrone that "our preferred course of action is to withdraw our shareholder resolution prior to the printing of your proxy statement," and "there are three issues we need to see progress on in order to make that possible." Those were the search for two new directors; progress on finding a new CEO and assurance that that person would be free to revise the recently announced restructuring plan; and follow-through on the promise to destagger the board.

On March 11, Waste Management announced the selection of two outside directors. They were Robert "Steve" Miller, most recently acting chief executive of Federal-Mogul Corporation, and Steven Rothmeier, chairman and CEO of Great Northern Capital and former CEO of Northwest Airlines. A few days later, Lens withdrew its shareholder resolution.

But Lens remained a thorn in the company's side, hoping to drive Buntrock out. The Lens partners had hired lawyers to help them investigate a rumor that Buntrock was involved in some sort of deceptive practices linked to the chemical Waste Management lawsuit. Monks was afraid Lens was being set up by the source of this information. Instead of making any direct accusations himself, Monks wrote to board member Jerry Dempsey, on March 17, "In light of the findings of the court in that case . . . we think it is essential for the credibility of the company—and the board—that the outside directors establish a special committee, with its own counsel, to examine compliance issues throughout the company."

Meanwhile, Minow inserted herself into the process of searching for a CEO. She called the head of the board's search committee, Peer Pederson, a friend of Buntrock's. The thrust of her remarks, she recalls, was, "The person you need for this job will not take the job if Buntrock is the chairman. The person you need for this job will show he's the person for this job by making sure that Buntrock leaves. I'm not here to tell you who to hire. I'm here to tell you what the process should be. Lanese is your floor. He's pretty darn good. You don't want him, okay. But then, you have to come up with someone better." Then she asked Pederson to contact the 17 largest shareholders to hear what kind of CEO they wanted, and he said he would. Minow next contacted the chief of the headhunting firm that was conducting the search for Waste Management, Gerard Roche, chairman of Heidrick & Struggles, and told him the same thing she had told Pederson.[8]

She then sent the 17 names to Pederson and notified all 17 that they would be getting a call from him. But within a few days, Minow started getting angry calls from these investors. Instead of getting a phone call from Pederson, they had received a letter from Buntrock. "It said thank you for your interest in our search, we have it under control, we always like hearing from our shareholders," Minow sums up. "I was really angry." She picked up the phone and called Pederson.

"I'm sorry. That was unacceptable," she told him.

"Well, 17 people is a lot of people," he objected.

"You've got five people on your committee. You can split it up."

"How about if I write them a letter?" Pederson asked.

"That would have worked if they hadn't already gotten this offensive letter from Buntrock," Minow blurted. "You know, you personally are up for reelection this year, and we don't want it to be ugly. We could have a record-breaking withhold vote on the directors if you're not careful." He agreed to make the calls.

A few minutes after Minow hung up, the phone rang. It was head-hunter Roche. "Oh my god, what did you say to Pederson?" he asked. He told her that Pederson wanted him to call the 17 investors. Anyone who was unhappy with that could talk to Pederson directly. That was fine with her.[9]

So, the investors had their opportunity to give some input. In many cases, their input was that Buntrock would be an obstacle for any self-respecting CEO. One day Minow got two phone calls from Chicago reporters who both used exactly the same words. "That led me to believe it was a plant," she said. They both asked me, 'How would you feel if Dean Buntrock stayed on in a purely symbolic advisory role on the board?' To both I said, 'There is no such job. He has to be off the board. Period.'"

In mid-April, Buntrock announced that he would step aside as chairman if doing so would attract the best candidates to be CEO. Not until July did the company announce the appointment of a new Chairman, CEO, and President: Ronald LeMay, former president of Sprint Corp. Buntrock stepped down as chairman but remained on the board.

Shortly after taking the job, LeMay phoned Monks to introduce himself and made arrangements to meet in Chicago at the end of July. In the interim, Monks hosted a lunch with several of the top institutional shareholders—all big New York money managers—"to make sure the owners were in agreement with what we were doing and to avoid conflicting messages with individual [institutional] shareholders," he explains.

Monks took Minow and Lens sales executive Charlie Woodworth with him to Chicago. "Bob really didn't like LeMay," Minow recalls. "I thought he was all right. We asked him to do a few things—replace some directors right away, buy stock, get off other boards—none of which he did. We also said Buntrock had to go. LeMay said, 'If I didn't feel I had full authority, I wouldn't have taken the job.'" While driving to the airport, Monks remarked, "That guy's not going to make it." He saw LeMay as an executive who was not willing to roll up his sleeves.

Buntrock and LeMay did not hit it off. Indeed, some directors were alarmed that LeMay, who was from a different industry, did not avail himself of the store of knowledge and experience Buntrock offered. Certainly, things were not going well for Waste Management as LeMay continued trying to get his footing. He announced that third quarter earnings would not meet forecasts and disclosed the possibility of a big charge in the fourth quarter to write down the value of some assets.

LeMay lasted only a few months. At the end of October, he announced he would be returning to Sprint. The news came as a complete surprise to the board and the shareholders. What made it all the more shocking to Lens was that EVP Koenig and CFO Sanford resigned on the same day. Why did LeMay leave so abruptly? According to Steve Miller, the director who recruited and would succeed him, LeMay was homesick—for his wife, who had stayed in Kansas City, and for the telecommunications business. But also, Miller adds, "As he dug into it, it became clear that the earnings in the prior year weren't what they were cracked up to be. He knew the accounting had some irregularities."[10] The extent of the irregularities would not be fully known until February 1998.

Miller, a turnaround manager by profession, took over as acting CEO right away. "He wouldn't even have been on the board if it hadn't been for us pushing for new directors," Minow crows. His first act of business was to announce that the company would adopt more conservative accounting practices, which would lower earnings expectations in an industry already plagued with overcapacity and high costs. That announcement on top of LeMay's departure pushed the stock to new lows.

Just after his appointment as interim CEO, Miller got a call from his friend Jerome York, who was on the board of USA Waste, the country's third largest, and most profitable, waste hauler. York asked Miller to sit down with John Drury, CEO of USA Waste, and within days they met. Drury was interested in a merger. Miller was not. Drury's suggestion of a merger-of-equals at existing stock prices did not sit well with Miller, who believed that once Waste Management had a new CEO, its stock would improve markedly. "We'll go hire a new CEO and then talk," he told Drury.[11]

Miller was more than happy to entertain Lens's desire to talk. "They have an agenda to enhance the quality of corporate governance in America," he says. "And it's a worthy goal. They are trying to do the right thing. They're worth talking to only for that. But also, they have a strong following in the press. You quite often seen Lens quoted, mostly Nell. It's in our interest to talk to Nell and find out where they're coming from."

Indeed, Minow immediately told the reporters who called that Lens felt it was in good hands with Miller. When she spoke with him shortly afterward, he thanked her for the nice things she had said about him in the papers. That set a good tone for the conversation, though Minow talked tough, as she recounts: "I said get rid of Buntrock. He said it's not that easy. I said he's simply got to go. Then he said Lens would be involved in the search for some more new directors." Within a day or two, however, Minow heard that Waste Management had just added two new directors, including former SEC chairman Roderick Hills, who would head an investigation into the accounting irregularities. "I just was furious," she says. "Betrayed." In the heat of her anger, she sat down and updated the "Long-Term Liabilities" advertisement depicting the company's board that Lens had tabled after Rooney's resignation.

Then she faxed Miller a letter. "Shareholders need clearer answers now, and we cannot wait through yet another CEO selection process before we get them," she asserted. Since Lens had already reserved November 18 for a discussion with LeMay, she proposed Miller meet with shareholders that day in New York. On her agenda for a discussion were, in part: (1) When will Dean Buntrock leave the board? (2) What is the process for selecting the new directors? What plans are under way for finding new director candidates, and what will be the process and criteria in selecting them? (3) How will this CEO selection process differ from the last one? (4) What steps are being taken to secure all documentation required for a thorough review of the accounting issues scheduled for change? . . . We need better information about the changes in accounting treatment. And (5) Why have margins gone down or stayed flat at a time when low margin businesses have been sold? What is the schedule for the long-promised cost-cutting plan?

In response, Miller called her. First, he clarified that the two new directors were not the ones he had in mind when he said Lens would be involved in director selection. Those two were both people he knew who had indicated to him that they were willing to join Waste Management's board right away. Miller intended to find another two directors—with her help. That appeased Minow. Concerning the meeting, he said he could not make it on the 18th. Minow's response was, "If we don't have this meeting, I'm running my ad in the *WSJ* calling your board long-term liabilities. I've got the ad ready to go, I've reserved space in the *Journal*."

"I'll be there," Miller said.

He arranged two meetings in New York, each with 10 large or, in Lens's case, influential WMX shareholders. Minow and Holmes were in attendance. Miller started out by stating, "I'm the interim chairman. You are the owners. What kind of a CEO would you like? And what kind of a strategy would you like to see us pursue?" He listened to a lot of opinions and answered a lot of questions. Someone asked what Miller would do if USA Waste made an offer for the company. Miller ducked that one. Someone else suggested hiring Al Dunlap as CEO. Miller agreed to consider Dunlap (He did meet with Dunlap in Florida the following Sunday. But he concluded that the man who had earned the nickname "Chainsaw Al" for his vigorous cost-cutting at other companies was not the right answer for Waste Management.) For the most part, Miller and the investors were pleased with the day's meetings, simply because they had participated in a civil discussion. "The attitude of the previous management had been very defensive," he says. "They tended to react negatively toward anyone who was critical." And he understood why. They had created the bad situation. "Being new here, I don't have to apologize for what happened."[12]

Minow kept in close touch with Miller to stay updated on the search for a new CEO. She wrote him that December: "We liked Ron LeMay very much, but we were concerned that he was unwilling to buy stock or resign from all of his other boards, as we repeatedly requested. In retrospect, those may have been indicators that his commitment was less than it should have been." She suggested that the new candidate follow through on both of Lens's requests.

In mid-November 1997, Waste Management announced a dramatic round of layoffs and cost cuts, plus moves to modernize its truck fleet and procurement and computer systems. And, the company noted that Buntrock would be off the board by the end of the year, though Miller wanted to continue using him as a consultant.

On December 8, the Waste Management board formally decided to tell USA Waste, in Miller's words, "to go fly a kite."[13] Around that time, Minow received a call from Ralph Whitworth, the former head of the United Shareholders' Association, who was now heading his own activist investment fund, Relational Investors. Whitworth had made a sizable investment in USA Waste, and after LeMay's departure sent Waste Management's stock reeling, he also invested in that company. He told Minow that USA Waste's John Drury was keen on merging with Waste Management. "I'd be happy with that," Minow recalls her response. More than her approval, Whitworth wanted her help in convincing Miller to play ball. If she could arrange for an introduction to the Soros group, and the Soros group liked Whitworth and the merger idea, the Waste Management shareholders could get the talks moving.[14]

No problem. She phoned Monks, who arranged to take his friend Whitworth and his partner David Batchelder to Soros' 7th Avenue headquarters to meet Druckenmiller on December 16. They talked about the potential synergies between the two companies; Whitworth cited USA Waste board member Jerry York's figure of $800 million in savings. There was also discussion of the elimination of the Oak Brook headquarters and the opportunity to close duplicated dumps. Monks, who had known Whitworth for years, recommended that Druckenmiller support him by informing Miller that he wanted Waste Management to negotiate. Shortly thereafter, Druckenmiller and Minow each called Miller to stress that they wanted him to take this offer very seriously.[15] Miller responded that he would. But at the time he really was not inclined to do so.

On December 30, Drury wrote a letter to the Waste Management board, again proposing a merger of the companies, but this time with Waste Management shareholders receiving a premium to the market price. As Miller recalls, "I said that's a concept we can work with." First, however, he needed to complete the accounting review "to find out where the bedrock [value] was."

Early in 1998, Miller called Minow on another matter: to seek her advice on the composition of Waste Management's board of directors. "We are on the ten worst boards in America and I want to be on the list of the ten best boards," he told her. "What do you use to test? Give me the template." Delighted to receive this call, Minow sent a three-page letter containing her recommendations. Among them: that directors have a significant personal stake in the company and receive all fees in stock; outside directors confer with each other privately; the nominating committee use an executive search firm and consult with major shareholders; all directors should serve on no more than three boards; the board should regularly evaluate the CEO, directors, and board. Minow referred to the recommendations issued by the National

Association of Corporate Directors, which she helped prepare as a member of the Blue Ribbon Commission on Director Professionalism. After reading her pointers, Miller resolved to use them.

He had a few other things to take care of before he did so. After USA Waste's Drury had met each Waste Management director, the board concluded that he would be capable of handling the combined companies. Miller's team also determined that the assumed $800 million in cost savings from the merger were real. In February, Waste Management took a grand total of $3.54 billion in pretax charges and write-downs for the fourth quarter, and restated results going back to 1991 as it completed its reform of once-aggressive accounting methods. The corrective action indicated that in the early 1990s as the industry became more competitive, the company had been bolstering profits with deceptive accounting practices. For all of 1997, Waste Management took a loss of $1.18 billion compared with a $39.3 million loss the year earlier. The board immediately launched an investigation into how earnings became so overstated for so long.

Early in March, USA Waste and Waste Management announced a deal, to mighty applause from shareholders. They would merge in a $13.5 billion transaction with the astute Drury becoming CEO of the new Waste Management and Miller serving as chairman of the board. In shaping the new board, seven directors would be plucked from each company's board. "It is important to recognize that this is a real victory for shareholders," Lens wrote on its Web site. "Without pressure from shareholders, the old management team and the old board and the old accounting assumptions would still be in place."

The story was not over for Lens. It would maintain its investment until the merger was accomplished and make sure that things were on the right track. But, if all went well, the days and nights of letter writing and phone calls and meetings were in the past. (By the fall of 1998, Lens had sold some stock at a 33% profit.) "We really have been able to put ourselves right inside of the company, and we made changes where we wanted to," Monks says. "I never thought governance would get to this stage. It's beyond the huff and puff stage, beyond send a petition to the board or a resolution to the shareholders. You have to do that in case they back down. In a company like WMX, our access to the institutions means that we've got more power than the management does."

Epilogue

Beyond Boundaries

> *In the century to come, as multinational companies create the borderless world of global markets, the focus will be on ensuring that corporate power is compatible with the rights of individuals in a democracy. The challenge is to encourage the creative energy of corporations without imposing unacceptable costs on individuals and society.*
>
> Watching the Watchers[1]

For two years, Lens had devoted all of its resources to the Waste Management effort. But Monks himself was dividing his time between that and a number of other ambitious projects. It seemed as if after the grueling Senate race and its disheartening conclusion, Monks had more energy than he did before. Some credited his uncanny ability to bounce back from defeat. Others said it was a sort of mad rush to restore his name and his confidence after a crushing blow. Monks himself would say that he was just continuing the crusade where he left off, which to him means recognizing what needs to be done and, if others are not already moving to fill the need, doing so himself. Whatever the reason, he has been taking shareholder activism and corporate governance in new directions.

One chief direction has been across the Atlantic. Early in 1996, just as he began thinking about launching another Senate race, Monks donated $1 million to establish a corporate governance center at Cambridge University's Judge Institute of Management Studies. Monks had long pondered the need for an academic program in corporate governance that took a broad view, approaching the issue from a global perspective and examining its ramifications in other realms, such as law, ethics, management, economics, and public policy. "If we want trustees and money managers to act as responsible trustees, we need to have some place where they can be trained," he says. For a long time, he thought about taking his idea and his money to a U.S. university—and tried unsuccessfully to interest his alma mater, Harvard, in some governance curriculum—but sensed that ties between academia and business would make objective study impossible. Instead, he began seriously considering the United Kingdom, where academia has kept its distance from corporations. Besides, as commerce had become global, it seemed to matter less and less where a governance center was located.

Ever since meeting the Bank of England's Lord Henry Benson in 1984, while traveling in his capacity as U.S. pensions administrator, Monks felt inspired by the progress corporate governance efforts had made in that country. He kept in close touch with him—the founder of Pro-Ned, the group that selected candidates to be nonexecutive directors—and others he had met over the years in the United Kingdom's governance vanguard. They included Sir Adrian Cadbury, the first chairman of Pro-Ned and the author of the groundbreaking 1992 Cadbury Report, which pressed corporations to formulate boards that are genuinely independent and responsive to shareholders; Jonathan Charkham, a governance advocate and the first director of Pro-Ned; Sir David Walker, chairman of Morgan Stanley UK, who had also been head of the country's securities regulation agency; and Alastair Ross Goobey, the activist CEO of Hermes Pensions Management, the manager of Postel, the post office and telecommunications systems' pension funds.

In recent years, thanks to Monks and others, as well as the information revolution, U.S. shareholder activists have developed a voice that is much louder and more effective than its counterpart in the United Kingdom. Still, there were clear indications that things were proceeding apace there, and that as investing has become increasingly global, the advancing U.S. shareholder activism/corporate governance movement was being felt in the United Kingdom and spreading to continental Europe. Partly as a result of some major corporate scandals and failures as well as the raging success of U.S. corporations on the international stage, shareholders in France, Italy, and even Germany were agitating at corporations where managements and directors were long accustomed to having complete authority and where social concerns were often paramount. In March 1997, Monks spoke at a forum in Berlin that addressed the general subject of the ethical responsibilities of multinational corporations. His talk focused on the role of activist institutions, particularly pension funds, in monitoring managements, and afterward he was mobbed by interested listeners. A year later, Calpers, which had more than $2 billion invested in Germany, adopted a set of corporate governance principles for German companies, including better disclosure and more independent directors, that would require dramatic change for many of the country's corporations. In the future, European corporations that wanted capital undoubtedly would have to demonstrate that they deliver value for shareholders.[2]

Driving that point home was a recommendation to the Organization for Economic Cooperation and Development, an association of 29 leading industrial countries, to adopt minimum corporate governance standards. After two years of study, a six-member advisory group to the OECD, chaired by Ira Millstein, issued its report in April 1998. The group had agreed on three main principles to be adhered to by member countries and their corporations. First: The chief objective should be to maximize shareholder value; that had not traditionally been the priority for companies in Europe and Japan, where such stakeholders as employees held superior status. The 1997–1998 Asia crisis, said Millstein, can only represent an argument for this principle. "Nobody was watching management," he said. "They were growing for the sake of growth with no concern for shareholder value." Second: Boards of directors need to exercise independent oversight of management. That was something Monks had been demanding at target corporations in the United States, including Sears, and that his British friends had also been rallying for. There could be no assurance of a focus on shareholder value unless the board was independent. Third: Governments should aim to preserve free markets and refrain from interfering in them. These standards, proclaimed the advisory commission, would "promote fairness, transparency, accountability and responsibility." The OECD was expected to issue final guidelines in the spring of 1999. Importantly, investors in a four-country survey by Russell Reynolds Associates, the executive search firm, indicated a strong desire for a global set of corporate governance standards.[3]

In July 1996, just after suffering defeat at the polls, Monks delivered a speech at Cambridge as the Judge Institute began the process of deciding its approach to governance. His own view was that the program should look at the corporation's lack of accountability to anyone in society. "The prevailing governance system in the U.S. boils down to the chief executive acting as a trustee for the public good," he charged. To guide the program's administrators, Monks chose a blue ribbon advisory board consisting of Cadbury, Charkham, Walker, Ross Goobey, and himself. By 1998, the school had established a Master in Philosophy Program in Governance and was about to begin offering a Doctoral degree.

Having established a center for the study of global governance matters at a major university to help provide a backbone for the growing movement, Monks then made his own contribution to shareholder activism's great leap abroad. In March 1998, Lens announced a joint endeavor with Hermes. The venture was essentially a British Lens fund. The first fund formed by the joint venture, the Hermes UK Focus Fund, was launched in the summer of 1998 with 100 million pounds ($165 million) from the Hermes funds. Monks first met the people at what was then called Postel when he was at ISS and prospecting in the United Kingdom for clients; Postel was among those that did sign up with ISS. Later, the phone system was privatized and its pension fund acquired the rest of Postel, formerly owned by the post office, and renamed itself Hermes. Ross Goobey, the manager of Hermes, became a prominent British activist investor, moving publicly against particular companies and even hiring a "governance executive." At one point, he told Monks that he was starting a Lens fund of his own, devoted solely to activism. Later, they negotiated a joint venture in which Hermes would be able to benefit from the experience and advice of Monks and his partners as well as acquire the Lens-developed computer and Internet technology.

The new fund is devoted solely to institutional activism. "The UK fund is a critical step toward globalization of governance," Monks says. He hoped it would be the template for similar specialist funds in other countries. In the United Kingdom, Hermes and Lens did not have the first activist fund. In fact, three months before their announcement, Calpers announced a commitment of at least $200 million to Active Value Capital, another firm using shareholder activism to coax value out of corporations.

Twenty-three years earlier, in 1973—when Monks was a delegate to the United Nations Environmental Protection Agency meeting in Geneva—he had first realized that any action on the environment would have to be a global effort, or polluting companies would be able to move. He later reached the same conclusion with the shareholder activism movement; it was necessary for shareholders to act on a global scale to make corporations truly accountable. Over the years, he spoke in Japan, Germany, and England to spread the governance gospel. Now, it was happening, and Monks was continuing to play a major role in its inspiration and guidance.

Another direction for Monks: fostering a discussion of how shareholders should involve themselves regarding corporations' ethical conduct as well as their financial performance. In this endeavor, he will be working with Marcy Murninghan, a former lecturer on religion and society at the Harvard Divinity School. Murninghan met Monks in the early 1980s after she had earned a doctoral degree from the Harvard University Graduate School of Education and gone on to help launch a socially responsible mutual fund. In the course of her work, she had read about Monks and was introduced to him by a colleague, and they began sharing their thoughts about corporate social responsibility. She began to realize that the way corporations were governed was an important determinant in how they behaved in society; she wanted to do further research on values, which prompted her move to Harvard Divinity School to do postdoctoral work. Sounding a lot like Monks, she began to ask, "How can a corporation be managed and governed so that the public is served as well as the fiduciary duty met?" When she mentioned to Monks her idea of developing the concept of what she called the corporate covenant, "a voluntary corporate commitment to a set of civic moral principles and ideals," he offered to help fund the research with a gift of $10,000.

In 1994, she produced an occasional paper for the John W. McCormack Institute of Public Affairs at Boston University on the potential for cultivating moral and ethical integrity in corporate ownership, governance, and accountability. It was called "Corporate Civic Responsibility and the Ownership Agenda: Investing in the Public Good." In it, she addressed ways in which the rise of shareholder activism and the prominence of the institutional owner could lead to a corporate covenant, and interviewed a number of thinkers and players on the topic, including Monks. "My style is to get owners to identify normative standards, in addition to financial ones, to define core ethical values that can be used as standards for judging corporate behavior," she says. "Monks and Minow are changing the paradigm, by providing both a legal and political justification for opening the corporate structure to greater scrutiny. They set the stage for someone like me. You can't make moral arguments in a vacuum. I want to stretch the definition of 'fiduciary responsibility' to accommodate 'stewardship' objectives." Monks was thrilled with the paper, also viewing Murninghan's work as complementary to his own. "It provided the analytical spiritual base that I was looking for to complete my own fiduciary approach," he says. In 1998, Monks and Murninghan were coediting a special issue of the *New England Journal of Public Policy* on corporate governance. And they had started planning a longer term collaboration, developing a think tank of a dozen or so major pension funds to elicit discussion of what a corporation means to them as citizens, and how their power as good investors might be used to assure good governance.

The next frontier for the team of Monks and Minow is addressing the conflict of interest that keeps major financial institutions, including corporate pension funds, from being involved owners of companies for fear they will lose business. This issue is Monks' Moby Dick. It eluded him while he was at the Labor Department, when Carter Hawley Hale got away. It taunted him in the Sears battle, in the form of BankAmerica, the trustee to the employee profit sharing plan, a huge shareholder, and in Stone & Webster as well. His only relief has been in the form of Lens's partnership with Hermes, which is a money manager with only two clients—the postal and telecommunications pension funds—and therefore no conflict of interest.

"We will not have a really durable activist investor climate until the mainstream firms are fully and competitively involved," he says. "Even the best people running conventional institutions do not dare associate themselves with activism for fear of customer backlash." Monks had hoped to take this issue on as a U.S. Senator—hold hearings, write legislation. This was not going to be. Instead, the partners are starting from an intellectual base by organizing a forum, commissioning papers on the topic from recognized scholars in corporate law. The idea is to publish the forum in a law journal and then make it news. Because the thinkers involved are so well regarded—and because they are not Bob Monks once again making the same arguments he's made before—their discussion may attract the attention of the press and policy makers. Monks is optimistic that it will provide the basis for further study, perhaps even in the form of congressional hearings.

Monks' ultimate solution for the conflict of interest problem is the establishment of special purpose companies devoted to voting. This is the conclusion he reaches in his fourth, and first sole-authored, book, *The Emperor's Nightingale,*[4] published in the spring of 1998. The book describes Monks' vision of shareholder activism as the best reconciler of a corporation's two contrasting qualities: the mechanistic and the human. This time, Monks takes a new approach to the whole subject of corporate governance. In the fall of 1996, his friend LeBaron took him to the Santa Fe Institute, a think tank in the emerging field of complexity. In essence, complexity is the notion that you cannot take things apart to study them; you have to study them as a whole. Monks took to it at once, for to him complexity seemed to be a wonderfully fresh way of looking at the modern corporation. "I've spent so much time trying to understand corporations, from a lawyer's point of view, a manager's point of view, an economist's point of view, an ethics point of view, and none of these languages work," Monks says. "What you need is a dynamic language. A corporation is a dynamic thing. This is a way I can tell the story that is more accessible." By November, he was working on the book, which took him only 10 months to write.

As a literary analogy for his message, Monks uses the myth of the Emperor's Nightingale, in which a mechanical bird's song cannot replace that of the live bird, but both are shown to have their place. He goes on to explain the mechanistic and "living" qualities of the corporation; although it is artificial, it is also a lifelike creature. The corporation is neither a machine of production as it is often perceived to be nor a living being with such qualities as emotion, compassion, or imagination. Rather, it is a "system" with potential for both. Left to its own devices, as Adam Smith noted, a corporation would follow four dangerous mechanistic tendencies: "unlimited life, size, power, and license." One by-product of these is the "externalizing machine" that Monks and Minow introduced in *Power and Accountability*. In its search for profits—and greater size—a company will place such costs on society as pollution, medical treatment from workplace injuries or harmful products, retraining, and unemployment. The four mechanistic tendencies can overpower a corporation's more dynamic, "living" side, which has such qualities as spontaneity, creativity, and accommodation.

Monks concludes that the four tendencies must somehow be watched and controlled by a human element, or corporations will exact harm on society. "To restore integrity to the corporate form, we must reconcile its programmed, mechanical drives with its nature as a lifelike system in touch with human needs," Monks writes. Government regulation does not offer a good enough solution, since corporations have shown that they can elude it. The best solution, as he has argued in his other books, is accountability to institutional shareholders. If a corporation has shareholders who are actively involved as owners—supported by a federal standard of ownership recognizing the importance of having informed, involved owners—it can have the human traits necessary to guide the corporation so that it operates in the interest of society, Monks says. What they should do, is compel corporations to follow the three principles outlined by David Engel, Monks's colleague at The Boston Company: obey the law, make full disclosure about the corporation's impact on society, and refrain from involvement in politics. Monks believes that with proper shareholder monitoring and adherence to these precepts, market value will more accurately reflect the costs companies foist on society and make them more likely to reduce these costs.

In a rather unusual epilogue, Monks envisions, with his idiosyncratic optimism, the evolution of the corporate governance movement to a point where "special purpose trust companies" are created that will discharge institutional investors' ownership responsibilities without conflicts of interest and will enforce what Monks calls the Engel Triad. The reason the chapter is unusual is because he unabashedly casts himself in the protagonist's role using a barely camouflaged character he calls Ruth. "Born and raised in New England, Ruth possessed a pilgrim-like commitment to personal improvement and a thirst for reform slaked only through constant involvement in public service," Monks writes. She ran a money management fund called PRISM and "detested the term 'gadfly.'" Elsewhere, he credits her as an "innovator and catalyst" with "boundless energy" and "a gift for analogy from the everyday world." And finally: "It could be said that the evolution of the post-Communist development of corporate accountability owed as much to Ruth as to any other individual." Surely, this is Monks' tendency for self-promotion run amok. For his part, he claims that he was writing about his partner Nell Minow, not himself. But at best, Ruth is a combination of Monks and Minow, since Minow is from Chicago and since they run Lens together (with others).

In this semi-imaginary world, Ruth is counsel for beneficiaries of Carter Hawley Hale employee benefit plans in a DOL lawsuit charging conflict of interest by the plan's trustee, the Bank of America. This is the case that Monks was prevented from bringing when he was pensions regulator. In the book Hawley has avoided a hostile takeover with the help of the plan trustee; but in making an aggressive defense, it drives itself into bankruptcy, ravaging the pension fund. "Ruth kept in mind the picture of a pensioner impoverished by lack of corporate accountability," Monks writes. Eventually, the Supreme Court rules that financial organizations with a conflict of interest would have to prove themselves free of conflicts or face the risk of losing the right to do any fiduciary business. Thus is born the special purpose trust company. And so the book ends.

The final aspect of corporate governance that Monks hopes soon to begin addressing is encouraging the involvement of pension plan participants in the governance process. These are the ultimate owners, and in his view they need to be not only informed but allowed to contribute to the decisions made by the trustees of their funds. "I have used the trustees as the owners for these many years, not because I have any respect for their omniscience—quite the contrary—but because I can legally get their attention," Monks says. "Now it is time to move to the real beneficial owners." He hopes the Internet can become one way to keep beneficiaries informed and foster communication from them.

"I feel that a significant plateau has been achieved," Monks wrote in his 1998 Agenda distributed to a number of contacts. "It is now universally accepted that corporate governance is linearly related to shareholder value and is an essential component of the permanent business syllabus." Near the end of the century, shareholder activism and corporate governance have come a long way. As the *Wall Street Journal* of June 8, 1998, proclaimed: "The bull market of the 1990s has coincided with a surge in shareholder activism that appears to have spurred remarkable performance in many stocks and contributed to the overall market's gains as well. . . . The fact that companies are simply paying more attention to what shareholders want appears to have given the bull market some extra oomph." Monks believes a bear market could advance the movement even more.

Monks' stamp could be seen in many places. The Lens Fund has proved that activism, and in turn improved corporate governance, creates value. Its six-year record as of July 31, 1998: 23.8 percent compounded annually versus 22.9 percent for the S&P 500. It was then involved in new investments such as Reader's Digest and Juno Lighting. Monks' imitators—Ralph Whitworth's Relational Investors, Alfred Kingsley's Greenway Partners, and others—are the best proof of praise for his approach. But studies of activist funds also have confirmed its value. Both CEOs and investors in a 1996 McKinsey Quarterly survey indicated that they value good governance in terms of a solid 11 percent premium on the stock price.

An important part of what Lens has brought to shareholder activism is cybertechnology: a communication capability through the Internet. Through Lens's Web site, investors can research governance and keep track of ongoing shareholder activism at Lens companies as well as others. Its private intranet networks foster communication among shareholders of its portfolio companies. The technology is cheap and fast and could represent a huge leap for the practice of active ownership.

TIAA-CREF, the country's largest pension system, which got involved in filing proxy resolutions at Monks' suggestion, has continued to break new ground for activism. In 1995, it pressured management at W. R. Grace & Company in private meetings to overhaul the board. In a proxy contest in May 1998, it succeeded in ousting the board of the ailing

cafeteria operator, Furr's/Bishop's Inc.—the first time that a pension fund
had replaced an entire board. It remained to be seen whether the shake-up
would boost the company and its stock; but doing nothing in the face of a
deteriorating situation did not seem to be a viable alternative.

Meantime, Calpers, which Monks had educated in the minutiae of activism, is still perceived as the leading activist institution in the United
States. However, in Monks' not unbiased view as well as that of some others,
it has lost much of its effectiveness. While the fund has continued to convince corporations to change governance provisions, that is fairly easy for
companies to do, he says. He objects that Calpers has not asked more of corporations. Naturally, Calpers CEO Burton has a different impression. "My
view of Calpers' effectiveness is, it is in the doing of it," he says. "If Calpers
abandoned the field, governance as a movement would not die, but would be
significantly less. There is a need for strong leadership in holding corporations accountable, and that's what we do." In any case, others, including
TIAA-CREF and major investment managers, are also in the vanguard.

Often, they are running behind Lens or other activist funds. Indeed,
the same *Wall Street Journal* story observes: "The activist torch now is being
carried by specialized investors who buy stakes in undervalued companies
aiming to shake up management." In Calpers' defense, then, the fund is a
major investor in Relational Investors as well as in Active Value Investors in
the United Kingdom. An example of Relationship's recent endeavors is that
besides helping to negotiate the merger of USA Waste and Waste Management, in May 1998, the fund successfully pushed 5 of 11 directors off the
board of Apria Healthcare Group. Relational holds 9.9 percent of the troubled Costa Mesa, California-based home healthcare provider, and Whitworth is now chairman.

It could also be argued that by simply getting the press it gets for its initiatives and its annual list of target, underperforming companies, Calpers
continues to have a sizable impact on corporations. Companies and their
boards just do not want to be highlighted in the press and involved in a public battle with activists, and will do what they can to avoid that—including
everything from changing governance provisions to, in a few cases, changing management and directors. The fact that the media now gives activists
great credence is in large part due to Monks' painstaking efforts since 1984
to encourage and assist reporters.

Meanwhile, ISS has grown in influence to the point where some are
asking whether it has too much. Today, the firm advises 700 clients, mostly

institutional investors—largely public and private pension funds and index funds—but also corporations, on the entire gamut of proxy issues, in the United States and abroad. Its opinions are potent when it comes to proxy battles, approval of executive stock options, or controversial management or shareholder resolutions. Even when clients have proxy voting guidelines of their own, they will often follow ISS's counsel. The *Wall Street Journal* of November 10, 1997, read: "Given the growth of institutional stock ownership and the increasing use of ISS as a guidepost, the firm has become a power in its own right in merger-and-acquisition circles."

Monks is proud but at the same time humble about these accomplishments, because he sees that shareholders have such a long way to go. He is particularly troubled by what he sees as "CEO hegemony," given their ever-rising compensation levels and their success in avoiding any accounting of executive stock options. "Options are a free ride for management—no cost, no risk on the down side, only wins—and in those cases where the market goes the wrong way, repricing and a new start," Monks wrote in a professional paper in July 1998.[5] "Only a few years after the fall of the Berlin Wall, it would be supreme irony if Karl Marx's ultimate prophecy comes true and capitalism fails because of its inner contradictions—the inability of flesh and blood human beings to threaten their own comfort by effective confrontation of a system of power." This is a glimpse of Monks' dark side. It is not the quality that keeps him going despite the odds.

In considering his agenda for the future, Monks reflects briefly on his own restless energy, which both drives and torments him. "It haunts me to think that in my sixty-fifth year, I am spending time doing what I did last year. I ought to be able to figure out a higher priority and to allocate my energy more appropriately. I do not want to get dragged into the conventional agenda; I do not want to spend my time on commissions that are reviewing what is past—even those that are concerned with restating the present; I need to take advantage of my time, experience, and energy and be sure that the really important issues are being raised." There should be much more to come from Robert A. G. Monks.

Notes

Much of the material in this book is based on interviews with Robert A. G. Monks and numerous other people conducted from 1995 through 1998.

CHAPTER 1

1. G. Gardner Monks, *Beginnings* (Portland, Maine: Colonial Printing, 1978), p. 3.
2. John Peabody Monks, *History of Roque Island, Maine* (Boston: Colonial Society of Massachusetts, 1971).
3. G. Gardner Monks, *Beginnings,* p. 81.
4. Ibid., p. 4.
5. Ibid., p. 251.
6. David Halberstam, The Amateurs (New York: Ballantine Books, 1985), p. 30.

CHAPTER 2

1. Peter Amory Bradford, *Fragile Structures* (New York: Harper's Magazine Press, 1975), p. 172.
2. Interview with R. Monks, February 1998.
3. Bradford, *Fragile Structures,* p. 173.
4. From interviews with R. Monks, December, 1996.

CHAPTER 3

1. Interview with H. Goldenfarb, February 17, 1998.
2. Interview with E. Higgins, January 28, 1998.
3. Bradford, *Fragile Structures,* p. 268.
4. Bradford, *Fragile Structures,* p. 269, and interview with H. Goldenfarb, January 7, 1998.
5. Bradford, *Fragile Structures,* p. 267.
6. Interview with R. Monks, December 10, 1997.
7. Interview with R. Monks, March 3, 1998.

CHAPTER 4

1. Account of sealing the deal with Shearson, from interviews with R. Monks (February 28, 1998); D. Allison (December 13, 1996); Arthur Dubow (October 30, 1996); D. Engel (March 1998); and J. Berman (November 5, 1996).

2. Ibid.

3. Howard Kurtz, "Synfuels Corp. President Resigns under Board Members' Pressure," *Washington Post,* August 19, 1983, p. A4.

4. Letter from R. Monks to David S. Broder, December 15, 1987. Letter from Broder to R. Monks, December 17, 1987.

CHAPTER 5

1. "ERISA Administrator Plans Review of Law," Interview with Robert Monks, *Labor & Investments,* May 1984, p. 1.

2. Conversation from interview with F. Lilly, January 22, 1997.

3. Interview with former DOL staff member, March 1997.

4. Joel Chernoff, "Monks Sets Sights High," *Pensions & Investments Age,* February 6, 1984, *Business Week,* October 8, 1984, and National Pension Forum hearings.

5. Fran Hawthorne, "How Bob Monks Plans to Shake Up Pensionland," *Institutional Investor,* March 1984.

6. James Flanigan, "Pension Funds Are Full of Potential—and Problems—for U.S. Business," *Los Angeles Times,* March 21, 1984.

7. Hawthorne, *Institutional Investor,* March 1984.

8. *Barron's* April 8, 1991, p.15.

9. Letter from R. Monks to John Welch and Randall Bassett of Latham & Watkins, regarding Carter, Hawley, Hale case, April 30, 1984.

10. Interview with R. Monks, November 8, 1997.

11. *Barron's* April 8, 1991, p. 15.

12. James Flanigan, "A Long-Term Rule Would Stifle Raiders," *Los Angeles Times,* May 13, 1984.

13. "Erisa Administrator Plans Review of Law," interview with R. Monks, *Labor & Investments,* May 1984, p. 1.

14. Frank Sleeper, "Monks Makes Waves in Pension Fund Field," *Maine Sunday Telegram,* July 8, 1984, p. 4C.

15. R. Monks, "Policy Implications of Failure of Pension Funds' Investment Performance," Speech before the Institutional Investor Washington Pensions Seminar, October 16, 1984.

16. U.S. Department of Labor, Office of Pension and Welfare Benefit Programs, Public Hearing on Pension Fund Investment Performance, January 9, 1985.

17. The National Pension Forum, Washington, D.C., September 19, 1984.

18. Chernoff, *Pensions & Investment Age,* February 6, 1984.

19. Joel Chernoff, "Monks Resigns Pension Post," *Pensions & Investment Age,* December 10, 1984, p. 8.

20. Randall Smith and Cathy Trost, "Labor Department's Pension Watchdog, Robert Monks, Plans to Resign in January," *Wall Street Journal,* December 3, 1984.

21. Ibid.

22. Interview with O. Berg, February 6, 1998.

CHAPTER 6

1. Joe Kolman, "The Proxy Pressure on Pension Managers," *Institutional Investor,* July 1985, p. 147.

2. Nancy Perry, "Newsman Says Pension Funds Sway America," *Portland Press Herald,* July 1985.

3. Introduction to R. Monks draft of autobiography, unpublished, June 7, 1994.

4. Letter from R. Monks to J. Berman, October 3, 1985.

5. ISS business plan, November 1985.

6. Ibid.

7. "ISS—Corporate Governance Principles," December 30, 1985.

8. Interview with R. Monks, September 23, 1996.

9. ISS draft of letter to shareholders of the Potlatch Corp., November 15, 1985.

10. ISS strategy memo from R. Monks, January 30, 1986.

11. Memo from ISS staff member to R. Monks, March 19, 1986.

12. Letter from ISS to shareholders of Chase Manhattan Corp., March 28, 1989.

13. James W. Hurst, "The Legitimacy of the Business Corporation in the Law of the United States, 1780–1970, University Press of Virginia, 1970, p. 89.

14. Daniel Hertzberg, "Chase Holders Narrowly Clear Defensive Steps," *Wall Street Journal,* April 16, 1986, p. 3.

15. Ibid.

16. Letter from R. Monks to John Shad, June 13, 1986.

17. ISS 1986 annual report to directors and advisers, August 4, 1986.

18. Ibid.

19. Ibid.

20. R. Monks draft autobiography, unpublished.

21. The Georgeson Report, Fourth Quarter, 1986.

22. August 1986 memo from R. Monks to ISS board and advisers.

23. Reference is made in October internal ISS memo from R. Monks to board, "The rescission/resolution program for TIAA/CREF. . . . " Also, Letter to Joshua Berman, from Marian Vobach of ISS; October 13, 1986. "I have revised the draft of the shareholder resolution we are writing for TIAA/CREF. . . . I spoke to Dick Schlefer at TIAA/CREF on Friday and he reiterated the points he

had covered with Bob. He wants the rescission resolution to include the following points." Draft follows.

CHAPTER 7

1. Letter to Joshua Berman from Marian Vobach of ISS, October 13, 1986.

2. Michael W. Miller, "Common Defense Against Takeovers Faces New Hurdle," the *Wall Street Journal,* November 4, 1986.

3. Hilary Rosenberg, "The revolt of the institutional shareholders," *Institutional Investor,* May 1987, p. 131.

4. "Proxy Battles Heating Up; More Chief Executives Join Letter Writing Campaign," Marcia Parker, *Pensions & Investment Age,* April 6, 1987, p. 1.

5. Robert A. G. Monks, "Will the Corporation's Real Owners Please Stand Up?" *Across the Board,* February 1987, p. 52.

6. Marcia Parker, "Proxy solicitation under fire as votes near," *Pensions & Investment Age,* March 23, 1987.

7. Marcia Parker and Marlene Givant, "Executives Warned of Proxy Vote Liability," *Pensions & Investment Age,* May 18, 1987.

8. Ibid.

9. Interviews with R. Monks, August–September, 1997.

10. Interview with M. Lipton, May 5, 1997.

11. Letter from M. Johnston to R. Monks, December 13, 1986.

12. "Institutional Shareholders—Resolutions Requesting Involvement in Decisions Affecting Their Ultimate Destiny," Speech by R. Monks to the American Society of Corporate Secretaries, New York, May 13, 1987.

13. Robert A. G. Monks and Nell Minow, "Indexing Boosts Long-Term View," *Pensions & Investment Age,* January 11, 1988.

14. Ellen Perlman, "The Largest Institutional Investor in the Country," *Pension World,* July 1987, p. 25.

CHAPTER 8

1. Internal memo from R. Monks, November 30, 1987.

2. R. Monks draft autobiography, unpublished, June 7, 1994.

CHAPTER 9

1. Nancy J. Perry, "Who Runs Your Company, Anyway?" *Fortune,* September 12, 1988, p. 140.

2. R. Monks speech to National Association of Corporate Directors, October 25, 1988.

3. Letter from R. Monks to F. Baxter, November 14, 1988.

4. Ibid.

5. Giving credit for victories, from ISS strategy memo, November 1988.

6. Interview with R. Monks, January 8, 1997.

7. ISS strategy memo from R. Monks to the board, November 30, 1988.

8. Letter from R. Monks to A. Dubow, February 3, 1989; Internal memo "The proxy process as seen through our Bergen Brunswig experience," February 13, 1989, and interviews with R. Monks.

9. Letter from R. Monks to L. Rawl of Exxon, October 26, 1988.

10. ISS memo on corporate crime, September 2, 1988.

11. ISS strategy memo to board, November 1988.

12. Interview with R. Monks, January 8, 1997.

13. Bob Ortega, "Louisiana Pacific Fined $37 Million," *Wall Street Journal*, May 28, 1998, p. A3.

14. John Dizard, "Staying in Control at Honeywell," *Corporate Finance*, December 1989, p. 49.

15. Interviews with R. Monks, January 20, 1997, and N. Minow, April 6, 1998. The author contacted Lampert for comments, but he did not return calls.

16. Brett D. Fromson, "How to Make a Million . . . Or, at Age 33, by Hunting Stock Bargains for the Wealthy," *Washington Post*, September 10, 1995, p. H01.

17. Letter from R. Monks to Richard Koppes, February 2, 1989.

18. On Ira Millstein's role, from interview with R. Monks, February 1997.

19. Letter from R. Monks to Frank Baxter, July 11, 1989.

20. Letter from R. Monks to A. Dubow, July 27, 1989.

21. Report on board meeting, October 11, 1989.

22. Letter from R. Monks to A. Dubow, January 17, 1990.

23. From letters from R. Monks to A. Dubow, January 5 and January 17, 1990.

24. "Improving Directors," *Pensions & Investments Age*, April 16, 1990, p. 14.

25. "Administration Views on Corporate Governance," *Insights*, September 1990, p. 37.

26. Marcia Parker, "Activists Get Not from Ball," *Pensions & Investments Age*, February 2, 1990.

27. Letter to A. Dubow, January 17, 1990; M. Parker, February 2, 1990.

28. From an interview with R. Koppes, April 2, 1997.

29. Letter from R. Monks to R. Koppes, December 29, 1989.

30. Smith's reaction, from James Treece and Judith Dobrzynski, "Can GM's Big Investors Get it to Change Lanes" *Business Week*, January 22, 1990, p. 30.

31. Mike Consol, "World War II: Lockheed Foes Lock Ads Again," *The Los Angeles Business Journal*, March 26, 1990, p. 1.

32. Leslie Wayne, "A Fervent Advocate of the Proxy Battle," *The New York Times*, May 8, 1990, p. D1.

33. Peter Riddell, "A crusader takes on corporate America," *Financial Times*, June 6, 1990.

34. ABC's *Business World*, May 6, 1990.

35. Interview with J. Wilcox, February 10, 1997 and R. Monks, June 9, 1997.

CHAPTER 10

1. Interview with M. Lipton, May 5, 1997.

2. R. Monks' account of Sears drama, unpublished, June 8, 1994.

3. Interview with R. Monks, April 9, 1997.

4. Interview with E. Brennan, May 19, 1997.

5. Interview with D. Martin, April 1, 1997.

6. Francine Schwadel, "Sears Roebuck Eliminates Five Seats of Inside Directors in Defensive Move," *Wall Street Journal,* March 13, 1991.

7. R. Monks' account of Sears drama, unpublished, June 8, 1994.

8. Ibid.

9. Ibid.

10. "Let Brennan's Record Start to Speak for Itself," *Crain's Chicago Business,* April 8, 1991, p. 14.

11. Interview with E. Brennan, May 19, 1997.

12. Account of Sears drama written by R. Monks, unpublished; interviews with R. Monks, October, 1996.

13. Interview with R. Monks, October, 1996.

14. Letter from S. Rich to Sears, Roebuck & Co., April 18, 1991.

15. Lisa Holton, "Gadfly or Giantkiller, Sears Doesn't Take Monks Lightly," *Chicago Sun-Times,* April 8, 1991, p. 35.

16. Regarding the other lawsuit, Diana B. Henriques, "A Lawsuit Sears Doesn't Mention," *The New York Times,* May 5, 1991, p. 15; "Two Sears Holders Accuse the Directors of Mismanagement," the *Wall Street Journal,* May 7, 1991; Eric N. Berg, "Shareholders at Sears Sue to Delay Meeting," *The New York Times,* May 7, 1991; Francine Schwadel, "Sears's Adviser Saw More for Holders from a Breakup than from Revamping," the *Wall Street Journal,* May 8, 1991; Eric Berg, "Judge Won't Delay Sears Annual Meeting," *The New York Times,* May 9, 1991.

17. Account of Sears drama written by R. Monks, unpublished, June 8, 1994.

18. Ibid.

19. A. Dubow nominating speech at Sears, Roebuck & Co. annual meeting, May 8, 1991.

20. R. Monks' speech to Sears, Roebuck & Co. annual meeting, May 8, 1991, and R. Monks' account of Sears drama, unpublished, June 8, 1994.

CHAPTER 11

1. Michael Klein quotes from an excerpt from a letter to R. Monks, quoted in account of Sears drama by R. Monks, unpublished, June 8, 1994.

2. Account of Sears drama written by R. Monks, unpublished, June 8, 1994.

3. Interview with R. Monks, October, 1996.

4. From interview with J. Heard, August 25, 1998.

5. Meeting with D. Shute, from account of Sears drama by R. Monks and letter from R. Monks to J. Berman.

6. Account of Sears drama by R. Monks.

7. Meeting with Shute, from interviews with R. Monks, account of Sears drama by R. Monks, and letters from R. Monks to J. Wilcox (March 16, 1992) and J. Berman (March 19, 1992).

8. Francine Schwadel, "Big Sears Holder Decides to Vote Against Board," *Wall Street Journal,* April 30, 1992.

9. "Profits and Promises," Roundtable discussion, PBS, March 1, 1995.

10. R. Monks' account of Sears drama, unpublished.

11. Interview with E. Brennan, May 19, 1997.

12. Account of annual meeting from R. Monks' account of the Sears drama and interviews with R. Monks, K. Bingham (December 16, 1997); and A. Towers (April 29, 1997).

13. Ellen Neuborne and Michelle Osborn, "Mutual Funds, Pension Funds Lead the Charge," *USA Today,* May 15, 1992.

CHAPTER 12

1. Account of conversations with Jim Robinson from interviews with R. Monks.

2. Account of meeting with P. Lego and Westinghouse annual meeting from internal Lens memos and interviews with R. Monks.

3. Interviews with R. Monks, October, 1997, N. Minow, September 9, 1996, and R. Holmes, January 20, 1998.

4. "Looking Ahead with Lens Inc.," interview with Robert Monks, *Directorship,* May 1993, p. 3.

5. Account of meeting with Kodak executives, from internal Lens memos, November 16, 1993, and interviews with R. Monks and J. Higgins.

6. Interviews with R. Monks and J. Higgins, March 13, 1998.

7. J. Burton's comments recalled by R. Monks in interviews, and by J. Burton, July 28, 1998.

8. From interviews with R. Monks, J. Pannell (March 17, 1998) and J. Burton (July 28, 1998).

9. S. L. Mintz, "True Lies: How GAAP Conceals the Real Story at Stone & Webster," *CFO* magazine, September 1994, p. 49.

10. Account of pre-annual meeting confrontation, from interview with N. Minow, April 20, 1998.

11. Interview with N. Minow, April 20, 1998.

12. Interview with H. K. Smith, April 25, 1998.

13. Ibid.

14. Robert A. G. Monks and Nell Minow, *Corporate Governance,* Oxford, Blackwell Publishers, 1995.

15. Robert A. G. Monks and Nell Minow, *Watching the Watchers,* Oxford, Blackwell Publishers, 1996.

CHAPTER 13

1. Interview with R. Monks, spring 1996.

2. Interview with R. Monks, April 6, 1998.

3. Interview with S. Miller, April 6, 1998.

4. Interview with campaign staff officer, June 1, 1996.

5. Interviews with campaign staff and Steve Campbell; "Awkwardness, Negative TV Ads Pull Down Monks," *Portland Press Herald,* June 16, 1996, p. 9A.

6. Interview with campaign advisor, January 21, 1998.

7. Quotes from *Boston Globe* are from Sara Rimer, "Maine Candidate Again Faces 1990 Child-Sex Accusation," *New York Times,* June 6, 1996.

8. Interview with H. Goldenfarb, January 7, 1998.

9. Regarding accusations aimed at Hathaway, from interviews with S. Miller, April 6, 1998, H. Goldenfarb, January 7, 1998, R. Monks, June 1996, and press reports.

10. Interview with R. Monks, April 26, 1998.

11. Christian P. Potholm, *An Insider's Guide to Maine Politics, 1946–1996,* New York, Madison Books, 1998, p. 198.

CHAPTER 14

1. Interview with C. Woodworth, March 5, 1998.

2. Interview with N. Minow, April 6, 1998.

3. Interviews with R. Monks, December 18, 1986, N. Minow, April 6, 1998, and J. Higgins, August 28, 1998. Also, memo written by R. Monks on November 21, 1996.

4. Account of conference call and conversation with Rooney and conversation with analyst from Goldman Sachs, from interviews with R. Monks.

5. James L. Tyson, "Garbage Collection King Gets Dumped On," *Christian Science Monitor,* January 6, 1997, p. 9.

6. Memo written by R. Monks, February 7, 1997, and interview with J. Higgins, August 28, 1998.

7. Internal Lens memos and Soros Group 13D filing, February 11, 1997.

8. Interview with N. Minow, April 6, 1998.

9. Ibid.

10. Interview with R. Miller, April 23, 1998.

11. Interview with R. Miller, June 18, 1998.

12. Interview with R. Miller, April 23, 1998.

13. Interview with R. Miller, June 18, 1998.

14. Interview with N. Minow, April 6, 1998.

15. Ibid.

EPILOGUE

1. Robert A. G. Monks and Nell Minow, *Watching the Watchers* (Cambridge, MA: Blackwell Publishers, 1996) p. 261.

2. John Tagliabue, "Compliments of U.S. Investors: New Activism Shakes Europe's Markets," *The New York Times,* p. D1.

3. Kenneth N. Gilpin, "Shareholders Push for Tighter Rules Abroad," *The New York Times,* p. D.1.

4. Robert A. G. Monks, *The Emperor's Nightingale,* Oxford, Capstone Publishing, 1998.

5. Robert A. G. Monks, "Executive and director compensation—1984 REDUX," Corporate Governance, Professional Papers, Volume 6, Number 3, July 1998.

Acknowledgments

Bob Monks could have written this book himself. He had drafted a few chapters of an autobiography by the time I came along in the spring of 1995 with the idea to write his story as a way to record the rise of shareholder activism. He gave me his full cooperation, even though my approach was to interview both those who credit him with helping to create a movement that seeks better corporate governance as well as those who disagree with him and discount his influence. Beyond that, he offered all his vast resources and a great deal of his time. I spent countless hours interviewing him in person, by phone, and by e-mail, and he always had patience to spare. It was invigorating to be with someone who has so much energy and optimism and who seems always to be looking forward to the next adventure, whatever it may be. My appreciation is without bounds.

I owe many thanks to Bob's wife Milly Monks and the rest of his family, who gave generously of their time in repeated interviews. Bob's longtime collaborator Nell Minow was an invaluable source, and her vitality was infectious. All of Bob's colleagues at Lens, Bob Holmes, John Higgins, and Charlie Woodworth, were extraordinarily helpful and available.

Bob's assistant Barbara Sleasman not only helped me sift through files in Lens's Washington office and sent me many packages of documents. But she also spent more than one evening in her garage going through old papers from Bob's days at the Department of Labor and Institutional Shareholder Services that were to be transferred to Lens's office in Maine. I owe her a great debt.

I want to express my gratitude to the following people who gave their time to be interviewed: Dwight Allison, Dr. French Anderson, Frank Baxter, Olena Berg, Joshua Berman, Kit Bingham, Gordon Binns, Edward Brennan, Jim Burton, Charles Clough, William S. Cohen, T. Jefferson Coolidge, Arthur Dubow, David Engel, Howard Goldenfarb, Alistair Ross Goobey, Anne Hanson, Dale Hanson, Jamie Heard, Ellen Higgins, Alan

367

Kahn, Morton Klevan, Richard Koppes, Dean LeBaron, Alan Lebowitz, Charles Lerner, Frank Lilly, Martin Lipton, Willis Lyford, Ben Makihara, Greta Marshall, David Martin, Sharon Miller, Steve Miller, Ira Millstein, George Monks, Robert Monks Jr., Marcy Murninghan, Torquil Norman, Jim Pannell, Ned Regan, Richard Schlefer, Jim Severance, Howard Sherman, Harold Simmons, Barbara Sleasman, H. Kerner Smith, Al Sommer, Alan Towers, David Walker, William Webster, Ralph Whitworth, John Wilcox, and C. Howard Wilkins.

This book would never have happened without Myles Thompson at Wiley, who encouraged me to pursue an idea to capture the essence of a movement in the life of one of its leaders. I also owe great thanks to my editor Jennifer Pincott, who helped me develop and polish the story.

Finally, I want to thank my husband, Ed Hersh, who is my best friend and wisest adviser, and who, with my son Aaron, keeps me laughing.

HILARY ROSENBERG

Index

Scott Paper Company, 322
Sea-Land Corp., 207
Sears, Roebuck & Co., xiii, xiv, xv, 95–96,
 215–252, 253–279, 282, 284, 287, 296,
 331, 347, 350
Seattle, Battle in, 59
Securities Exchange Commission (SEC), 60,
 91, 128, 138, 139, 140, 141, 142, 143,
 149, 151, 152, 153, 154, 156, 169, 174,
 175, 177, 187, 191, 195–201, 209,
 211–212, 220, 222, 224, 225, 231, 232,
 234, 240, 256, 262, 268, 279, 290, 297,
 304, 306, 308, 332, 341
Sellin, Eric, 13
Senior Power, 50
Severance, James, 296
Shad, John, 140, 222
Shames, Ervin, 298
Shapiro, Stuart, 125
Shaw, James, 2
Shearson, 68, 71, 130, 187, 282, 283
Shearson American Express, 68, 166
Shearson Lehman Hutton, 186
Shearson Loeb Rhodes, 67
Shell Oil, 12, 30, 33. *See also* Royal Dutch
 Shell
Sherman, Howard, 175, 182, 195, 196, 197,
 198
Shute, David, 223–224, 231, 234, 239, 240,
 251, 264, 265, 266, 272, 273, 274, 278
Siegel, Mayer, 203
Sigler, Andrew, 204
Simmons, Hardwick, 67
Simmons, Harold, 181, 206–208, 209, 211,
 212, 221, 245, 296
Skadden Arps Meagher & Flom, 125, 172
Sleasman, Barbara, 85, 120, 123–124, 146, 214
Small Business Investment Company, 19
Smith, Adam, 351
Smith, H. Kerner, 310, 311–312
Smith, Margaret Chase, 38–45, 52, 55
Smith, Roger, 204, 205, 206
Smith, William French, 96
Sommer, Al, xi, 191
Soros, George, 34, 35, 295, 322
Soros Fund Management, 295, 296, 322, 323,
 326, 328, 331, 332, 333, 334, 337, 343
South Africa, 62, 63, 65, 72, 73
Spangler, Meredith, 308
Spencer Stuart (headhunting firm), 331, 335
Sprague, Charles Hill, 10. *See also* C. H.
 Sprague & Son
Sprague, Phineas Shaw. *See* Sprague, Shaw
 (father-in-law)

Sprague, Phineas W., 10, 82
Sprague, Shaw (father-in-law), 10, 21, 22–23,
 27, 33, 42. *See also* C. H. Sprague & Son
Sprague, Shaw, Jr., 42
Sprague Corporation, 42
Sprint Corp., 339, 340
Spurwink School, 80
State of Wisconsin Investment Board (SWIB).
 See Wisconsin public fund (SWIB: State
 of Wisconsin Investment Board)
Steffen, Christopher, 289, 290
Stempel, Robert, 267, 287
Sterling Drug, 288
Stilatis, Eddie, 31
Stone & Webster, ix, xiv, 299–312, 323, 350
St. Paul's school (Concord, New Hampshire),
 7, 8, 12, 172, 222
Sugarman, Burt, 170
Sullivan & Cromwell, 203
Sulpetro of Canada, 48–50, 221
Sunbeam, 322
SWIB. *See* Wisconsin public fund (SWIB:
 State of Wisconsin Investment Board)
Synfuels, 69, 70, 71, 72, 73, 74, 77, 78, 79,
 80, 99, 316

Teachers' pension fund. *See* TIAA-CREF
 (Teachers Insurance and Annuity
 Association—College Retirement Equities
 Fund)
Teamsters Central States Pension Fund, 89
Telling, Edward R., 226, 227, 228, 230
Tellup, Daniel, 207, 209
Tenneco Corp., 300, 301, 306, 307, 322
Tettamanti, Tito, 169
Texaco, 99, 122, 170, 171, 172, 173, 174,
 175, 181, 204
Texas Teachers, 276
Thibeau, Donald, 99, 109
Thompson Financial, 213
"Thugs in pin stripes," 89
Thurow, Lester, 175, 256
TIAA-CREF (Teachers Insurance and
 Annuity Association—College
 Retirement Equities Fund), xi, 142, 145,
 149, 152, 154, 155, 159, 160, 175, 176,
 189, 209, 271, 353, 354
Times Mirror, 133–134
Time-Warner, 322
Tomabechi, Mr., 29, 30, 34
Tonight Show, 239, 240
Tower, John, 208
Towers, Alan, 223, 232, 266, 269, 272, 273
Toys "R" Us, 322